EIGHTEENTH-CENTURY CONTEXTS

Eighteenth-Century Contexts

Historical Inquiries in Honor of Phillip Harth

Edited by
Howard D. Weinbrot,
Peter J. Schakel,
and Stephen E. Karian

The University of Wisconsin Press

The University of Wisconsin Press
1930 Monroe Street
Madison, Wisconsin 53711

3 Henrietta Street
London WC2E 8LU, England

5 4 3 2 1

Printed in the United States of America

Library of Congress Cataloging-in-Publication Data
Eighteenth-century contexts: historical inquiries in honor of Phillip Harth
edited by Howard D. Weinbrot, Peter J. Schakel, and Stephen E. Karian
pp. cm.
"Phillip Harth: a bibliography": p.
Includes index.
ISBN 0-299-17480-8 (alk. paper)
1. English literature—18th century—History and criticism. 2. Literature and history—Great Britain—History—18th century. 3. Great Britain—Civilization—18th century. I. Harth, Phillip, 1926– II. Weinbrot, Howard D. III. Schakel, Peter J. IV. Karian, Stephen E.
PR442.E39 2001
820.9′005—dc21 2001000746

To Phillip and Sydney Harth

Contents

Acknowledgments

The Editors wish to thank the following for generous subventions that helped to make this book possible: Chancellor John Wiley and the William Freeman Vilas Trust of the University of Wisconsin–Madison; Provost Jacob Nyenhuis and the Collegial Faculty Development Fund at Hope College, Holland, Michigan; the Department of English at the University of Wisconsin–Madison, and its Chair Thomas H. Schaub; and the Institute for Research in the Humanities at the University of Wisconsin–Madison, and its Director Paul S. Boyer and its Administrative Assistant Loretta K. Freiling. The Editors also wish to thank Jeffrey Theis and Charles A. Hutlar for valuable help with the index, and especially the University of Wisconsin Press and its able staff for consistently helpful and professional work with this book.

Introduction

This volume, written by colleagues, friends, and former students of Phillip Harth, honors his many contributions to the understanding and appreciation of the Restoration and early eighteenth century. The title and the unifying motif in the volume acknowledge that as teacher, scholar, and editor, Phillip Harth has been devoted to the practice and methodology of historical inquiry.

In *Contexts of Dryden's Thought* (1968), Phillip Harth spelled out explicitly the historical method he employed in his research and taught in his classes. His approach, he wrote, was not a "history-of-ideas exercise in the Basil Willey tradition." Rather, sound historical scholarship makes no assumptions about commonality. Each author invoked, each position, each statement must be examined independently, in its context, in order to determine its precise meaning. The scholar should be alert to subtle nuances that create differences in thought. Only by so doing can one reliably open up and clarify a work's relation to its historical contexts.

Phillip Harth's first book, *Swift and Anglican Rationalism: The Religious Background of "A Tale of a Tub"* (1961), provides specific application of that approach. One does not begin with the assumption that a single milieu exists for writers living at the beginning of the eighteenth century and that this milieu therefore explains Swift's attitudes. Such a uniform milieu can be constructed only at the unacceptable cost of eliminating necessary qualifications and exceptions. Nor can a writer's milieu be determined solely by focusing on the figures or positions he or she attacks, and by assuming that the writer shares the values or beliefs held by others who attack the same figures or positions. Any figure or position can be attacked for a variety of reasons and from a variety of viewpoints. In order to determine a precise milieu, one must attempt to relate a writer to others who attack the same objects for the same reasons from the same philosophical point of view.

Phillip Harth learned from his mentor, R. S. Crane, the danger of starting from a priori positions. Harth joined with Crane in advocating for historical research, and for the humanities generally, the standard of the sciences: one posits multiple hypotheses and considers counter-possibilities until one finds disbelief in a hypothesis more difficult to maintain than belief. Beginning with the text of Swift's *Tale of a Tub, Swift and Anglican Rationalism* involves a search by trial and error, looking for writers who attack the same groups or ideas, make the same specific charges against those groups or ideas, and argue from the same premises. When identified and analyzed, the writers thus isolated should constitute the most favorable hypothesis for determining the intellectual and moral position underlying the *Tale*'s religious aspect.

Harth's subsequent books, *Contexts of Dryden's Thought* (1968) and *Pen for a Party: Dryden's Tory Propaganda in Its Contexts* (1993), show similar concerns and use similar approaches. *Contexts* examines the religious controversy that gave rise to *Religio Laici* and *The Hind and the Panther. Pen for a Party* considers the political propaganda that shaped *Absalom and Achitophel.* In these books, in numerous scholarly articles and reviews, and in his edition of Mandeville's *The Fable of the Bees* (1970), Phillip Harth emphasizes the need for rigor and care in advancing historical argumentation. In doing so, he has guided and deeply influenced scholarship of the Restoration and eighteenth century.

The essays that follow are arranged in chronological order, in keeping with the volume's historical emphasis. The first three reflect Phillip Harth's work on Dryden and the religious backgrounds of the Restoration. James A. Winn undertakes a historical and critical inquiry into the nature of musical dissonance in the long eighteenth century, comparing and contrasting it to efforts to achieve analogous effects in that era's poetry. Maximillian E. Novak argues for the presence of hidden political meanings, or anti-Williamite "innuendos," in *The Old Batchelour,* added to Congreve's text by Dryden as he revised the play to prepare it for stage performance. Gerard Reedy, S. J. shows that the works of "Anglican rationalists" can be misinterpreted if their historical context is not taken into account—the occasions for which they were preached or written, for example, or the order in which they were subsequently published.

The next six essays, each undertaking a historical inquiry into the life and work of Jonathan Swift, recognize the centrality of Swift in Phillip Harth's career. Claude Rawson's demonstration of patterns of similarities in thought and language between Swift and Mandeville, "a reciprocal array of undeclared allusion," is particularly appropriate as a tribute to Phillip Harth as editor of *The Fable of the Bees.* Frank H. Ellis shows how Swift, in *Mr. C——ns's Discourse of Free-Thinking,* created a mock-abstract of Anthony Collins's *Discourse* through "additions" which both politicize Collins and reduce his work to nonsense while revealing Swift's own religious convictions. Hermann J. Real examines why, although *Gulliver's Travels* has often been labeled a utopia because of Swift's emulation of More, the seeming correspondences and similarities between the two men, and the dichotomous and paradoxical structure of their books, the label is inappropriate and the books pursue quite different ends.

Three essays deal with Swift's poetry. Peter J. Schakel shows that the poems Swift wrote at Market Hill develop techniques—particularly a polyphonic approach featuring voices other than the poet's—that characterize his finest later poems. Michael J. Conlon argues that Swift's ambivalent representations of his authority as a poet reflect a deliberate philosophical position regarding the meaning and value of authority: he chose to be authoritative in style and originality, but not in his person. James Woolley provides a thorough assessment of the origins, nature, and contents of the manuscript collection "The Whimsical Medley," its use by John Barrett in 1808 to make new attributions to Swift, its contributions to Swiftiana, and the research still necessary to determine its reliability and full value today.

Two essays deal with Pope, another of Phillip Harth's scholarly interests. David L. Vander Meulen uses the editorial policies enunciated by Martinus Scriblerus in *The Dunciad Variorum* as a vehicle for describing the fundamental approaches available to editors and illustrates those possibilities by connecting them to the ways the several *Dunciad*s have been or might be edited. Howard D. Weinbrot examines the reasons for and nature of Madame Dacier's attacks on Pope's translations of Homer (his supposedly inadequate understanding of Homer and Aristotle and alleged disloyalty to his own monarch) and the nature of Pope's reply and defense of his work and his patriotism.

Two essays deal with the novel and one with Johnson. Patricia C. Brückmann examines the way the story of Noah was interpreted in Renaissance and post-Renaissance commentaries and uses that context to clarify why in *Sir Charles Grandison* Clementina brings an unfinished needlepoint of Noah's ark rather than a book when Sir Charles offers to continue her lessons in English. Brian Corman shows that the critical history of the novel in English was established in the first two decades of the nineteenth century, in the work of Anna Laetitia Barbauld, John Colin Dunlop, and Sir Walter Scott, and that its impact was especially great and long-lasting in advancing the reputations of several early women novelists. Bruce Redford provides a close analysis of how Boswell functioned like a playwright in the *Life of Johnson,* constructing dramatic scenes and conversations through careful, deliberate reshaping and revision of his earliest notes and the original manuscript of the *Life*.

The final essay, by Eric Rothstein, redescribes the history of literary theory from the mid-seventeenth century to beyond 1800, even to the present, by addressing the problem of change. Basing his analysis on immanent principles and logic, Rothstein demonstrates a gradual shift from preeminently "Civic" ideals to a preeminently "Personal logic" which underlies virtually all innovations in literary theory after Dryden. In its theoretical subtlety and recollection of Phillip Harth's mentor R. S. Crane, it is a fitting conclusion to this collection of contextual and historical inquiries.

In a review of Phillip Harth's first book, Hoyt Trowbridge noted that "in a field which has had so much historically naive criticism, [Harth's] investigation is notable for its methodological sophistication and scholarly responsibility" (*Philological Quarterly* 41 [1962]: 631). The essays in this volume pay tribute to Phillip Harth by continuing in the tradition of his contextual studies and by emulating the methodological and scholarly care that has marked all of his work.

Phillip Harth: A Bibliography

BOOKS

Swift and Anglican Rationalism: The Religious Background of "A Tale of a Tub." Chicago: University of Chicago Press, 1961.

Contexts of Dryden's Thought. Chicago: University of Chicago Press, 1968. Chapter 1, "The Sceptical Critic," reprinted in *Critics on Dryden: Readings in Literary Criticism.* Ed. Robert McHenry and David G. Lougee. London: George Allen and Unwin, 1973. 63–75.

The Fable of the Bees, by Bernard Mandeville. Edited with an introduction and notes by Phillip Harth. Pelican Classics. Harmondsworth, Middlesex: Penguin Books, 1970. Reissued in Penguin Classics, 1989.

New Approaches to Eighteenth-Century Literature: Selected Papers from the English Institute. Edited with a foreword by Phillip Harth. New York: Columbia University Press, 1974.

New Homage to John Dryden: Papers Read at a Clark Library Conference, February 13–14, 1981. By Phillip Harth, Alan Fisher, and Ralph Cohen, with an introduction by Alan Roper. Los Angeles: William Andrews Clark Memorial Library, 1983.

Pen for a Party: Dryden's Tory Propaganda in Its Contexts. Princeton, N.J.: Princeton University Press, 1993.

ARTICLES AND REVIEW ARTICLES

"The Satiric Purpose of *The Fable of the Bees.*" *Eighteenth-Century Studies* 2 (1969): 321–40.

"Swift's *Project:* Tract or Travesty?" *PMLA* 84 (1969): 336–43 (with rejoinders by Leland D. Peterson).

"Ehrenpreis's *Swift:* The Biographer as Critic." *Modern Philology* 67 (1970): 273–78.

"Empson's Interpretation of *Religio Laici*." *Essays in Criticism* 20 (1970): 446–50.

"Religion and Politics in Dryden's Poetry and Plays." *Modern Philology* 70 (1973): 236–42.

"Legends No Histories: The Case of *Absalom and Achitophel*." *Studies in Eighteenth-Century Culture.* Vol. 4. Ed. Harold E. Pagliaro. Madison: University of Wisconsin Press, 1975. 13–29.

"The Problem of Political Allegory in *Gulliver's Travels*." *Modern Philology* 73 (1976): S40–S47.

"Studies in Restoration Literature." *Philological Quarterly* 55 (1976): 489–506.

"Studies in Restoration Literature." *Philological Quarterly* 56 (1977): 427–37.

"Clio and the Critics." *Studies in Eighteenth-Century Culture.* Vol. 10. Ed. Harry C. Payne. Madison: University of Wisconsin Press, 1981. 3–15.

"The New Criticism and Eighteenth-Century Poetry." *Critical Inquiry* 7 (1981): 521–37.

"Dryden's Public Voices." *New Homage to John Dryden.* Los Angeles: William Andrews Clark Memorial Library, 1983. 1–28. Reprinted in *Critical Essays on John Dryden.* Ed. James A. Winn. New York: G. K. Hall, 1997. 104–22.

"Dryden in 1678–1681: The Literary and Historical Perspectives." *The Golden and the Brazen World: Papers in Literature and History, 1650–1800.* Ed. John M. Wallace. Berkeley: University of California Press, 1985. 55–77.

"Swift's Self-Image as a Satirist." *Proceedings of the First Münster Symposium on Jonathan Swift.* Ed. Hermann J. Real and Heinz J. Vienken. Munich: Wilhelm Fink, 1985. 113–21.

"Political Interpretations of *Venice Preserv'd*." *Modern Philology* 85 (1988): 345–62.

"Friendship and Politics: Swift's Relations with Pope in the Early 1730s." *Reading Swift: Papers from the Third Münster Symposium on Jonathan Swift.* Ed. Hermann J. Real and Helgard Stöver-Leidig. Munich: Wilhelm Fink, 1998. 239–48.

"Recent Religious History and *A Tale of a Tub*." *Swift Studies* 14 (1999): 29–36.

"The Text of Dryden's Poetry." *Huntington Library Quarterly* 63 (2000): forthcoming.

REVIEWS

Theme and Structure in Swift's "Tale of a Tub," by Ronald Paulson. *Modern Philology* 58 (1961): 282–85.

Jonathan Swift as a Tory Pamphleteer, by Richard I. Cook. *Modern Language Quarterly* 29 (1968): 493–95.

Man versus Society in Eighteenth-Century Britain: Six Points of View, edited by James L. Clifford. *Philological Quarterly* 48 (1969): 295–97.

The Portraits of Alexander Pope, by William Kurtz Wimsatt. *Modern Philology* 65 (1969): 395–96.

John Dryden: Four Comedies and *John Dryden: Four Tragedies,* edited by L. A. Beaurline and Fredson Bowers. *Modern Philology* 67 (1970): 379–82.

Lemuel Gulliver's Mirror for Man, by W. B. Carnochan. *Modern Language Quarterly* 31 (1970): 118–21.

Dryden and the Abyss of Light: A Study of "Religio Laici" and "The Hind and the Panther," by Sanford Budick. *Philological Quarterly* 50 (1971): 424–26.

Dryden's Criticism, by Robert D. Hume. *Philological Quarterly* 50 (1971): 427–28.

Jonathan Swift: A Critical Introduction, by Denis Donoghue. *Eighteenth-Century Studies* 4 (1971): 484–85.

The Other End of the Egg: Religious Satire in "Gulliver's Travels," by Martin Kallich. *Modern Philology* 69 (1971): 165–69.

The Works of John Dryden, vol. 17, *Prose 1668–1691,* edited by Samuel Holt Monk and A. E. Wallace Maurer. *Philological Quarterly* 51 (1972): 672–74.

The Works of John Dryden, vol. 2, *Poems 1681–1684,* edited by H. T. Swedenberg, Jr. *Philological Quarterly* 52 (1973): 492–93.

Satires against Man: The Poems of Rochester, by Dustin H. Griffin. *Philological Quarterly* 53 (1974): 788–89.

Dryden's Classical Theory of Literature, by Edward Pechter. *The Eighteenth Century: A Current Bibliography,* n.s., 1 (1975): 283–85.

The Ambivalence of Bernard Mandeville, by Hector Monro, and *Bernard Mandeville,* by Richard I. Cook. *Modern Language Review* 72 (1977): 659–62.

Dryden: The Public Writer, 1660–1685, by George McFadden. *Journal of English and Germanic Philology* 78 (1979): 128–30.

Gulliver's Progress, by L. J. Morrissey. *Eighteenth-Century Studies* 12 (1979): 403–5.

Essays in Eighteenth-Century English Literature, by Louis A. Landa. *English Language Notes* 20 (1982): 61–63.
The Faith of John Dryden: Change and Continuity, by G. Douglas Atkins. *Eighteenth-Century Studies* 15 (1982): 210–15.
John Toland and the Deist Controversy, by Robert E. Sullivan. *The Journal of Modern History* 55 (1983): 697–99.
The Diary of Samuel Pepys, vol. 10, *Companion;* vol. 11, *Index,* edited by Robert Latham and William Matthews. *Eighteenth-Century Studies* 18 (1985): 232–34.
Probability and Certainty in Seventeenth-Century England: A Study of the Relationships between Natural Science, Religion, History, Law, and Literature, by Barbara J. Shapiro. *Isis* 76 (1985): 279–80.
Swift: The Man, His Works, and the Age, vol. 3, *Dean Swift,* by Irvin Ehrenpreis. *Eighteenth-Century Studies* 18 (1985): 406–9.
The Map of Time: Seventeenth-Century English Literature and Ideas of Pattern in History, by Achsah Guibbory. *The Eighteenth Century: A Current Bibliography,* n.s., 12 (1986): 331.
Order from Confusion Sprung: Studies in Eighteenth-Century Literature from Swift to Cowper, by Claude Rawson. *Modern Language Review* 82 (1987): 706–8.
John Dryden and His World, by James Anderson Winn. *Modern Philology* 86 (1989): 425–27.
"When Beauty Fires the Blood": Love and the Arts in the Age of Dryden, by James Anderson Winn. *The Eighteenth Century: A Current Bibliography,* n.s., 18 (1992): 366.

EIGHTEENTH-CENTURY CONTEXTS

1

Dissonance

1613–1798

JAMES A. WINN

1. MUSICAL DISSONANCE

In 1613, Don Carlo Gesualdo—poet, composer, prince, and murderer—published his sixth book of madrigals, including this astonishing passage:[1]

This brief, expressive moment may serve as a convenient opening exhibit, a basis on which to make some fundamental observations. Although the concept of dissonance is important for music, poetry, and early modern culture more generally, it is musical in origin, and our exploration of its many meanings must therefore start with some strictly musical observations.

True dissonance requires polyphony. In single-line music, such as Gregorian chant or troubadour song, a melody may surprise us with an unexpected interval, but dissonance as we normally understand it, and as practiced by early modern composers, requires at least two parts. Two-part or dyadic counterpoint, with clear rules for the resolution of tensions between the two parts, was the fundamental grammar of medieval music, even when third and fourth parts were added. As sixteenth-century composers gained sensitivity to more complex simultaneities, a syntax of triads, resembling but not yet identical to the familiar tonal harmony of the eighteenth century, began to replace the older practice, again with recognizably regular rules of resolution.

The same composers who developed imitative melodic devices or "madrigalisms"—rapid notes for running, high notes for references to heaven, and so forth—also began to develop expressive uses for harmonies. During the sixteenth century, conventions linking specific sonorities with specific emotions, such as the association of happiness with major triads or sadness with minor triads, grew stronger. Once those triads began to function syntactically as goals or endpoints for harmonic motion and metaphorically as generalized signifiers for classes of emotion, listeners could hear more complex chords as dissonant. The most dissonant chords in our example from Gesualdo, voiced so that two adjacent parts are singing notes one half step apart, are extreme but by no means unique.

Harmonic devices sometimes developed from melodic devices. One of the most common madrigalisms was a convention treating a falling half step in a melody line as a signifier for sorrow or death. Composers soon discovered that if they harmonized such a melodic moment in a way that left the higher pitch still sounding in another line, they could increase the effect of sorrow through that powerful dissonance, which could appear as a direct clash of two adjacent pitches, as in this chord from our Gesualdo example—

—or as a major seventh, the interval one half step less than an octave, as in this chord from the same passage:

Dryden invokes these "dying notes" in his "Song for St. Cecilia's Day, 1687":

> The soft complaining FLUTE
> In dying Notes discovers
> The Woes of hopeless Lovers,
> Whose Dirge is whisper'd by the warbling LUTE.[2]

The first composer to set those words, Giovanni Baptista Draghi, was probably not an expert speaker of English, but he knew the conventions. Each time the voice articulates the word *dying*, he provides a falling half step, and the first flute part also frequently repeats that interval, producing an unsettling series of dissonances:[3]

The first of the "dying" chords, which we might describe as an F minor chord with both the seventh and the sixth sounding,

is an even more dissonant simultaneity than the chords in our example from Gesualdo, but Draghi resolves it quickly, passing through two progressively less dissonant chords on the way to a triad. Although this moment is a particularly poignant example of the harmonic consequences of an imitative melodic device, it remains isolated, as do other instances of harmonic or melodic word-painting in Draghi's score. Other composers, as we shall see, went beyond Draghi in learning how to use dissonance structurally.

Dissonance requires some implicit standard of consonance. Dissonances like Gesualdo's and Draghi's can only be perceived as straining tonal grammar or striving to express emotion if they are understood against a background of consonance. Those of us who grew up listening to Western tonal music are so familiar with both kinds of meaning that it may be hard to accept the truth that both are entirely conventional. Despite various attempts to generate the tonal system out of acoustical physics, there is no compelling reason why music should have defined triads as consonant; in other periods, and certainly in other cultures, those chords, familiar to our ears, are strange. Similarly, our conventions linking major triads with happiness and minor triads with sadness, which we teach to our children, are simply conventions; there is no compelling intrinsic or "natural" reason why those chords should have those meanings. We cannot even label the twelve-tone compositions of Schoenberg and his followers as truly dissonant, however surprising their sonorities may be to ears accustomed to tonal music, because there are no triads or key centers against which dissonance clashes. The works begin and end in a harmonic idiom divorced from tonality. Gesualdo and Draghi, by contrast, are recognizably tonal composers; their pieces typically begin and end in the same key and reach cadences on the primary triads that shape normal tonal grammar. In our first example, Gesualdo's strange harmonies lead fairly quickly to a decisive cadence in the home key, G major, on *Felice sorte* ("happy fate"). In our second, Draghi treats the word *notes* as requiring consonance, moving rapidly from the strange sonorities on *dying* to resolutions on the dominant and the relative major when he reaches *notes.* If Draghi's dissonances, taken out of context, are harsher, Gesualdo's dissonances are actually stranger because of their greater distance from the home key; in both cases, the process of return or resolution, typically quite rapid in seventeenth-century music, gives us a sensory way of measuring that distance. Leonard Meyer has identified tension and release as a primary mechanism by which music expresses and induces emotion;[4] dissonance within a tonal framework, dissonance that leads to resolution, is an especially powerful example of this process.

In vocal music, dissonance is usually mimetic. It may be associated with either a specific word or phrase in the text or with the general occasion or mood of the text. The word *crucifixus* in the Nicene Creed, for example, provided many composers with opportunities for dissonances intended to express pain. More generally, references to death, madness, despair, and primal chaos were all occasions for expressive dissonance. As we have seen, such mimesis depended upon convention, and one especially powerful convention linked dissonance with the kind of emotional conflict poets had expressed through oxymoron. The phrase Gesualdo sets with those dissonant chords is *Dolcissimo il languire* ("sweetest is the languishing"), and I believe he placed the dissonant chords where he did for two reasons. They occur on a textual elision merging two adjacent vowels—"mo‿il"—a moment when two words melt into each other, and in emotional terms, they represent the merging of pleasure and pain in the moment of orgasm. The whole text turns on that bittersweet, oxymoronic state: "I burn for you, my dear, but the burning breathes a sweet spirit into my heart; I die for you, my life, but the dying is divine joy." As we shall see, the history of dissonance is intimately entwined with the history of the erotic. In both cases, extreme tension, even pain, may lead to a release intense in its sweetness.

The history of dissonance is not teleological. We cannot twist the evidence to fit either an imperialistic metanarrative in which chaotic, undisciplined noises become civilized and ordered, producing the classical tonal system as an end-product, or a radical metanarrative in which heroic composers break free from the chains of dull, conventional harmony. Though demonstrably incorrect, both of these narratives have been seductive and influential. The first accounts in part for the frequent invocation of dissonance as a metaphor for political unrest in the eighteenth century, with harmony serving as a figure for hierarchical order. The second helps to explain the rage for disorder that we encounter even in the most orderly of eighteenth-century composers and poets. But neither narrative fits the actual history, which is local, particular, and messy. In the long eighteenth century, we may trace a general motion away from the extremes of local dissonance that occasionally appear in earlier music. I know of no eighteenth-century piece containing a harmonic sequence as dissonant as the example from Gesualdo or a local clash as shocking as the example from Draghi. Yet as pieces grow longer and more complex in their structure, composers learn to produce tension on a larger scale by staying away from home keys for longer periods, delaying resolution and release. A growing interest in harmonic ambiguity replaces the earlier fascination with isolated, intensely expressive moments of dissonance.

As with so many other fundamental shifts occurring during the long eighteenth century, we can easily find simultaneous examples of the new and the old—especially in England, where older musical forms and styles lingered long after they had been abandoned on the Continent. My examples here come from a pair of short operas, probably first performed at the English Court during the 1680s, though the dates in both cases are now hotly disputed. John Blow's *Venus and Adonis,* for which the libretto remains stubbornly anonymous, is a good instance of English nostalgia for a late Renaissance theory of dissonance. Here is a truly amazing moment in the final chorus, in which Venus and her attendants ask the mourning Cupids to bear her soft Adonis "through the yielding air":[5]

As in our example from Gesualdo, the linkage between death and eroticism licenses the dissonance. The most excruciating chords come on the word *yielding,* which applies to the parting of the air as the body of Adonis floats toward heaven, but also suggests the earlier yielding of the goddess Venus to the charms of her mortal lover. Here Blow manages to write a series of suspensions that point toward a major seventh without ever quite reaching it, so that the chord previously treated as a shocking dissonance appears to function as a harmonic goal. But as in our other examples, dissonance finally yields to consonance, with a satisfying dominant cadence on the word *air.*

The companion piece, another short, through-sung court opera, is Purcell's *Dido and Aeneas.* Like his friend and colleague Blow, Purcell could write local dissonances with wonderfully expressive effect, and did so throughout his career. But in his best works, he moved toward a more structural use of dissonance, in which both musical grammar and emotional expression remain unsettled for much longer stretches of time. My example is Dido's first aria, "Ah Belinda." The librettist, Nahum Tate, provided a typical seventeenth-century song text: five lines, rhyming AABBA, in trochaic tetrameter, with a trimeter line for a cadence:

> Ah! *Belinda* I am prest
> With Torment not to be Confest.
> Peace and I are Strangers grown,
> I Languish till my Grief is known,
> Yet wou'd not have it Guest.[6]

A straightforward song following that poetic rhythm would have given Purcell no chance to dramatize Dido's torment. In typical fashion, he chose to rearrange the text. Here is what Dido actually sings:

> Ah, ah, ah! Belinda, I am prest, with torment,
> Ah, ah, ah! Belinda, I am prest, with torment, not to be confest.
> Ah, ah, ah! Belinda, I am prest, with torment,
> Ah, ah, ah! Belinda, I am prest, with torment, not to be confest.
> Peace and I are strangers grown,
> Peace and I are strangers, strangers grown.
> I languish till my grief is known,
> I languish [long melisma] till my grief is known,
> Yet would not, yet would not, would not have it guess'd.
> Peace and I are strangers grown,
> Peace and I are strangers, strangers grown.[7]

This is not merely a matter of stretching out the text by repetition in order to write a longer aria. The repeated "Ah" at the beginning gives Purcell a chance to establish Dido's emotional state before she even sings a meaningful word; it empowers musical, rather than verbal expression. The enjambment, splicing "with torment" right into the first line, gives us a longer, more expressive phrase, and softens Tate's obvious rhyme between "prest" and "confest." The most daring change is the repetition of Tate's third line at the end of Purcell's aria. That change denies the neat cadence of Tate's poem and leaves Dido's grief unresolved. On the evidence of this rewriting, I would argue that Purcell is a considerable poet. He recognizes that Dido's restlessness is a more important point than her secrecy, her desire not to have her torment "guess'd," and he moves that restlessness to the end, deliberately and dramatically unsettling the poetic form. In metaphorical terms, we might say that Purcell has made Tate's regular and consonant text more dissonant.

If we look at musical structure, Purcell initially seems quite conservative. Continental opera composers at this time were already using the *da capo* form that would be normative from Handel through Mozart. In this form, a substantial first section moves toward a decisive cadence, followed by a shorter contrasting section, often in a different key, with a different texture and sometimes even a different tempo, followed by a complete repeat of the first section. Purcell uses a much more static and old-fashioned form, writing his aria on a "ground bass," a short, repeating pattern, here just four bars:

In this instance, there are twenty-one repetitions of the same ground bass: eleven repetitions in the tonic, two in the dominant minor, then eight more in the tonic. Purcell escapes from this potentially boring structure in several ways. We are unlikely to hear the repetitions of the ground bass as repetitious because the phrase-lengths of the vocal line seldom coincide with the four-bar pattern of the ground bass. Dido begins singing in the middle of the bass pattern, and her lines stretch across and overlap the bass in what we might call a dissonance of phrase-length, an avoidance of symmetry closely analogous to the rewriting of Tate's text to subordinate its predictable meter. Only in the lines declaring that "Peace and I are strangers grown," perhaps with conscious irony, does Purcell allow symmetry between the phrases of the vocal line and the bass.

He also finds a way to make his expression of the text relate organically to his ground bass. The word-painting convention most strongly suggested by Tate's text is the falling half step of grief, dying, languishing, and so forth. On her second "ah," Dido gives us that expected pattern.

But we have already heard it two bars earlier in the bass, because Purcell has used the expressive falling half step, then its upwards inversion as the fundamental shaping idea of his ground bass. An idea derived from word-painting thus becomes a structural principle, and the chromaticism introduced into the bass line has far-reaching harmonic consequences. In the concluding passage in the strings, for example, Purcell includes some surprising harmonies that will remind us of Blow's choral harmonies:

Looked at as isolated chords, several of these sonorities are powerful local dissonances, but Purcell can afford to downplay them, adding them almost as an afterthought, because the piece as a whole sustains and extends the kind of tension that was merely local in our other examples. Where Gesualdo and Blow used particular dissonances to dramatize single words or phrases, Purcell uses larger strategies of structural dissonance to express Dido's restless, unsettled state of mind. The climax of the piece is the long melisma on the second "languish," another piece of expressive word-painting, significantly enough on a word Gesualdo had also used:

In Purcell's aria, however, this moment gains structural importance by occurring at the largest harmonic turning point, the moment where the second dominant ground returns to the tonic. What we can hear at that moment is the structural expansion of the idea of dissonance. Eighteenth-century composers, as we shall see, continued this process, though they increasingly shied away from strong local dissonances of the kind we have noticed in Gesualdo, Draghi, and Blow.

2. POETIC RESPONSES TO DISSONANCE

I have often argued for analogies between musical and poetic practice, and for patterns of influence running in both directions; but in the case of dissonance, the differences between poetry and music are more immediately obvious than the similarities.[8]

Because poetry cannot be truly polyphonic, *poetic dissonance must be imagined.* A spoken poem presents only one sound at a time. An acute sense of that limitation may help explain why popes and poets opposed polyphony from its invention in the Middle Ages well into the Renaissance, and why puritans enthusiastically joined that opposition. Although almost all of the attacks on polyphony complain that it obscures the words of the sung text, some of this hostility must have come from the recognition that polyphony gave composers expressive resources for which there were no obvious poetic equivalents. Outdone by their rivals, poets sought formal and metaphorical analogues in technique; when writing about music, they fell back on the ancient and Christian traditions associating it with the temptations of the flesh. In Spenser's Bower of Bliss, for example, the fleshly temptation of the naked damsels in the fountain immediately reappears in the form of explicitly polyphonic music:

> . . . a most melodious sound,
> Of all that mote delight a daintie eare,
> . . . .
> Was there consorted in one harmonee,
> Birdes, voyces, instruments, windes, waters, all agree.[9]

The next stanza is a poetic attempt to suggest polyphony:

> The joyous *birdes* shrouded in chearefull shade,
> Their notes unto the *voyce* attempred sweet;
> Th' Angelicall soft trembling *voyces* made
> To th' *instruments* divine respondence meet:
> The silver sounding *instruments* did meet
> With the base murmure of the *waters fall:*
> The *waters fall* with difference discreet,
> Now soft, now loud, unto the *wind* did call:
> The gentle warbling *wind* low answered to all.
> (2.12.71, emphasis mine)

This stanza attempts to provide a verbal equivalent for the actual complexity of polyphonic music. What Spenser suggests by repetition and overlap, polyphonic music accomplishes by simple simultaneity; Spenser helps us imagine the consorting together of the various parts, while a composer could simply write multiple parts. In the next stanza, "Many faire Ladies, and lascivious boyes . . . [mix] their song with light licentious toyes" (2.12.72). Music, especially polyphonic music, is thus equivalent to sexual temptation and sorcery; the poet demeans as sinful what he cannot quite accomplish by his own art.

Such opinions had real consequences. When parliamentary soldiers dismantled the cathedral organs and disbanded the choirs in English cathedrals during the 1640s, they were overtly attacking polyphony, which one puritan preacher described as "empty tautologies or chaunting over and over the same things, tossing of the Word of God like a tennis-ball from one to the other like that Cathedrall Musick intended onely to please the eare."[10] By referring to "empty tautologies," this writer treats the contrapuntal devices of polyphonic music as if they were failed rhetoric and denies the very different role played by repetition in musical and literary expression. In fact, as our example from Spenser suggests, it was poets who had to use repetition to suggest or imply simultaneity.

In seeking modes of expression analogous to dissonance, poets also needed an implicit standard of consonance. In rhythmic practice, for example, meter is the implicit, normative standard against which the actual rhythm of the poetic line is measured. Sheridan Baker once quipped that the only truly regular line of iambic pentameter would read "Detroit, Detroit, Detroit, Detroit, Detroit," but all sensitive poets hear such regularity as the implicit norm against which the rhythms of actual poetry struggle.[11] The relations between poetic meter and rhythm resemble those between musical consonance and dissonance only by analogy—especially because poets have to induce their readers to hear both the actual rhythm of the line and (in their imagination) the underlying regular meter. But without a real principle of dissonance, poets sought an equivalent expressiveness through straining meter. Donne's characteristic roughness, for which Ben Jonson thought he "deserved hanging," suggests a tolerance for rhythmic irregularity in the service of emotional expression, a practice loosely analogous to the harmonic irregularity of Gesualdo. Milton's obsessive habit of enjambment suggests an interest in stretching out phrases and avoiding symmetry between line-length and syntactic phrase length, a practice loosely analogous to Purcell's treatment of both Tate's text and his own repeating ground bass. Similar analogies obtain in other areas. A poetic line with many different vowel sounds will sound more troubled than a line restricted to one or two vowels; a line with inversions and distortions of normal prose word order will sound more troubled than a line with normal syntax. In all these cases, however, the analogy between musical and poetic practice is limited not only by the absence of true polyphony in poetry, but by the absence of a poetic effect as powerful and kinetic as the resolution of dissonance in music. When Donne writes a regular line after an irregular one, or when Milton follows a series of enjambments with an endstopped line consisting of one syntactic unit, the return to regularity does not carry with it the intense sense of relief that we feel when a musical dissonance resolves to a consonance.

We might consider the most self-consciously "irregular" poems of the long eighteenth century, the free pindarics initiated by Cowley and imitated by many later poets, analogous to those musical pieces that extend dissonance over longer stretches of time, except for the important fact that those musical pieces provide a much stronger principle of resolution. Here, for example, is a passage from Cowley's ode "To the Royal Society," praising the telescope and the microscope:

> Natures great Workes no distance can obscure,
> No smalness her near Objects can secure.
>   Y' have taught the curious Sight to press
>   Into the privatest recess
> Of her imperceptible Littleness.
> She with much stronger Art than his who put

All th' *Iliads* in a Nut,
The numerous work of Life does into Atomes shut.
Y' have learn'd to Read her smallest Hand,
And well begun her deepest Sense to Understand.[12]

These lines are dissonant in having clumsy rhythm, irregular line-lengths, awkward syntax, poor decorum, and a cacophonous collection of sounds; but the closing lines of the poem, where we might hope for some sense of resolution, continue to exhibit all those forms of dissonance. Cowley flatters Sprat, the author of the book in which this poem appears as front-matter:

His candid Stile like a clean Stream does slide,
And his bright Fancy all the way
Does like the Sun-shine in it play;
It does like *Thames,* the best of Rivers, glide,
Where the God does not rudely overturn,
But gently pour the Crystal Urn,
And with judicious hand does the whole Current Guide.
T' has all the Beauties Nature can impart,
And all the comely Dress without the paint of Art.
(sig. B3^{v})

The only principle of consonance in this poem is rhyme, and if the arrival of an expected rhyme sometimes provides a feeling analogous to that sense of relief we feel when a musical dissonance resolves to a cadence, the analogy here is pretty faint. There are more satisfying examples, such as the rhyming couplets with which Shakespeare often concludes an act of blank verse, providing a stronger sense of closure, or the deft use of a triplet with an Alexandrine to signal the end of a verse paragraph in a couplet poem. Although the degree of resolution a reader or hearer may experience at such moments differs widely according to form, content, and context, *rhyme is the closest poetic equivalent to the resolution reached in a musical cadence.*

Indeed, some poets have insisted on this analogy. Dryden's defense of rhyme in the *Essay of Dramatick Poesie,* perhaps the most enthusiastic in the period, invokes musical terminology and alludes to the erotic, which was closely connected in his imagination, and the imagination of the period, with the power of musical dissonance and resolution. Neander, the Dryden figure, argues that artful rhyme is the best imitation of intense passion.

I acknowledg the hand of Art appears in repartee, as of necessity it must in all kind of verse. But there is also the quick and poynant brevity of it (which is an high imitation of Nature in those sudden gusts of passion) to mingle with it: and

> this joyn'd with the cadency and sweetness of the Rhyme, leaves nothing in the soul of the hearer to desire.[13]

In invoking "cadency," Dryden borrows a term from music, though the analogy between cadence and rhyme had long been recognized. Thomas Morley, the composer who set a number of Shakespeare's songs, defined cadence in 1597: "A Cadence we call that when, coming to a close, two notes are bound together and the following note descendeth."[14] George Puttenham had claimed the term for poetry eight years earlier, in 1589, defining cadence as rhyme: "This cadence is the fal of a verse in every last word with a certaine tunable sound which being matched with another of like sound, do make a concord."[15] Dryden's claims, however, go well beyond noticing the "concord" of "like sound[s]" in rhyme. In claiming that "the cadency and sweetness of the Rhyme [will leave] nothing in the soul of the hearer to desire," he insists that rhyme provides the same satisfaction as musical cadence, and his description of satisfied desire is not the only gesture toward eroticism in this passage. When Neander argues that "the quick and poynant brevity" of rhymed dialogue is "an high imitation of Nature in those sudden gusts of passion," he repeats a phrase Eugenius has already used in discussing the emotions imitated in ancient plays.

> To speak generally, their Lovers say little, when they see each other, but *anima mea, vita mea;* ζωὴ καὶ ψυχή, as the women in *Juvenal*'s time us'd to cry out in the fury of their kindness: Any sudden gust of passion (as an ecstasie of love in an unexpected meeting) cannot better be express'd than in a word and a sigh, breaking one another. (*Works* 17:31–32)

The Greek phrase, lifted from Juvenal's notorious satire against women, directs our attention to the cries of ecstasy that women make "in the fury of their kindness," in orgasm. A "sudden gust of passion," the phrase Neander will later associate with rhyme, "cannot better be express'd than in a word and a sigh, breaking one another." But surely our first example of dissonance, in which Gesualdo places a sighing dissonance at the point where one word breaks another, is a far more poignant expression of such passions than the predictable rhymes of Dryden's heroic plays.

If Dryden's claims on behalf of the "cadency and sweetness of the Rhyme" are less than convincing, they nonetheless reveal his hope that rhyme *might* generate an affective power akin to that produced by dissonance and resolution. Twenty years after the *Essay,* in his pindaric "Song for St. Cecilia's Day, 1687," he used a complex pattern of rhyming to exemplify the ordering of chaos by harmony, making the power of rhyme analogous to musical resolution, and to God's power at the moment of Creation. Although it is far more beautiful than anything dreamt of in

Cowley, the opening stanza is dissonant not only in irregular line-lengths, but in appearing to be unrhymed. Yet once the first rhyme appears, this apparent chaos resolves into elaborate concord, best described in Earl Wasserman's diagram:[16]

From Harmony, from heav'nly Harmony,	5A
This universal Frame began	4B
When Nature underneath a heap	4C
Of jarring Atomes lay,	3D
and cou'd not heave her Head,	3E
The tuneful Voice was heard from high,	4F
"Arise ye more than dead."	3E
Then cold, and hot, and moist, and dry,	4F
In order to their stations leap,	4C
And Musick's pow'r obey.	3D
From Harmony, from heav'nly Harmony	5A
This universal Frame began:	4B
From Harmony to Harmony	4A'
Through all the compass of the Notes it ran,	5B'
The diapason closing full in Man.	5B"

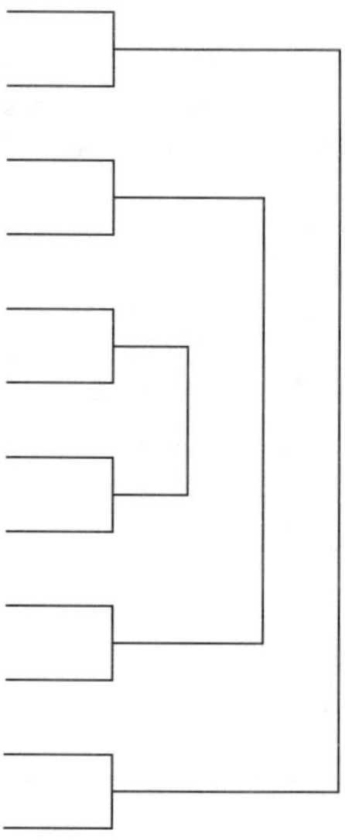

The concluding coda, repeating the first two rhymes and providing the only couplet in the stanza, insists on resolution and cadence. I offer this stanza as a maximum instance of poetry approximating dissonance and resolution.

Yet even this example, cunning as it is, is more intellectual, less visceral, than our musical examples. I have argued elsewhere that Dryden's mathematical structures constitute a booby trap for the composer, whose attention to local imitative effects and word-painting will inevitably lead him to obscure the poetic form.[17] Both Giovanni Baptista Draghi, who set the poem in 1687, and George Frederick Handel, who set it some thirty years after Dryden's death, ignore the careful symmetries on which Dryden's mimetic form depends. Handel sets the first ten lines as a recitative, the last five as a chorus, and repeats several lines within the recitative, thus obscuring the grouping of the lines in pairs and Dryden's complex metrical pattern. Composers could afford to override poetic form, as we have seen in Purcell's treatment of Tate, because they had different expressive powers at their disposal, including the dissonance and resolution made possible by polyphony. In setting the opening lines, Handel uses local dissonances to express the jarring atoms of chaos, but his dissonances will strike us as palpably different from those used by Gesualdo, Blow, and Purcell. Where those earlier composers had favored semitone clashes, major sevenths, and cross-relations, Handel mainly uses the diminished seventh chord:

This pile of minor thirds is so familiar to our ears from its excessive use in nineteenth-century music that it may take some effort to recover the feeling of strangeness it produced when first used in a triadic context. Although it does not involve a semitone clash, the diminished seventh chord includes two intervals of a tritone or augmented fourth, an unstable and dissonant interval crying out for resolution. As composers quickly discovered, it was also a marvelous tool for achieving structural dissonance. Unlike our earlier examples of dissonance, which normally resolved in only one predictable way, the diminished seventh could plausibly lead to several different triads; this harmonic ambiguity made it possible to move smoothly to distant keys, and to suspend real harmonic resolution for longer stretches of time. In this case, those long periods of ambiguity enact primal chaos, so that the large cadence on the dominant at "Arise, ye more than dead" becomes a highly satisfying event, truly leaving "nothing in the soul of the hearer to desire."[18]

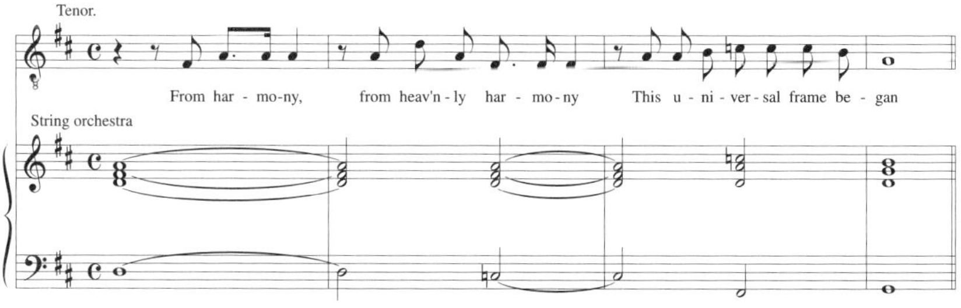

When Na - ture, un - der - neath a heap Of jar - ring a - toms
lay, When Na - ture un - der - neath a
heap Of jar - ring a - toms lay, And could not heave her head,
The tune - ful voice was heard from high, A -

While composers like Handel sought to expand and extend the principle of dissonance, *poets embraced a false teleology in which expression was supposed to be evolving toward smoothness and correctness.* What came to be the conventional narrative of smoothness and correctness, the long eighteenth century's sense of its own poetry as an improvement over past practice, correctly reflects a decreasing tolerance for the forms of poetic dissonance apparent in our examples from Cowley. As early as 1667, Dryden speaks of "the happiness of some Writers yet living; who first taught us to mould our thoughts into easie and significant words; to retrench the superfluities of expression, and to make our Rime so properly a part of the Verse, that it should never mis-lead the sence, but it self be led and govern'd by it" (*Works* 17:14). He is thinking of Waller, the patron saint of the cult of smoothness. Walsh's famous advice to the young Pope is part of the same narrative: "we ha[ve] had several great poets," he told the precocious boy, "but never had any one great poet that was correct."[19] Although Pope set out to be the most correct of poets, valuing consonance highly in his youthful *Pastorals,* he was already expressing scorn for mere sweetness in the *Essay on Criticism,* where he criticizes predictable rhymes and overly regular versification. Significantly for our purposes, music in this passage functions as a metaphor for consonance:

> But most by *Numbers* judge a Poet's Song,
> And *smooth* or *rough,* with them, is *right* or *wrong;*
> In the bright *Muse* tho' thousand *Charms* conspire,
> Her *Voice* is all these tuneful Fools admire,
> Who haunt *Parnassus* but to please their Ear,
> Not mend their Minds; as some to *Church* repair,
> Not for the *Doctrine,* but the *Musick* there.
> These *Equal Syllables* alone require,
> Tho' oft the Ear the *open Vowels* tire,
> While *Expletives* their feeble Aid *do* join,

And ten low Words oft creep in one dull Line,
While they ring round the same *unvary'd Chimes,*
With sure *Returns* of still *expected Rhymes.*
(337–49)[20]

Wickedly accurate as a critique of smoothly empty coffee-house couplets, this passage misrepresents music as pure, predictable consonance. As Pope continues, he claims for poetry the languishing power more easily achieved by musical dissonance:

Leave such to tune their own dull Rhimes, and know
What's *roundly smooth,* or *languishingly slow;*
And praise the *Easie Vigor* of a Line,
Where *Denham*'s strength, and *Waller*'s Sweetness join.
(358–61)

The link between languishing and the slowing down of poetic tempo, the delaying of resolution, shows Pope's desire to appropriate for poetry the power of tension and release. He expands the word *languish,* which we have already encountered at expressive moments in Gesualdo ("dolcissimo il languire") and in Purcell ("I languish till my grief is known") into a four-syllable adverb ("languishingly") that functions as a poetic equivalent for the kind of sensuous delay achieved by musical dissonance. Like Dryden, from whom he learned versification, Pope realized that unrelieved consonance was boring, that poetry needed not merely the sweetness signified by Waller but the strength signified by Denham.

In *The Dunciad,* Pope even embraced chaos, for example in the contest of the noisy poets:

Now thousand tongues are heard in one loud din:
The Monkey-mimics rush discordant in;
'Twas chatt'ring, grinning, mouthing, jabb'ring all,
And Noise and Norton, Brangling and Breval,
Dennis and Dissonance, and captious Art,
And Snip-snap short, and Interruption smart,
And Demonstration thin, and Theses thick,
And Major, Minor, and Conclusion quick.
(2.235–42)[21]

Of course this version of discord is not nearly as dissonant as our examples from Cowley. Pope orders his noisy material through alliteration, couplet rhymes, and careful modulation of the rhythm. Unlike Cowley, he also matches his sound to his subject, delighting in hitching the names of his enemies into a context of controlled cacophony. The concluding joke, which turns on the fact that *major* and *minor* are terms used for both premises in logic and keys in music, directs our attention to the virtuosity of this celebration of noise.

Incongruous or jarring content of this kind often served poets as a metaphorical equivalent for dissonance. The verbal excesses of the heroic play, in which the rant of the Almanzors and Maximins often produces bizarre imagery, may derive not only from the belated metaphysical practice of poets like Cowley, but also from the musical origins of the genre, which I have explored elsewhere.[22] What the lost music for Davenant's *Siege of Rhodes* probably accomplished by local dissonance, Dryden and his contemporaries had to accomplish by verbal dissonance. Here, for example, is a speech given by Creon in the version of *Oedipus* that Dryden wrote in collaboration with Nathaniel Lee:

> Am I to blame if Nature threw my body
> In so perverse a mould? yet when she cast
> Her envious hand upon my supple joints,
> Unable to resist, and rumpled 'em
> On heaps in their dark lodging, to revenge
> Her bungled work she stampt my mind more fair:
> And as from Chaos, huddled and deform'd,
> The God strook fire, and lighted up the Lamps
> That beautify the sky, so he inform'd
> This ill-shap'd body with a daring soul:
> And making less than man, he made me more.[23]

Nature first "throws" Creon's body, as if it were a pot, then shapes it in a mold, then does something strange with "her envious hand," so that his joints wind up in heaps in a "dark lodging"; then she stamps his mind, a process somehow analogous to the striking of fire from chaos. The vocabulary this passage shares with the St. Cecilia ode is not accidental, but in this case there is no ordering or shaping, only a deliberate mixing of "huddled and deform'd" images. The creation of a stage villain licensed such excess. In other contexts, such as satire, poets often treated ugly, obscene, or incongruous matter as a form of cognitive dissonance, which in turn called forth formally dissonant verse. The dissonance was always associated with the target, though often enjoyed by the poet.

3. CODA

Although the histories of musical and poetic dissonance are not parallel, they have frequent productive intersections. We may conclude with one telling example. Handel's setting of Dryden's ode for 1687, with wind parts added by Mozart, was performed under the patronage of Baron van

Swieten in Vienna in 1790; the same van Swieten was responsible for the German libretto for Haydn's *Die Schöpfung* (*The Creation*), first performed in 1798. Haydn's remarkable instrumental overture to that work, the *Vorstellung des Chaos,* extends techniques of harmonic ambiguity learned from Handel's setting of Dryden, including frequent and creative use of the diminished seventh chord. Although Haydn's piece, not least because of the absence of a text, signals the increasing freedom and power of orchestral music, it draws upon a harmonic convention developed in an attempt to find a musical equivalent for a poetic evocation of dissonance; but that poetic text itself was an attempt to find a verbal equivalent for musical dissonance. As is so often the case in the larger histories of music and poetry, the limitations of one art form, creatively confronted by an authentic genius, may ultimately have expressive consequences for another.

NOTES

1. Don Carlo Gesualdo, "Ardo per te"; music and text from the "*Gesamtausgabe*" of the *Works of Gesualdo* (Hamburg: Ugrino Verlag, 1957–1967), 6:63–64.
2. "A Song for St. Cecilia's Day, 1687," in *Poems, 1685–1692,* ed. Earl Miner, vol. 3 of *The Works of John Dryden,* ed. Edward Niles Hooker et al. (Berkeley: University of California Press, 1969), 202 (33–36).
3. Following my transcription of the manuscript at the Royal College of Music, London.
4. Leonard B. Meyer, *Emotion and Meaning in Music* (Chicago: University of Chicago Press, 1956).
5. Music and text from *Venus and Adonis,* ed. Bruce Wood (Aberystwyth, Wales: privately printed, 1992), 70–71.
6. Nahum Tate, *Dido and Aeneas* (London, 1689), 3.
7. This and all citations of the music from Henry Purcell, *Dido and Aeneas,* ed. Curtis Price (New York: Norton, 1986), 6–9.
8. See especially my *Unsuspected Eloquence: A History of the Relations between Poetry and Music* (New Haven, Conn.: Yale University Press, 1981).
9. Edmund Spenser, *The Faerie Queene,* 2.12.70. This and all citations of Spenser follow the text given in *Spenser: Poetical Works,* ed. J. C. Smith and E. De Selincourt (London: Oxford University Press, 1970); I have normalized v and u, i and j.
10. Thomas Ford, *Singing of Psalms the Duty of Christians . . . In V. Sermons* (London, 1653), 68. The metaphor of the tennis ball was a commonplace in Puritan attacks on polyphony. For an earlier instance, see Nathanael Homes, *Gospel Music; or, The singing of Davids psalms, &c. in the publick congregations, or private families asserted, and vindicated* (London, 1644): "first one sings an An-

them, then half the Chore, then the other, tossing the Word of God like a Tenice-ball" (19).

11. Sheridan Baker, "English Meter *Is* Quantitative," *College English* 21 (1960): 311. As Baker notes, he assumes standard northern pronunciation of the city's name, not the "*Dee*troit" often heard in the South.

12. Abraham Cowley, "To the *Royal Society*," in the front-matter of Thomas Sprat, *History of the Royal Society,* ed. Jackson I. Cope and Harold Whitmore Jones (St. Louis, Mo.: Washington University, 1958), sig. B3^{r}.

13. *Prose, 1668–1691: An Essay of Dramatick Poesie and Shorter Works,* ed. Samuel Holt Monk, vol. 17 of *The Works of John Dryden* (1971), 76–77.

14. Thomas Morley, *A Plain and Easy Introduction to Practical Music,* ed. R. Alec Harman (New York: Norton, 1952), 145.

15. George Puttenham, *The Arte of English Poesie* (London, 1589), 66.

16. Earl Wasserman, "Pope's *Ode for Musick,*" *ELH* 28 (1961): 163–86, here quoting 167.

17. James A. Winn, *"When Beauty Fires the Blood": Love and the Arts in the Age of Dryden* (Ann Arbor: University of Michigan Press, 1992), chapter 3.

18. George Frederick Handel, *Ode on St. Cecilia's Day* (New York: H. W. Gray, n.d.), 6–8.

19. Anecdote no. 73 in Joseph Spence, *Observations, Anecdotes, and Characters of Books and Men, Collected from Conversation,* ed. James M. Osborn (Oxford: Clarendon Press, 1966), 1:73.

20. *Pastoral Poetry and An Essay on Criticism,* ed. E. Audra and Aubrey Williams, vol. 1 of *The Twickenham Edition of the Poems of Alexander Pope,* ed. John Butt et al. (London: Methuen, 1961), 276–79.

21. I quote the version given in *Dunciad* B (1743), from *The Dunciad,* ed. James Sutherland, vol. 5 of *The Twickenham Edition of the Poems of Alexander Pope,* 3d ed. (1963), 307. The text in *Dunciad* A (1728), 2.227–32 (5:128), lacks the final couplet here quoted.

22. James A. Winn, "Heroic Song: A Proposal for a Revised History of English Theatre and Opera, 1656–1711," *Eighteenth-Century Studies* 30 (1997): 113–37.

23. *Plays: All for Love, Oedipus, Troilus and Cressida,* ed. Maximillian E. Novak, vol. 13 of *The Works of John Dryden* (1984), 126 (1.1.145–55).

2

The "fashionable cutt of the town" and William Congreve's The Old Batchelour

MAXIMILLIAN E. NOVAK

The Romantic critics, led by Charles Lamb, advanced the argument that the scenes portrayed in Restoration drama belonged to a kind of imaginary world having no relationship to reality. They did so by way of searching for a method of defending these plays against the charges of obscenity and immorality leveled against them by a variety of moralists who followed Jeremy Collier's examination and condemnation of these works in 1698.[1] As Jonas Barish has demonstrated, "anti-theatrical prejudice" has always accompanied stage productions; in the middle of the eighteenth century even Jean-Jacques Rousseau had weighed in against stage performances.[2] If many thought of the theater as objectionable in principle, how much more unacceptable were plays that dealt openly with sexuality and with the details of contemporary life? The Romantic approach prevailed for a time, but it eventually brought with it the possibility of dismissing these plays on the grounds that they had no relevance to ordinary life. Such an attitude dominated the middle of the twentieth century and it has only been during the last twenty-five years that these plays have been regarded as seriously reflecting the Restoration experience. More particularly, critics have become aware of how thoroughly politics pervaded the drama of the time and how entirely the playwrights devoted themselves to political statement and attacks upon the attitudes of their opponents.[3]

1.

By now almost all of William Congreve's plays have been subjected to political readings. Many years ago I suggested that his sole tragedy, *The Mourning Bride* (1697), might be read in terms of a Whig allegory in which the old forces of repression are swept away by the triumph of the young lovers, and somewhat later, I argued that *The Double Dealer* (1694) was essentially about the survival of the English Family over the conspiracies of "Jack" (Jacobite) Maskwell.[4] Even more recently, Richard Braverman has maintained that *The Way of the World* (1700) embodies another Whiggish triumph—this time over another conspirator, Fainall, and his attempt to take over the wealth of Lady Wishfort.[5] Much the same might be said for *Love for Love* (1695) with the victory of the true lovers, Valentine and Angelica, over the Hobbist ideas of the tyrannical patriarch, Sir Sampson Legend. The play that involves the greatest problem for political interpretation, however, is *The Old Batchelour* (1693), for most contemporaries appeared to think that for Congreve's stage debut, he had written a play that avoided the type of backbiting, lampooning, and political innuendoes that distinguished the comedies of the early 1690s.

Such a judgment, however, must be viewed in the context of the times. Satire had emerged as the form, which, to paraphrase Juvenal, writers could not avoid if they wanted to do so. Dryden had given satire a new prominence with his translations of Juvenal and Persius accompanied by his "Discourse" concerning satire, in which he had written some of his most acute criticism. For Jacobites such as Dryden and his sometime collaborator, Thomas Southerne, half concealing satiric barbs under seemingly innocent historical parallels became an art in itself. As Phillip Harth has pointed out, the enterprise was very different in nature from Dryden's direct party propaganda during the 1680s, but through allusion, parallels, and innuendoes, he continued to wage poetic warfare against the government of William and Mary and William III throughout the entire decade of the 1690s.[6] The audience for Dryden's poems, translations, and plays and, indeed, the audience for every work of the time came to the literary experience prepared to discover every possible innuendo, social as well as political. This was particularly true of theatrical presentations. For example, during the 1690s, the playwright Thomas D'Urfey frequently added disclaimers to his printed plays, insisting that he was not lampooning individuals who thought they had been attacked in his comedies.[7] On at least one occasion, when Queen Mary went to the theater, the audience apparently turned to her to see how she might be reacting to lines that could be interpreted as reflecting upon her relationship to her deposed father, James II.[8] The response of the audience was symptomatic of the expectation for political innuendo at the time.[9]

It is not surprising that the word "innuendo" was given its modern meanings at around this time. Formerly it had a meaning equivalent to "in other words" by way of explaining a difficult or ambiguous concept. During the political squabbles at the end of Charles II's reign two related meanings emerged. According to the *Oxford English Dictionary,* an innuendo might be, as it is usually today, an "oblique hint, indirect suggestion . . . esp. one of a depreciatory kind," or it might be "an interpolated or appended explanation of, or construction put upon a word, expression, or passage; esp. the injurious meaning or signification alleged to be conveyed by words not *per se* injurious or actionable." Although the *OED* gives the usage of Roger L'Estrange in 1678 as its point of origin, its popular usage as a kind of hint or implied meaning dates from the trials associated with the Rye House Plot and the persecutions of those considered enemies of the crown in and after 1683. The most famous use of "innuendo" as extrapolated meaning came in the trial of Algernon Sidney, who was convicted on the basis of an interpretation of a reading in a manuscript found on his desk. Chief Justice Jeffreys maintained that a general argument about the rights of the people to remove tyrants might be constructed to be a direct attack on Charles II.[10] Thereafter, contemporary writers on politics spoke of his being convicted on the basis of an "innuendo."[11]

In some ways, however, an even more elaborate use of "innuendo" came in the trial of the dissenting minister Thomas Rosewell around the same time (1684). As in the case of Sidney, the presiding judge was the infamous Jeffreys. He used the concept of innuendo in its original meaning as well as in both of its contemporary meanings. Jeffreys accused Rosewell of hinting at Charles II's sexual life in his references to Samson and Delilah and of "imagining" the death of Charles in allusions to the deaths of wicked kings, even though Rosewell stated that Ahab and his son Ahaziah were intended.[12] The prosecution argued that Rosewell's case was similar to the trial of Algernon Sidney and that the jury should come in with another guilty verdict. Rosewell's side argued that words should not be drawn out of their proper signification, that in matters of law, one should not "press Words, or strain them to speak more than willingly they mean or intend."[13] At one point, both Jeffreys and the defence became so entangled in the problems of determining the exact meaning of an innuendo that Rosewell's lawyer expressed his wish that all discussions of innuendoes might be dropped from the trial. Although Rosewell was found guilty, Charles II pardoned him and reduced his sentence to a fine, after Sir John Talbot had appealed to the King and convinced him that if the principles applied in the Rosewell case were allowed to stand, no Englishman would feel safe from prosecution.[14] Why Talbot felt this way is easy enough to ascertain. At one point during the trial, Jeffreys had speculated that the audience which had listened to Rosewell's sermon might be presumed to have been infected by his alleged innuendoes and therefore be as guilty of treason as the unfortunate preacher. Algernon Sidney became a Whig martyr and Thomas Rosewell a hero to the Dissenters, but their cases, in addition to popularizing new meanings to an old word, may have given some impetus to a literary culture in which the audience, already attuned to discovering hidden meanings and political references, was even more eager to search for concealed allusions.

As has been suggested, after the Glorious Revolution, the Jacobites became most skillful at the game of hidden meanings, but if satire was the most obvious vehicle for attacking William and Mary it was also the most dangerous. As an alternative, playwrights opposed to the regime often turned to historical plays that could offer political parallels to contemporary events. If audiences might make the application, it was surely not the fault of the author or so, at least, Dryden would argue in his defence.[15] If the playgoer wished to construe a contemporary political parallel from an old play such as *The Spanish Fryar,* how much the more might they look for it in contemporary performances?

In Dryden's case, the question is: could he ever resist the temptation to hint at a subversive political meaning? Recently, in watching a delightful, if abridged, performance of Dryden's *King Arthur* by Les Arts Florissants, I found myself very much in the position of what must have been that of the audience that heard it in 1691.[16] I had not read the play for several years and had never seen it performed. Of course Purcell's music was wonderful, but what of the politics? Shortened as it was, the text still seemed to bristle with possible political significance. Was this simply a story of a legendary Arthur who restores Britain to its true greatness, or was it all about the deposed James II, and his true claim to the nation? Were the "Saxon" hordes really William's Dutch soldiers? Was it an accident that the names of both the evil enchanter and the leader of the enemy forces had names beginning with O—like William of Orange? Doubtless most members of the audience were content to listen to the wonderful music and watch the spectacle, but surely Dryden hoped the audience could take away some kind of political message. Later in this paper I will discuss some of Dryden's use of the drama for more overt attacks upon the government, but I choose to start with *King Arthur* because it might be read as entirely innocent of political propaganda.

Although James Winn admits that *King Arthur* was "open to a Jacobite reading," he argues that the opera was so balanced in its possible political ramifications that supporters of William could read it in a positive way and the Jacobites could read it as an anti-Williamite play.[17] Everything suggests that Winn reads Dryden's intentions correctly, but who in the audience did not know of Dryden's political position? In his dedication to Halifax, Dryden himself speaks of how he felt obliged to alter the politics of the work from his original draft that had been written in 1684, but his claim to have had the full approbation of Queen Mary for his work has been greeted with considerable skepticism.[18] While modern readers might find his references to the strength of the navy protecting England's shores a simple statement of patriotism, what contemporary reader did not know of the defeat inflicted by the French upon the combined British-Dutch fleet at Beachy Head on 30 June 1690? Not until after the end of the naval battle at La Hogue on 20 May 1692 was it evident that James II was not going to be capable of launching an invasion of Britain. Vinton Dearing's notes to the play suggest the possibility of irony in several places, but the various parts of the published text, including the prologue, epilogue, and its dedication read more like a work written in coded language, with the knowledgeable audience having no difficulty supplying the true meaning of what might seem innocuous enough to many readers.[19]

It was not merely in the theater and in satires that the Jacobite message was conveyed. The author of *Antiquity Reviv'd, or, The Government of a Certain Island Antiently Call'd Astreada* (1693) put his criticism of the new world of William and Mary into a prose utopia. Any punishment that might have followed the publication of this work was deflected by the notation that the society being described dated "Some hundreds of yrs before Christ." It begins innocuously enough with the story of how some Athenians fled their city by sea after the conquest by Alexander. Blown to an unknown island, the Athenian exiles encounter the world of the Astreadans and are immediately enchanted by their ideas on religion and philosophy. Only after more than fifty pages might readers become aware that they were not reading the kind of imaginary voyage which, in the hands of Gabriel Foigny and Denis Vairasse, insinuated certain deistical and radical political notions at the end of the seventeenth century. After a discussion of the religion of the Astreadans, which consists of a general worship of "Providence," without any belief in miracles, the text veers suddenly to a discussion of politics clearly representative of the Jacobite viewpoint. There is no "original Contract" between the monarch and the people. The system is entirely patriarchal with the monarch having absolute power. The notion that the people would have the right to make laws is viewed as absurd, and the monarch, who represents virtue in the nation, has the power to crush any kind of popular threat to his family or the state. Of course there were direct attacks upon the government along with advocacy for the return of James II, such as *Great Britain's Just Complaint for Her Late Measures, Present Sufferings, and Future Miseries She Is Exposed To* (1691?), but most of the writers who opposed the reign of William and Mary appeared to believe that indirect methods were best. Religion, warfare, the rise of the moneyed interests, and foreign domination were all subjects that could be hinted at in utopias, vaguely parallel dramatic plots, or verse satires containing obscure references.

2.

Congreve's prologue to *The Old Batchelour* describes the new satiric mode, which might be found in its quintessential state in the prologues to these contemporary plays, and tries to distinguish his play from these bitterly satiric comedies:

> But now, no more like Suppliants, we come;
> A Play makes War, and Prologue is the Drum:
> Arm'd with keen Satyr, and with pointed Wit,
> We threaten you who do for Judges sit,
> To save our Plays, or else we'll damn your Pit.
> But for your Comfort, it falls out to day,
> We've a young Author and his first born Play;
> So, standing only on his good Behaviour,
> He's very civil, and entreats your Favour.[20]

Congreve was successful in this attempt at presenting his play as an example of "Humour" without any elements of satire or serious themes.[21] For all its apparent apolitical surface and its charming allusiveness to earlier comedies, however, *The Old Batchelour* contains much topical satire along with an unusually ambiguous ending for Vainlove and Araminta, who share the main love interest of the play with Bellmour and Belinda. Like many texts, both those favorable to the reign of William and Mary and the political principles of the Glorious Revolution and those favorable to the Jacobite cause, this play has a feeling about it of cynicism, open-endedness, and particularly in the Heartwell plot, bitterness. Its enormous success, though dependent in part on the expectation aroused over a play that had been long in preparation as well as upon the play's intrinsic excellence, had to be linked to its ability to capture the mood of the times.

Congreve's biographer, John Hodges, was convinced that Congreve wrote the play in 1689, based on the assertion in his dedication that the original version had been written four years earlier.[22] Congreve later remarked that he had composed it during a "slow Recovery from a Fit of Sickness," and the place of composition was likely to have been outside of London in either Ilam, Derbyshire, or in the nearby Stretton Hall, Staffordshire.[23] D. Crane Taylor suggested that William accompanied his father and mother there after the death of his grandfather in August 1688, but Hodges also speculated that, like so many others, the Congreve family fled Dublin for political reasons.[24] The Earl of Tyrconnel had been rooting out Protestants from the army as early as 1686, and in 1689 Congreve's father was listed as an unemployed army officer in the London environs. Tyrconnel's vendetta extended itself to the Protestant Trinity College, where Congreve was studying. With both students and tutors fleeing precipitously during the months preceding William of Orange's landing at Taunton on the fifth of November 1688, it must have seemed as if Ireland would be an uncomfortable place for those who did not support James II. Under these circumstances, Congreve would have seemed an unlikely writer to have demonstrated unhappiness with James II's departure from England or to have written a comedy that would have been skeptical about William III's war against Louis XIV, James's chief defender on the continent.

At any rate Congreve appears to have written the first draft of his play in a place that he described as "so much out of the world that nothing but . . . great news could have reacht it."[25] That he would have known every detail about all the "Murmurers," who were to be so critical of the Glorious Revolution and publish their discontent in satires and lampoons, seems improbable.[26] Yet Congreve's play is very much the product of 1691 and 1692, when anti-clerical satire was all the rage and when Jacobites saw the country as still "unsettled" and ready for a new restoration of the Stuarts. Even if Congreve was not following the news closely, his situation and that of his family would have meant that the outlines of the political situation would have been clear and inescapable to him.

Thomas Southerne, a constant supporter of the House of Stuart both before and after James II fled England, described how he helped Congreve "in the whole course of his play," which may mean that he acted as a kind of contact with the managers of the theater or that he added something to the writing. Southerne also turned it over to John Dryden, the disgruntled former laureate, for revision. Dryden, Southerne tells us, thought it an admirable "first play," but judged that "the Author not being acquainted with the Stage or the town, it woud be pity to have it miscarry for want of a little Assistance: the stuff was rich indeed, it wanted only the fashionable cutt of the town." Southerne continued, "To help that Mr Dryden,

Mr Arthur Manwayring, and Mr Southerne red it with great care, and Mr Dryden put it in the order it was playd."[27]

The passage is puzzling. Mainwaring was to become one of the most effective of Whig polemicists during the party wars of Queen Anne's reign, but at this time he, like Dryden and Southerne, was a Jacobite. Although the notion that Dryden rearranged the play has been greeted with skepticism, it is possible that he reshaped the play in many ways.[28] After all, how could Congreve, then a young and completely inexperienced playwright, resist the help of the best poet and one of the best dramatists of the Restoration? The deposed laureate had returned to writing for the stage with *Don Sebastian* (1689) and *Amphytrion; or the Two Sosias* (1690) both of which had considerable success.

On the other hand, both of Dryden's plays have strong Jacobite subtexts. If, as has been suggested, *King Arthur* appeared to deliver an anti-Williamite message by innuendoes and coded language, the intent of a number of Dryden's other plays are apparent enough. The government originally barred his *Cleomenes* (1691) from the stage for just such a reason. Under such conditions, we may well wonder whether, when Dryden remarked that the play "wanted only the fashionable cutt of the town," he might not have meant that it needed a strong dose of the kind of innuendo and satire that the Jacobites and enemies of William were spreading throughout the nation—satire upon the clergy, most of whom had turned their backs upon James II to take oaths of loyalty to King William, and upon the war against Louis XIV, which the Jacobites argued to be unwinnable, costly from the standpoint of English lives lost, and generally futile.

Amphytrion was typical of such propaganda.[29] The story of how Zeus took the place of Amphytrion as the legitimate husband of Alcmena, had intercourse with her, and through this action eventually produced Hercules may be open to any number of interpretations, but in Dryden's hands, the play becomes a vehicle for raising questions about William III's claims to the throne and about England's role in the process. The wife's willingness to accept a surrogate lover, a being of great power, in place of her authentic husband provides a jarring note to the low comedy of the servants. Though Hercules was traditionally to become a benefactor to mankind, his role is also put in doubt in Dryden's rendering of the theme. Since William III was frequently associated with Hercules in the propaganda written in his praise, few of the knowledgeable members of the audience would have missed the allusion.[30] In addition, Dryden's attack upon the very notion of the hero resonated with specific acerbity throughout the play. Dryden, like Hamlet, could claim that the story was well known and that he was innocent of any kind of malice, but the play was nevertheless a trap for the ruling king. As has been mentioned, audiences of the 1690s went to the theater expecting just such a thrill afforded by parallel stories of this kind.[31] But if Dryden's *King Arthur* depended on coded references and innuendo, his *Amphytrion* was closer to true irony.

Paradoxically, *The Old Batchelour* was both the most contemporary of Congreve's plays, from the standpoint of its allusions to current topics, and the most formulaic, in many ways a pastiche of the dozens of previous comedies written after the Restoration of Charles II. This seeming contradiction may be compared to the dilemma in Jorge Luis Borges's "Pierre Menard, Author of the *Quixote*." Borges suggests that if *Don Quixote* might be approached as a modern text, the language and meaning of Cervantes's masterpiece would be transformed and our understanding of it entirely changed.[32] Similarly, in the context of the 1690s, the comic situations and wit of the 1670s and 1680s assumed entirely new meanings in Congreve's reshaping of the older material. That at the very beginning Congreve's Vainlove should argue that his pursuit of pleasure was a form of business might sound like a fairly traditional opening for a Restoration play, a variation on Thomas Shadwell's introduction of his young wits in *Epsom-Wells* (1672–1673) and *The Virtuoso* (1676) as well as being the credo of his villain in *The Libertine* (1675–1676), but in his defense of fashion and luxury as promoting the economic growth and well being of society, Vainlove appears to be echoing a contemporary debate. Nicholas Barbon had recently argued the radical notion that the pursuits of pleasure, new fashions, and luxury were vital to the economic health of the country.[33] Although Bernard Mandeville was later to publicize and elaborate upon this paradox in the various versions of the *Fable of the Bees* (1705, 1714, 1723, etc.), Barbon, with his stress upon encouraging consumption, had already given currency to this idea. The opening of the play, then, with its ironic emphasis on ways of enriching the nation through the search after luxury and pleasure, placed it squarely in the world of the 1690s, that time of the Financial Revolution, lotteries, and projects.

On the other hand, the criticisms of Fondlewife, the banker, and his pursuit of money belong to the counter-attack upon the new commercialism and the rise to importance of those dealing in finance.[34] Ned Ward's *The Miracles Perform'd by Money* (1692) viewed the entire society as corrupted by the emphasis upon wealth. Money, he argued, will transform workers into gentlemen; mothers will betray their daughters for money; and the displacement of a respect for authority by money will eventually turn the manners and morals of the society upside down. Ward specifically complains about situations such as that which prevails between Fondlewife and Laetitia, in which an old, impotent husband, who is rich, may purchase a young wife.

> Women like *Books* and Pictures now a Days,
> Are put to Sale, and who the Price can raise,
> Not he whose merits decently can Crave 'em,
> No, no, the Lucky He bids most shall have 'em:
> Youth, Wit and Valour will not now prevail:
> But yet *Almighty Mony* cannot fail.[35]

A similar lament by Robert Gould, in his poem *The Corruption of the Times by Money* (1693), placed the character of men such as Fondlewife among the destroyers of the country.[36] William III's Holland may have been content to think of itself as a commercial country, but England had some time to go before it would be entirely content with such a designation.

Even Fondlewife's designation as a "banker" is significant because it functions in an entirely new context. The play was performed one year before the establishment of the Bank of England, but discussions concerning various forms of banks were everywhere.[37] While the Bank was instrumental in enabling William to finance the War of the Grand Alliance, the Tories and Jacobites were to regard it with suspicion and hostility. Although the departure of the husband to his scene of business and the abandonment of the young wife recalls Wycherley's *The Country Wife* (1676), the general anti-commercial context of such an action was now much richer. Fondlewife's business is obscure, but it does have to do with a shipping investment at a time when the complaints about the losses at sea, through the depredations of the French fleet and privateers, fueled the criticism of the Murmurers and Grumbletonians.[38] There were some specific scandals that appear to have informed Congreve's text as well. In *The Trimming Court Divine* of 1690, the Jacobite author drew an analogy between the political situation and a recent event involving the young wife of an old lawyer who had been carried off by a gallant.[39] In fact the author of *The Trimming Court Divine* touched on most of the problems of the time. Some of these involved England's war on the continent, which the Jacobites argued to be endless, incapable of ending in victory for the English, and a drain of English money and lives.

The characters of the cowardly Captain Bluffe, who claims to have fought in Flanders, the timid Sir Joseph Wittol, who longs to be associated with a heroic soldier, and Sharper, who cheats Sir Joseph out of his money, have to be read within these contexts. That figures such as Sharper, who is little better than a con man, appeared everywhere in the plays of these years, whether by Whig or Tory playwrights, is hardly surprising since everyone viewed this as a time of dubious schemes and projects. The government itself was constantly promoting schemes to raise money for the war including unusual forms of taxation and lotteries. Sharper's proverbial "'Tis an ill wind that blows nobody good," aside from expressing the prevailing views of self-interest and opportunism, might well have been heard by the audience as a reference to those who flourished after the famous "Providential" wind that blew William to England.[40]

Echoes of the ongoing war emerge everywhere in the text of Congreve's play, and there is no heroic soldier in the play to counter the cowardice of Sir Joseph Wittoll and his protector Bluffe. The audience had to perceive the ambiguity in Bluffe's boast that he fought only for "Justifiable" causes such as his "Country" or "Religion" (51 [2.1.159–60]). Was the war on the continent, sometimes called the War of the Grand Alliance, sometimes the Nine Years War, and in America referred to as King William's War, justifiable from an English standpoint? Certainly the Jacobites implied that it was not, but even strong supporters of the Glorious Revolution had their doubts. Many felt that England should limit itself to a naval war.[41] Such an attitude became even more popular after the stunning victory of the Dutch and English fleet at Cape La Hogue on 19 May 1692, which nullified James II's planned invasion of England.

The ground war in Flanders seemed to many to be too distant a matter to involve the expenditure of English blood and English money. After the violent standoff at Steenkirk on 24 July 1692, which resulted in eight thousand casualties, it was rumored that the Dutch commander, Graf van Solms-Braunfels, was accused of "allowing the British to die on the Plaine St. Martin out of hatred and callousness."[42] Rumors of this kind were spread by leaders of the English troops such as Thomas Talmash and John Churchill in an effort to wrest power over the allied army from the Dutch, but they had some basis in fact. Following the battle of Steenkirk, British wounded were left lying in the streets of Brussels while the Dutch troops were being cared for in the Grootlegerhospitael. The British troops had fought bravely in a losing cause, as they were to do at Landen in 1693, and there was great pride in England at the courage they had shown.[43] Although the Jacobites and Tories were successfully arguing that Steenkirk had been a defeat that questioned William's abilities as a leader, his supporters attempted to show that Steenkirk was actually close to being a victory, that the French suffered greater casualties, and that the British troops "have shewn by the Blood they have so chearfully spilt, what Affection and Fidelty they have to his [William's] Service."[44]

As a dramatic type, Bluffe much resembles the Pistol of *Henry V*, but whatever his pedigree, he is used for some distinctly anti-Williamite satire on the indecisive and bloody Flanders campaign of 1691–1692 during which, in addition to the indecisive battle of Steenkirk mentioned above, the allies lost the fortress of Namur. Sir Joseph Wittol may be seen as any Englishman so cowardly as to need a soldier who had fought in Flanders to protect him, and Bluffe's anger against the *London Gazette* for failing to mention his name in its accounts of battles, aside from the likelihood that he was never near a battlefield, seems to suggest that soldiers are dominated by a desire for fame and that the reputation of someone such as William III might be more a matter of publicity than reality.[45] Bluffe's final speech, "No more Wars, Spouse, no more Wars" (111 [5.2.147]), may be taken as an inoffensive, comic resolution on his part to avoid becoming a cuckold, but it does have larger connotations about war and its evil influence upon private life. Such satire might be the "fashionable cutt of the Town," but it was hardly what might have been expected from the son of an army officer and the future poet who was to celebrate William's later victory at Namur in 1695 with a grandiose ode.

The attack upon the war is linked to the wickedness of the Clergy in Bellmour's remark upon Bluffe as a fraud and a "pretender" who "wears the habit of a Soldier, which now a'days as often cloaks Cowardice, as a Black Gown does Atheism" (46–47 [1.1.366–68]). Although there was much fault found with the behavior of the clergy toward James II after many had gone back on their expressions of complete obedience, most criticisms of the clergy during the 1690s alluded to the crisis in the Church of England created by William Sherlock's decision to take the oaths of loyalty to William and Mary.[46] Sherlock had originally refrained from taking the oaths.[47] He had let the deadline pass before expressing his loyalty to the reigning monarchs, and many felt that his actions demonstrated that the leaders of the Church of England were acting entirely on the basis of self-interest rather than conviction.[48] Although Sherlock was to explain his decision on theological grounds—that the clergy had the duty to obey the established monarch—many of the satirists blamed Sherlock's decision on his wife, who was supposed to have insisted upon it.[49] Her motivation had nothing to do with theology. Thomas D'Urfey's *The Weesils* (1691) depicts her as objecting to the loss of income ("Cheese") that might result from her husband's initially principled stance.[50] The decision seemed to throw doubt upon all religious principles. The author of *The Moralists* (1691) put the matter succinctly. After having a pastor attack the morals of the age, the author remarks that the clergy had lost the credibility necessary for commenting convincingly upon ethical matters: "And yet 'tis thought by more than half the Nation, / That you have lately lost some Reputation."[51] Visions of a world of cheat and deceit were ubiquitous in contemporary literature. Of course the satire in Congreve's play seems mostly aimed at the Dissenters, but Jeremy Collier was right when he argued that Congreve had managed to "hook the *Church* of *England* into the Abuse."[52]

In Congreve's comedy, on the suggestion of Laetitia, Vainlove (for whom

Bellmour acts as a substitute when Vainlove expresses a lack of interest) is supposed to come to her dressed as Parson Spintext while her husband Fondlewife is away. The very name Spintext suggests misusing holy texts, and like his disciple Fondlewife, he appears to be married to a woman of easy virtue. His wife's name, Comfort, and his name, Tribulation, suggests much about their relationship. Bellmour's use of the cloak of religion to gain his ends with Laetitia also might be seen to have general implications at a time when, as one writer argued, the clergy of the Church of England appeared to be practicing "Sanctity in Masquerade," hiding their self-interest behind their clerical gowns.[53] Indeed, as Bellmour admits, had he carried *The Practice of Piety* with him instead of the novels of Scarron, he would never have been detected by Fondlewife. Similarly, the "Blessing of an easy Faith" (96 [4.4.271]) that allows Fondlewife to believe in Laetitia's innocence might seem to apply more generally to the faith of a Sherlock, who could discover reasons for taking the oath of loyalty to the reigning monarch. The "Act of Oblivion" (110 [5.2.103]) which pardons Captain Bluffe and Sir Joseph at the end, clearly alludes to the pardons extended to those who took the oaths. If Jeremy Collier was to perceive much in the play that he thought anti-clerical and blasphemous, he was certainly right to the extent that Congreve's comedy added to undermining the credibility of both the Dissenters and those who had taken the oaths. In this *The Old Batchelour* was, as has been mentioned, much in the same vein as D'Urfey's *The Moralists* with its attack upon "Sanctity in Masquerade."

What I am suggesting, then, is that by the time Congreve's Jacobite friends had finished with *The Old Batchelour,* it had some distinct features that are little in keeping with Congreve's other writings. I do not find even a hint of politics in his first publication, the novella *Incognita,* unless one would want to politicize the innocuous theme of reconciliation, but in *The Old Batchelour* satirical implication manages even to invade the traditional love plot with Bellinda using the imagery of creditors and debtors in speaking of Bellmour's love, and Araminta remarking "Every Man, now, changes his Mistress and his Religion, as his Humour varies or his Interest" (58 [2.2.148–49]). Even Araminta's refusal to take Vainlove up on his proposal, for fear that her very act of consenting would cause him to repent, suggests mental hesitations and an unsettled condition that may be seen to have larger implications for the state of England as a whole.

Would Congreve have permitted such rewritings? He may have been aware that he had fallen into a nest of Jacobites, but to repeat, this was, after all, his first play. What beginning playwright in England would have rejected suggestions from the nation's greatest poet? Besides, Congreve was famous for being inoffensive and able to get along with people of all political convictions.[54] Doubtless most of Congreve's "rich" dialogue that so impressed Dryden, Southerne, and Mainwaring remained, and the sensibility of Araminta was very much part of Congreve's gift to the comedies of the 1690s. But who can doubt that, given his convictions, Dryden would have wanted to provide the play with a little of the political thrust to be found in his reworking of Plautus's innocuous comedy into his ironic *Ampyhtrion; or The Two Sosias*?

NOTES

1. "On the Artificial Comedy of the Last Century," in *The Works of Charles and Mary Lamb*, ed. E. V. Lucas (London: Methuen, 1912), 161–68.

2. Jonas Barish, *The Antitheatrical Prejudice* (Berkeley: University of California Press, 1981), especially 256–94.

3. See for example Susan Owen's excellent discussion of the theater during the years of the Exclusion Crisis, *Restoration Theatre and Crisis* (Oxford: Clarendon Press, 1996).

4. Maximillian E. Novak, *Congreve* (New York: Twayne, 1970), 122–37 and "The Discourses of Criticism and the Discourses of History in the Restoration and Early Eighteenth Century," in *Theory and Tradition in Eighteenth-Century Studies*, ed. Richard B. Schwartz (Carbondale: Southern Illinois University Press, 1990), 104–11.

5. Richard Braverman, *Plots and Counterplots: Sexual Politics and the Body Politic in English Literature, 1660–1730* (Cambridge: Cambridge University Press, 1993), 213–37.

6. Phillip Harth, *Pen for a Party: Dryden's Tory Propaganda in Its Contexts* (Princeton, N.J.: Princeton University Press, 1993), 271. Of course there was a major difference between writing satire with the full support of the government and writing as an opponent of the regime. Dryden could hardly have written a satire such as *The Medal* during the 1690s.

7. See for example the preface to D'Urfey's *Love for Money: or, The Boarding School* (London, 1691), sig. A3v. For a complaint against contemporary satirists, especially D'Urfey, see [Thomas Brown?], *Wit for Money: or, Poet Stutter* (London, 1691), 11.

8. *The London Stage 1660–1800 A Calendar of Plays, Entertainments & Afterpieces Together with Casts, Box-Receipts and Contemporary Comment*, ed. William Van Lennep et al. (Carbondale: Southern Illinois University Press, 1960–1968), 1:371. The play was John Dryden's *The Spanish Friar*. The audience turned to observe Queen Mary's reaction "whenever their fancy led them to make any application."

9. For a discussion of the use of coded language and parallelism, see Richard

Ashcraft and Alan Roper, *Politics as Reflected in Literature,* introduction by Maximillian E. Novak (Los Angeles: William Andrews Clark Memorial Library, 1989).

10. See H. B. Irving, *The Life of Judge Jeffreys* (London: William Heinemann, 1898), 176.

11. The *OED* gives Bishop Gilbert Burnet's statement from 1715 on this subject, but Burnet was simply repeating the use of innuendo at the time the event occurred. See Burnet's *History of His Own Time* (London: Samuel Bagster, 1815), 2:220.

12. See *The Arraignment and Tryal of the Late Reverend Mr. Thomas Rosewell, for High-Treason; before the Lord Chief Jefferies* (London, 1715), 242, 247.

13. Ibid., 271.

14. Despite Jeffreys's well-earned reputation for ferocity toward defendants, he was genuinely concerned about the legal ramifications of convicting Rosewell on innuendoes, and at one point, when the government's solicitor blandly stated that a particular innuendo was clear, Jeffreys appeared to reject the entire notion of conviction on the basis of innuendo. "You have *Innuendo'd* it too much I do doubt," remarked Jeffreys, "for all the Facts are laid under an *Innuendo,* without a positive Averment." On the basis of being unable to determine whether an innuendo was intended, Jeffreys allowed Rosewell to obtain counsel to argue the point. See *Arraignment and Tryal of Thomas Rosewell,* 250.

15. See Dryden's preface to *Cleomenes* in *Plays: King Arthur, Cleomenes, Love Triumphant, Contributions to the Pilgrim,* ed. Vinton A. Dearing, vol. 16 of *The Works of John Dryden,* ed. Edward Niles Hooker et al. (Berkeley: University of California Press, 1996), 79.

16. The original performance was some time in May 1691. The performance I witnessed was on Tuesday, 16 November 1999 at the auditorium of Santa Ana High School in California. The group has recorded their version on the Erato label under the direction of William Christie.

17. James Winn, *John Dryden and His World* (New Haven, Conn.: Yale University Press, 1987), 448–49.

18. See Dearing, ed., vol. 16, *Works of John Dryden,* 309.

19. For example, in the dedication, Dryden praises Charles II's "Clemency and Moderation," adding in parentheses "the inherent Virtues of his Family." The reference could be to Charles I, who was certainly often praised for such qualities, but it must also apply to James II, advancing the argument that, were he to return to England, he would be generous and forgiving. How such a view would have been supported by James's past behavior, particularly his treatment of the Duke of Monmouth and his followers, is obvious enough.

20. *The Complete Plays of William Congreve,* ed. Herbert Davis (Chicago: University of Chicago Press, 1967), 35. Subsequent references to *The Old Batchelour* refer to this edition and are included in my text within parentheses.

21. For this attitude, see *The Town Display'd in a Letter to Amintor in the Country* (London, 1701), 15. Comparing *The Old Batchelour* to Congreve's serious attempt at tragedy, *The Mourning Bride,* the critic advised: "Let him forsake

the lofty Tragick Scene, / And the dull Town with Humour Entertain; / For the *Old Batchelour,* without a Plot, / Will Live, when the poor *Mourning-Bride's* forgot."

22. John C. Hodges, *William Congreve the Man* (New York: Modern Language Association, 1941), 30.

23. See *William Congreve: Letters and Documents,* ed. John C. Hodges (New York: Harcourt, Brace, and World, 1964), 8, referred to hereafter as Hodges, *William Congreve.* For Congreve's description of the composition of *The Old Batchelour,* see his *Amendments of Mr. Collier's False and Imperfect Citations,* in *The Mourning Bride, Poems, and Miscellanies,* ed. Bonamy Dobrée (London: Oxford University Press, 1928), 2:423.

24. D. Crane Taylor, *William Congreve* (1931; reprint New York: Russell and Russell, 1963), 15; and Hodges, *William Congreve the Man,* 29.

25. See Hodges, *William Congreve,* 8.

26. For this term, see for example *A Modest Enquiry into the Causes of the Present Disasters in England* (London, 1690), 34. It was also the title of a poem written "soon after the late Revolution" by Robert Gould. See *The Works of Robert Gould* (London, 1709), 119–43.

27. Hodges, *William Congreve,* 151. Thomas Southerne prepared his statement for Thomas Birch, who was writing a brief biography of Congreve which appeared in the fourth volume of the *General Dictionary, Historical and Critical* (London, 1736).

28. Charles Gildon claimed that it was "in nothing alter'd but in the Length" by the trio of friends. Since written versions are usually longer than the final acting version, they probably did do some cutting, but Southerne's emphasis upon the care with which the manuscript was read suggests many more revisions. For Gildon's comments, see the excerpt from *Lives and Characters of the English Dramatic Poets* (1699), in *William Congreve: The Critical Heritage,* ed. Alexander Lindsay and Howard Erskine-Hill (London: Routledge, 1989), 174.

29. Herbert Davis, in his edition of Congreve's *Complete Plays,* indicates several places where he detects borrowings from Dryden's *Amphytrion* in *The Old Batchelour.* See for example, 105.

30. See for example the praise of William as "our Hercules" in "An Epistle to Mr. Dryden," in *A Collection of the Newest and Most Ingenious Poems, Songs, Catches, etc. against Popery* (London, 1689), 4. Richard Braverman maintains that James II was also occasionally compared to Hercules, but surely no one would have mistaken the allusion to William III in *Amphytrion.* See *Plots and Counterplots,* 182–83.

31. Of course some of the attacks upon William and Mary were entirely direct, arguing that the Glorious Revolution had been a mistake and that the nation should restore James. See for example Sir James Montgomery, *Great Britain's Just Complaint for Her Late Measures, Present Sufferings, and the Future Miseries She Is Exposed to* (no place but probably London, 1692).

32. Quoting the same passage twice, Borges dismisses Cervantes's meaning as mere rhetoric, while praising Menard's insight into modern thinking. *Labyrinths:*

Selected Stories and Other Writings, ed. Donald A. Yates and James E. Irby (New York: New Directions, 1964), 36–44.

33. Nicholas Barbon, *A Discourse of Trade* (London, 1690), especially 14, 35, 72–73.

34. For a general discussion of the ethical problems involved in a world devoted to self-interest and greed, see David Abercromby, *A Moral Discourse of the Power of Interest* (London, 1690), especially 87–118, 172–73.

35. Ned Ward, *The Miracles Perform'd by Money* (London, 1692), 15–16.

36. Gould, *Works,* 2:226–99. Since Gould's work was originally published in 1693, it probably appeared too late for anyone associated with the play to have read it. On the other hand, it was common for such works to circulate in manuscript. Such attitudes toward the commercial drift of England intensified. See also L. Meriton, *Pecuniae Obediunt Omnia: Money Does Master All Things* (London, 1696), especially 40–41 for comments on money and marriage.

37. For a summary of some of the schemes proposed at the time, see Defoe, "Of Banks," in *An Essay upon Projects,* ed. Joyce Kennedy, Michael Seidel, and Maximillian E. Novak (New York: AMS Press, 1999), 18–29.

38. For these terms, see for example, *Providence and Precept, or, The Case of Doing Evil that Good May Come of It* (London, 1691), 20, and *A Modest Enquiry into the Causes of the Present Disasters in England,* 34.

39. *The Trimming Court-Divine. Or, Reflexions on Dr. Sherlock's Book of the Lawfulness of Swearing Allegiance to the Present Government* (London, 1690), 19.

40. The first act contains a great deal of imagery about winds and fortune. See also *Complete Plays,* ed. Davis, 48 (2.1.32–33). Subsequent references to this work will appear within parentheses in my text as page number followed by act, scene, and line number in brackets.

41. See *The State of Parties, and of the Publick* (London, 1692), 12–13.

42. John Childs, *The Nine Years' War and the British Army, 1688–1697: The Operations in the Low Countries* (Manchester: Manchester University Press, 1991), 203.

43. It is not Bluffe, the pretended soldier, who comments on courage but Sharper, who remarks, "There is in true Beauty, as in Courage, somewhat, which narrow Souls cannot dare to admire" (86 [4.3.125]). The war has its influence on the imagery of the play, especially in the mention of the artillery used in the battles and sieges.

44. See *Memoires Concerning the Campagne of Three Kings, William, Lewis, and James in the Year 1692* (London, 1693), 63–69.

45. For an example of this kind of attack upon William III, see *Great Britain's Just Complaint,* especially 37, 59.

46. For general discussion of Sherlock and the political situation, see Charles Mullett, "A Case of Allegieance: William Sherlock and the Revolution of 1688," *Huntington Library Quarterly* 10 (1946): 83–103.

47. The fullest narrative about Sherlock appeared in *The Weesils* (London, 1691) ascribed to Thomas D'Urfey. An observer introduced into the poem as a

visitor to the Weesil home concludes that Sherlock abandoned the "plain Principles" of the Church. See especially 13.

48. See for example the broadside *Dr. Sherlock Vindicated, or Cogent Reasons Why that Worthy Person Hath Complied with the Necessity of the Times, and Why He at First Refused It* (London, 1691).

49. See *The Weesils,* 3–6. The wife in this allegory tells her husband that although conscience was a good thing, it was not important enough to deprive a family of a good income.

50. Ibid., 3.

51. *The Moralists* (London, 1691), 13. Both this work and *The Weesils* questioned Sherlock's motives.

52. Jeremy Collier, *A Short View of the Immorality, and Profaneness of the English Stage* (London, 1698), 102.

53. *The Moralists,* 15.

54. See Joseph Spence, *Anecdotes, Observations, and Characters of Books and Men,* ed. James Osborn (Oxford: Clarendon Press, 1966), 1:50 item 118, 1:208 item 488.

3

A Preface to Anglican Rationalism

GERARD REEDY, S. J.

Vast in volume and varied in genre, available almost entirely in printed sources yet insufficiently studied, the body of theological literature described and to an extent created by the term "Anglican rationalism" is the work of the most prominent clergymen, or divines, of the late seventeenth-century Church of England. Born before the civil wars, and tempered by the political upheaval of the mid-century, these divines include: John Tillotson (1630–1694), Archbishop of Canterbury, whose sermons formed the staple of clerical training for one hundred years; Edward Stillingfleet (1635–1699), Bishop of Worcester, historian, interpreter of church law, and highly intellectual preacher; Robert South (1634–1716), canon of Christ Church, Oxford, and Westminster Abbey, aligned with Tillotson and Stillingfleet in all but his political theory; Gilbert Burnet (1643–1715), Bishop of Salisbury and active supporter of the new administration of William III in 1688, preacher, advisor to clergy, historian, and author of a commentary on the thirty-nine articles of the Church of England; and Isaac Barrow (1630–1677), Cambridge mathematician and preacher whose works, after his early death, were edited by Tillotson. Many more divines contributed to the canon of Anglican rationalism, some of them only slightly less prominent than the above.

These prolific Anglican divines worked hard. We have over 250 of Tillotson's sermons; the first fifty-four, which he edited and arranged himself, amount to over 350,000 words. The sermons in Stillingfleet's *Fifty Sermons* (1710) range from 7,000 to 13,000 words in length, yet this folio volume is only one of six in the collected *Works* (1707–1710). Single interpretive frameworks cannot encompass the vast output of the divines between 1660 and 1700, because monist political, theological, and rhetorical categories tend to exclude as well as interpret what is there. Although interpretation of a body of work of this magnitude may be endless, common themes, responses to external events, and methodologies nevertheless suggest that a community of divines existed at this time. I will explore three shapes that community took: the occasional nature of its output and how occasions must influence interpretations; the synergy between the terms of the description, Anglican and rationalism; and the search for a plain sense in Scripture, on which the entire theological project was based.

1.

Many intellectual historians who refer to Archbishop Tillotson or other Anglican rationalists, because they have not read them in depth, misinterpret them; or, to put the matter in different terms, they create an interpretive framework that is narrow and inadequate to the fullness of the object of interpretation. In particular, interpreters overestimate the rationalism of the divines. It has been standard, for example, to isolate the chapters of the project that emphasize knowledge gained from the application of reason to human affairs without the help of Scripture and to make these chapters metonyms of the whole. With the help of this methodology, Anglican rationalism is enervated to become a code of belief and conduct whose verification rests on human reason alone. In this scheme Anglican rationalism, even if its authors were unconscious of their tendency, inevitably prefigured and abetted movement (always understood as progress) to Enlightenment.[1]

Over thirty years ago, two scholars of English literature, Phillip Harth and Irène Simon, explored Anglican rationalism in a fresh way. They took it seriously as an historical movement worth prolonged investigation in itself. They explored its themes, major works, proponents and opponents, and context. More importantly, they understood Anglican rationalism not as a passive substance in which a triumphant Enlightenment pressed its foot and moved on, but as an active agent in late seventeenth-century life and art. Harth's work especially shows how Dryden and Swift depended on Anglican rationalism as the undergirding ethic of their intellectual and political satire.[2]

Anglican rationalism occurs, first of all, in occasional forms. Although there seems to be an effort on the part of some of the major divines to suppress the dates of sermons in the final corrected *Sermons* or *Works,* and thus to sever the text from specific occasions, enough dated sermons remain to make us inquire about how occasion gives meaning. Stillingfleet dates a higher proportion of his sermons than other divines do; missing dates can often be filled in from the work of diarists who noted their attendance at sermons or from court, guild, or parish lists. Sermon listeners sometimes took notes. A sermon by a major divine may have been on a par, as a cultural event, with a play by Etherege or Dryden. Inquiry about occasion most easily rewards us when politics are involved. Certain dates implicate not only history, but also the preacher's place across the wide, late-Stuart political spectrum. For example, 29 May and 23 April, the anniversaries of Charles II's return to England in 1660 and of his coronation in 1661, are neutral dates; preaching about these anniversaries does not imply anything but support of the king and dynasty. To preach on 5 November, however, became a divine who looked favorably on building the power of Parliament; likewise, revisiting the Gunpowder Plot implicitly warned against the presence of Roman Catholics in the government and state. To preach on 30 January, on the other hand, the anniversary of the 1649 regicide, became a divine who stressed the sacred prerogatives of the king, and who perhaps felt that Protestant dissent was more threatening than Catholicism. Preaching on 30 January to commemorate the martyr-king after 1688 might even be considered a subtle act of opposition to the accession of William III and allegiance to James II and his son.

Even outside the political sphere, using sermons without reference to context or occasion can mislead. Some important questions to ask are: Where does the sermon occur in a divine's life—early or late? Does this sermon play a part in an ongoing controversy whose contours must be known to find the sermon's meaning? For example, a sermon against transubstantiation might praise individual reason and common sense as it attacks Roman Catholic authority; such praise of reason, when taken out of context, may falsify the general, lifelong views of this preacher about religious ways of knowing. At a later stage: does the placement of a sermon in the collected *Sermons* or *Works* add to its meaning in any way? Because unraveling an ongoing controversy can be difficult, the British Library catalogue of printed books, which often lists answers to or refutations of an entry, or library catalogues that list works chronologically, can be of great assistance. Since most references to Anglican rationalist sermons are brought in to supplement, in isolated form, the commentator's argument, students themselves must try to restore fuller meaning by rebuilding the philosophical or political occasion.

After Isaac Barrow died in 1677, his father Thomas published a sampling of his sermons. The pairing of the first two sermons shows how placement heightens meaning. The sermons are undated and of about the same length; the first is on the value of wisdom (after Prov. 3:17), the second on the profit of godliness (after 1 Tim. 4:8), a theme concluded in the third sermon. Both topics represent Anglican rationalists' habit of preaching on the moral life; other sermons explore the specifics of doctrine. By suppressing the dates, either Isaac Barrow or his father perhaps wanted to draw our attention away from an historical context for the sermons' counsels towards their universal import.

It is revealing to assess the Anglican rationalists' use of sources of evidence for their judgments: On what grounds does an individual author or sermon judge a statement to be true? The beginning three sermons of Barrow's 1678 *Sermons,* which contains fifteen sermons in all, use evidence in different ways: the first sermon refers to Scripture and other authors very few times as it lists sixteen uses of "wisdom" for a good life. Reason reflecting upon experience provides, without apparent external inspiration, the norms for a good life. In isolation, this sermon fulfills the narrow description often allowed for Anglican rationalism. Yet the second sermon's use of evidence takes us in another direction: marginal notes call attention to many Old Testament books as well as almost all of the New; classical and patristic authors like Juvenal, Salvian, Eusebius, Aristotle, Seneca, Tertullian, and Chrysostom also are assembled to affirm that godliness, or piety, profits a man or woman in several ways. As a matter of fact, this second sermon's methodology proves more indicative than that of the first of the volume of sermons' general evidentiary bent.[3]

The juxtaposition of two sermons reliant on very different types of evidence is not accidental: such juxtapositions occur throughout Anglican rationalism and point to its essence, the interdependence of evidentiary sources. Barrow does not appear to be saying in Sermon 1 that reason, logic, or experience can do without Scripture in advising for a good life; or in Sermon 2 that Scripture and tradition can do without reason. Interdependency and mutuality seem to be his point. Each sermon, like each kind of evidence, needs the other. The dramatic situation for these sermons, moreover, may help account for their placement. Because many of the sermons involved grand, public acts before audiences of notables, the juxtaposition of evidences may be for show: the speaker (and editor) shows his virtuosity by presenting matters argued from two points of view successively. Barrow's audiences were skilled in detecting the shifts a preacher made in his use of sources; perceived originality in those shifts gave pleasure to the alert congregation. Our great distance from these performances may keep us from sighting such causes and effects.

Since these sermons deal with life as well as art, Barrow calls his congregation back from the brink of aesthetic appreciation. At the end of the first sermon, wherein Barrow's observation of human nature stacks pleasure upon pleasure at wisdom's door, he moves to assemble varied evidence. We reach wisdom, he writes, "by the faithful exercise of our Reason, careful observations of things, diligent study of the Divine Law, watchful reflection upon ourselves, virtuous and religious practice; but especially, by imploring the Divine influence." The sermon then concludes with a prayer for wisdom. Likewise, Sermon 2, after an exploration of the profit of piety, doubles back, perhaps with its editor mindful of the previous sermon in the volume, to note that "Wisdom and impiety are incompatible things," that only the godly can be truly wise. Anglican rationalists like Barrow return again and again, in theme and method, to the mutuality rather than opposition of Scripture, faith and reason, of the traditional heritage and a contemporary approach to it. Thus, in Sermon 3, also on 1 Tim. 4:8 and godliness, Barrow writes that we would choose the "Precepts of Religion" even if there were no divine laws to dictate them; "common reason" and "daily trial" show these precepts conducive "to our welfare in all respects."[4]

No piece of Anglican rationalism has so suffered from misconstrual as its development of the subtle mix of Scripture, faith, reason, common sense, and experience. Although part of the problem surely lies in the divines' occasional overrepresentation of the reasonableness of their theology, the reader's ignorance of context, aversion from the hard work of remedially wide reading, and an anachronistic liberalism also come into play. A later humanism that seeks to read the best of the past as a progressive road to itself surely accounts for some of the wrongheadedness of the generalizing intelligence.

Discussion of two types of misinterpretation helps to illuminate the truth of Anglican rationalism. The first again concerns context. A recent commentator writes: "Isaac Barrow, John Tillotson, Edward Stillingfleet, and John Moore delivered sermon after sermon extolling the virtue of natural religion and morality. The years 1692–1710 were especially fruitful, since these were the days of the influential Boyle lectures, when many of the leading divines gave literally hundreds of lectures demonstrating the truth of Christianity on the basis of natural morality and religion."[5] Although an attempt is made to set Barrow, Tillotson, and Stillingfleet in the admirable context of the Boyle Lectures, the facts are inconvenient. Barrow died in 1677, and Tillotson and Stillingfleet never gave Boyle Lectures. One reason they did not was that by the early 1690s both were preoccupied with controversy about the mysteries of Christianity—writing, delivering, revising, and publishing thousands and thousands of words defending and exploring the orthodox position of a three-in-one divinity and a true incarnation of the second person.[6] In what Frederick C. Beiser calls "the classical age of English rationalism," at least two of the representative figures whom he cites were busy defending mysteries that they alleged were above the reach of human reason.[7]

In any interpretation of Anglican rationalism, Tillotson is the prize: if his main concerns are not caught in the net of interpretation, the net fails, as any interpretation that excludes key data must fail. Tillotson's discussion of the Christian mysteries defines himself as much as his (mostly) earlier essays in natural religion. In the first volume of the folio-collected sermons, the earlier sermons interact with the later as in a catechism: the natural religion draws the reader into a structure of belief whose mysterious essence is displayed later on—here, in Sermons 43 through 48 on mystery. The corrective to this first type of misinterpretation is not arcane: an individual sermon or set of sermons must be read in the context of all the sermons offered in the collected works to understand it and them more fully.[8]

A second area of misinterpretation lies in the mutuality of Scripture and what is usually called "reason," actually a dynamic complex of conceptual analysis, historical knowledge, and a common sense based in worldly experience. There is almost nothing in Anglican rationalism about a mathematical search for clear and distinct ideas as the principal process of gaining reliable knowledge. Although one often finds in Anglican rationalism the claim that Scripture is reasonable, or that reason must certify Scripture as an object of belief, the divines lend their own meaning to this claim. When they state the claim in its extreme form—that Scripture is governed by reason—they mean Scripture in gross, that is, Scripture taken as a whole, or as divided into books or groups of books. In the common theology of Anglican rationalism, reason judges the truth of Scripture or of a book thereof: when historical research convincingly shows that its contents conform to secular history; when its contents are as probable as can be expected from credible witnesses; when it can be shown that God's providence has protected the essential teaching of the text; and when the credibility of the authors can be corroborated by their miracles.

Although these analyses of reason may lack critical rigor, they are ubiquitous in the texts of Anglican rationalism. So far as I can see, what Anglican rationalism never does is to isolate an individual teaching of Scripture and measure its truth against a clear and distinct idea of the same alleged reality. Such a methodology does function in the late seventeenth century. I believe that it is the reading mode advocated by Baruch Spinoza (1632–1677) and John Toland (1670–1722), but on two grounds it is not the method of Anglican rationalists: for them, "reason" is more than a search for Cartesian certainty, and their submission of Scripture to reason involves Scripture as a whole, not its individual teachings or passages.

Anglicans recognized the heterogeneity of Scripture, especially in regard to genres, reader availability, and inspiration. Their response to this heterogeneity involves a theory of the plain sense of Scripture that all, learned or not, could understand. The most important parts of Scripture, its saving truths, had to be available to all; although all writers were reluctant to list these truths, for fear of limiting Scripture's freedom, the proclamation of saving truths to all was of course the purpose of Scripture's existence. The following description of the plain sense of Scripture as it is conceived by Anglican rationalism is based on a reading of a number of contemporary sermons and books, for though the theory is understood as a premise in many works, it is rarely fully outlined in any one source.[9]

An individual's salvation depends on accepting the essential, saving truths of Scripture that are contained in the plain or literal sense. By plain, the divines mean the sense usually gathered from a word or phrase—something untwisted by a contentious point of view and agreed to by educated people of good sense. Though the plain sense seems to be a concept deeply cast in one's own culture, the divines allege its universality and invincibility for rational believers. The plain sense usually endorses common sense, but if the plain sense challenges normal ways of thinking, divines are obliged to explain the discrepancy in favor of Scripture. It is not their duty to ignore or palliate the plain sense. For example, divines who explain the Trinity, a doctrine held to be in the plain sense, express their weariness at the task of explaining what is above reason, but they explain it nonetheless.

The literal sense of Scripture means the above, especially as it is distinguished from allegorical readings, for the Anglican rationalists firmly adhere to the literal side in the traditional division between literal Antioch and figurative Alexandria. Because sermons often begin with an explanation of the historical circumstances of a passage set for explication, the author's intention, say, Moses, David, Matthew, or Luke, so far as it can be determined, decides what a passage means. Reconstruction of historical context and intention, considered the distinguishing mark of "modern" divines, corrects a process of unmediated application of an historical text to modern circumstances.

Sermons after 1660 offer many examples of tropological, or moral, readings of the historical passages in Scripture: King David's sins, repentance, sadness, and joy offer examples for avoidance or imitation. In the normal course of things, however, preachers avoided typological readings of historical material, that is, the attempt to align biblical and contemporary events in such a way as to transfer divine approval or disapproval of past events to similar present events. Indeed, many felt that such crude treatment of history authorized the excesses of the past, especially the regicide of 1649. Although exceptions to this rule can be found, especially at times of high national emotion, as with Charles II's coronation or the Popish Plot, history is held not to repeat itself. Typological references to Jesus as Messiah are of course part of perennial Christian interpretation of the psalms and the prophetic books. Nevertheless, here and there in Anglican rationalist literature one finds warnings about excessive use even of messianic hermeneutic.

Belief in and retrieval of the plain sense of Scripture underlay Anglican theology in the second half of the seventeenth century. Inheriting the idea of the plain sense from a long tradition, expanding it and putting it repeatedly to practical use, Anglican preachers also found the plain sense useful in resolving contemporary arguments, from the left and right, on central theological questions. In the early years of the Restoration they countered advocacy of *ex tempore* preaching allegedly prompted by the Holy Spirit by arguing that a text of Scripture be studied carefully, out in the open, with great attention paid to the historical context of its composition. Toward the end of the century, in the face of Unitarian writing, they argued that Socinians and Unitarians either ignored doctrines in the plain sense or ingeniously explained away their plain meaning. In the early 1680s, awareness grows of the radically historical criticisms of the biblical text made by Spinoza and Richard Simon (1638–1712).[10] If we now understand how these criticisms undermine Anglican theories of the plain sense of Scripture, the divines in their day remained confident that history favored them. Although they heavily emphasized the a priori argument that Divine Providence would not allow the texts and versions of Scripture physically to degenerate, they also felt that the English Church had taken special care to reclaim original meanings. Two great English accomplishments testified to this care in building or restoring foundations that could withstand any historical criticism: the Authorized Version of 1611 and the *Biblia Sacra Polyglotta* of 1659.

In the 1650s, Brian Walton (1600–1661), later Bishop of Chester, assembled a team of scholars to edit and publish a variorum edition that in parallel columns of as many as ten different ancient languages gave the texts of the books of Scripture. Walton's lengthy prefatory essays told the Church of England what it needed to hear: although scribes and typesetters had perhaps introduced errors in these texts, "divine providence and the church's care have been so vigilant that all those matters that are necessary for salvation and regard faith and morals have stayed correct and whole."[11] It is likely that in any age or in any religious tradition believers refer to works whose methods and authenticity they could not adequately judge yet still thought of as the cornerstones of their way of life and belief: after 1660, for Anglicans, the Authorized Version and Walton's *Biblia Sacra Polyglotta* were such cornerstones.

The plain sense of Scripture rests not only on the accepted sense of the words of a passage: it also must agree with the rest of Scripture, an interpreting rule laid down by Article 7 of the Thirty-Nine Articles. Scripture is also consistent in moral teaching; no passage's plain sense can counsel immorality. For those who could read Latin and Greek, the plain sense of a passage ought to agree with how the Church Fathers of the first four centuries interpreted it; to help preachers of Scripture, John Wilkins (1614–1672), Bishop of Chester, in his *Ecclesiastes* (6th edition, 1675) lists eminent ancient and modern commentators for each book or group of books in the Bible. Not all of Scripture, of course, has a plain sense: especially in its poetic and prophetic passages, Scripture has many obscurities; but these obscurities involve only *adiaphora,* or indifferent matters, not the matters one has to believe to be saved. Like Reformation theology in general, the divines tend to have contempt for any who use Scripture to make indifferent matters a central issue; long-lived arguments about the dating of Easter provide their usual example of misplaced attention to *adiaphora.*

In a discourse entitled "Search the Scriptures" (1685), Simon Patrick (1626–1707), later Bishop of Ely, distinguishes between learned and unlearned readers of Scripture in a way that unites key parts of the Anglican rationalist project. Unlearned readers, he writes, are those "who are not skilled in the first principles of religion: men that know not, or mind not, those common natural truths upon which all religion is built."[12] Although you do not have to be learned to be saved, that is to accept and act upon the saving truths of Scripture, yet without learning you fail to appreciate how Scripture truth agrees with what philosophy teaches about history and human nature. Such appreciation undergirds, enriches, and strengthens belief. Patrick gives the correct context for us to understand Barrow and Tillotson as they begin their collections with sermons about natural religion: they by no means pretend that Christianity can stand solely on nature. They rather presume that their congregations value the unassailable theory of the essential truths in the plain sense and look for further enjoyment in a rational exercise that for the moment avoids revelation.

At the distance of more than three hundred years, the Anglican theory of the plain sense of Scripture seems to be forwarded with good intentions, but also with naiveté and even arrogance. Because it is so difficult to divest oneself of political or moral bias, is not the reader of common sense difficult to find? In our own time, one of hyperawareness of where the meanings of texts do and do not reside, when the politics and gender of author and reader offset professions of objective analysis and content, who is not a contentious interpreter? Moreover, one does not have to be a Marxist to note how elitist the Anglican rationalist project is: the sermons that teach and practice the plain sense were given in churches and by preachers directly supported by the labor of unlearned peasants; the preachers to a man went to two universities which, through various tests, maintained uniformity of class, religion, and gender; and appreciation of these sermons, in church or in a private library, reinforced the elite in their self-satisfied superiority.

The occasionally insightful John Toland (1670–1722) catches the presence of self-interest in the divines' reservation of interpretation, in the last analysis, to privileged persons like themselves. Toland writes that divines make "the most trifling things in the world *mysterious,* that we might constantly depend on them for the explication." He writes that "The learned will not, contrary to the experience of their own taste, take the brewer's or the baker's word for the goodness of bread or drink, though ignorant of their craft. And why may not the vulgar likewise be judges of the true sense of things, though they understand nothing of the tongues from whence they are translated for their use?"[13] Toland's simplification of the plain sense is difficult to encounter in simple terms, partly because his intuition of the kinship of learning and power approaches the divines' project in ways to which, consciously or not, they were blind.

2.

Lastly, where did Anglican rationalism come from, and where, after its flourishing between 1660 and 1700, did it lead? With roots in the Reformation and Catholic Reformation, also in the insights of Anglican authors in the earlier seventeenth century, Anglican rationalism keeps easy company with any theologian or theological school which experimented with the application of reason to Scriptural truths and respected the special discipline imposed by each. Thus I believe that it is directly counter to their project to ally Anglican rationalists with any before or after them who attempt to construct religion without Scripture, or who in an undifferentiated manner subjected Scripture to reason. Although interpretation of such a large body of literature may be endless, and while the richness of this literature ought always instigate further points of departure, a hermeneutic ought to be judged good, or not, to the extent that it liberates rather than restricts meaning. As Helen Vendler writes in another context: "Any number of interpretations, guided by any number of interests, can be built on the same foundation of evidence; but an interpretation ignoring that evidence can never be a defensible one."[14]

We often read that Anglican rationalism could not have developed as it did without the previous writings of a group of free-thinking philosophers and theologians who met in the 1630s at the Oxfordshire estate of Lucius Cary, Viscount Falkland (1610–1643). The circle famously included

Thomas Hobbes (1588–1679), William Chillingworth (1602–1644), John Hales (1584–1656), Edward Hyde (1609–1674), and Henry Hammond (1605–1660), all of whom had direct influence on Anglican rationalists in the latter part of the century. A recent commentator associates the idea of an English "Enlightenment," always a tenuous generalization, with the antidogmatism of Chillingworth and, later, of John Locke (1632–1704): this antidogmatism was tolerant, reasonable, minimal in its credal requirements, and unafraid to submit sectarian pieties to analysis.[15] The "fluid boundaries" of this tradition prominently contain Chillingworth's *Religion of Protestants* (1638) and Locke's letters on toleration (1690, 1692) and *Reasonableness of Christianity* (1695). They also contain the many Anglican rationalist writings that promote a plain sense of Scripture that teaches only a few saving truths. Perhaps because most of the builders of the antidogmatic tradition did not hold office in the church, the tradition is more free-thinking than that of Anglican rationalism, almost all of whose builders were canons, deans, or bishops with a vested interest in the status quo.

When John Tillotson complains that he is tired of theological controversy and wants simply to encourage himself and others in the Christian life, he speaks squarely in the antidogmatic tradition.[16] As his complaint indicates, this tradition was more easily sustained in principle than in practice, especially for a leader who felt a moral duty, as he did, to correct public heterodoxy. Freedom from divisive dogmas thrived more easily on Falkland's estate than in London where, especially at the end of the 1680s, Catholics and Unitarians had new license to publish, and where alternate doctrines might promote alternate polities. However, even Chillingworth's *Religion of Protestants,* the charter for antidogmatism, seems imprisoned by its arguments with Roman Catholic doctrine, rather than liberated by its call for freedom to read the Bible. Contrary to the antidogmatism Anglican rationalism half-espoused, it was fated to be involved in arguments about dogmas large and small. Its very occasional nature made it vulnerable to passing controversy; to be the voice of a national church, it had to speak about passing political and theological events. In a larger sense intervention was necessary if it did not wish to enervate one of the vital forces that had called it into being.

From a greater historical and philosophical distance, Melvyn New has suggested that the literature I have been prefacing here may, with its "constant translation of abstraction into the practicalities of sermon discourse," belong to a perennial (or anti-perennial) philosophy that eschews systems and stands "consistently opposed to Cartesian certainties."[17] Its natural generic homes are the sermon or a series of loosely connected sermons, the philosophical essay, and the aphorism. Truly, Cartesian certainty haunts Anglican rationalism as both desirable and impossible. Anglican rationalism often notes that the truth of Scripture—the foundation of all faith—is made from the softrock of moral not mathematical certainty; the divines knew that a harder kind of certainty was current in philosophy, indeed they may have longed for it. Moreover, the divines realistically assessed that the matters at hand for study—culminating in the divine mysteries—were only susceptible to modes of knowing and believing that were friendly to logic but not logically compelling.

The richness of the sermons always disrupts easy categorization. At times seventeenth- and eighteenth-century editors suppress dates and sites so as to create thematic groupings in collected *Sermons* or *Works*. Thus we can see the systematic impulse infiltrating itself into what had been a deeply nonsystematic, occasional enterprise. Desires for an Anglican *summa* especially moved editors of Barrow and Tillotson to group their works around theological topics.[18] One naturally finds change and even inconsistency within the forty year Anglican rationalist project. For example, the advent of William III and the taking of oaths necessary to maintain one's position made many 30 January and other political sermons a potential embarrassment. When Socinian rationalism received wider currency in a pamphlet skirmish in the 1690s, even leading divines carefully rewrote their previous opinions on the rational basis of Scripture. While Anglican rationalism indubitably stood for ascertainable, consistent doctrines and methodologies throughout its lifetime, changing events, arguments, audiences, and allegiances kept renewing its nonsystematic vivacity.

Achieved on a number of levels, the self-creation of the Restoration Church of England seems credible and compelling; it managed to foster an illusion of inevitability and invincibility. It successfully removed a significant number of its ministers in the early 1660s; it excluded others from the establishment in the 1670s and 1680s. It had the political will to frustrate the desires of two kings for easier ties with Catholics. Although such dominance of culture is impressive in itself, the illusion of inevitability would not have been complete without a theological content to its ideology, and a corresponding rhetoric. Strong leaders rose to fill this need. Energetic yet imperturbable, capacious yet not shrinking from theological squabbles, even by the late 1660s the work of the Anglican rationalists was perfecting the Restoration myth. Authors face their greatest challenge in creating compelling narrative and expository voices; in most literary forms, the artist's first task is to create such a voice. Anglican rationalists excelled at creating authoritative, consistent voices. Even as the parts of the project are being constructed, while major problems have yet to be addressed, the voices sound confident about the unassailability of the whole. Opponents appear and disappear into complicated rhetorical structures; opponents engender argument, but not doubt.

The Anglican rationalist divines, eminent advancers of print culture, were well aware of how to manipulate its power.[19] The divines gave careful instructions about their manuscripts, which except for a few remaining Stillingfleet and Tillotson manuscripts were destroyed after being edited for publication by close friends or by their chaplains. Thus Tillotson edited Barrow's collected works, and their chaplains edited Stillingfleet's and Tillotson's. Previous single publications were gathered and republished. If there had been any scribal circulation, the divines' final efforts seem intended to cancel its effects. The appearance of so many formidable folio and octavo sets around 1700 fulfilled their authors' intention to make the doctrine in and the establishment founded on their works seem inevitable and necessary.

The adversaries let into and smothered by these large rhetorical structures are at least twofold, those from the right, Roman Catholicism, and those from the left, rationalism. Encounters with rationalism, however, more interestingly introduce the continuing project of eighteenth-century Anglican theology, for one problem with some eighteenth-century theological texts is their apparent demand for a hermeneutical shift: how can they be Christian and Anglican when they do not explicitly argue from Scripture? Anglican rationalism sheds light on this interpretive problem. With various responses situated along a continuum from acceptance to rejection, it integrates various types of reason: arguments from experience and common sense, from ancient and modern history, from language, from necessity, from Aristotle, Hobbes, Spinoza, Locke, and the Socinians, and from many previous interpreters of Scripture whose interpretations themselves already rationalize Scriptural moral codes and narratives. When Scripture seems absent from a sermon or volume of Anglican rationalism's successors, the reader must search for the proper theological perspective, knowing that the terms of the search must be flexible. The absence of Scriptural argument need not signify that this is a deist text. The absence of Scripture may be simply a continuance of late seventeenth-century methodology, in that Anglican rationalism often dramatizes its self-conscious encounter with multivalent reason by such means. This dramatization, which has nothing to do with heterodoxy and everything to do with self-confident orthodoxy, seems to remain forceful in mainstream Anglican theology of the new century.

NOTES

1. Prominent examples of such interpretation include: Frederick C. Beiser, *The Sovereignty of Reason: The Defense of Rationality in the Early English Enlightenment* (Princeton, N.J.: Princeton University Press, 1996), 132–33; Gerald R. Cragg, *From Puritanism to the Age of Reason* (Cambridge: Cambridge University Press, 1950), 80–86, and *The Church and the Age of Reason, 1648–1789* (Harmondsworth, Middlesex: Penguin, 1960), 70–73; Horton Davies, *Worship and Theology in England: From Watts and Wesley to Maurice, 1690–1850* (Princeton, N.J.: Princeton University Press, 1960), 52–58, 67–70, 72–74; and Norman Sykes, *The English Religious Tradition* (London: SCM Press, 1953), 54–56.

2. See Phillip Harth, *Swift and Anglican Rationalism: The Religious Background of "A Tale of a Tub"* (Chicago: University of Chicago Press, 1961), 18–51, and *Contexts of Dryden's Thought* (Chicago: University of Chicago Press, 1968), 101–8, 152–73, 199–225. Harth does not use the term "Anglican rationalism" in *Contexts.* See also Irène Simon, *Three Restoration Divines* (Paris: Sociéte d'Edition "Les Belles Lettres," 1967–1976), 1:75–148. In this essay I do not use the term "latitudinarian," although scholarly use often takes it for substantially the same reality as Anglican rationalism; I believe that "latitudinarian" most often refers to the external relations of the movement whose content can be called Anglican rationalism. See also W. M. Spellman, *The Latitudinarians and the Church of England, 1660–1700* (Athens: University of Georgia Press, 1993), 11–32, 72–131; J. D. Spurr, *The Restoration Church of England, 1646–1689* (New Haven, Conn.: Yale University Press, 1991), 29–104; and John Walsh and Stephen Taylor, "Introduction: The Church and Anglicanism in the 'Long' Eighteenth Century," in *The Church of England, c. 1689–c. 1833: From Toleration to Tractarianism,* ed. John Walsh, Colin Haydon, and Stephen Taylor (Cambridge: Cambridge University Press, 1993), 35–43.

3. Isaac Barrow, *Sermons Preached upon Several Occasions* (London, 1678), 1–33, 34–71.

4. Barrow, *Sermons,* 33, 62, 82.

5. Beiser, *Sovereignty,* 270.

6. See Edward Stillingfleet, "The Mysteries of the Christian Faith Asserted and Vindicated," in *Works* (London, 1707–1710), 1:452–66, and John Tillotson, *Sermons Concerning the Divinity and Incarnation of Our Blessed Saviour,* 2d ed. (London, 1695).

7. Beiser, *Sovereignty,* 270.

8. For the full argument see Gerard Reedy, S. J., "Interpreting Tillotson," *Harvard Theological Review* 86 (1993): 96–103.

9. For the pre-1660 period sample works discussing the plain sense include: William Chillingworth, *Works* (Dublin, 1752), 1:24–131, 2:97–100; John Hales, *Works* (Glasgow, 1765), 2:1–46; Edward Hyde, "Contemplations and Reflections upon the Psalms of David," in *A Compleat Collection of Tracts* (London, 1747), 349–770, especially 379–82. For the post-1660 period see: Richard Allestree, *Forty Sermons* (Oxford, 1684), 2:1–20; Gilbert Burnet, *An Exposition of the*

Thirty-Nine Articles of the Church of England (London, 1699), 71–105, and *Four Discourses Delivered to the Clergy of the Diocese of Sarum* (London, 1694), 5–8, 48–52, 61–68, 140–41; Hugo Grotius, *The Truth of the Christian Religion,* trans. Simon Patrick (London, 1680), 114–18, 119–28, 272–77; William Lowth, *A Vindication of the Divine Authority and Inspiration of the Writings of the Old and New Testament* (Oxford, 1692), 31–40; Simon Patrick, *Works,* ed. Alexander Taylor (London, 1858), 6:517–49; John Sharp, *Works* (London, 1749), 1:172–205, 2:168–99; Edward Stillingfleet, *Works,* 1:393–409, 452–66; John Tillotson, *Sermons Concerning the Divinity and Incarnation of Our Blessed Saviour,* 14–15, 22–28, 32, 45–50, 60–68, 94–95, 105–8; John Williams, *Ecclesiastes,* 6th ed. (London, 1675), 57–79. For a recent collection of references to work on meaning and invention in Scripture in the late seventeenth century, see Marcus Walsh, *Shakespeare, Milton, and Eighteenth-Century Editing: The Beginnings of Interpretative Scholarship* (Cambridge: Cambridge University Press, 1997), 32–47.

10. See Harth, *Contexts,* 174–80; also Gerard Reedy, S. J., *The Bible and Reason* (Philadelphia: University of Pennsylvania Press, 1985), 104–18, for Anglican responses to Spinoza's *Tractatus Theologico-Politicus* (1670) and Richard Simon's *Critical History of the Old Testament* (1682).

11. *Biblia Sacra Polyglotta,* ed. Brian Walton et al. (London, 1657), 1:36. The Latin original reads: "Ita tamen invigilavit providentia Divina, Ecclesiaeque diligentia, ut in iis quae ad salutem necessaria sunt, et ad fidem et mores spectant, omnia pura et integra sint."

12. Patrick, "Search the Scriptures. A Treatise Showing that All Christians Ought to Read the Holy Books," in *Works,* 6:581.

13. John Toland, *Christianity Not Mysterious* (London, 1696), 26, xx. The Anglican rationalist and opposite position had been stated by, among others, John Sharp in a sermon, perhaps from the 1680s: "As a man is more or less furnished with proper Helps, and Means, and Instruments for the understanding of the Scripture; as he hath more or less improved himself, by acquiring Knowledge and Learning; so he shall in proportion understand more or less of those holy Books" (*Works* 7:75).

14. Helen Vendler, *The Art of Shakespeare's Sonnets* (Cambridge, Mass.: Belknap Press, Harvard University Press, 1997), 24.

15. B. W. Young, *Religion and Enlightenment in Eighteenth-Century England* (Oxford: Clarendon Press, 1998), 19–44.

16. John Tillotson, *Works,* ed. Thomas Birch, 5th ed. (London, 1752), 1:456, 471.

17. Melvyn New, "Benjamin Whichcote's Aphorisms and the Importance of Latitudinarianism," *1650–1850: Ideas, Aesthetics, and Inquiries in the Early Modern Era* 4 (1998): 89–104.

18. Tillotson's first biographer, Thomas Birch, provides the outline that Tillotson himself made in 1691 for a "summa theologiae Christianae"; his archiepiscopal duties prevented him from writing the full text before his death in 1694. Since the closer Tillotson is to an audience the livelier his writing becomes, our sense of loss for his summa need not be overwhelming. See Birch, *The Life of the Most*

Reverend Dr. John Tillotson, Lord Archbishop of Canterbury (London, 1752), 379–80.

19. For two recent discussions of the implication of print dominance, see Harold Love, *Scribal Publication in Seventeenth-Century England* (Oxford: Clarendon Press, 1993), 141–48, and Edward H. Jacobs, "Buying into Classes: The Practice of Book Selection in Eighteenth-Century Britain," *Eighteenth-Century Studies* 33 (1999): 43–46.

4

Mandeville and Swift

CLAUDE RAWSON

It was perhaps Basil Willey, in 1940, who was the first to notice a Mandevillian ring in a famous passage of Swift's ironical *Argument against Abolishing Christianity* (1708).[1] This occurs near the beginning, where the speaker explains that it is "nominal" Christianity that he is arguing for and not the real thing:

> I hope, no Reader imagines me so weak to stand up in the Defence of *real* Christianity; such as used in primitive Times (if we may believe the Authors of those Ages) to have an Influence upon Mens Belief and Actions: To offer at the Restoration of that, would indeed be a wild Project; it would be to dig up Foundations; to destroy at one Blow *all* the Wit, and *half* the Learning of the Kingdom; to break the entire Frame and Constitution of Things; to ruin Trade, extinguish Arts and Sciences with the Professors of them; in short, to turn our Courts, Exchanges and Shops into Desarts: And would be full as absurd as the Proposal of *Horace,* where he advises the *Romans,* all in a Body, to leave their City, and seek a new Seat in some remote Part of the World, by Way of Cure for the Corruption of their Manners. (*PW* 2:27–28)[2]

Prima facie this "closely resembles," as Willey said, "Mandeville's account of the effects of introducing virtue into the hive." There are few or no known references to Mandeville in Swift's writings and correspondence, though there is a glancing sneer at Mandeville in one of Sheridan's contributions to the *Intelligencer* in 1728.[3] Mandeville seems seldom to have been mentioned by anyone in print until the greatly enlarged 1723 edition of the *Fable of the Bees,* when his status as an ideological bogeyfigure, a Man-devil comparable to the Machiavel or Make-evil of an earlier time, became fully consolidated. Mandeville said the smaller edition of 1714 had "many Enemies," though it was "never carpt at, or publickly taken Notice of" (*F* 240, 408).[4] There may have been about him an aura of untouchability, comparable to that of Hobbes, with whom he was often associated, which made authors reticent of "taking Notice," as one might avoid naming a pornographer, even when attacking him, and especially when their views appeared to converge or overlap with any of his.[5]

Whatever the reasons, the works of Swift and Mandeville sometimes appear to show a pattern of tacit or interlocking awareness of one another, absorbing each other's language and reproducing it in what might seem to be a reciprocal array of undeclared allusion. Some of this may be fortuitous, though Mandeville was, as we shall see, certainly aware of *A Tale of a Tub* (1704), and mentioned other works by Swift occasionally.[6] In 1708, when Swift wrote the *Argument,* Mandeville was largely unknown, though it is possible that he may have been remembering the nuclear text of Mandeville's *Fable—The Grumbling Hive, or, Knaves Turn'd Honest*—which had appeared as a freestanding poem in 1705. Swift had, after all, published a famous bee fable of his own the previous year, and might be expected to take notice of analogues. Herbert Davis, quoting the same passage in the same year as Willey (1940), spoke in passing of the *Argument*'s "scepticism rather like Mandeville's," but didn't elaborate, while Willey appears to uncouple the two in a subsequent comment: Swift "does not believe, with Mandeville, that the hive must needs be vicious to be great; indeed, he is a satirist precisely because he feels that it should and could be directed by standards which would have been acceptable to Plato or Cicero—standards of rationality, 'nature' and civilization for which the great ancients stood, and for which the Church of England now stands."[7]

Reading these remarks today, one is struck by a certain blandness. They are not, in their way, untrue. Swift's "official" or overt beliefs correspond approximately to what Willey says, except that the texture of his writings has a different feel. The notional appeal is to these things, not perhaps with the comfortable complacency evoked by Willey's words, but with an insistence on their authority which is at the same time urgent and hopeless. These standards, it is implied, are vitally necessary in view of the character of the human animal, but that character simultaneously ensures that they will be continually violated. The disruptive energies of Swift's prose, the tearaway irony of *A Tale of a Tub* and its extraordinary absence of "positive" ideological bearings or resting-points, notably on the things "for which the Church of England now stands," are a remarkable demonstration of the "nominal" truth of Willey's description and of a certain inadequacy in "real" terms. The description brings out, with the unwitting simplicity of a textbook example, the poverty as well as the uses of that "world picture" approach to literary history of which Willey's "background" volumes may be counted among the more sophisticated examples. A single paragraph from Leavis's famous essay "The Irony of

Swift," to which Willey pays tribute in a footnote—the paragraph, for example, about Swift and Gibbon, or even a single affirmation that the Houyhnhnms "may have all the reason, but the Yahoos have all the life"—tells us more about prevailing ideologies and an author's relation to them than whole chapters in Willey's mode of patient exposition.[8]

Willey's uncoupling of Swift from Mandeville is only apparent or at least incomplete. It comes after the following passage, whose blandness is still more numbing, even as it registers a possibly disconcerting truth:

> [Swift's] writings in general show his attachment to reason and good sense, to the Anglican Church as their embodiment, and to settled and orderly government. He does not want a revolutionary Christianity; no one hates religious enthusiasm more than he, and no one has analysed more devastatingly the sources of fanaticism ("Aeolism") and of any kind of megalomania. As a Church of England man, a friend of Revolution principles, and a statesman, he accepts the splendid hive—"our present schemes of wealth and power," with which he says real Christianity is utterly inconsistent.[9]

Swift's attachment to "settled and orderly government" is much closer to the insistence on law and order that we nowadays hear from politicians of a certain sort than to the cosy Addisonian or perhaps Gibbonian perspective that Willey seems to imply. When the *Sentiments of a Church-of-England Man,* probably roughly contemporaneous with the *Argument* (that is, also said to have been "Written in the YEAR 1708") or alternatively somewhat earlier, speaks of the extermination velleities of fanatics of left and right towards one another, there is more than a hint that both sides deserve the punishment they wish upon each other (*PW* 2:13).[10] A dimension that Willey leaves out of account is precisely that element of unresolved contradiction, that intercrossing web of aggressions directed against all parties, and indeed against aggression itself, as often as not including the writer's own. Willey is of course right about the hatred for "revolutionary Christianity," "enthusiasm," and religious "fanaticism," but overlooks the element of extremism with which Swift entertained these views, and the immoderate rigor with which he asserted the need for moderation or ridiculed the moderation of others. Swift also shrank from devotional excesses, as well as theological niceties, even of an orthodox sort, regarding religion, which is always the state religion in a Platonic sense of these things, as a policing authority for the conduct of life rather than an arena of spiritual experience.

This view of the importance of the Church disconcertingly mirrors the idea that Religion was the "Invention of Politicians, to keep the lower Part of the World in Awe" (*PW* 2:34, 4:27, 40), which Swift satirically ascribed to "freethinkers" like Toland and Anthony Collins, and which, as Louis Landa said, "was frequently remarked on, though not always defended, by unorthodox writers, as Hobbes, Mandeville, Spinoza."[11] (It was eventually appropriated, in its now best-known form, in Marx's *mot* about religion being the "opium of the people."[12]) Swift typically repudiated the imputed cynicism of those who held this view, but wasn't altogether ready to deny its validity, and remained committed to his own supposedly sanitized version of it.

A parallel ambivalence, in a variant configuration, may be found in Mandeville. His version, as expressed in the "Enquiry into the Origin of Moral Virtue," first included in the 1714 edition of the *Fable,* cautiously displaces the scenario away from the Jewish and Christian religions to "the Idolatrous Superstitions of all other Nations," whose "pitiful Notions . . . of the Supreme Being were incapable of exciting Man to Virtue, and good for nothing but to awe and amuse a rude and unthinking Multitude." Moreover, the practical agency of these heathen religions and idolatrous superstitions in restraining man's "Appetites and subduing his dearest Inclinations" was nil. The moral excellence of Greece or Rome was not the product of their religious beliefs, but of "the skilful Management of wary Politicians" (*F* 86–87).

Mandeville's maneuver enables him to separate "true Religion" from these processes, though he clearly felt the need to affirm a disengagement, much as Swift had felt compelled, in the 1710 Apology to *A Tale of a Tub,* to defend his work against imputations that it attacked religion itself and not only its Papist or Dissenting abuses. Mandeville was sharply aware of Swift's vulnerability on this score. In Mandeville's last work, *A Letter to Dion* (1732), mainly concerned to defend the *Fable* against Berkeley's attack in the Second Dialogue of *Alciphron,* published earlier the same year ("You are not the first, Sir, . . . who has been very severe upon the *Fable of the Bees* without having ever read it"), he contends against Berkeley that:

> There are various Ways, by which Private Vices may become Publick Benefits, Ways more real and practicable, than what, some Time ago, was offere'd by that serious Divine, whose Religion and Piety are so amply set forth in that undisguised Confession of his Faith, *The Tale of a Tub.*[13]

It seems possible that, while incidentally directing his sarcasm at a notorious sensitive spot in Swift's reputation, Mandeville was mainly referring to what he would see as the misplaced irony of Swift's version of the "Private Vices . . . Publick Benefits" formula in the *Argument against Abolishing Christianity* itself. There is piquancy in this bravura obliquity at the expense of a writer who is perhaps the most versatile practitioner of stylistic indirection in the language. Its even greater interest is that it may represent an early perception of the *Argument,* rightly or wrongly, as a deliberately perverse reading of the Mandevillian doctrines of the *Fable.*

Mandeville's disengagement of true religion from false superstitions in the *Enquiry,* even as it proclaims appropriate allegiances, tilts the reasoning towards a subtle endorsement of the main argument, so that "True Religion" is itself properly served by the kind of management of frailties and imperfections which his entire *Fable* is expounding:

> If the too scrupulous Reader should at first View condemn these Notions concerning the Origin of Moral Virtue, and think them perhaps offensive to Christianity, I hope he'll forbear his Censures, when he shall consider, that nothing can render the unsearchable depth of the Divine Wisdom more conspicuous than that *Man,* whom Providence had designed for Society, should not only by his own Frailties and Imperfections be led into the Road to Temporal Happiness, but likewise receive, from a seeming Necessity of Natural Causes, a Tincture of that Knowledge, in which he was afterwards to be made perfect by the True Religion, to his Eternal Welfare. (*F* 92)

It is evident that these obeisances are not designed to negate "the skilful Management of wary Politicians" working to keep the multitude in awe, but only to say in the last analysis that such management collaborates with the divine wisdom (*F* 87). The overriding momentum of the "Enquiry" is concerned to refute those who hold that "no Society was ever any ways civilis'd before the major part had agreed upon some Worship or other of an over ruling Power, and consequently that the Notions of Good and Evil, and the Distinction between *Virtue* and *Vice,* were never the Contrivance of Politicians, but the pure Effect of Religion" (*F* 86). The bottom line, as he says in Remark L, was that "The Multitude must be aw'd . . . and the Clergy allow'd no greater Share in State Affairs than our Saviour has bequeathed them in his Testament" (*F* 142). It is a fairly short step from this, in Mandeville's scheme, not only to the notion of divine wisdom as part of the management that keeps the multitude in awe, but of the tactical discriminations themselves as belonging to the same project, and designed for those sections of the multitude less easily awed.

The view, discussed in Swift's *Argument,* that religion was the "Invention of Politicians, to keep the lower Part of the World in Awe," thus anticipates Mandeville's wordings as well as parroting the freethinkers'. It is a view from which the fictive author of the *Argument* professes a judicious disengagement, even as he admits to "conceiv[ing] some scattered Notions about a superior Power to be of singular Use for the common People, as furnishing excellent Materials to keep Children quiet, when they grow peevish; and providing Topicks of Amusement in a tedious Winter Night" (*PW* 2:34. Mandeville was also to speak both of *awing* and *amusing* his unthinking multitude, *F* 86). The double-take, more insinuatingly elusive than anything Mandeville typically goes in for, makes the speaker appear as an unreservedly committed freethinker, not to be taken in even by such a modest view of the uses of Christianity, but settling nevertheless for a lowered version of it. That move, a routine of Swiftian irony most fully deployed in *A Modest Proposal* (1729), exhibits the speaker as a moderate and committed to current versions of political correctness but not to be numbered among extremer ideologues; and Mandeville was to develop his own version of it in *A Modest Defence of Publick Stews* (1724). But the Swiftian signature is variously distinctive, especially in the manner in which the graduated and selective mock-adoption of unacceptable views intimates a teasing convergence with a primary element of Swift's own thinking, seriously entertained. It brings to the surface a paradox, now well-recognized in Swift studies, of an aggressively slippery identity of views between Swift and the things or people he rejects.

The relation of this to Mandeville's notions about the role of religion is complex. Establishing his credentials as a defender of education in the essay on charity-schools, Mandeville declares that "There is no Faculty so immediately necessary to the Government of a Nation as that of Theology, and as we ought to have great numbers of Divines for the Service of this Island, I would not have the meaner People discouraged from bringing up their Children to that Function" (*F* 300). This is not, as we have seen, because Mandeville had a highly developed regard for the importance and prerogatives of the clergy, who, in his view, must be "allow'd no greater Share in State Affairs than our Saviour has bequeathed them in his Testament" (*F* 142). Like Swift in the *Project for the Advancement of Religion* (1709), Mandeville thought the number of clergy could usefully be increased. Swift thought the present shortage reflected an ignominious neglect of religion (*PW* 2:45). Mandeville's argument for having "great numbers of Divines" drawn from "the meaner People" is instead based on the fact that "Among the midling People of all Trades there are Bigots who have a Superstitious Awe for a Gown and Cassock," who long to see their child elevated to the clergy, and who thus provide the nation with a labor-force that is likely to be content with the low clerical pickings which the speaker of Swift's *Argument* described as a socially beneficial arrangement and which were a perpetual source of Swiftian dismay. Mandeville explains:

> It is to this Religious Zeal, or at least the Human Frailties that pass for and represent it, that we owe the great plenty of poor Scholars the Nation enjoys. For considering the inequality of Livings, and the smalness of Benefices up and down

> the Kingdom, without this happy Disposition in Parents of small Fortune, we could not possibly be furnish'd from any other Quarter with proper Persons for the Ministry, to attend all the Cures of Souls, so pitifully provided for, that no Mortal could Live upon them that had been Educated in any Tolerable Plenty, unless he was possess'd of real Virtue, which it is Foolish and indeed Injurious, we should more expect from the Clergy than we generally find in the Laity. (*F* 300–301)

This is more sophisticated than Swift's speaker, though not than Swift's perception into that speaker. Had the essay on charity-schools been available at the time, one may suppose that the sarcasms of the *Argument* would have been the more stingingly intricate for it. Still, the *Argument*'s reasonings about the advantages of keeping in business some "ten Thousand Persons reduced by the wise Regulations of *Henry* the Eighth, to the Necessity of a low Diet, and moderate Exercise" (*PW* 2:30), may be taken as one of Swift's many parodic anticipations. And Mandeville's reflections later in the essay on the use of Sunday worship for keeping the children of the poor out of mischief would also not be out of place in the *Argument*'s scenario (*F* 311–12).

Nevertheless there is an important sense, glimpsed even in Willey's shallow account, in which "our present Schemes of Wealth and Power" (*PW* 2:28) remain important to Swift, in a quasi-Mandevillian way and in the teeth of his own sarcasms, although they are at the same time the prime targets of some of his most biting satirical works. The case is again characteristic of a well-established tendency for Swiftian satire both to turn against itself and to shadow very closely some Swiftian values not offered up for castigation. When the *Argument* contends that the continued use of Sunday as a day of rest has specific advantages for the pursuit of business, litigation, gallantry, and fashion, it is easy to detect parody, actual or potential or proleptic, of Mandevillian utilitarianism. But in those derisive enumerations one hears not only the moralist or the divine denouncing worldly ways, but the spokesman of a patrician establishment doing his number with merchants at their greasy till. The quip at the end of the *Argument* that abolishing Christianity may not have the "great Advantage to Trade" that some expect, and that the "Bank and *East-India* Stock may fall, at least, One *per Cent,*" is partly directed at what in Swift's perspective would be considered to be "alternative" or adversarial wealth (*PW* 2:38–39): at the takeover by the money-men of the privileges of a landed or notionally court-centered nexus of "Wealth and Power," with its traditional alliances with *ancienneté* and the kind of Church that gave men like Swift their livelihood, their forum for literary expression, and what passed for a political power-base. The "nominal" or mock-preoccupation in the *Argument* with the preservation of the Church as a material, secular, or political institution is the flip side of Swift's "real" and unwavering championship of the clergy's financial prerogatives and of the Church as a secularly established embodiment of institutional authority.

Swift, unlike Mandeville, might be described as a radical satirist, in the etymological sense which implies a concern with the roots of human nature and a feeling that they are irremediably depraved. An un-Mandevillian pessimism follows from this, but the social or political radicalism which might demand a root-and-branch destruction of the existing order is as alien to Swift's vision as any corresponding ardors of revolutionary hope. There is no demand for a new world order, at best a hopeless nostalgia for the virtuous arrangements of an older time, classical republicanism, the gothic institution, English yeomen of the old stamp. The incurability of human nature makes irrelevant "radical" solutions of any sort, so that the ruthlessness of the Swiftian anatomy settles paradoxically for a conservatism of accommodation, concerned with management rather than eradication of human depravity. It is this moral territory that he shares with Mandeville, though he arrives at it by a different route. The term "Management," often accompanied by the adjective "dextrous" (sometimes "skilful"), is a frequently recurrent one in Mandeville, applicable to private morals (the "dextrous Management of ourselves") as well as to the religious, social, political, and economic spheres, and to their interactions with one another and with the private (*F* 87, 102, 141, 410). Mandeville's usages tend overtly to the preservation of those "present Schemes of Wealth and Power" which come under fire in Swift's *Argument*. But if Swift's dismissal of these is absolute, there is also a practical concern to maintain them against the destabilising pressures of an adversarial extremism, itself a product of the restless depravity that brought them into being in the first place, and that is simultaneously constrained into survivability by their structural force as institutions.

Swift's project as a satirist purports to expose, unmask, dissect, rejecting the prettifying fictions which disguise the Kurtzian "horror" beneath the "present Schemes." But this has little in common with that cult of unmasking which produced Rousseau's *Confessions* on the personal or introspective plane and the appropriations of Rousseau by soul-baring rituals of French (and later) revolutionary ideologues on the political plane. Swift had none of the rooted contempt prescribed by revolutionary ideology for "hypocrisy" as the cardinal political offence. He disliked "hypocrites," but conceded, in the *Project for the Advancement of Religion* (another work with Mandevillian associations) and elsewhere, a need to protect society from certain open professions of viciousness.[14]

Consider the actual fortunes of unmasking, especially in its guise of dissection, in *A Tale of a Tub*. The genial speaker of the Digression on

Madness, upholding the advantages of "*the Possession of being well deceived,*" reports in the "modern" way that outward appearances are always better than the inner reality, it being one of Nature's "Eternal Laws . . . to put her best Furniture forward." In what is perhaps the best-known sentence Swift ever wrote, the speaker reports in evidence that "Last Week I saw a Woman *flay'd,* and you will hardly believe, how much it altered her Person for the worse"—probably an evocation of a whipped and carted whore, and complemented by the male example of a dissected beau, whose organs are laid open to reveal "Defects encreas[ing] upon us in Number and Bulk" (*PW* 1:109–10).

The 1714 Preface to the *Fable of the Bees* has a passage that it is instructive to compare with this:

> Those that study the Anatomy of Dead Carkasses may see, that the chief Organs and nicest Springs more immediately required to continue the Motion of our Machine, are not hard Bones, strong Muscles and Nerves, nor the smooth white Skin that so beautifully covers them, but small trifling Films and little Pipes that are either overlook'd, or else seem inconsiderable to Vulgar Eyes; so they that examine into the Nature of Man . . . may observe, that what renders him a Sociable Animal, consists not in his desire of Company, good Nature, Pity, Affability, and other Graces of a fair Outside; but that his vilest and most hateful Qualities are the most necessary Accomplishments to fit him for the largest, and according to the World, the happiest and most flourishing Societies. (*F* 53)

Mandeville's particular spin makes of this a parallel view to that of Swift (not Swift's speaker), but with a reverse valuation: it is good to be bad inside. The fact that the *Tale*'s speaker wants this hidden, using the discoveries of science as a motive for retreating from fact, while Mandeville delights in exposing it, treating the discovery as something to celebrate, may be what distinguishes them from each other. But both are in another way distinguished from Swift, whose posture is that you don't need scientific experiments to discover the obvious. The speaker learns from science that ugly truths should be kept hidden, deploring dissectors as men who hold "*Anatomy* to be the ultimate End of *Physick*" (*PW* 1:110), whereas Mandeville the real-life physician adopts the stance of the value-free scientist for whom anatomy can indeed be an end in itself. That good news may be found in smelly innards would have delighted Swift's speaker and been rejected by Swift. It has something of the neutrally complacent view of the pre-Houyhnhnm Gulliver, like Mandeville a surgeon educated at Leyden, whose scientist's composure is itself one of the signs of his boneheadedness. (It is worth recalling, among the affinities between Mandeville and *Gulliver's Travels,* the proto-Lilliputian fiction of the *Fable of the Bees*).

This boneheadedness, like that of the *Tale*'s speaker, has paradoxical relations with the "*Superficies* of *Things*," which "creams off Nature, leaving the Sower and the Dregs, for Philosophy and Reason to lap up" (*PW* 1:110). Gulliver has progressed a little beyond the *Tale*'s speaker and found, in a Mandevillian sort of way, that "the Sower and the Dregs" have their point. In Gulliver's perspective, before he becomes misanthropically disillusioned, the innards might be said to have come to the surface, and are found beautiful. That too is unacceptable to Swift, who exposes it as idiotic in an equal and opposite way. But the third way, which you think to be implicit all along, is the supposedly good kind of "unmasking," that which consists of an unflinching exposure of the horror within, which the *Tale*'s speaker, at least in the Digression on Madness, seems philosophically opposed to. In his capacity as scientific hack, he performs the experiments, notably on the carcass of the Digression's beau, and is found, as we saw, foolish for doing so, foolish for needing to do so in order to discover what he does, and foolish for insisting on the preferability of surfaces and refusing the satirist's truth-telling project. That he can't win if he dissects and can't win if he doesn't is a version of a familiar Swiftian trap, and the bind is replicated in all those Swiftian places where ambitions of exposure give way to images of covering and containment, like those poems in which the fact that Celia shits must be faced but also kept out of sight if society is to go on.[15]

In an earlier Digression, "in the Modern Kind," the speaker again reports some scientific dissections, and mostly sounds his usual fatuous self. But the blending of tones is subtly different, and in a passage of heightened rhetoric, what Leavis might have called one of Swift's "intensities," the speaker seems to speak for his author in an unusually direct way when he says he has, "with a World of Pains and Art, dissected the Carcass of *Humane Nature* . . . till at last it *smelt* so strong, I could preserve it no longer" (*PW* 1:77).[16] There are revealing *pensées* in which Swift, like Johnson, concedes the presence of subversive or disruptive sentiments in his own psyche, and disclaims answerability to God for them provided he conceals and endeavors to subdue them, and does not allow them to influence the conduct of his life (*PW* 9:261–62).[17]

The *Project for the Advancement of Religion* rests on assumptions and purposes of this sort. Its tolerance of a managed species of hypocrisy is actually fairly traditional, and is found in Pascal, La Rochefoucauld, and others.[18] Modern readers, marked by an ideology of sincerity which ultimately derives from French revolutionary thought, are sometimes shocked into a mode of denial which, as also with Book 4 of *Gulliver's Travels,* makes them unable to accept that Swift can possibly mean what he seems to be saying, and argue that the proposal must have been ironically intended. But it derives in part from the same sense, identified by Willey in Mandeville, that the human mind is an impure place, that judging it by its motives inevitably and correctly invites radical condemnation, but that "impure motives can and do produce beneficial results."[19]

Mandeville has some formulations that superficially resemble these notions, but should not be confused with the position of Pascal or Swift:

> Vertue, who from Politicks
> Had learn'd a Thousand cunning Tricks,
> Was, by their happy Influence,
> Made Friends with Vice.
>
> (*F* 68)

This has to be distinguished from the traditional paradox about hypocrisy being the vice that is a friend to virtue. Swift's version rests on a psychology of habituation in which the artificial pretence turns to a kind of second nature: the positive form is given in the *Project,* and there is a negative obverse, in which dissembling at last grows real in a bad sense, in the *Mechanical Operation of the Spirit* (*PW* 2:57, 1:175–76).[20] Mandeville's version of emotions worked on by art doesn't entertain these notions of a naturalising and habituating process, which, from Swift to Burke and Yeats, are the basis of a paradoxical and would-be aristocratic conception of organic acculturation ("How but in custom and in ceremony / Are innocence and beauty born?").[21]

The Mandevillian scheme isn't concerned with habituation but with civil adaptation, and does not presuppose a merging of the spheres of virtue and social requirement: "Virtue bids us subdue, but good Breeding only requires we should hide our Appetites." For a moment, as he goes on to enunciate the principle that "A fashionable Gentleman may have as violent an Inclination to a Woman as the brutish Fellow; but then he behaves himself quite otherwise," the plain-spoken Dutch doctor sounds a bit like the Earl of Chesterfield. But Chesterfield's seigneurial advocacy of certain styles of courtship has none of Mandeville's open acceptance of the commercial value of sensual pleasures. When Mandeville says that "by being well bred, we suffer no Abridgment in our sensual Pleasures, but only labour for our mutual Happiness, and assist each other in the luxurious Enjoyment of all worldly Comforts," he is not educating his son or godson in the arts of pleasing but presupposing the apology for "luxury" which becomes the principal preoccupation of Remark L (*F* 106, 136 ff). His own mildly raffish, proto-Chesterfieldian "Wishes to a Godson" (published with other poems of would-be libertine sentiment in 1712) shows less concern with Chesterfieldian breeding than with good burgher comforts:

May your Whores be prudent, true,
And Coquets to all but you,
Cleanly, Buxom, Gen'rous taking
And be sure of your own making;
May you never stick to one,
Or, by fondness be undone.[22]

This genial merchant-replica of the Chesterfieldian ethos is as remote from Swift as both are from the real Chesterfieldian product. Mandeville doesn't accept even the lowered version implied in the Swiftian idea of hypocrisy, or the negative scenario of a hideous sincerity achieved through the manipulations of mechanical operators of the spirit. In the "Essay on Charity, and Charity-Schools" he offers a quite different conception of the artificial stimulation of responsive minds, a comment whose closing instance looks forward to some well-known preoccupations of Burke[23]:

> Those who have a strong and lively Imagination, and can make Representations of things in their Minds, as they would be if they were actually before them, may work themselves up into something that resembles Compassion; but this is done by Art, and often the help of a little Enthusiasm, and is only an imitation of Pity: the Heart feels little of it, and it is as faint as what we suffer at the acting of a Tragedy. (*F* 266–67)

Swift was as vigilant as Mandeville on the dangers of a misplaced softness towards the poor, and only a little less hardline on the subject of charity schools.[24] He also undoubtedly shared in some form an unillusioned sense of the need for management of human behavior of the sort which included a massaging of moral imperatives for the sake of civil order and civic well-being. This included low-key scenarios for transforming vices into virtues which should not be confused with Mandeville's idea of how impure motives served the public good while actually retaining their full impurity. Swift's view of hypocrisy as a friend to virtue rests on quite different foundations from those by which, in Mandeville's poem, "Vertue . . . Made Friends with Vice." Mandeville's emphasis, as he explains in Remark F, is on a process in which the friendship between virtue and vice is a matter not of mental processes but of market situations, "when industrious good People, who maintain their Families and bring up their Children handsomely, pay Taxes, and are several ways useful Members of the Society, get a livelyhood by something that chiefly depends on, or is very much influenc'd by the Vices of others" (*F* 117). Swift's interest is in the psychological process by which morality and immorality enter into strange and transforming alliances, whereas Mandeville's is in the economic mechanisms by which immorality may serve the public good while remaining morally untransformed.

Mandeville's version is a mercantilist variation of Pope's *Essay on Man,* or the kind of Thatcherite theodicy which the modern term "sociodicy" describes most accurately. The term, said to have been coined by Raymond Aron, is nowadays applied to the secularized version of theodicy of which Mandeville himself is sometimes described as the "founder."[25] But it was the economist F. A. Hayek who, without using the word, most clearly brought out Mandeville's sense of an order that formed itself without divine design or systematic human planning. Hayek regarded Mandeville as a "master mind" not for his contribution to economics, but for his recognition that society was formed by agencies which "had never been deliberately invented but had grown up by the survival of what proved successful," and his "awareness of the spontaneous order which the market produces" without "government interference or intervention." That such language has been vulgarised into a clarion call of Thatcherism does not diminish the insight and eloquence of Hayek's claim that Mandeville "made Hume possible . . . the greatest of all modern students of mind and society," and thence led to the social thought of Adam Smith and Herder, and to Darwin's extension of the evolutionary idea to biological organisms.[26]

This would not have been visible to Swift or his contemporaries, and the differences between Mandeville and Swift I am discussing are, along with important convergences, clearly discernible on the issue of licensed prostitution. Swift could not, modestly or otherwise, advocate the institution of public stews on the grounds of its public benefits. His dismay at the sight of "the streets of *London* . . . full of Common Whores" transcends the ironical contexts in which it is expressed in *Mr. Collins's Discourse* (1713) or the *Project for the Advancement of Religion* (*PW* 4:40, 2:55). In both places, as in *A Tale,* sarcasms are directed at others than the "infamous Women," without any abatement of distaste for these. It seems evident that he did not, as Mandeville seemed to do, deplore the whipping and "Carting of Bawds":

> What better could we expect from Your Carting of Bawds, than that the Great Leviathan of Leachery, for Want of these Tubs to play with, should, with one Whisk of his Tail, overset the *Vessel* of Modesty?

But it is interesting that Mandeville in this passage shows no more compassion for the carted victim than Swift does for the *Tale of a Tub*'s flayed woman. The passage, moreover, employs such a pointedly Tubbaean vocabulary, along with its not un-Swiftian conceptual apparatus concerned with the tactical diversion of destructive energies, that it is hard to resist the suspicion of a glancing shot at the Digression on Madness's evocation of a whipped and carted whore, or at least a deep verbal assimilation of *A*

Tale and its most famous passage.[27] And, as Richard I. Cook has pointed out, Swift's own *Project for the Advancement of Religion* was concerned with some of the same problems Mandeville was to address in the *Modest Defence,* including that of religious societies profiteering from the lucrative business of informing on moral offenders.[28] The project of the *Modest Defence* would not commend itself to Swift in its specific operational features. At the same time, the idea of managing an unstoppable depravity so as to protect certain public decencies and stabilities was not foreign to his essential outlook.

Mandeville's notions of virtue are in principle as absolute as Swift's, though he appears more relaxed in the application. Both made a big production of the importance of chastity, but Swift didn't propose licensed brothels. The Mandevillian project (he did call it that) claimed paradoxically to protect virtue by confining lechery to a manageable sphere,[29] and it seems to run against the spirit of Swift's seemingly absolute refusal, in the *Project for the Advancement of Religion,* to concede that there might be a "certain Point where Gallantry ends, and Infamy begins; or that an Hundred criminal Amours were not as pardonable as Half a Score" (*PW* 2:46). I have tried to show elsewhere that Swift's moral absolutism, the flip side of an unillusioned sense of human depravity, produced a species of pragmatic morality, content to settle for piece-meal accommodations, including the concealments of a managed "hypocrisy," which seems to contradict the rigorism of such an observation.[30] The two occur side by side in the same *Project,* however, and demonstrate his disenchanted conviction that concealment and containment, rather than eradication, are the best that can be expected from any programme for the "reformation of manners."

This is broadly the Mandevillian view, converging with Swift's even on the issue of "concealment," though Mandeville wrote at the end of the Preface to the *Modest Defence* against affecting "*to conceal that which cannot be concealed,*" and claimed that public prostitution was better than private. The idea was to get prostitution off the streets and out of the normal stream of social life by removing it to a few discreet houses.[31] The point is also made in Remark H (*F* 128–29). And the refusal to conceal must be understood as both limited and rhetorical. Thus when, in Remark C and elsewhere, he expounds the value, in shame cultures (I think that for Mandeville all cultures are shame cultures), of concealing rather than suppressing vices deemed unsocial, he is making the point that what he refuses to conceal is only the fact of the prevalence or necessity for concealment, for the sake of civic harmony, productive circulation, and the creation of wealth: this underlies the insistence on pretences to virtue, profit-motivated subterfuges like the one in the anecdote about

Decio and Alcander in Remark B or the reticence about profits themselves in the verse text, the use of euphemisms about perquisites and emoluments, as well as the regulation of whoring (*F* 106, 96–97, 66–67). And for all his scorn of the practice of carting and whipping, on grounds of its uselessness, Mandeville is willing to contemplate a repressiveness of *unlicensed* whoring wholly commensurate with the practical rigorism of Swift, as when he thus addresses the reforming societies to which his tract is dedicated:

And here it is to be hoped, that those worthy *Gentlemen* of the *Society* who have hitherto distinguish'd their *Zeal* to so little Purpose, will now exert themselves where they have so good a Prospect of Success; for altho' a poor Itinerant Courtezan could not by any Means be persuaded to starve at the Instigation of a *Reforming* Constable, yet a little *Bridewell* Rhetorick, or the Terrors of a Transportation, will soon convince her that she may live more comfortably and honestly in a *Publick Stew.*[32]

There is even a sense in which the institution of the public stews comes unexpectedly to address one of the problems identified in the *Argument against Abolishing Christianity.* Mandeville argued that the unlicensed state of whoring has contributed to the "Propagation of that infectious Disease, called the *French Pox,* which, in two Centuries, has made such incredible Havock all over *Europe,*" with the result that "In these Kingdoms it so seldom fails to attend Whoring, now-a-days mistaken for Gallantry and Politeness, that a hale, robust Constitution is esteem'd a Mark of Ungentility; and a healthy young Fellow is look'd upon with the same View, as if he had spent his Life in a Cottage."[33] One is reminded of the *Argument*'s plea in favor of maintaining ten thousand clergymen, bound by necessity to "a low Diet, and moderate Exercise," as "the only great Restorers of our Breed," since we have otherwise "nothing to trust to, besides the scrophulous consumptive Productions furnished by our Men of Wit and Pleasure; when having squandered away their Vigour, Health, and Estates; they are forced, by some disagreeable Marriage, to piece up their broken Fortunes, and entail Rottenness and Politeness on their Posterity" (*PW* 2:30–31).

The *Modest Defence* appeared five years before Swift's *Modest Proposal.* The adjective was not uncommon in pamphleteering convention, though its use in works which, in the words of Richard I. Cook, advocate "shocking violations of accepted moral practice" distinguishes both authors from the more usual kind of pamphleteer. The difference between the two is that Swift isn't proposing his scheme straight while Mandeville is, though Cook again says well that Mandeville's "satirically exaggerated pragmatism is designed not so much to undercut that scheme as to bait the tender-minded reader."[34] The latter is itself a not un-Swiftian enterprise. The hint of bumptious positiveness as Mandeville declines "to dwell upon those many Advantages that will accrue to the *Nation* by this admirable Scheme," thereby dwelling on them, affirms that "I have fully prov'd what I at first propos'd in this Treatise," and expresses puzzlement that anyone "could possibly object" to his scheme, are tailor-made for retrospective inclusion in the parodic mayhem of *A Tale of a Tub*.[35] One is almost tempted to suppose that Mandeville was deliberately outfacing, as Sterne was later and more overtly to outface, Swift's extraordinary act of preemptive mockery. The temptation, in Mandeville's case, should probably be resisted, even as some relation to Swift's *Tale* is actively evident. A recent critic's reference to the *Modest Defence*'s "obviously Swiftian pose" also has a point, though the comment suggests an impoverished sense of the workings of Swift's irony.[36] The heavy irony of the Dutchman who signs his Dedication "Phil-Porney" and asks such billowing rhetorical questions as "Now, if those Reverend School-Masters of Antiquity, were so Loose in their Seminals; shall we, of this Age, set up for Chastity? . . . Or, is an *Officer* of the Army less Ticklish in the Shoulder than *Socrates?*" suggests that its author's aptitude for subtleties of ironic indirection had its limits.[37] It's likelier that when Swift came to write *A Modest Proposal* he may have had in mind not only bland uses of the modesty formula but also provocative ones like Mandeville's, and that the paucity or absence of direct references to Mandeville by Swift has the teasing uncertainty which similarly surrounds the possible relation of *Robinson Crusoe* to *Gulliver's Travels*.

There are, at all events, enough elements in common to suggest the possibility, starting with the mercantilist axiom that people are the riches of a nation, which Swift literalized in the way we all know, and to which Mandeville appealed at the outset of his argument against the practice of unrestricted prostitution, as distinct from the kind proposed by his own modest defence:

> Since the Prosperity of any Country is allow'd to depend, in a great measure, on the Number of its Inhabitants, the *Government* ought, if it were possible, to prevent any Whoring at all, as it evidently hinders the Propagation of the Species.[38]

Both Swift and Mandeville stood in an essentially non-adversarial relation to the axiom. Swift's point was not that it was untrue but that Ireland was such an odd place that it was true in an unusually literal way, while Mandeville is doggedly promoting a more usual version, though it involves him in some bizarre argumentation. Phil-Porney can't have been unaware of his power to shock, and I've already suggested that Mandeville's literalness carried its own North European blend of pedantry and broad humor. Swift's subsequent parody, if that is what it was, might or might not have taken these features on board, but it's certainly inclusive enough to take in innocent as well as loaded versions, or normal as well as outlandish ones, while not dissociating itself from the root proposition.

When Swift speaks in *A Modest Proposal* of his ambition to eliminate "that horrid Practice of *Women murdering their Bastard Children*" (*PW* 12:110) he is echoing almost verbatim Mandeville's repeated concern that unrestricted whoring leads to the "murdering of Bastard Infants." Mandeville tended to be obsessive about the issue of women murdering their bastards, and he seemed generally to have an accentuated interest, perhaps bordering on obsession, with prostitution, which he wished to liberalize.[39] His immediate argument about the murder of bastards is that it depletes the population, which is notionally one of Swift's speaker's points. But the latter seems principally to mimic the tender-hearted, with talk of "sacrificing the *poor Innocent Babes,* I doubt, more to avoid the Expence than the Shame; which would move Tears and Pity in the most Savage and inhuman Breast" (*PW* 12:110). Contrary to a lingering sentimentalization of Swift's views on poverty, Swift's irony is just as concerned as Mandeville's "to bait the tender-minded reader," whatever differences there are between them in nuance or emphasis.[40] It should by now be well-established that Swift isn't exhibiting a compassion of his own, but exposing misplaced sentiments by do-gooders towards social groups whose personal morals and social nuisance-value the *Modest Proposal,* as well as some of Swift's more literal tracts, go to some lengths to denounce (*PW* 9:129–30, 136).[41] Mandeville might be hardline in not dissimilar ways, but with rather less investment in emotional affect, whether compassionate or anti-compassionate. (Of compassion he took, in "An Essay on Charity, and Charity-Schools," a Jonathan-Wild-like view: "all Mankind are more or less affected with it; but the weakest Minds generally the most." This is by no means the only instance of formulations which suggest that Fielding might have been mimicking Mandeville in his early novel, as he overtly attacked him in his last.)[42]

The casualness with which Mandeville speaks of wishing to stop "this Practice, which, besides the Barbarity of it, tends very much to dispeople the Country," may well have provided a subsidiary ingredient to the blend of styles that goes into Swiftian parody, with its fluid and proliferating population of victims.[43] The Modest Proposer's concern to dissociate himself from any practice which might be thought "(although indeed very unjustly) as a little bordering upon Cruelty; which, I confess, hath always been with me the strongest Objection against any Project, how well soever intended" (*PW* 12:113) might be set beside Mandeville's declaration in the "Essay on . . . Charity-Schools" that he "would not advance any thing that is Barbarous or Inhuman" (*F* 318). Swift's line against charity-schools is, as I said, a shade less hardline than Mandeville's, but Mandeville is here advocating a plan to keep the poor content in their lowly station which is quite close to Swift's own position on the charity-school issue, much as Mandeville's opposition (*F* 322) to charity for undeserving beggars (and for both Mandeville and Swift most beggars were undeserving) is close to the position implied in *A Modest Proposal* and fully elaborated in Swift's later *Proposal for Giving Badges to the Beggars.* If Swift is parodying Mandeville, or any generic category of hardline mercantilist thinker to which he might be assimilated, it is not because of any compassionate "humanity" which might lie behind the assertions of dislike for cruelty, as Paulette Carrive, among recent Mandeville scholars, seems to suppose, but because of the routine character of such rhetoric, its staleness and its humbug.[44] On the substantive issue they were very close, and if Mandeville succumbed to the rhetoric of humbug, he wore the fact on his sleeve, offering a brashly cynical testimony, almost as clear-eyed in its way as Swift's parodic exposure, to the threadbare prevalence of such *façons de parler.* It would be just like Swift to take a swipe at this stylistic maneuver too.

NOTES

1. Basil Willey, *The Eighteenth Century Background: Studies on the Idea of Nature in the Thought of the Period* (London: Chatto and Windus, 1940), 102–3.

2. The following editions have been used, unless otherwise noted: *The Prose Works of Jonathan Swift,* ed. Herbert Davis et al. (Oxford: Basil Blackwell, 1939–1968), abbreviated *PW;* Bernard Mandeville, *Fable of the Bees,* ed. Phillip Harth (Harmondsworth, Middlesex: Penguin, 1970), abbreviated *F.*

3. Thomas Sheridan, *Intelligencer,* No. 13, 22–26 October 1728, in Swift and Sheridan, *The Intelligencer,* ed. James Woolley (Oxford: Clarendon Press, 1992), 159 (162 n. 98 reports another sarcasm by Sheridan against Mandeville).

4. F. B. Kaye knew "of no reference to the *Fable* earlier than 1723." *Fable of the Bees,* ed. Kaye (1924; Indianapolis: Liberty Press, 1988), 1:230 n. Kaye (2:418–53) gives a chronological list of references to Mandeville from 1716 to 1923, including a single non-canonical instance attributed to Swift (2:426). For an extremely useful collection of responses to Mandeville, see *Private Vices, Publick Benefits? The Contemporary Reception of Bernard Mandeville,* ed. J. Martin Stafford (Solihull: Ismeron, 1997); for a summary, see General Introduction, xi–xxiv.

5. The most tellingly vivid sketch known to me of Mandeville's furtive notori-

ety, as "an author whom one might read in secret," overtly viewed as a "moral monster" while "almost everybody read him," may be found in F. A. Hayek's British Academy Lecture on a Master Mind, "Dr. Bernard Mandeville," *Proceedings of the British Academy* 52 (1966): 125–41, esp. 127–28.

6. "Preface" and "Dialogue I," in *The Fable of the Bees. Part II* (1729), ed. Kaye, 2:27, 33–34.

7. Davis, *PW,* 2:xix; Willey, *Eighteenth Century Background,* 103.

8. F. R. Leavis, *The Common Pursuit* (London: Chatto and Windus, 1952), 73–87, esp. 75, 84; Willey, *Eighteenth Century Background,* 106 n.

9. Willey, *Eighteenth Century Background,* 103.

10. The date of 1708, usually accepted, has been challenged by Irvin Ehrenpreis in favor of 1704. For references, and a rebuttal, see Frank T. Boyle, "Ehrenpreis's *Swift* and the Date of the *Sentiments of a Church-of-England Man,*" *Swift Studies* 6 (1991): 30–37.

11. Jonathan Swift, *Gulliver's Travels and Other Writings,* ed. Louis A. Landa (Boston: Houghton Mifflin, 1960), 541 n. 418.

12. Karl Marx, *Critique of Hegel's "Philosophy of Right"* (1843–1844), ed. Joseph O'Malley (Cambridge: Cambridge University Press, 1970), introduction, 131. (A similar comment by Charles Kingsley is reported in the *Oxford Dictionary of Quotations,* 4th ed., ed. Angela Partington [Oxford: Oxford University Press, 1992], 398/1.) For Marx's interest in Mandeville, see S. S. Prawer, *Karl Marx and World Literature* (Oxford: Clarendon Press, 1976), 319–20; Louis Dumont, *From Mandeville to Marx: The Genesis and Triumph of Economic Ideology* (Chicago: University of Chicago Press, 1977), 150, 219–20 n. 3; Paulette Carrive, *Bernard Mandeville: Passions, Vices, Vertus* (Paris: Vrin, 1980); E. G. Hundert, *The Enlightenment's Fable: Bernard Mandeville at the Discovery of Society* (Cambridge: Cambridge University Press, 1996), 183, 219–20, 248.

13. *A Letter to Dion, Occasion'd by his Book call'd Alciphron, . . . : By the Author of the Fable of the Bees* (1732), in *Private Vices, Publick Benefits?,* 579, 597.

14. On the cult of unmasking in Rousseau and ideologues of the French Revolution, see Claude Rawson, *Satire and Sentiment, 1660–1830,* new ed. (London and New Haven, Conn.: Yale University Press, 2000), 180–89. For an additional resemblance or convergence of Swift's *Project* with Mandevillian thought, see the introduction to Mandeville's *A Modest Defence of Publick Stews* (1724), ed. Richard I. Cook (Los Angeles: Augustan Reprint Society No. 162, 1973), ii. See also Cook, *Bernard Mandeville* (New York: Twayne, 1974), 97.

15. See "The Lady's Dressing Room" (1730), "Cassinus and Peter" (1731), and especially "Strephon and Chloe" (1731), in *The Poems of Jonathan Swift,* ed. Harold Williams, 2d ed. (Oxford: Clarendon Press, 1958), 2:524–30, 593–97, 584–93.

16. Leavis, *Common Pursuit,* 76.

17. For a Johnsonian analogue, and for convergences between the thought of Swift and Johnson on the one hand, and between both authors and Hobbes and Mandeville on the other, see Claude Rawson, *Order from Confusion Sprung,* new

ed. (Atlantic Highlands, N.J.: Humanities Press, 1992), 3–9, 98, 141 n. For Mandevillian elements in Johnson, despite Johnson's expressions of disapproval, see James Boswell, *Boswell's Life of Johnson: Together with Boswell's Journey of a Tour to the Hebrides,* ed. George Birbeck Hill, rev. L. F. Powell (Oxford: Clarendon Press, 1934–1964), 3:291–93 and nn, a passage whose pertinence to this discussion was kindly pointed out to me by Howard Weinbrot.

18. For some references, see Rawson, *Satire and Sentiment,* 183 and n. 168.

19. Willey, *Eighteenth Century Background,* 98.

20. See Rawson, *Order from Confusion Sprung,* 29 and *Satire and Sentiment,* 162, 177.

21. For a full discussion of this topic, see Rawson, *Satire and Sentiment,* 133–96; see 185 n. 175, for the passage from Yeats, "A Prayer for My Daughter" (ll. 77–78).

22. Mandeville, *Wishes to a Godson, with other Miscellany Poems. By B.M.,* Facsimile Reprint (1712; Exeter: The Rota [University of Exeter], 1975), 5.

23. For Burke's and his opponents' uses of the theatrical analogy, see Rawson, *Satire and Sentiment,* 194–95 and nn.

24. For a somewhat different view of Mandeville and Swift on charity schools, see Cook, *Bernard Mandeville,* 100–102, 124–28 (including an interesting connection between Mandeville's educational thought and Swift's ancient Utopian Lilliput in *Gulliver's Travels,* 1.6 [*PW* 11:63]), 128, 161 n. 15.

25. See Jon Elster, "Snobs," an extended review of Pierre Bourdieu's *La Distinction: Critique sociale du jugement* (Paris: Editions de Minuit, 1979), *London Review of Books,* 5–18 November 1981, 10–12, esp. 10; Raymond Aron, *De la Condition historique du sociologue: leçon inaugurale au Collège de France* (Paris: Gallimard, 1971), 41.

26. Hayek, "Dr. Bernard Mandeville," 125–41, esp. 125–27, 129, 134, 139–41.

27. Mandeville, "Dedication," in *Modest Defence,* ii–iii, x–xi. For Swift's flayed woman, and his use of the traditional image of a diversionary tub thrown at Leviathan, see Section 9 (Digression concerning . . . Madness) of *A Tale,* and its preface respectively (*PW* 1:109, 24–25).

28. Mandeville, "Introduction," in *Modest Defence,* ii.

29. Mandeville, *Modest Defence,* 50–51.

30. Rawson, *Order from Confusion Sprung,* 34.

31. Mandeville, *Modest Defence,* [xvi] and 2, 15.

32. Ibid., 15.

33. Ibid., 2–3.

34. Ibid., "Introduction," v.

35. Ibid., 65–66.

36. Hundert, *Enlightenment's Fable,* 121.

37. Mandeville, *Modest Defence,* xii, ix.

38. Ibid., 5; The classic statement of Swift's conception of the mercantilist axiom is contained in two essays by Landa, "Swift's Economic Views and Mercantilism" and "*A Modest Proposal* and Populousness," in his *Essays in Eighteenth-Century English Literature* (Princeton, N.J.: Princeton University Press, 1980), 13–48.

39. Mandeville, *Modest Defence,* 4, 8–10, 26, and *F,* 107–8, 127 ff.

40. For the view being contested here, see Cook, *Bernard Mandeville,* 102, 100–102.

41. For a just sense of the play of compassion and denunciation in Swift's writings on beggars, see Ehrenpreis, *Swift: The Man, His Works, and the Age* (Cambridge, Mass.: Harvard University Press, 1962–1983), 3:811–19, esp. 814–17. On Swift's hard-line views on the treatment of beggars, see David Nokes, "Swift and the Beggars," *Essays in Criticism* 26 (1976): 218–35; Rawson, *Order from Confusion Sprung,* 131–44, and "Killing the Poor: An Anglo-Irish Theme?" F. W. Bateson Memorial Lecture, *Essays in Criticism* 49 (1999): 101–31.

42. Mandeville, *F,* 264; see also 289, for passages which sound like *Jonathan Wild* and whose idiom Fielding may have been mimicking in his novel. In "An Enquiry into the Origin of Moral Virtue" Mandeville had already spoken of pity as characteristic of "weakest Minds," and also as the "most amiable" of "all our Weaknesses" (*F* 91), a vocabulary that Fielding was to harp on. A later and more explicit attack on Mandeville occurs in *Amelia.* For an extended recent discussion of Fielding and Mandeville, see Hundert, *Enlightenment's Fable,* 153–68.

43. Mandeville, *Modest Defence,* 4.

44. Carrive, *Bernard Mandeville,* 113, 119–20; this author's writings on Mandeville, including also her *La Philosophie des Passions chez Bernard Mandeville* (Paris: Didier Erudition, 1983), are full of references to Swift, not usually reflecting an accurate sense of his ironic register.

5

What Swift Did to Collins's Discourse of Free-Thinking *and Why*

FRANK H. ELLIS

> To answer a Book effectually, requires more Pains and Skill, more Wit, Learning, and Judgement than were employ'd in the Writing it.
>
> Jonathan Swift, *A Tale of a Tub*

1. WHAT SWIFT DID TO COLLINS'S DISCOURSE

This is by no means the first attempt to describe in words exactly what Swift did to Anthony Collins's *Discourse of Free-Thinking* (1713). The first attempt may have been made by Swift himself. *The Examiners* of 1712–1714 were written by William Oldisworth, but the announcement in *The Examiner* of 19–23 January 1713 that *Mr. C——ns's Discourse of Free-Thinking, Put into Plain English, by Way of Abstract, for the Use of the Poor* "is now in the Press" may have been sent to Oldisworth by Swift[1]: "If the Writer strips that adventurous Piece of its Disguises, and leaves it naked and exposed in full Light, he will amply deserve a perusal, and cannot fail of being *Useful or Entertaining,*" or "*useful and diverting,*" as Swift said in *A Tale of Tub.*[2]

In 1957 Herbert Davis tried to describe exactly what Swift did: he "relies on a congenial device, the *reductio ad absurdum,* achieved by a slight distortion of Collins's text, a twist of his meaning here or there, and the addition or omission of a word" (*PW* 4:xix). Ten years later Irvin Ehrenpreis says almost the same thing: "Swift's main method of ridiculing Collins is to pretend to give objective summaries of many of his propositions but to twist their sense so as to make them sound heavily irreligious and absurd. The satirist adds examples, explanations, and transitions of his own."[3]

"Reductions," "twists," and factitious "additions," however, are not what readers experience and do not describe the uniqueness of Swift's work. *Mr. C——ns's Discourse* may be *sui generis.* Only an edition in parallel columns would allow the curious reader to see exactly what Swift did to Collins's *Discourse of Free-Thinking.*[4] Failing such an edition we may try again to describe in words what Swift did to Collins's *Discourse.*

What we can be sure of is that *Mr. C——ns's Discourse* is not what the Abstracter says it is, "*a brief, but faithful Abstract*" of Collins's essay (*PW* 4:48). It is brief all right, 31 pages to Collins's 178, and it is a crazy kind of "Abstract," whereby Swift makes available to the satirist a new subgenre, the mock-abstract; but "*faithful*" it is not. Nor is the Abstracter "*a Friend*" of Anthony Collins. He is Jonathan Swift.

Irony, as we do not need to be reminded, is read "just contrary," as Defoe reminds us in his *Review* for 16 April 1713, and *Mr. C——ns's Discourse* is a "contrary" abstract of Collins's essay. "*I have all along,*" the Abstracter says, "*religiously adhered to our Author's Notions, and generally to his Words, without any other Addition than that of explaining a few necessary Consequences, for the sake of ignorant Readers*" (*PW* 4:48). But this is not true. Mr. Collins is almost swamped by Swift's "*Additions,*" which add up to nearly two-thirds of the text of Swift's work.[5] This enables Swift to "correct" Collins and to substitute his own mock-summary for Collins's text. These "*Additions,*" moreover, are privileged, for they are Swift's innocent revelations of religious conviction—innocent because he had other things in mind when he wrote them, that is, "*explaining a few necessary Consequences, for the sake of ignorant Readers.*" But these unguarded casualties come closer than *The Sentiments of a Church-of-England Man with Respect to Religion and Government* (1708; published in *Miscellanies* 1711) or Swift's sermons to disclosing his private religious beliefs.

The most obvious of Swift's "*Additions*" to Collins's essay are a preface and conclusion, in which these false, that is, ironic, claims about "*a brief, but faithful Abstract*" are made. What Swift does in the preface is first, to establish a persona for himself and second, to politicize the argument. A persona begins to emerge on the title page: "*Put into plain English . . . By a Friend of the Author.*" Collins's alleged friend, or the Abstracter as I have called him, identifies himself as a Whig in his first utterance: "*Our Party,*" he says, by which he means the Whigs in general and the Whig Junto in particular: Somers, Halifax, Orford, Wharton, Sunderland, and their Tory recruits, Marlborough and Nottingham. These, "*having failed, by all their Political Arguments,*" now turn to religious argument "*to re-*

establish their Power" lost in the summer of 1710 when Queen Anne allowed Harley to form the "Moderate" coalition ministry that Swift defends in *The Examiner* (1710–1711). The "*compleat Body of* Atheology" in Collins's *Discourse of Free-Thinking* seems to the Abstracter to be just what is needed to restore "*our* [Whig] *Friends* [to] *Place and Power*" (*PW* 4:27). Swift's mock-abstract of Collins's essay is clearly not intended "*for the Use of the Poor*"; it is intended for the use of the Whig "*Nobility and Gentry*" who caucus at "*the* Kit-Cat *and* Hannover *Clubs*" and who refresh themselves at "White's *and* Tom's," and ultimately of course for the political nation, "*the Publick*" (*PW* 4:28, 48).

Collins tried to position *A Discourse of Free-Thinking* above politics, calling "*a blind Zeal to . . . Party*" "the worst of all Vices," but Swift would not let him.[6] Collins mentions "certain half-witted Politicians" (*Discourse* 24), but neglects to tell us whether he means Whig politicians or Tory politicians. The Abstracter makes it clear that Collins means half-witted Tory politicians. If the King of Siam should send a boatload of Buddhist monks to "spread *Free-thinking* among us," the Abstracter says, "then the War [of the Spanish Succession] would go on, [and] the late [Whig] Ministry be restored" (*PW* 4:31; added by Swift). The Abstracter repeats this in the preface, where he says, "*I am sensible that nothing would more contribute to the* continuance of the War, *and the Restoration of the late Ministry, than to have the Doctrines delivered in this Treatise well infused into the People*" (*PW* 4:28).

If Edward Brown, an Anglican rector of Sundridge in Kent, in his translation of Paolo Sarpi's *Letters* (1693), leaves out a passage reflecting on James I, that proves "he was an Enemy to *Political Free Thinking*" (*PW* 4:38; added by Swift). Anglican priests, the Abstracter observes, "are not ours" (*PW* 4:40; added by Swift). This is enough, I think, to demonstrate that despite his assurance to Stella and Mrs. Dingley that his "little Pamphlet is . . . not Politicks" (*Journal* 2:608), Swift's "*Additions*" unequivocally politicize Collins's text. Collins conceives of his work as "*Polemick Divinity*"; Swift brings it down to what Collins calls "the worst of all Vices," party politics (*Discourse* 101, 120).

Besides politicizing Collins's text, Swift nonsensifies it. Unlike other answerers—an *anonyme* once thought to be Defoe, Richard Bentley, George Berkeley, Thomas Cockman, the anonymous author of *Free Thoughts,* Benjamin Hoadly, Benjamin Ibbot, the anonymous author of *A Letter to the Free-Thinkers,* William Oldisworth, Richard Steele, William Whiston, and Daniel Williams—Swift refuses to take Collins seriously. With what dead seriousness the other answerers read Collins's text may be judged by some of their remarks: Cockman, Hoadly, Ibbot, Steele, Whiston, and Williams, for example, all agree that Collins's book was, in the words of *Free Thoughts upon the Discourse of Free-Thinking* (London, 1713), "a violent Attack upon all Reveal'd Religion" (1). *An Answer to the Discourse of Free-Thinking* (London, 1713) observes that the dispute is not about politics or adherence to a specific religion, but that "Religion in general is the Question, Religion is the Thing stabb'd at" (sig. A2^{r})—a remark with which Hoadly and the author of *Free Thoughts* would have agreed (1). As Bentley complains, Collins offers only a life without heaven or providence, a "Death without hope like that of Asses and Dogs."[7] The elimination of providence, the writer of *A Letter to the Free-Thinkers* (London, 1713) recognizes, must "carry us back to Chance, Atoms, [and] Fatality" (35). Ibbot fears that Collins's work will "undermine and shake the Foundations of All."[8]

But Swift will have none of this.[9] He nonsensifies Collins, making him say that "a great deal of *Free-thinking* will at last set us all right, and every one will adhere to the *Scripture* he likes best; by which means Religion, Peace, and Wealth, will be for ever secured in Her Majesty's Realms" (*PW* 4:32–33; added by Swift).

The author of *A Farther Discourse of Free-Thinking* agrees with Swift. "I would not," he says, "that [the clergy] should write against this Book; for that way will only spread it further, and make it read the more." He remembers that "'twas the Notice which was not long since taken of a Discourse [Locke, *The Reasonableness of Christianity* (1695)], which, when it came out first, was generally thought but a very ordinary Performance, which in a short time gain'd an extraordinary Credit."[10] Similarly, with the help of sober Anglican clergymen like those cited above, Collins's *Discourse of Free-Thinking* "gain'd an extraordinary Credit." Four or five octavo editions were published in London in 1713. It was "more than once re-printed abroad" in 1713. French translations were published in 1714, 1717, and 1766 and a facsimile edition with a German translation appeared in Stuttgart in 1965 (see Appendix 1 below).

Swift's work, on the other hand, was a failure. "If it takes I say again, you shll hear of it," he tells Stella, but he never mentions it again (*Journal* 2:608). It "*s[a]nk into waste Paper and Oblivion, after the usual Fate of Common Answerers to Books*" (*PW* 1:4). It received no critical notice, and was not reprinted until long after Swift's death, in John Nichols's collection, *A Supplement to Dr. Swift's Works* (1776). It was not mentioned in *Gleanings from the Writings of the Celebrated Dean Swift* (1802) and in the last century it was rejected by *Reader's Digest.*

2. AND WHY

No, . . . I am not Dean of Wells. (Swift, *Journal* 2:518)

Mr. C——ns's Discourse is by no means Swift's first encounter with Anthony Collins. Free-thinking is not mentioned in *A Tale of a Tub* (1704), but "*Atheists, Deists, Socinians, Anti-Trinitarians,* and other Subdivisions of Free-Thinkers" (*PW* 2:36) figure largely in *The Sentiments of a Church-of-England Man* (written 1708) and *An Argument against Abolishing Christianity* (1708). In April 1708 when he was writing *An Argument against Abolishing Christianity,* Swift had not yet promoted Anthony Collins to the select company of "*Asgill, Tindall, Toland, Coward*" (*PW* 2:29).[11] But he could not have failed to notice Collins's demolition of a printed sermon by Swift's pontifical friend and sometime patron, William King, Archbishop of Dublin. In this sermon delivered in Christ Church Cathedral before a very skeptical Lord Lieutenant of Ireland, Thomas, Earl of Wharton, in May 1709, King

> reason'd high
> Of Providence, Foreknowledge, Will and Fate,
> Fixt Fate, free will, foreknowledge absolute,
> And found no end, in wand'ring mazes lost.
> (*Paradise Lost* [1674], 2.558–61)

Collins, who was eager to promote the "clear and distinct Method of Reasoning introduced by [John Locke's] new Philosophy" (*Vindication* 3) and who had been reading Pierre Bayle's article on Manichaeans in the *Dictionnaire historique et critique* (1695–1697; enlarged ed. 1702), published *A Vindication of the Divine Attributes, in some Remarks on His Grace the Archbishop of Dublin's Sermon Intituled "Divine Predestination Consistent with the Freedom of Man's Will"* (London, 1710).

Just as Dr. South, in the Trinitarian controversy of 1690–1696, "proved there is but One *God;* and [Dr. Sherlock], That there are Three,"[12] so Archbishop King, undertaking to resolve the contradiction between God's foreknowledge and man's free will, proved that God is "only figuratively Merciful, Just, Intelligent or Foreknowing."[13] But if God is not literally, or really, foreknowing, the contradiction ceases to exist. "His Grace's Meaning may perhaps shock the Reader," Collins observes (*Vindication* 10).

Collins is promoted to the select company of Asgill et al. in the early numbers of *The Examiner,* which Swift took up in November 1710.[14] By 29 March 1711 Swift had learned that Collins was a member of the Unbelieving Club that met at the Grecian Coffee House in Devereux

Court near Temple Bar (*Examiner* 331n). In September 1711 Swift received Archbishop King's fatuous letter reminding him of his "duty, to set [himself] to some serious and useful subject in [his] profession."[15] As Swift reported to his ladies in Dublin, "He advises me . . . to think of some new subject in Divinity not handled by others. . . . A rare spark this, with a pox!" (*Journal* 1:358–59).[16] By this time Swift may have made his "crucial decision" *not* to devote his life to "*Polemick Divinity,*" in Collins's phrase.[17] "The Grand points of Christianity," Swift said, "ought to be taken as infallible Revelations" (*Corr.* 4:7). So instead of "some new subject in Divinity," Swift wrote hoaxes like *A New Journey to Paris* (1711), political ballads only "two degrees above Grubstreet" (*Journal* 2:431), such as *The Description of Dunkirk with Squash's and Dismal's Opinion How Easily Prince Eugene May Retake It, and Many Other Matters of the Last Importance* (1712), mock-progress poems such as *Phillis, or, The Progress of Love* (1711–12?), and a mock-abstract like *Mr. C——ns's Discourse.* Swift's ultimate reply to the Archbishop's demand for something "serious and useful" may be *A Serious and Useful Scheme, to Make an Hospital for Incurables* (1733): "He gave the little Wealth he had, / To build a House for Fools and Mad."[18] But his immediate reply to the Archbishop was the publication on 27 November 1711 of *The Conduct of the Allies,* which George M. Trevelyan calls "the greatest of his pamphlets," of which one thousand copies were sold in two days and 11,000 in two months.[19]

In January 1713, when Swift wrote *Mr. C——ns's Discourse,* he was "a clergyman of five-and-forty" not settled "in a station wherein he may be easy to himself, and useful to the public," as the Archbishop pointedly reminded him (*Corr.* 1:326, 318). He was still the vicar of Laracor, to which he had been appointed nearly thirteen years before by Charles Berkeley, Earl of Berkeley, one of the lords justices of Ireland. To Laracor, a parish in the diocese of Meath, James Butler, second Duke of Ormond, added a prebendal stall in the Cathedral of St. Patrick's, Dublin. The two posts together yielded little more than £200 a year, compared to the Archbishop's annual stipend of £5,000. The sixteen Protestant families in the parish of Laracor made it possible for Swift to preach on Sunday to as many as "fifteen people most of them gentle, and all simple."[20]

In January 1713 Swift was denizened in "an ordinary room [up] two pair of Stairs" at Mrs. Hubbot's in Little Rider Street, a few doors from fashionable St. James's Square (*Journal* 2:565, 581; 1:143n). Of the ten previous years (1702–1712) Swift had spent more of them in London than in Ireland. Before November 1707 his visits to London were personal and occasional, but after November 1707 he came to London on official business for the Church of Ireland, under orders from Archbishop King.

Although an unreconstructed high churchman, Swift was from the beginning known in London as a Whig in politics, which "even in Bad times . . . [was] a Monstrous Composition."[21] He had been secretary to Sir William Temple, a notorious Williamite and a Hobbist, and chaplain to the Earl of Berkeley, another Whig. Swift's first published prose work, *A Discourse of the Contests and Dissentions* (1701), defended the Whig Junto who were under impeachment by the House of Commons for high crimes and misdemeanors. *A Tale of a Tub* (1704) was dedicated in the most fulsome terms to John Somers, Lord Somers, the Whig *capo di capi.*

In October 1710 Robert Harley, an "Old Whig," recruited Swift to defend the ministry that Harley had put together that summer. Under the influence of Henry St. John, Harley's secretary of state, and a huge Tory majority in Parliament, however, Harley's "Moderate" ministry had careened heavily to starboard. Before he knew it, Swift was *chef de propagande,* speech writer, almoner, and appointments secretary for a Tory ministry that was threatening to self-destruct. The warring chiefs, Harley and St. John, had been richly rewarded for their services. Harley was now the Earl of Oxford (May 1711) and St. John was Viscount Bolingbroke (July 1712), but in January 1713 Swift was still the vicar of Laracor, at the foot of "the Ladder Ecclesiastical" (*PW* 12:44). "They call me nothing but Jonathan," he told Stella, but they will "leave me Jonathan as they found me" (*Journal* 1:193–94). In the last five years Swift had been passed over for five rich livings in England and Ireland.[22]

Queen Anne allowed Swift to accomplish his mission for the Church of Ireland by remitting payment to the crown of taxes called First Fruits and Twentieth Parts, but she would not allow him to kiss her hand or to preach at court, much less to sit in the House of Lords as an English Bishop. Oxford, who was angry if Swift did not dine with him every other day, wanted to keep Swift in England, of course (*Journal* 2:588, 616). He favored the prebendal stall at Windsor that Swift fancied:

> *S——t* much admires the Place and Air,
> And longs to be a *Canon* there;
> In Summer round the Park to ride,
> In Winter—never to reside.
>
> (*Poems* 1:173)

Bolingbroke told Swift that he had turned down a very good living for him without even asking Swift because it was in a place that Bolingbroke did not like (*Journal* 1:314).

So in the end Swift had to accept the fact of Oxford's "want of power to keep me in what I ought to call my own Country" (*Corr.* 5:46). On 28 October 1712 he told Stella that his friend Marmaduke Coghill, Justice of the Prerogative Court in Dublin, suggested that Swift solicit the post of Dean of St. Patrick's Cathedral, if the bishopric of Raphoe could be got for another of Swift's friends, John Stearne, the incumbent dean (*Journal* 2:567). Since the deanery of St. Patrick's was in the gift of a third friend, James Butler, second Duke of Ormond, Lord Lieutenant of Ireland, with the consent of course of the "Royal Prude" (*Poems* 1:193), Swift began to solicit an Irish bishopric for his friend Stearne.[23] In January 1713, when he was writing *Mr. C——ns's Discourse,* Swift, like the rest of the political nation, was in a paroxysm of suspense: Swift for the Queen's consent, and the political nation including Swift for news of the signing of the Treaty of Utrecht, ending the ten-year War of the Spanish Succession.

With the foregoing data in mind some guesses can be made about why Swift wrote his "little Whim," as he called his abstract (*Journal* 2:603). Swift's first awareness of Collins's existence, and ambition to defend his friend, Archbishop King, may have developed in 1710 with the publication of Collins's *Vindication.* Swift's animosity would have been notably raised in March 1711 when he learned that Collins was a member of the Unbelieving Club at the Grecian Coffee House. If Swift had made his "crucial decision" not to devote his writing career to "*Polemick Divinity*" by the first weeks of January 1713, the opportunity of writing a mock-abstract of Collins's *Discourse of Free-Thinking* would have appealed to him as soon as it occurred to him. Since the *Discourse* is sustained anti-Anglican-clerical satire, there can be no doubt that Swift wanted to answer it and that his answer was much more than "a little Whim."

The standard format for answering political pamphlets in verse or prose was that of William Pittis's *The True-Born Englishman: A Satyr, Answer'd, Paragraph by Paragraph* (London, 1701), which required reprinting all 1,216 lines of Defoe's poem.[24] Swift wanted to defend the Anglican clergy who were ridiculed in *A Discourse of Free-Thinking;* he wanted to associate "*the Sect call'd Free-Thinkers*" of Collins's title with the Whigs; he wanted his readers to carry away his "correct" evaluation of deism, not Anthony Collins's, but he did *not* want to give double exposure to something that would soon "*be utterly unknown*" if "*not kept alive by his Replies*" (*PW* 1:4). A mock-abstract in which nearly two-thirds of the words are Swift's is obviously an economical way to do this.

What finally determined Swift to write against *A Discourse of Free-Thinking* may have been Collins's representation of Swift in the *Discourse.* Swift is mentioned by name twice, once as a representative high churchman, in illustration of Collins's familiar argument that religions are taken up like fashions: "[if] Men may chuse their own Priests, as they chuse their Lawyers and Physicians . . . then one Man will chuse [the Quaker] WILLIAM PENN, another [the Presbyterian] DANIEL BURGESS, a third Dr. SWIFT, . . . and so on" (*Discourse* 110–11).[25] Earlier in his book, however, Collins attacks Swift at Swift's most vulnerable point in the closing weeks of 1712: his failure to be provided for in the Church. This was a matter of acute embarrassment to Swift.[26] "As soon as ever things are given away, & I not provided for," he told Stella, "I will be gone" (*Journal* 2:633). The delay in receiving his "Due" reward for services to the ministry was so widely known that Swift might have heard it sung in the streets in Tom D'Urfey's words: "Let *Prior* and *Swift* now receive their Due, / . . . And all the rest of the High-Church Crew."[27] Even though it seems unlikely that Collins knew of efforts being made in the winter of 1712–13 to exile Swift to Ireland, his pointed suggestion that Swift be exiled to America must have been doubly ironical and doubly painful for Swift.

The Society for the Propagation of the Gospel in Foreign Parts, based on missionary work of Dr. Thomas Bray in Maryland, received a royal charter in London in June 1701. Its purpose was to supply and maintain Anglican clergy, under the jurisdiction of Henry Compton, Bishop of London, in frontier towns (such as Northampton in the Massachusetts Bay Colony) that were "wholly destitute and unprovided with Means for the Maintenance of Ministers and the public worship of God."[28] "AND Oh!" Collins exclaims

> that the proper Persons were but employ'd for the Execution of so glorious a Work! That such zealous Divines as our S[ACHEVEREL]LS, our A[TTERBUR]YS, our S[MALRID]GES, our S[TUB]BS, our HIGG[O]NS'S, our M[EA]RNS, our SW[I]FTS, were drawn out annually, as our *military Missionarys* are, to be sent into *foreign Parts to propagate the Gospel!* (a Service in which such conscientious Men must rejoice, since preaching the Gospel to infidel Nations is no doubt contain'd in *Christ's Commission,* whatever *haranguing upon a Text* among Christians, by some call'd *preaching the Gospel,* may be) we might then hope to see blessed Days, the *Doctrine and Discipline of the Church of England* triumph throughout the World.[29] (*Discourse* 43)

If Swift could feel no joy at passing his days in Dublin (*Journal* 2:662), we can imagine his feelings at the prospect of passing his days in Northampton. This was the "Countercheck Quarrelsome" to which Swift could not fail to reply. What Swift finally did to *A Discourse of Free-Thinking* was to qualify Collins for a dunce, as Alexander Pope recognized when he included Collins in the six editions of the 1728 *Dunciad.*[30]

3. POSTSCRIPT

A Fool may sometime put forth a Word in Season. (*A Farther Discourse* 35)

But Collins was not a dunce. He was a country gentleman, educated at Eton, King's College Cambridge, and the Middle Temple, with "an estate in the Country, a Library in Town, [and] Freinds every where," as John Locke observed.[31] Befriended by Locke, Collins commissioned Sir Godfrey Kneller to paint Locke's portrait in 1704. In his chambers at Lincoln's Inn and his house in Harley Square, Collins collected the third largest private library in Britain, of about 10,000 volumes.[32] Of the sixteen books that he wrote himself, *A Discourse of Free-Thinking* is said to be the worst, but a copy of it survives in Voltaire's *Kabinet* in St. Petersburg. German graduate students in the eighteenth century wrote doctoral dissertations "*contra Antonium Collinum.*" [33] In the interminable wars of Free Will vs. Determinism, Collins is a notable skirmisher in the ranks of Determinism and is still cited in the literature.[34] But no one seems to have noticed the supreme irony that the propagandist for free thinking is a determinist who believes that thinking is not free.

One hundred and nine pages are devoted to Collins in Jean André Naigeon's *Encyclopédie méthodique* (1791); Hume rates only forty pages, Locke twenty-eight, and Descartes seventeen.[35] Collins's *Discourse concerning Ridicule and Irony* (1729) was reprinted as recently as 1970 and his own ridicule and irony (very) occasionally remind us of Swift. For example, "*His Sacred Majesty King* JAMES the First . . . employ'd his Royal Pen always on Subjects worthy of a Prince, viz. *a Paraphrase on the Revelation, A counterblast to Tobacco-taking,* and *Love-Letters* to the Duke of Buckingham" (29). The difference, however, lies in the fact that Swift is defending the past—"I look upon myself, in the capacity of a clergyman, to be one appointed by providence for defending a post assigned me" (*PW* 9:262)—while Collins is anticipating the future.

APPENDIX 1

The bibliography of *A Discourse of Free-Thinking* remains a desideratum. The first edition—London, M.DCC.XIII, iii–vi, 3–178 pp.—is distinguished by an errata list on the last page of the "Contents" (p. 6; copies: Yale Coll. Pamph. v. 160; Harvard AND. H.). In the second edition—London, M.DCC.XIII. iii–vi, 3–178 pp.—the errata are corrected, requiring sigs. $C4^v$–$C8^v$ and $I4^r$–$I6^r$ to be reset (copies: Yale Coll. Pamph. V. 531, K8.C69.g713; Harvard *EC7.C6922.713db, *EC65.B4465.B715f). The third edition—London, M.DCC.XIII, 3–178 pp., omitting the "Contents"—is a line-by-line resetting of the second edition (copy: Yale Coll. Pamph. v. 991). There is also said to be an edition of 173 pp.[36] The octavo edition of 140 pp. with London, 1713 (in arabic numerals) on the title page may be the edition described by Richard Lort: "Collins had this book more than once re-printed abroad, though in the title-page said to be at London" (copy: Harvard *EC7.C6922.713dc).[37] The edition of 149 pp. with no title page and no place or date of publication but with a caption title, *A Discourse of Free-Thinking, in a Letter to ***** Esquire* is "almost certainly" an edition published by Henry van Dole at The Hague: "on leaf A1 there is an ornamental capital identical with one of leaf A1 of the French translation of Algernon Sidney's *Discourse concerning Government,* published by Henry van Dole at The Hague in 1702, and a headpiece that is identical (though inverted) with one that appears in leaf A1 of the second volume of the same translation" (copies: Leeds Reference Library; Harvard Lp 20.161.3).[38] "Another edition, in 12 mo," is probably the 1713 edition published at The Hague by T. Johnson "avec des Additions nombreuses."[39] A French version—*Discourse sur la Liberté de Penser . . . Traduit de l'Anglois & Augmenté d'une Lettre d'un medecin Arabe,* A Londres [The Hague], MDCCXIV—in which Collins silently corrects some of the errors exposed by Bentley, was translated under Collins's direction by Henry Scheurléer and Jean Rousset de Missi (copy: Harvard Phil 8610.713.10).[40] A second edition of the French translation was published in 1717 (copy: Yale K8.C69.gf717) and a third in 1766. A facsimile edition, edited by Günter Gawlick, was published in Stuttgart in 1965 (copy: Harvard Phil 8610.713.5).

APPENDIX 2

Collins was twenty-seven when *A Tale of a Tub* was published anonymously in May 1704. If he read it as a deistical tract, that might explain why there seem to be echoes of *A Tale of a Tub* in *A Discourse of Free-Thinking* written nine years later. And he could not have failed to learn that the anonymous author was a high churchman, Jonathan Swift, "that Orthodox Divine who . . . was never half so witty upon any other Subject, as upon that of Rcligion" (*The British Academy* [1712], 10), "thc ingcnious Divine . . . who . . . derives the Succession of his own Church from the *D—l,* if there be any truth in his 'Tale of a Tub'" (*The Flying Post,* 7–10 February 1712).

Swift complained that "Some have endeavour'd to squeeze out a dangerous Meaning" from *A Tale of a Tub* (*PW* 1:4) and Collins may be one of these. The parallel columns below suggest possible echoes worth bringing to readers' attention; they will judge for themselves whether these are present by accident or design.

A Tale of a Tub	*A Discourse of Free-Thinking*
Happiness . . . is a perpetual Possession of being well Deceived. (*PW* 1:108)	Fools . . . well pleas'd in being deceiv'd. (4)
Homer . . . design'd his Work for a compleat Body of all Knowledge. (*PW* 1:79)	all Arts and Sciences are contain'd in him [Homer]. (10)
without [enthusiasm] . . . all Mankind would . . . be reduced to the same Belief in Things Invisible. (*PW* 1:107)	a fancy . . . that all Men should have the same Belief with relation to certain Objects of the Eyes. (15)
had my Eyes been open . . . the Business might have been a great deal worse. (*PW* 1:123)	I should walk abroad with my Eyes shut, because of the possibility of falling if I should walk abroad with my Eyes open. (26–27)
New Schemes in Philosophy . . . New Religions. (*PW* 1:102)	new Doctrines . . . new Ceremonies, and new Modes of Worship. (40)

NOTES

1. Cf. "I gave the Examiner a hint about this Prorogation [of Parliament]" (Swift, *Journal to Stella*, ed. Harold Williams [Oxford: Clarendon Press, 1948], 2:603. Cited hereafter as *Journal*).

2. *The Prose Works of Jonathan Swift*, ed. Herbert Davis et al. (Oxford: Basil Blackwell, 1939–1968), 4:xvi, emphasis added, and 1:1. Cited hereafter as *PW*.

3. Irvin Ehrenpreis, *Swift: The Man, His Works, and the Age* (Cambridge, Mass.: Harvard University Press, 1962–1983), 2:588.

4. Swift may not have wanted us to see exactly what he did to Collins's *Discourse*. What he wanted us to see and remember was his "corrected" and reductive mock-abstract of Collins's work.

5. As Johnson observes, "To count is a modern practice, the ancient method was to guess." See *A Journey to the Western Islands of Scotland*, ed. Mary Lascelles, vol. 9 of *The Yale Edition of the Works of Samuel Johnson*, ed. John H. Middendorf et al. (New Haven, Conn.: Yale University Press, 1971), 98. Of the 713 lines of *Mr. C——ns's Discourse* in *PW* 4:27–48, by a generous count only

300, or 42 percent, are Collins's. If the preface and conclusion are added in, Swift's "*Additions*" constitute 63 percent of the text of *Mr. C——ns's Discourse.* The remaining 37 percent is just enough to recall the original.

6. *A Discourse of Free-Thinking. Occasion'd by the Rise and Growth of a Sect call'd Free-Thinkers* (London, 1713), 120. Cited hereafter as *Discourse.*

7. Richard Bentley, *Remarks upon a Late Discourse of Free-Thinking: In a Letter to F[rancis] H[are]. D. D. By Phileleutherus Lipsiensis* (London, 1713), 1:14.

8. Benjamin Ibbot, *A Course of Sermons Preach'd at the Lecture Founded by the Honourable Robert Boyle Esq; in the Year 1713* (London, 1727), 1:9. See also George Berkeley, *The Guardian,* No. 55, 14 May 1713; Thomas Cockman, *Free-Thinking Rightly Stated; Wherein a Discourse (Falsly So Called) Is Fully Considered* (London, 1713), 130; Benjamin Hoadly, *Queries Recommended to the Authors of the Late Discourse of Free Thinking. By a Christian,* 2d ed. (London 1713), 5; William Whiston, *Reflexions on an Anonymous Pamphlet, Entituled a Discourse of Free Thinking* (London, 1713), 46.

Lot 1667 in the sale of Collins's library was "Tracts of Sixteen different Authors against the Discourse of Free-Thinking 1713" (Thomas Ballard, *Bibliotheca Antonij Collins, Arm.* [London, 1731], 147), but only fourteen of these are identified herein. For a more complete list, see Robert Phiddian, "The Reaction to Collins's *A Discourse of Free-Thinking:* 'Not Politics'?" *Swift Studies* 4 (1989): 68–71.

9. This is the only point at which this essay confronts Michael DePorte's outstanding essay "Contemplating Collins: Freethinking in Swift": "Swift's elaborations on [Collins's] *Discourse* are not calculated to make it seem more ridiculous, but to seem more dangerous." See *Reading Swift: Papers from the Third Münster Symposium on Jonathan Swift,* ed. Hermann J. Real and Helgard Stöver-Leidig (München: Wilhelm Fink, 1998), 115. Danger magnifies; Swift belittles.

10. *A Farther Discourse of Free-Thinking: In a Letter to a Clergy-Man. With some Considerations on Mr. Pyecroft's Treatise upon the same Subject* (London, 1713), 35–36, 37. Although attributed to Collins in the *National Union Catalog* and *English Short-Title Catalogue,* it is not by Collins. It is an answer to Collins's *Discourse of Free-Thinking:* "what I had learned by reading this Book? And my Answer was, just nothing at all; 'tis a silly book" (35).

11. See Frank H. Ellis, "*An Argument against Abolishing Christianity* as an Argument against Abolishing the Test Act," in *Reading Swift: Papers from the Second Münster Symposium on Jonathan Swift,* ed. Richard H. Rodino and Hermann J. Real (München: Wilhelm Fink, 1993), 134 n.

12. 1709 Key to *The Dispensary,* quoted in *Poems on Affairs of State: Augustan Satirical Verse, 1660–1714,* vol. 6, *1697–1704,* ed. Frank H. Ellis (New Haven, Conn.: Yale University Press, 1970), 105 n, 726.

13. William King, *Divine Predestination and Foreknowledge. Consistent with the Freedom of Man's Will. A Sermon Preach'd at Christ-Church, Dublin; May 15, 1709* (Dublin, 1709), 22.

14. See *Swift vs. Mainwaring: The Examiner and the Medley,* ed. Frank H. Ellis (Oxford: Clarendon Press, 1985), 98, 149. Cited hereafter as *Examiner.*

15. *The Correspondence of Jonathan Swift,* ed. Harold Williams (Oxford: Clarendon Press, 1963–1965), 1:254. Cited hereafter as *Corr.*

16. Archbishop King did not like satire: "I would wish . . . some of my friends . . . would not show the ugly shocking face of things," he wrote to Swift (*Corr.* 1:332).

17. Frank H. Ellis, "Swift's Phillis, or, The Progress of Self-Deception," in *Swift and his Contexts,* ed. John Irwin Fischer, Hermann J. Real, and James Woolley (New York: AMS Press, 1989), 59–60; Collins, *Discourse,* 101.

18. *The Poems of Jonathan Swift,* ed. Harold Williams, 2d ed. (Oxford: Clarendon Press, 1958), 2:572. Cited hereafter as *Poems.*

19. George M. Trevelyan, *England under Queen Anne* (London: Longmans, Green and Co., 1930–1934), 3:192; *Journal,* 2:422, 423, 474.

20. Louis A. Landa, *Swift and the Church of Ireland* (Oxford: Clarendon Press, 1954), 36; Robert Beatson, *A Political Index,* 2d ed. (London, 1788), 2:146. The quotation appears in Landa, *Swift and the Church of Ireland,* 38.

21. Landa, *Swift and the Church of Ireland,* 73.

22. Sir Charles H. Firth, "Dean Swift and Ecclesiastical Preferment," *Review of English Studies* 2 (1926): 1–17.

23. Andrew Carpenter, "Archbishop King and Swift's Appointment as Dean of St. Patrick's," *Long Room* 11 (1975): 11–13.

24. See *Poems on Affairs of State,* 6:763–64.

25. Compare *A Tale of a Tub,* "Is not Religion a *Cloak*" (*PW* 1:47). See Appendix 2 within.

26. That *A Tale of a Tub* imposed a "sort of an Impediment to a Dignity" was reported in *The Britain,* No. 4, 13–17 January 1713.

27. *Poems on Affairs of State: Augustan Satirical Verse, 1660–1714,* vol. 7, *1704–1714,* ed. Frank H. Ellis (New Haven, Conn.: Yale University Press, 1975), 588–89. Anne delayed her consent until 18 April 1713 (*Journal* 2:662).

28. *Encyclopaedia Britannica,* 11th ed. (London: Encyclopaedia Britannica, Inc., 1910–1911), 17:935.

29. This is the point of departure for Clive T. Probyn's provocative study of parody as "refunctioning" an original text: "'Haranguing upon Texts': Swift and the Idea of the Book," in *Proceedings of the First Münster Symposium on Jonathan Swift,* ed. Hermann J. Real and Heinz J. Vienken (München: Wilhelm Fink, 1985), 187–97.

30. *The Dunciad,* ed. James Sutherland, vol. 5 of *The Twickenham Edition of the Poems of Alexander Pope,* 3d ed., ed. John Butt et al. (New Haven, Conn.: Yale University Press, 1963), 144 n. In the *Dunciad Variorum* (1729) Collins was replaced by a greater dunce, Matthew Tindal.

31. *The Correspondence of John Locke,* ed. E. E. de Beer (Oxford: Clarendon Press, 1976–1989), 8:189.

32. When Collins's library was sold in 1731, fifty-six days were required to auction 6,893 lots, some of which included ten to twenty items (Ballard, *Bibliotheca Antonij Collins, passim).*

33. James O'Higgins, S. J., *Anthony Collins: The Man and His Works* (The Hague: Martinus Nijhoff, 1970), 219, 234, 204–5.

34. Compare William L. Rowe, "Causality and Free Will in the Controversy between Collins and Clarke," *Journal of the History of Philosophy* 25 (1987): 51–67; Paul Russell, "Epigram, Pantheists and Freethought in Hume's *Treatise:* A Study in Esoteric Communication," *Journal of the History of Ideas* 54 (1993): 659–73.

35. O'Higgins, *Anthony Collins,* 218.

36. Ibid., 80.

37. John Nichols, *Literary Anecdotes of the Eighteenth Century* (London, 1812–1815), 2:673 n.

38. O'Higgins, *Anthony Collins,* 80 n.

39. Richard Bentley, *La Friponnerie Laïque des Pretendus Esprits-Forts d'Angleterre: ou Remarques de Phileleuthere de Leipsick sur le Discours de la Liberté de Penser, Traduites de l'Anglois . . . par Mr. N.N.* [Armand de la Chapelle] (Amsterdam, 1738), xxiii; Nichols, *Literary Anecdotes,* 2:675 n.

40. Bentley, xxvi, xxix; O'Higgins, *Anthony Collins,* 206.

6

Voyages to Nowhere

More's *Utopia* and Swift's *Gulliver's Travels*

HERMANN J. REAL

I' th' commonwealth I would by contraries
Execute all things.
Shakespeare, *The Tempest* 2.1.143–44

Gulliver's Travels has been given many names in its critical history. It has been designated a "novel," an "allegory," and an "extraordinary voyage" as well as a "fable," a "parody," and a "satire," not to mention "philosophical treatise" and "scientific discourse."[1] Moreover, it has been described as "paradoxical," as "grotesque," and, most recently, as "picaresque," as well as "utopian" in mode, or alternatively, a "utopia," and even "a series of Utopias."[2]

Since in Swift scholarship little, if anything, is uncontested, the utopian angle on *Gulliver's Travels* also presents the familiar picture of a battleground. "I think that none of the accepted sources for *Gulliver's Travels*," one critic categorically rules, "presents a closer parallel [than *Utopia*] for the basic situation of a political and ethical attack on our society by juxtaposition with that of an imaginary one."[3] Another reader endorses this position, also placing the *Travels* against the single foil of More's *Utopia* ("The whole mad vision of utopia . . . lies behind [Swift's] passion and More's"), and a third invokes the entire matrix of utopian fiction: "The author of *Gulliver's Travels* benefits from as rich a grounding as any of his contemporaries," this critic writes. "In Swift's case, there are . . . texts which he cannot be proved to have read, but which are contextually interesting (and which could conceivably have been among the 'diverting books' or 'abundance of Trash' he soaked up when working on his own fiction)."[4] By contrast, a dissenting voice holds that the "parallels," that is narrative devices, as well as thematic and structural features, between *Gulliver's Travels* and its utopian pre-texts, including the ones Swift is known to have admired and relished, originated not in any generic repertoire but in Swift's very philosophy: "Es ergibt sich, daß wir die utopischen Gedanken Swifts, da sie auf 'Quellen' nicht zurückzuführen sind, anders erklären müssen. Deshalb sind bei der Besprechung des utopischen Staates die Gedanken und utopischen Motive unmittelbar aus Swifts Weltanschauung abgeleitet worden."[5]

It is of course true that *Gulliver's Travels* is a "whole array of genres," a literary heterocosm in which generic categories interact and overlap.[6] To revitalize the culinary metaphor familiar from accounts of the etymology of satire, it may perhaps be called a nutritious mixed stuffing, a ragout, as it were, which is as "assorted" as it is "spicy" and "peppery."[7] Even mixed stews, though, do not take everything, or anything for that matter, and while the desire to "season" the profusion of generic ingredients which is *Gulliver's Travels* with an additional pinch of "utopia" or "dystopia" seems natural enough, I hope to show that a dash of these stands to render the whole dish distasteful. In fact, the view that *Gulliver's Travels* is utopian in character and intent is interesting only inasmuch as it raises the question how such a "misprision" could originate with educated people.[8]

To me, there are three reasons. The first is of a biographical nature and is to be sought in the specific affinity of the intellectual and moral temperament that Swift seems to have felt for Sir Thomas More. "By the time he was fifty-five," Irvin Ehrenpreis says, "[Swift] liked to imagine he was emulating Cato or Thomas More, and devoting his life to preserve a people on the edge of ruin."[9] Significantly, More is the only political leader of the modern age to belong to that legendary sextumvirate of ancient political heroes whom Gulliver calls up in Glubbdubdrib, "a *Sextumvirate* to which all the Ages of the World cannot add a Seventh" (3.7.10).[10] The Dean of St. Patrick's admired the author of *Utopia* profoundly, presumably because of More's principled steadfastness during the controversy about Henry VIII's divorce proceedings. In the marginalia of his own copy of Lord Herbert's *Life and Raigne of Henry VIII* (1649), he described More as the "only Man of true Virtue tha[t] ever Engl[an]d produced," and a few pages later, he noted in a gloss on Cherbury's account of More's execution: "[H]ere the detestable [Ty]rant murdred [Vir]tue her self."[11] It comes as no surprise, therefore, that the special affinity between the two men has suggested a special relationship between their two works. However, we remember that Swift, in "A Letter from Capt. Gulliver to his Cousin Sympson," has Gulliver indignantly dismiss any reputed similarity between his travels and More's *Utopia*.[12]

The second reason for misapprehending the relationship between *Utopia* and *Gulliver's Travels* is to be found in the great number of correspondences, similar, or ostensibly similar, components of narrative strategy and philosophical content; more specifically, the seeming intertextuality of framework and narration, of "realism" and authenticity, of motifs and themes like reason and paradox.[13] This intertextuality seems especially prominent in the two protagonists, Raphael Hythlodaeus and Lemuel Gulliver, travelers both and first-person narrators, unreliable though they are, whose characterization is "dramatic in method," and whose most distinguishing trait is their thirst for knowledge, their curiosity.[14]

Gulliver spends but two months with his family after his return from Lilliput: "My insatiable Desire of seeing foreign Countries would suffer me to continue no longer" (1.8.11). Before he sets out on the journey which eventually takes him to Laputa, he confesses that not even the remembrance of his past misfortunes could abate his curiosity (3.1.2). In the countries Gulliver visits, he always shows himself eager "to see the Curiosities" (3.3.1), he lets his "Curiosity prevail" over others (3.7.6), and he feels contempt for people who do not appear "to be curious in any Part of Knowledge" (3.4.1). In short, he is "condemned by Nature and Fortune to an active and restless Life" (2.1.1).

Like Gulliver, More's Hythlodaeus is goaded on by indomitable wanderlust. Unlike Gulliver, however, who is wont to justify his "insatiable Desire of seeing foreign Countries" with "advantageous Offers" designed to improve the family fortune,[15] Raphael is indifferent to money. He leaves his patrimony to his brothers, and "being eager to see the world," he joins Amerigo Vespucci and becomes "his constant companion." In Raphael, curiosity, the "Lust of the mind," as Hobbes was to call it in *Leviathan* (1651), is even stronger than the fear of death.[16] "Being more anxious for travel than about the grave," he is in the habit of pointing out that "from all places it is the same distance to heaven."[17] Not coincidentally, Peter Giles, when introducing Hythlodaeus to "More," compares him with Ulysses, the archetype of all restlessly inquisitive travelers.[18]

These presumed parallels or analogues indeed suggest a particular proximity of the two works; but on closer inspection they turn out to be incidental rather than central.[19] It is important to remember that although both Hythlodaeus and Gulliver visit fantastic, imaginary countries, they never leave the real world to which they belong and to which they return while they are still on their voyages. The accounts they give of these voyages invite readers to compare favorably and unfavorably the prevailing conditions of their native country with the ones reflected in the reports' truthful memoirs of the "foreign" lands.[20] The alternative worlds both the inquisitive Hythlodaeus and Gulliver chance upon are alternative versions of England, with this decisive difference: in the *Travels,* Gulliver voyages into the English past, the history of recent English politics and science, there to be confronted with the dismal record of his "dear native Country" (2.6.6). In *Utopia,* Raphael voyages into the future, there to encounter a "hallucinated world," a model of the state of England as it might be or, perhaps, even should be. Whereas *Gulliver's Travels* is a satirical allegory in which the surface structure of characters, actions, and events refers to a superimposed "real" structure of "discernible historic particulars," *Utopia,* the account of "a very good state of the commonwealth" in Nowhere-Land, is the secular variant of a chiliastic vision.[21]

This brings me to the third reason that has led critics to posit a utopian quality in *Gulliver's Travels:* the dichotomous structure of either book.[22] Gulliver journeys into the past three times. On his first journey, he re-experiences the most significant events in a period of English political history which was of particular importance to Swift. On Gulliver's second voyage, the dissection of the intellectual and moral shortcomings of Whig politics in Lilliput is supplemented by a satirical anatomy of the corruptions in the English system of government, its legislative, executive, and judiciary. On his third trip, Gulliver witnesses a cascade of follies committed in the name of science, exposing its inane futility and tyrannical hubris. In history, and in particular the history of recent English politics and science, Gulliver encounters man and his deeds; in history he confronts the discrepancy between man's assessment of himself as a rational being and man's accomplishment. The human pretence to be *animal rationale* is refuted by the historical record. However, even though Gulliver has the opportunity to see how corrupt human nature is, he does not recognize it and history does not teach him anything: "In Book IV, [Gulliver] is three books behind the reader's awareness."[23]

If the lesson of Gulliver's excursions into history is not to be lost, somebody will have to "enlighten" him. The historical *exempla* of Books 1–3 need interpreting; they have to be supplemented by a concise statement in which the lesson of history is driven home to Gulliver, mediocre representative of mankind that he is.[24] The moral of history is presented in Book 4. Here, the Houyhnhnm master instructs Gulliver about man's "true" nature. Neither Books 1 plus 2 nor 3 plus 4, therefore, cohere in the overall design of the *Travels;* nor do Books 1 plus 3 and 2 plus 4. Their relationship is a different one. Books 1–3 are closely related; Book 4 is set apart, yet by no means complete in itself. On the contrary, Book 4 is a compendium, a summary which presents the bill, or balance, of Gulliver's journeys throughout man's "vulgar errors." The dichotomous macro-structure of *Gulliver's Travels,* then, combines the rhetorical forces of historical experience with those of philosophical reason: *homo non est animal rationale sed rationis capax.*

In *Gulliver's Travels,* I suggest, Swift writes a new and paradoxical, that is, heretical anthropology.[25] Its central tenet is that philosophy does man no favor by defining him as *animal rationale.* Pure rationality is incommensurate with the nature of man. As Gulliver's fate reveals, man cannot live by reason alone. Preferring to live with his stallions rather than with his family, he is, "by any recognizable standard, mad."[26] Gulliver, not Swift, is "mad" for reason. As Gulliver's final scenes demonstrate, man's desire to be regarded as reasonable is a symptom of madness.

In parading the Houyhnhnms, the epitome of virtue and rationality, before and for Gulliver, Swift exhibits the ideal which the philosophy of the schools, the "orthodox" anthropology of the age, claimed for man's nature. While the bestial Yahoos are the image of man as he has documented himself within history, the rational horses image man as he appears in his own view, as he should be in his own assessment of himself. Their sole function is to remind Gulliver of his own ideal, his own standard. If the Yahoos' task is to present Gulliver with the devastating balance sheet of man's presumed historical accomplishment, the satirical thrust gains momentum if the accomplishment does not in the least measure up to the standard which man boasted he was capable of achieving.

Swift's satire is double-edged, however. In a first cut, he shows that man does not measure up to his own standard; in a second, that this standard is not for man. As the conclusion of the *Travels* proves, it is neither possible nor desirable for Gulliver to qualify for a rational community. When Gulliver tries to live a life of reason, "the results are disastrous."[27] The ending of the travels is also the end of Gulliver, if not physically, at least emotionally, morally, and intellectually. Seen as a "Roman model," Books 1–3 are identical with the "destructive" A-Part, the satiric scene; Book 4, the community of the rational horses, is not a "utopia" but the "constructive" B-Part, the satiric norm.[28]

However, it is crucial to remember here that a satire's norms are relative to the object of its attack, not necessarily relative to its author. As a result, the norms of Gulliver and *Gulliver's Travels* need not be identical with Swift's. In fact, his stance is not at all as straightforward as these observations might suggest. The most one can say is that his position is negative: the definition of man as a reasonable animal is not commensurate with man's nature. Not even the "truth" of this simple sentence remains unquestioned at the end, for two reasons. First, although Gulliver is taught history's lessons, his illumination results in darkness. Since history teaches

Gulliver nothing, he continues to worship the ideal which, his travels should have taught him, only rational animals could live. Second, Swift nowhere speaks *in propria persona;* all information and accompanying judgments are transmitted through Gulliver, unreliable narrator that he is or progressively becomes. The panegyric of reason into which Gulliver bursts thus is spoken by somebody who apparently has lost his wits or no longer is in his right mind. As in the early stroke of genius, *A Tale of a Tub* (1704), the collapse of norms seems to be complete. Where is Swift?

Like *Gulliver's Travels, Utopia* is bipartite in structure. In either case, a seemingly ideal alternative world succeeds the satiric scene, even if in inverse proportion. It is not without reason, therefore, that *Utopia* has been described as an inverted satire: "It is as though the normal proportions of satire were here reversed, with part B—the positives—in preponderance."[29] After the political and social problems of contemporary England have been introduced in the narrative framework of Book 1, the narrated narration of "Utopia/Eutopia" in Book 2 provides one answer, though not *the* answer: Raphael "rehearsed not a few points," the narrator "More" notes at the beginning of their conversation, "from which our own cities, nations, races, and kingdoms may take example for the correction of their errors." Yet at the end "More" insists, "I cannot agree with all that he said, but I readily admit that there are very many features in the Utopian commonwealth which it is easier for me to wish for in our countries than to have any hope of seeing realized."[30] The conclusion is obvious: the text itself induces skepticism towards Utopia's putative ideality. The commonwealth of Utopia, which contrasts with the body politic of England, and to which this has to measure up, is not an ideal model but an alternative society, excellent though this may be. At best, Utopia is an ideal in relation to England's anarchic, sordid reality.[31] Otherwise, it is impossible to determine "what the ideal is ideal in respect to."[32] All the more reason to render *Utopia's* title, *De optimo reipvblicae statv,* not as "the best state" but as "a very good, or excellent, state of the commonwealth."[33]

The fact that Utopia is indeed an alternative vision of England follows from Raphael's stay with Cardinal Morton, Archbishop of Canterbury and Lord Chancellor at the time, in whose household More had served.[34] This visit, more particularly its "debates within the discourse" at the cardinal's table, is the centerpiece of Book 1.[35] In essence, these debates focus on three closely interrelated themes—views of legal and military policy as well as aspects of socio-economic order—and they present a satirical anatomy of England. As Raphael's name suggests, he turns out to be the physician who opens up wounds and proposes remedies, especially for three cancers that are about to destroy the English body politic.[36]

The first issue to be raised is the inhumanity of criminal law and capital punishment. Here, "a layman, learned in the laws of [the] country," who happens to be at the cardinal's table, is Raphael's adversary:

> Availing himself of some opportunity or other, he began to speak punctiliously of the strict justice which was then dealt out to thieves. They were everywhere executed, he reported, as many as twenty at a time being hanged on one gallows, and added that he wondered all the more, though so few escaped execution, by what bad luck the whole country was still infested with them.[37]

Raphael's refutation points out that the general formula, such as the criminal offence of theft, does not do justice to the individual case. All offences are not equal, and each case has to be judged on its own merits. If a man, for example, steals because he lives in poverty, he is not an offender but a victim. Necessity knows no law. The social conditions in which thievery originates, Raphael continues, are poverty and unemployment. The blunt facts reveal that have-nots are aggressors against what they take to be not a social but an antisocial order that enforces the theft which leads to capital punishment: "You ordain grievous and terrible punishments for a thief when it would have been much better to provide some means of getting a living, that no one should be under this terrible necessity first of stealing and then of dying for it."[38] The lawyer at the cardinal's table has to face up to the charge that the cure is worse than the disease, that the system whose justice he extols deliberately trains the thief in order to execute him.[39] *Summum ius, summa iniuria.*

The second issue to be raised at Cardinal Morton's table is the controversy about mercenary standing armies, which beset the majority of European nation-states at the time, and which was to leave its mark on English military policy for more than two hundred years.[40] In Raphael's criticism of standing armies, he recalls a warning from St. Augustine: "If justice is left out, what are kingdoms except great robber bands?" (*Remota itaque iustitia quid sunt regna nisi magna latrocinia*), Augustine exclaims in the *City of God,* "for what are robber bands except little kingdoms?" (*quia et latrocinia quid sunt nisi parva regna*?).[41] In times of peace, standing armies effect the opposite of their purpose. Rather than prevent war, they provide an occasion or a pretext for war. Whoever has arms and soldiers at his disposal desires to make use of them: "This attitude obliges [the kings] always to be seeking for a pretext for war just so they may not have soldiers without experience," Raphael remarks sarcastically. More importantly, he continues, in times of peace, a standing army is likely not to be a militia defending its country in an emergency but rather a threat to the peace and liberty of its people: "Not only the supreme authority [of several countries] but their land and even their cities have been more than once destroyed by their own standing armies."[42] Of all forms of injustice, however, Aristotle had ruled in the *Politica,* "nothing is so difficult to subdue as injustice in arms" (1.2; 1253a).[43]

Finally, the party at the cardinal's table discuss aspects of England's socio-economic (dis)order, more especially the social and economic grievances resulting from the history of enclosure, that movement which was extended as it was extensive, and by which "strictly private ownership and use supplanted the system of commonfields."[44] Again, Raphael speaks to the point, presenting a precise and pithy summary of most basic arguments deployed against enclosure:

> Your sheep . . . which are usually so tame and so cheaply fed, begin now . . . to be so greedy and wild that they devour human beings themselves and devastate and depopulate fields, houses, and towns. In all those parts of the realm where the finest and therefore costliest wool is produced, there are noblemen, gentlemen, and even some abbots . . . who are not satisfied with the annual revenues and profits which their predecessors used to derive from their estates. They are not content, by leading an idle and sumptuous life, to do no good to their country; they must also do it positive harm. They leave no ground to be tilled; they enclose every bit of land for pasture; they pull down houses and destroy towns. . . . And, as if enough English land were not wasted on ranges and preserves of game, those good fellows turn all human habitations and all cultivated land into a wilderness.[45]

The concatenation of social misery and wretchedness becomes only too manifest in this analysis: the conversion of tillage into pasture, itself rooted in the greed and avarice of the aristocracy and higher clergy, is succeeded by the eviction of tenants; eviction not only results in the destruction of cottages and villages but also in the depopulation of the countryside as well as in the rise of unemployment and the increase of poverty; poverty, in turn, leads straight into the familiar vicious circle of necessity and thievery, to which the authorities know no answer but oppression and deterrence. Raphael seems to anticipate the England of Disraeli's *Sybil,* in which the country is divided into the rich and the poor, and even the most cursory of glimpses at the evidence shows that Raphael has history on his side.[46] "England was a nation in distress," one historian writes,

> uprooted from its past and reeling along a wayward path toward certain destruction. It was a nation of decaying towns and deserted farms and villages, a nation swarming with vagabonds, masterless men, and starving wretches. Traditional rights and relationships were cast aside and trampled by a new species of rapacious tyrants: landlords and merchants who laid house to house and field to field, sending England's raw wealth abroad or squandering it at home on luxuries. England's peasant laborers and small leaseholders were reaping the old, mean har-

vest of dearth, homelessness, and disease, but on a scale so unprecedented as to mark a momentous historical change.[47]

The corollary is equally manifest. In a society like England, whose most characteristic feature is the struggle for survival, all hallmarks of civilization, which so visibly constitute the commonwealth of the Utopians, are conspicuously lacking. In a society like England, there is no room for education and religion, for peace and toleration, for family life and health care, for pleasure and for virtue. Such a society is rich only in privation.

It is useful to remember at this point that Book 1, more precisely the Dialogue of Counsel, though written later than Book 2, the Discourse on Utopia, was placed before the account of the Utopian commonwealth, and that More decided not to publish Book 2 separately, "finished" though it may have seemed.[48] The interpretative significance of this decision is worth noticing: "Whatever else the dialogue may be, it was evidently intended as an *introduction* to the account of Utopia."[49] In other words, the later Book 1 was important to More, as important as Book 2, and was neither occasional nor extemporized. On the contrary, Book 1 is intellectually if not chronologically prefigured in Book 2. One cannot be read without the other; both are as complementary as they are contrastive.

If Book 1 opens up the wounds in England's body politic, then Book 2 proposes the remedy, the methods how they may or should be healed. However, Raphael's therapy does not design only to alleviate the symptoms; he is eager to root out the disease. Like Hippocrates, the most famous physician of classical antiquity, More makes Raphael endorse the principle of allopathic medicine, *contraria contrariorum esse remedia.*[50] Thus after diagnosing greed and rapacity as the causes underlying the English malady, Raphael outlines the treatment which would make these causes disappear. As in Utopia, "all greed for money [would be] entirely removed with the use of money," and as a result, "poverty . . . forthwith would itself dwindle and disappear."[51] Seen in this light, the Utopian commonwealth is a trope of contrast, an anti-world. "What sets [*Utopia*] apart from the more usual social criticism of its time," Richard Helgerson rightly says, "is that it—or at least its chief speaker—finally rejects [any] partial solutions." Instead, "*Utopia* undertakes a global analysis that . . . points toward a general transformation of society as the unique remedy."[52]

Perhaps the most salient feature of this anti-world is the practice through which the Utopian state has codified, and guaranteed, specific human rights that are all violated in then contemporary England: the rights to work, to property, to liberty, to peace, to self-preservation, and to equality before the law. For example, "agriculture [being] the one pursuit" in which all citizens are trained and engaged, there is "no danger of anything going wrong with the annual food supply through want of skill." Besides agriculture, "each is taught one particular craft as his own," and although no one is allowed "to sit idle," all citizens are encouraged to devote as much time as possible "to the freedom and culture of the mind." Even if all Utopians work, they "never claim payment" for their services, in accordance with their most important belief that gold "by its very nature is useless." As a paradoxical result, there is no poverty in Utopia: "Though no man has anything, yet all are rich." For military reasons only "they keep a vast treasure," using it "above all to hire . . . foreign mercenaries (whom they would jeopardize rather than their own citizens)." On principle, however, they regard war "with utter loathing," as an "activity fit only for beasts," deeming war justified merely "to protect their own territory" or "to deliver [a people oppressed by tyranny] by force of arms from the yoke and slavery of the tyrant." As they take care of their country, Utopians care for the members of their national family. In well-furnished hospitals, "constant attendance" is ministered to the sick "by expert physicians," and the legal system ensures that punishment is commensurate with the crime: "There is no law prescribing any fixed penalty, but the punishment is assigned by the senate according to the atrocity, or veniality, of the individual crime."[53]

"More's" final remark to Raphael reveals how More the historical author intended this vision of the Utopian anti-world to be read: not as a patent remedy for England's ills but as a means of orientation, not as a blueprint to be executed but as a draft to be debated in the future. Taking Raphael by the hand and leading him into the house to supper, "More" expresses his hope "that there would be another chance to think about these matters more deeply and to talk them over with him more fully."[54] If the commonwealth of England is not as it should be, it is necessary first of all to talk about its shortcomings. Though English society badly needs correction, its subjects do not wholly have to discard the idea of a better society. Before statesmen set to work, however, they need to engage in conversation and debate. There seems little point in acting before things have been finally considered.[55] Words, therefore, are bound to come before the deed.

In More's view, then, *Utopia* was intended as a means to initiate the debate by questioning the social and economic status quo and by arguing *contra opinionem*: "*Utopia*, in the last analysis, is a cry of distress over the exploited poor and a call to reform in every department of human endeavor in England and in Europe."[56] In this regard, More is as paradoxical and heretical as the Dean of St. Patrick's, even if his concern is not anthropology but social ethics, and as a result, nothing could be less conducive to a better understanding of the work than a criticism like this:

> Let us list some of the inconsistencies which have been detected between the practices of Utopia and More's own conduct. First, the Utopians have few laws and small regard for lawyers: More devoted most of his life to the law and became England's chief law officer. Secondly, Utopians despise the precious metals, while regarding ascetic practices as a mark of folly; More, in and out of office, wore a golden chain, and beneath it a shirt of hair to tame his flesh. In Utopia, thirdly, it is lawful to follow, peaceably, any religion one chooses; More prided himself on his reputation as a severe castigator of heretics. Fourthly, in *Utopia* the clergy are allowed to marry, and indeed to select the choicest partners; More, in controversy with Luther, harps beyond the bounds of taste on his marriage with a nun as nullifying all his doctrinal claims. Fifthly, divorce is permitted in Utopia on comparatively easy terms; in life More went to prison rather than consent to a divorce which half the divines of Christendom thought was allowable according to Scripture and canon law. Sixthly, suicide in Utopia, in appropriate circumstances, is regarded as permissible and even laudable; More, however weary of life in the Tower, was scrupulously careful not to utter a word that would bring him within the death penalty and thus create a risk that he would face God before God had called him. Seventhly, the constitution of Utopia is radically egalitarian; More, right up to his death, behaved to the tyrant Henry with an obsequiousness bordering on servility which could not, as it could in the case of others less brave, be attributed to fear. Finally, in *Utopia* the Papacy is spoken of with contemptuous irony; it was, in the end, for the prerogatives of the Pope that More gave his life. It would not be difficult to prolong such a list of paradoxes. How are they to be resolved?[57]

These apparent contradictions between "More," the participant in the dialogue, and More, the historical personality, are easy to account for if one accepts that the text intends to be paradoxical. *Utopia,* the book, is the logical paradox of the *eutopia* which is "nowhere." Nowhere-Land is the place where ideals exist.

One element common to all types of paradox is the fact that paradoxes invariably kick against the pricks of some orthodoxy; they challenge prevailing assumptions, conventions, and norms. One chief function is to surprise, to provoke, and to confuse. Above all, they are meant, Charles Estienne reminds us, "to stir [their readers] into debate" and thus to make them think again. Paradoxes never hold positions or assert views, and they never commit themselves to anything.[58] For this reason there is no sense of resolution at the end of *Utopia.*[59] Paradoxically, in *Utopia,* the debate has not yet begun although the conversation is over. By contrast, in *Gulliver's Travels,* the conversation is over, and nothing else remains to be said.[60]

NOTES

1. For "novel" see Dieter Mehl, *Der englische Roman bis zum Ende des 18. Jahrhunderts* (Düsseldorf, Bern, München: August Bagel und Francke Verlag, 1977), 85–92; J. Paul Hunter, "*Gulliver's Travels* and the Novel," in *The Genres of "Gulliver's Travels,"* ed. Frederik N. Smith (Newark, N.J.: Associated University Presses, 1990), 56–74, cited hereafter as Smith, *Genres;* J. A. Downie, "Swift and the Making of the English Novel," in *Reading Swift: Papers from the Third Münster Symposium on Jonathan Swift,* ed. Hermann J. Real and Helgard Stöver-Leidig (München: Wilhelm Fink, 1998), 179–87. For "allegory" see Brean S. Hammond, "Applying Swift," in *Reading Swift: Papers from the Second Münster Symposium on Jonathan Swift,* ed. Richard H. Rodino and Hermann J. Real, with the assistance of Helgard Stöver-Leidig (München: Wilhelm Fink, 1993), 185–97. For "extraordinary voyage" see the fullest and most comprehensive account by Dirk F. Passmann, *"Full of Improbable Lies": "Gulliver's Travels" und die Reiseliteratur vor 1726* (Frankfurt am Main: Peter Lang, 1987). For "fable" see Albert Ball, "Swift and the Animal Myth," *Transactions of the Wisconsin Academy of Sciences, Arts, and Letters* 48 (1959): 239–48. For "parody" see Friedrich Krey, *Interpretationskommentar zu "Gulliver's Travels": Vorspann und Buch I,* Dissertation (Berlin, 1969), 76–77, and C. J. Rawson, *Gulliver and the Gentle Reader: Studies in Swift and Our Time* (London: Routledge and Kegan Paul, 1973), 10–11. For "satire" see Edward W. Rosenheim, Jr., *Swift and the Satirist's Art* (Chicago: University of Chicago Press, 1967 [1963]), 90–102 and passim, and Bernhard Fabian, "*Gulliver's Travels* als Satire," *Poetica* 3 (1970): 421–34. For "philosophical treatise" or "scientific discourse" see the essays by Frederik N. Smith and William Bowman Piper, respectively, in Smith, *Genres,* 139–62, 179–202, as well as Frederick M. Keener, *The Chain of Becoming: The Philosophical Tale, the Novel, and a Neglected Realism of the Enlightenment* (New York: Columbia University Press, 1983), particularly 89–126.

2. For "paradoxical" see Hermann J. Real, "The Dean's European Ancestors: Swift and the Tradition of Paradox," in *La Grande-Bretagne et l'Europe des Lumières,* ed. Serge Soupel (Paris: Presses de la Sorbonne Nouvelle, 1996), 135–42. For "grotesque" see, among others, Christian W. Thomsen, *Das Groteske im englischen Roman des 18. Jahrhunderts: Erscheinungsformen und Funktionen* (Darmstadt: Wissenschaftliche Buchgesellschaft, 1974), 15–92. For "picaresque" see Maximillian E. Novak, "*Gulliver's Travels* and the Picaresque Voyage: Some Reflections on the Hazards of Genre Criticism," in Smith, *Genres,* 23–38. For "utopia" or "series of Utopias" see A. L. Morton, *The English Utopia* (London: Lawrence and Wishart, 1969), 132; Raymond Smith, "Swift's Utopias," *Discourse* 9 (1966): 389–98; Milton Voigt, "*Gulliver's Travels* in a Utopias-Dystopias Course," in *Approaches to Teaching Swift's "Gulliver's Travels,"* ed. Edward J. Rielly (New York: The Modern Language Association, 1988), 117–20; Annemarie Pieper, "Gullivers Reisen: Märchen oder brauchbare Staatsutopie?" *Innovatio* 5 (1989): 50; and Terry Siu-Han Yip, "The Juxtaposition of Utopia and Dystopia in Chinese and English Literature: A Comparative Study of *Flowers in the Mirror* and *Gulliver's Travels,*" in *Proceedings of the XIIth Congress of the*

International Comparative Literature Association, ed. Roger Bauer et al. (München: Iudicium Verlag, 1995), 2:467.

3. Brian Vickers, "The Satiric Structure of *Gulliver's Travels* and More's *Utopia,*" in *The World of Jonathan Swift: Essays for the Tercentenary,* ed. Brian Vickers (Oxford: Basil Blackwell, 1968), 241. See also J. R. Brink, "From the Utopians to the Yahoos: Thomas More and Jonathan Swift," *Journal of the Rutgers University Libraries* 42 (1980): 59–66.

4. For "another reader," see John Traugott, "A Voyage to Nowhere with Thomas More and Jonathan Swift: *Utopia* and *The Voyage to the Houyhnhnms,*" in *Swift: A Collection of Critical Essays,* ed. Ernest Tuveson (Englewood Cliffs, N. J.: Prentice-Hall, 1964), 160. For "a third," see Christine Rees, *Utopian Imagination and Eighteenth-Century Fiction* (London: Longman, 1996), 123–24.

5. "Since Swift's utopian thoughts cannot be reduced to 'sources,' we have to account for them in a different way. That is why in the discussion of the utopian society ideas and utopian motifs have been directly deduced from Swift's *weltanschauung*" (my translation). See Charlotte Dege, *Utopie und Satire in Swifts "Gulliver's Travels"* (Frankfurt/Oder: Trowitzsch and Sohn, 1934), 59–60. Another dissenting voice, Dorothy F. Donnelly, claims that "the *Travels* is more anti-utopian in outlook than is generally acknowledged." See her "*Utopia* and *Gulliver's Travels:* Another Perspective," *Moreana* 25 (1988): 115–24.

6. Smith, "Afterword: Style, Swift's Reader, and the Genres of *Gulliver's Travels,*" in Smith, *Genres,* 246.

7. See, in particular, Ulrich Knoche, *Roman Satire* (Bloomington: Indiana University Press, 1975), 7–16.

8. See also David Fishelov, "*Satura contra Utopiam:* Satirical Distortions of Utopian Ideas," *Revue de littérature comparée* 67 (1993): 463–71.

9. Irvin Ehrenpreis, *Swift: The Man, His Works, and the Age* (London: Methuen, 1962–1983), 3:187. See also R. W. Chambers, *Thomas More* (London: Jonathan Cape, 1967 [1935]), 365: "From some aspects Swift seems to be More come to life again. . . . Swift has been described as the soul of Rabelais in a dry place; we might think of him as the mind of Sir Thomas More without More's patience or More's faith, wandering through desert places seeking rest, and finding none."

10. *Gulliver's Travels (1726),* vol. 11 of *The Prose Works of Jonathan Swift,* ed. Herbert Davis et al. (Oxford: Basil Blackwell, 1959), 196. All quotations are from this edition, cited hereafter as *PW.* Numbers given in parentheses refer to book, chapter, and paragraph.

11. *Miscellaneous and Autobiographical Pieces, Fragments and Marginalia,* ed. Herbert Davis, vol. 5 of *The Prose Works of Jonathan Swift* (1962), 247, 248. In these excerpts square brackets signify editorial inference, with the exception of my own inference of "Engl[an]d." See also *Miscellaneous and Autobiographical Pieces,* 84, and "Concerning that Universal Hatred, which Prevails against the Clergy," in *Directions to Servants and Miscellaneous Pieces, 1733–1742,* ed. Herbert Davis, vol. 13 of *The Prose Works of Jonathan Swift* (1964), 123. Swift's own copy of Lord Herbert's *Life* is now in the Rothschild Collection, Trinity College, Cambridge; see *The Rothschild Library* (London: Cambridge University Press, 1954), 2:626–27, no. 2313.

12. See *PW,* 11:8.

13. It is impossible to list all of the criticism that bears on these aspects here; see, for example, Gabrielle Bersier, "Reise als Umrahmung der Utopie: einige Überlegungen zum utopischen Reiseroman bis zum Ausgang des 18. Jahrhunderts," in *Reise und soziale Realität am Ende des 18. Jahrhunderts,* ed. Wolfgang Griep and Hans-Wolf Jäger (Heidelberg: Carl Winter, 1983), 292–301; Hermann J. Real and Heinz J. Vienken, *Jonathan Swift, "Gulliver's Travels"* (München: Wilhelm Fink, 1984), 34–43; Eugene R. Hammond, "Nature-Reason-Justice in *Utopia* and *Gulliver's Travels,*" *Studies in English Literature* 22 (1982): 445–68; and Jenny Mezciems, "Utopia and 'The Thing Which Is Not': More, Swift, and Other Lying Idealists," *University of Toronto Quarterly* 52 (1982–83): 40–62.

14. Hythlodaeus is the "expert in trifles" or the "nonsense-peddler," and Gulliver is the "gullible" one. See, respectively, *Utopia,* vol. 4, *The Yale Edition of the Complete Works of St. Thomas More,* ed. Edward Surtz, S. J., and J. H. Hexter (New Haven, Conn.: Yale University Press, 1965), 301–2 (cited hereafter as *Utopia*); *Utopia,* trans. and ed. Robert M. Adams, 2d ed. (New York: Norton, 1992), 5 n. 9; and Paul Odell Clark, "A Gulliver Dictionary," *Studies in Philology* 50 (1953): 599. For the interpretative consequences of this view, see pages 105–6 of this essay. For "dramatic in method" see *Utopia,* cxxxiv–cxxxviii, and for *Gulliver's Travels* see the convenient summary in Real and Vienken, *Jonathan Swift,* 51–52. For "curiosity" see Real and Vienken's summary in "The Structure of *Gulliver's Travels,*" in *Proceedings of the First Münster Symposium on Jonathan Swift,* ed. Hermann J. Real and Heinz J. Vienken (München: Wilhelm Fink, 1985), 202–3.

15. See *Gulliver* 1.1.3; 1.8.11; 3.1.1–2; 4.1.1.

16. Thomas Hobbes, *Leviathan,* ed. C. B. Macpherson (Harmondsworth, Middlesex: Penguin Books, 1986 [1968]), 124.

17. *Utopia,* 51.

18. I adopt the distinction, common in More scholarship, between "More," fictional character in, and More, Lord Chancellor of England and author of, *Utopia.* For the Ulysses comparison, see *Utopia,* 49, 301.

19. In addition, and irrespective of the question whether *Gulliver's Travels* is in the "Utopian" mode at all, the majority of the "parallels" are not restricted to *Utopia* and *Gulliver's Travels,* as Dege already has emphasized, *Utopie und Satire,* 55–59. See also Rees, *Utopian Imagination,* 123–24. As a result, *Utopia* does not provide a more privileged and more authoritative context for the *Travels* than, say, Plato's *Republic* and Harrington's *The Commonwealth of Oceana,* both of which also were in Swift's library. See also William LeFanu, *A Catalogue of Books Belonging to Dr Jonathan Swift, Dean of St Patrick's, Dublin, Aug. 19. 1715* (Cambridge: Cambridge Bibliographical Society, 1988), 21, 26; Irène Samuel, "Swift's Reading of Plato," *Studies in Philology* 73 (1976): 440–62; Myrddin Jones, "Swift, Harrington, and Corruption in England," *Philological Quarterly* 53 (1974): 59–70.

20. See *Utopia,* 39, and *PW,* 11:9–10, 291.

21. For "discernible historic particulars" see Edward Rosenheim's use, though the context in which it occurs is different. See *Swift and the Satirist's Art,* 31. The

Latin title of *Utopia, De optimo reipvblicae statv,* is as a rule translated as "the best state of a commonwealth" (see the editions by Surtz and Hexter, 1, and Adams, 3). For reasons that will become obvious in the course of my interpretation, I prefer "a very good state of the commonwealth," a variant which is grammatically possible, too. Surtz and Hexter suggest the translation of Utopia as "Nowhere-Land," 274. For "secular variant" see, among others, J. C. Davis, *Utopia and the Ideal Society: A Study of English Utopian Writing, 1516–1700* (Cambridge: Cambridge University Press, 1981), 42–43; Werner von Koppenfels, "Thomas Morus und die humanistische Utopie der Renaissance," in *Alternative Welten,* ed. Manfred Pfister (München: Wilhelm Fink, 1982), 99.

22. In what follows, I rely, in part, on my monograph of 1984, co-authored with Heinz J. Vienken; see *Jonathan Swift,* 54–115. I add that this reading rests on an historical interpretation of the political and scientific allegory of the *Travels* with which Phillip Harth would not agree. He argues for a more "modernized" significance in "The Problem of Political Allegory in *Gulliver's Travels,*" *Modern Philology* 73 (1976): S40–S47.

23. Philip Pinkus, "Jonathan Swift, *Gulliver's Travels,*" in *Studies of Major Works in English,* ed. John Orrell (Toronto: Oxford University Press, 1968), 144.

24. I endorse the position widespread in Swift studies that Gulliver's "role is rather to represent all of us," and that "he is the hero as synecdoche rather than exemplar." See Thomas E. Maresca, *Epic to Novel* (Columbus: Ohio State University Press, 1974), 168. The relevant criticism is conveniently summarized in Real and Vienken, *Jonathan Swift,* 48–53.

25. Anthropology is here used not in its narrow meaning of "study of the human race," but in the wider sense of "science of [the nature of] man, or of mankind" (*OED, s.v.*). "Paradoxical" is here intended to mean "contrary to received opinion or expectation," as its etymology suggests.

26. Andrew Carpenter, *The Irish Perspective of Jonathan Swift* (Wuppertal, Germany: Peter Hammer, 1978), 15.

27. Kathleen Williams, *Jonathan Swift and the Age of Compromise* (Lawrence: University Press of Kansas, 1958), 199.

28. For the "Roman model," see Mary Claire Randolph, "The Structural Design of the Formal Verse Satire," *Philological Quarterly* 21 (1942): 368–84, and Howard D. Weinbrot, *The Formal Strain: Studies in Augustan Imitation and Satire* (Chicago: University of Chicago Press, 1969), 59–75; for "satiric scene," see Alvin Kernan, *The Cankered Muse: Satire of the English Renaissance* (New Haven, Conn.: Yale University Press, 1959), 16–21. The same confusion of "utopia" and "satiric norm" is to be held responsible for the assessment of further passages of the *Travels* as "utopian"; see, for example, Dirk F. Passmann, "The Lilliputian Utopia: A Revised Focus," *Swift Studies* 2 (1987): 67–76.

29. Robert C. Elliott, *The Shape of Utopia: Studies in a Literary Genre* (Chicago: University of Chicago Press, 1970), 40. See also Northrop Frye, "Varieties of Literary Utopias," *Daedalus* 94 (1965): 325.

30. *Utopia,* 55, 245–47.

31. See the introduction to *Literarische Utopien von Morus bis zur Gegenwart*

by Klaus L. Berghahn and Hans Ulrich Seeber (Königstein, Taunus: Athenäum, 1983), 16–17. See also Jürgen Mittelstrass, *Neuzeit und Aufklärung: Studien zur Entstehung der neuzeitlichen Wissenschaft und Philosophie* (Berlin: Walter de Gruyter, 1970), 365: "Man muss im Falle der Utopie . . . die Behauptung fallenlassen, man wisse schon, wie ein *bester* Zustand aussähe. Hier genügt es vielmehr, von einem gegenüber dem jetzigen Zustand *besseren* Zustand zu sprechen. . . . Utopien sind Entwürfe, die anzugeben suchen, wie man gemeinsam besser leben kann" ("In the case of utopias, we have to discard the view that we already know what the *best* state looks like. It is sufficient to speak of a *better* state in relation to the present one. . . . Utopias are imagined forms which seek to describe how we may live in a better way"). As a result, I agree with Holger Klein that "for most people living around 1500, including More and the *Utopia*'s target readership . . . life in Utopia would altogether have been a splendid thing, a grand liberation." See "*Ille locus, illud tempus:* Sir Thomas More's *Utopia* and the Pastoral," in *Anglistentag 1998 Erfurt: Proceedings,* ed. Fritz-Wilhelm Neumann and Sabine Schülting (Trier: Wissenschaftlicher Verlag, 1999), 163.

32. What Robert C. Elliott has beautifully formulated for the "utopia" of the Houyhnhnms is equally valid for *Utopia;* see his *The Shape of Utopia,* 60.

33. See also note 21 of this essay.

34. See *Utopia,* 59, 314. See also for the identity of Utopia and England, how "shadowy" so ever, Alistair Fox, *Thomas More: History and Providence* (New Haven, Conn.: Yale University Press, 1983), 56–57.

35. See, for the structure of the talks, *Utopia,* cxxv–cxxix, and R. Bracht Branham, "Utopian Laughter: Lucian and Thomas More," *Moreana* 22 (1985): 23–43, particularly 32–34. Some scholars prefer the phrase "Dialogue of Counsel" for these debates at the cardinal's table.

36. Surtz and Hexter point out that Raphael could mean "the physician of health," suggesting his "role of salvation-bringer." See *Utopia,* 301–2.

37. Ibid., 61, 315–16.

38. Ibid., 61.

39. See also Davis, *Utopia and the Ideal Society,* 46–47; George M. Logan, *The Meaning of More's "Utopia"* (Princeton, N.J.: Princeton University Press, 1983), 53–59.

40. In addition to the notes by Surtz and Hexter, *Utopia,* l–liv, see Paul D. Solon, "Popular Response to Standing Military Forces in Fifteenth-Century France," *Studies in the Renaissance* 19 (1972): 78–111, and in particular, Lois G. Schwoerer, *"No Standing Armies!": The Antiarmy Ideology in Seventeenth-Century England* (Baltimore, Md.: Johns Hopkins University Press, 1974).

41. Augustine, *The City of God against the Pagans,* vol. 2, trans. William M. Green, Loeb Classical Library (Cambridge, Mass.: Harvard University Press, 1963), 4.4.16–17. See also *Utopia,* 321.

42. *Utopia,* 65.

43. William Ellis, *A Treatise on Government: Translated from the Greek of Aristotle* (London: J. M. Dent, 1931 [1912]), 5.

44. See in particular the annotations provided by Surtz and Hexter in their

edition of *Utopia,* 325–36, and passim, as well as the rich material in Richard Marius, *Thomas More: A Biography* (London: J. M. Dent and Son, 1984), 155–57.

45. *Utopia,* 65–67.

46. See Ibid., 69: "Alongside this wretched need and poverty you find wanton luxury."

47. Lawrence Manley, *Literature and Culture in Early Modern London* (Cambridge: Cambridge University Press, 1995), 64; see also T. S. Dorsch, "Sir Thomas More and Lucian: An Interpretation of *Utopia,*" *Archiv für das Studium der Neueren Sprachen* 203 (1967): 352.

48. On the composition of *Utopia,* see *Utopia,* xv–xxiii. I do not agree, however, with the editors' conclusion on the interpretative significance of their results.

49. Logan, *The Meaning of More's "Utopia"*, 17; see also R. J. Schoeck, "'A Nursery of Correct and Useful Institutions': On Reading More's *Utopia* as Dialogue," in *Essential Articles for the Study of Thomas More,* ed. R. S. Sylvester and G. P. Marc'hadour (Hamden, Conn.: Archon Books, 1977), 285–86.

50. In my view, this attitude largely accounts for the well-known "radicalism" of *Utopia.* See, for example, *Utopia,* cv–cxxiv.

51. Ibid., 241–43.

52. Richard Helgerson, "Inventing Noplace, or the Power of Negative Thinking," *Genre* 15 (1982): 106.

53. The quotations from the Surtz and Hexter *Utopia* occur in the following order: 125, 115, 125, 127, 135, 149, 157, 239, 151, 149, 199, 201, 149, 141, 191. This précis is not in any way intended to reflect the sequence of topics in Book 2, which some scholars have found confusing. See, in addition to the Surtz and Hexter introduction to *Utopia,* cxxix–cxxxiv, Jenny Kreyssig, *Die "Utopia" des Thomas Morus: Studien zur Rezeptionsgeschichte und zum Bedeutungskontext* (Frankfurt am Main: Peter Lang, 1988), 3–4. Rather, I have tried to focus on the pairs of related passages in Books 1 and 2.

54. *Utopia,* 245.

55. Raphael's many counterarguments notwithstanding, the fact that things have not yet finally been considered, I think, may explain Raphael's repeated, and to many More scholars irritating, refusal to take up "More's" invitation "to apply [his] talent and industry to the public interest," that is, to turn acting politician; see *Utopia,* 57. See, for example, J. H. Hexter, *More's "Utopia": The Biography of an Idea* (London: Oxford University Press, 1952), 127; David M. Bevington, "The Dialogue in *Utopia:* Two Sides to the Question," *Studies in Philology* 58 (1961): 501, 508–9; and Ed Quattrocki, "Injustice, Not Councilorship: The Theme of Book One of *Utopia,*" *Moreana* 6 (1971): 19–28.

56. For a dissenting view regarding More's initiation of debate, see Peter Nitschke, *Staatsräson kontra Utopie? Von Thomas Müntzer bis zu Friedrich II. von Preußen* (Stuttgart: J. B. Metzler, 1995), 69; see also Jenny Mezciems, "Swift and Orwell: Utopia as Nightmare," *Dutch Quarterly Review* 15 (1985): 93–94. For the quotation above, see Edward Surtz, S. J., *The Praise of Pleasure: Philosophy, Education, and Commission in More's "Utopia"* (Cambridge, Mass.: Harvard University Press, 1957), 199.

57. Anthony Kenny, *Thomas More* (Oxford: Oxford University Press, 1983),

98. The complaint is common; see, in addition to Kenny, Willi Erzgräber, *Utopie und Anti-Utopie in der englischen Literatur* (München: Wilhelm Fink, 1980), 26–28; Fox, *Thomas More,* 60; Bernd-Peter Lange, "Thomas More, *Utopia,*" in *Die Utopie in der angloamerikanischen Literatur: Interpretationen,* ed. Hartmut Heuermann and Bernd-Peter Lange (Düsseldorf: Bagel, 1984), 15, 22.

58. See my summary in "The Dean's European Ancestors," 141–42, in note 20 above.

59. See also Klein, "*Ille locus, illud tempus,*" 160.

60. This is the revised version of a paper I gave at the conference on *Staatstheoretische Diskurse im Spiegel der Nationalliteraturen von 1500 bis 1800,* which was hosted by the Herzog August Bibliothek, Wolfenbüttel, in November 1995. It was subsequently published, in German, under the title "Reisen ins Nirgendwo: Mores *Utopia* und Swifts *Gullivers Reisen,*" in *Staatstheoretische Diskurse im Spiegel der Nationalliteraturen,* ed. Barbara Bauer and Wolfgang G. Müller, Wolfenbütteler Forschungen, no. 79 (1998), 445–68.

7

Swift's Voices

Innovation and Complication in the Poems Written at Market Hill

PETER J. SCHAKEL

Of the twenty-eight months between June 1728 and the end of September 1730, Jonathan Swift spent at least fifteen at Market Hill, the estate of Sir Arthur and Lady Acheson.[1] Swift had been acquainted with Lady Acheson's father, the Right Honorable Philip Savage, Chancellor of the Exchequer of Ireland from 1695 until his death in 1717, and tells Stella about dining with him in London in December, 1712.[2] Sir Arthur entered the Irish House of Commons in 1727, and the invitation to visit Market Hill may have grown out of encounters with Swift in Dublin. Swift wrote to Pope concerning his first visit, of some eight months, "I lived very easily in the country: Sir Arthur Acheson is a man of Sense, and a scholar, has a good voice, and my Lady a better; she is perfectly well bred, and desirous to improve her understanding, which is very good, but cultivated too much like a fine Lady. She was my pupil there . . . ; with that, and walking and making twenty little amusing improvements, and writing family verses of mirth by way of libels on my Lady, my time past very well and in very great order."[3]

The "libels on my Lady" are part of a group of poems written "by Way of Amusement, in the Family of an honourable Gentleman in the North of *Ireland*."[4] Harold Williams groups fifteen of these poems into a section labeled "Poems Relating to Market Hill" (*Poems* 3:845–908), and he notes that "Swift's friendship with Sir Arthur and Lady Acheson was productive of some of his best verse." Williams establishes a precedent by treating the poems as "place" poems. Thus, he notes, "other pieces written during these years at Market Hill, but unrelated to the place, appear elsewhere" (*Poems* 3:847).[5] This editorial decision, pulling the poems about Market Hill from the generally chronological arrangement of the *Poems* and separating them from the other eight or nine poems written at Market Hill, has obscured the importance of the Market Hill visits in the development of Swift's work as a poet. These poems mark a decisive turn in Swift's poetic style and influence the directions his writing took in the years immediately following.

While the poems about Market Hill have received much scholarly attention, the poems written at Market Hill have not been considered as a group.[6] Swift wrote mostly poetry during his months at Market Hill.[7] Apart from *Intelligencer* no. 19 (3–7 December 1728), he wrote little prose there; even his correspondence drops off markedly during his months in residence. He did have the manuscript of *History of the Four Last Years of the Queen* (published in 1758) and two other pieces sent to him (*Corr.* 3:297), but there is no evidence he worked on them. He was, after all, "a very busy Man," occupied with "Planting and Pruning" (*Corr.* 3:296), and generally not in good health, suffering "at least half a dozen returns of my giddiness and deafness, which lasted me about three weeks a piece" (*Corr.* 3:312; also 3:304). He nonetheless had to make time to write verse: "If I do not produce [a lampoon] every now and then of about two Hundred Lines, I am chid for my Idleness" (*Corr.* 3:297). In a letter to Pope on 16 March 1729, he dismisses the results: "I was dwindled to a writer of libels on the lady of the family where I lived, and upon myself" (*Corr.* 3:313). Although on 26 February 1730 he complains to Pope that "I find neither prose nor Rime will come to me as it used" (*Corr.* 3:375), the poems written at Market Hill show confidence, care, and several characteristics that signal new directions in his verse.

Until the Market Hill poems, most of Swift's poetry was largely monophonic. With a few exceptions, he spoke either in his own voice or in the voice appropriate for an historical genre like the celebratory ode or a classical author to whom his own voice was at least in part subordinate. The Market Hill poems, however, place Swift in a social setting that helps to develop the set of conventions for which he has become deservedly famous. Here his poetic performances drew his hosts into the poems with his hosts' own voices, but made more complex by Swift's ventriloquism. Such practice demonstrably complicated both his immediate readers' or auditors' response as well as our own far later response. The social context required that his poems be conversational rather than literary and allude to immediate family events—like Lady Acheson having stepped in dung while on a country walk. In short, the poems written at Market Hill were testing grounds for several devices that Swift would fully mature in later works: assumption of someone else's personal voice; manipulation of readers; and scatological references.

Most significant of these devices is a new way of engaging with his readers. The first step involves developing further an approach he had adopted a few times before, namely the use of his intended initial reader as a speaker in the poem.[8] Such use of the speaker appears in the earliest of the Market Hill poems, "My Lady's Lamentation and Complaint against the Dean" (1728). The poem, in dimeter lines of an iamb and an anapest, or two anapests, is undistinguished apart from the way it causes its initial reader, Lady Acheson, to listen to a representation of her own voice as she reads, the aural equivalent of looking into the proverbial satiric mirror. "She" criticizes both the Dean and herself:

> He comes with his whims,
> I must move my limbs;
> . . . .
> And, say what I will,
> Haul'd up every hill;
> 'Till, draggled and tatter'd,
> My spirit's quite shatter'd,
> I return home at night,
> And fast out of spite:
> For I'd rather be dead,
> Than it e'er should be said
> I was better for him,
> In stomach or limb.
> (*Poems* 3:852–53)

Lady Acheson's initial experience in reading the poem must have been, on the one hand, simultaneous delight and incredulity at hearing an exaggerated reproduction, purportedly in her own voice, of things she had said or thought, or could have been forgiven for thinking or saying, and, on the other, mock-protest that she had not said or thought such things. Swift's letters supply evidence that the poems circulated freely in manuscript and attest to Lady Acheson's appreciation of his efforts: "My Lady . . . shews every Creature the Libels I have writ against her" (*Corr.* 3:298).[9]

Such use of the initial reader as the putative author forces subsequent readers to assess the relationship of the poem's voice to the author and initial reader, a process analogous to that required by the polyphonic *A Tale of a Tub* (1704) but not by most of Swift's earlier poetry. The pre–Market Hill verse typically addresses a universal reader through the author's voice or that of a speaker resembling the author, as for example in

Baucis and Philemon (1708–1709) or these lines from "A Description of a City Shower":

> CAREFUL Observers may fortel the Hour
> (By sure Prognosticks) when to dread a Show'r:
> While Rain depends, the pensive Cat gives o'er
> Her Frolicks, and pursues her Tail no more.
> (*Poems* 1:136)

The reader is concerned with form and content, not the poem's speaker. The author's voice in the poem is appealing, but not complex and does not require the reader's attention. Reaction to the poem by readers who encountered it initially in the *Tatler,* no. 238 (October 1710), is not a significant part of the later reading experience. Similarly, in poems intended for a particular initial reader, such as "To Lord Harley . . . on His Marriage" (1713) or "To Mr. Delany" (1718), the poetic voice is that of a genial familiar author. It was, and is, not significant in understanding or responding fully to the poem.[10] The Market Hill poems, in contrast, do require attention to voice and context. Part of the enjoyment of "My Lady's Lamentation and Complaint" for subsequent readers is imagining Lady Acheson's initial reaction to the poem, as well as listening to the interplay between the voices of the author and the speaker, and at times the speaker's voice supposedly dramatizing the author's:

> He haws and he hums,
> At last out it comes.
>
> What, Madam? No walking,
> No reading, nor talking?
> You're now in your prime,
> Make use of your time.
> (*Poems* 3:854)

Writing personal poems to an identifiable initial reader was not new for Swift; he had done so in personal poems to Stella Johnson and Esther Vanhomrigh, for example. However, beyond the addressee, those poems assumed a general reading audience of anyone who might eventually see the poem in manuscript or in print. Though "My Lady's Lamentation and Complaint" is addressed to a specific initial reader, it also assumes as audience the other occupants of the country house, to whom it was probably read aloud. His awareness of that additional audience creates a further response layer: later readers are led to wonder not just how the addressee responded to the poem, but also how others in the household reacted to it.

The new effect in the Market Hill poems is one Swift capitalized on and developed further. He uses the same technique to better effect in "Lady A—s—n Weary of the Dean" (1728?), where upon first seeing the poem Lady Acheson found herself reading what she would not have said but might have thought about Swift:

III.
After a Week, a Month, a Quarter,
And Day succeeding after Day,
Says not a Word of his Departure
Tho' not a Soul would have him stay.

VI. [IV.]
I've said enough to make him blush
Methinks, or else the Devil's in't,
But he cares not for it a Rush,
Nor for my Life will take the Hint.
(*Poems* 3:860)

Much of the distinctive flavor of the Market Hill poems is achieved through interaction between the initial reader and subsequent readers aware that they are reading a text intended for a specific person incorporated within the poem. We watch Swift expressing what we too feel the lady probably thought, we cannot help feeling the tension the poem expresses, and we then wonder if the tension was genuine or to what degree it was present. Swift makes himself vulnerable in more ways than just the "Tallow Face and Wainscot Paws" and "Beetle-brows and Eyes of Wall" he has the Lady's voice attribute to him; he also risks making himself appear selfish and insensitive. The humor and good-natured tone projected through creation of the Lady's exasperated voice, however, deflect such criticism, and leave one asking if the good company of someone able to achieve such effects and willing to risk such self-denigration would not make ample amends for an extended stay.

All of this is apparent in what could be thought of as paired poems, "A Panegyrick on the D—n, in the Person of a Lady in the North" (1730) and *An Epistle to a Lady, Who desired the Author to make Verses on Her, in the Heroick Stile* (1730?, 1733?), though placement in the Williams and Horrell editions obscures the possible linkage.[11] In "A Panegyrick on the D—n," like the earlier "Lady A—s—n Weary of the Dean," Swift has Lady Acheson hear her own voice, but this time supposedly praising the Dean instead of criticizing him:

My Heart with Emulation burns
To make you suitable Returns;
My Gratitude the World shall know:

And, see, the Printer's Boy below:
Ye Hawkers all, your Voices lift;
A Panegyrick on D—n *S*—.
And then, to mend the Matter still;
By Lady *Anne* of *Market-Hill.*
(*Poems* 3:887–88)

The lady ironically praises Swift as dean, butler, usher, jester, tutor, gardener, dairyman, and architect. The reader enjoys hearing the satirist satirized and appreciates Swift's self-awareness and willingness to acknowledge his own foibles and eccentricities, but also imagines the delight of its initial audience hearing or reading that satire in the presence of the author and the supposed speaker.

In *An Epistle to a Lady,* Swift has Lady Acheson, as a speaker within the poem, ask him to reciprocate, to write a panegyric on her: "Have I nothing then to praise? / . . . / . . . I beg, suspend a While, / That same paultry *Burlesque* Stile: / . . . / SING my Praise in Strain sublime" (*Poems* 2:630–31). The lady evinces the same self-awareness and willingness to acknowledge her own foibles and eccentricities that Swift did in "A Panegyrick on the D—n":

Follies, from my Youth instill'd,
Have my Soul entirely fill'd:
In my Head and Heart they center;
Nor will let your Lessons enter.
(*Poems* 2:630)

The delight of the poem for initial and later readers arises first from irony—the fact that the lady's admissions have been given her by Swift—and then from raillery, backhanded praise leading into what may be genuine instruction, or additional irony:

THO' you lead a blameless Life,
Are an humble, prudent Wife;
Answer all domestick Ends,
What is this to us your Friends?
. . . .
Tho' you . . .
Load our Plates from ev'ry Dish;
This is not the Thing we wish.
Col'nel . . . . . . may be your Debtor;
We expect Employment better.
You must learn, if you would gain us,
With good sense to entertain us.
(*Poems* 2:633)[12]

The Journal of a Modern Lady (1729), which Williams places among general poems of 1729 and not with the Market Hill group, also profits from being considered as a Market Hill poem.[13] Nothing in the poem identifies Lady Acheson as the addressee of the opening lines or signals that it was written at Market Hill; but awareness of an actual initial reader and her presumed reaction upon reading or hearing the poem for the first time are important aspects of the reading experience. When Lady Acheson was given the poem at Market Hill or listened to Swift read it aloud there, the original title, "The Journal of a Dublin Lady," might have led her to expect another poem in her own voice; instead she finds herself addressed directly by Swift and immediately put on the defensive:

> It was a most unfriendly Part
> In you, who ought to know my Heart,
> So well acquainted with my Zeal
> . . . .
> How cou'd it come into your Mind,
> To pitch on me, of all Mankind,
> Against the Sex to write a Satyre?
> (*Poems* 2:444–45)

The accusations are rendered comic by the ironic intervening line—"Zeal / For all the Female Commonweal"—and subsequent lines:

> On me, who think them all so fair,
> They rival *Venus* to a Hair;
> Their Virtues never ceased to sing,
> Since first I learn'd to tune a String.

Regardless of whether Lady Acheson actually set Swift such a topic, or whether he only imputes it to her, he makes her as initial reader an active participant in the reading process: first by accusing her of dictating his subject—"'Twas you engag'd me first to write, / Then gave the Subject out of Spite: / The *Journal of a Modern Dame*"—and then by warning her that "perhaps you may be bit," for "the Guilt is yours" (*Poems* 2:445).

Lady Acheson's experience as she read or heard the poem initially had to have been complex. The title suggests that the poem is a journal, but instead it contains a journal, the journal of a typical modern lady, "The modern Dame" (*Poems* 2:446). Lady Acheson knows that the descriptions in the journal do not apply to herself. After all, Swift would hardly have referred to his host as "the Booby Husband" who sits "In Admiration at her Wit" (2:448). Yet she would also know that the journal is to some extent her journal. Some three years later, Swift writes to Charles Ford that "Lady Acheson . . . is an absolute Dublin rake, sits up late, loses her money, and goes to bed sick" (*Corr.* 4:92). The wording corresponds closely to that of the poem, whether deliberately or not, and indicates that in 1732, at least, Swift saw similarities between Lady Acheson and the Dublin lady he had satirized in the poem. As she read or heard the poem in 1729, Lady Acheson must have felt some uneasiness, wondering to what extent the poem was a serious expression of what Swift thought she was or was capable of becoming. For later readers, awareness that the poem was written at Market Hill and addressed to Lady Acheson raises speculation about reactions to the poem at Market Hill: the household surely enjoyed the humor, but must also have felt a certain ambivalence as they watched for Lady Acheson's response. The poem's initial context, therefore, affects the experiencing of it and complicates the reading process.

The Market Hill context is one of several characteristics which force an active role upon its readers, then and now. The poem requires readers to recognize ironic implications and fill narrative gaps, as in the *Tale of a Tub*-like gap between lines 19 and 20, where readers are forced to provide their own analogies:

> Sooner shall, *&c.*
> [*Here several Verses are omitted.*]
> The Hound be hunted by the Hare,
> Than I turn Rebel to the Fair.
> (*Poems* 2:445)

Readers also are forced to deal with the indeterminacy of the poem's genre, for Swift does not give a clear, stable set of generic conventions with which one can rest comfortably. The modern lady's journal begins at line 36, with the poem as a whole starting off as a personal, conversational poem, similar to "My Lady's Lamentation and Complaint" or "Lady A—s—n Weary of the Dean." It has an unusually dramatic quality for a journal, with a great deal of dialogue; that, together with the reference to "Rake" and the line "Now to another Scene give Place," suggest an affinity to Restoration comedy in form as well as content (*Poems* 2:446, 447). The "train" of allegorized figures (2:448–49) invokes the grand style momentarily (Rogers, 789) and echoes of *The Rape of the Lock* (2:450–53; Rogers, 789) add a touch of mock epic. Thus neither initial nor later reader is allowed to settle into comfortable conventions and assumptions. Instead, the poem forces readers to be flexible and adjust to shifting and unspecified generic codes, just as the interplay between voices does not allow readers to slip into a passive and merely receptive role.

The manipulation of voice and readers in the poems written at Market Hill becomes characteristic of Swift's poems of the early 1730s. Such pieces as "To Mr. Gay on his being Steward to the Duke of Queensbury" (1731) and "On Mr. *P—y* being put out of the Council" (1731) show a similar strength of voice and attention to the poem's initial reader. The techniques initiated at Market Hill are used to stunning effect in *Verses on the Death of Dr. Swift* (1731). It establishes a powerful "I" and its voice moves aggressively to engage the reader; the reader, addressed as "you," is forced to assess from section to section whether to accede to the speaker's controversial assertions, as he or she is expected to do:

> DEAR honest *Ned* is in the Gout,
> Lies rackt with Pain, and you without:
> How patiently you hear him groan!
> How glad the Case is not your Own!
> (*Poems* 2:554)

The interaction between initial and later readers is made more complicated by an implied inversion: setting much of the poem after Swift's death means the actual reader of 1739 had to imagine an "initial" reader experiencing the poem after Swift died. The "initial" reader, paradoxically, is a later reader than the actual reader. Subsequent readers must both determine a satisfactory way of dealing with the complex ironies of the poem and imagine how other eighteenth-century readers experienced lines like these when the poem first appeared and, later, after Swift died: "One Year is past; a different Scene; / No further mention of the Dean; / Who now, alas, no more is mist, / Than if he never did exist" (*Poems* 2:562). *Verses on the Death of Dr. Swift,* in its intricacies and sophistication, lies far beyond the pieces written at Market Hill, but descends from them. Nothing prior to the Market Hill visits prepared Swift for it technically, and it is reasonable to assume that without Market Hill it would not have been written as it was.

The voice of the poems written at Market Hill developed in part through a second characteristic, the conversational style Swift perfected in them. Swift had employed conversational speech previously, but in the personal poems written and read aloud at Market Hill Swift captures the phrases and inflections of those around him more skillfully and blends them into verse forms more effectively than he ever had before. Even in tetrameter quatrains, he succeeds in making Lady Acheson's voice sound colloquial and authentic:

> But you, my Life, may let him know,
> In civil Language, if he stays
> How deep and foul the Roads may grow,
> And that he may command the Chaise.
> (*Poems* 3:860)

Particularly interesting in the poems written at Market Hill is the use of one conversational voice to convey the speech of another voice. We hear Swift's voice conveyed through Lady Acheson's, as in this passage from "My Lady's Lamentation and Complaint":

> And then he grows mild;
> Come, be a good child:
> If you are inclin'd
> To polish your mind,
> Be ador'd by the men
> 'Till threescore and ten,
> And kill with the spleen
> The jades of sixteen,
> I'll shew you the way:
> Read six hours a-day.
> The wits will frequent ye,
> And think you but twenty.
> (*Poems* 3:855)

Some of the finest of Swift's conversational verse appears in "The Grand Question debated. Whether *Hamilton's Bawn* should be turned into a *Barrack* or a *Malt-House*" (1729).[14] It opens with the voices of Sir Arthur and then Lady Acheson, the former laying out the benefits of a malt-house, the latter arguing ineffectually for a barracks. As Nora Crow Jaffe says, however, the poem belongs to the third speaker, the maid Hannah, who shows her mistress how the argument should have been conducted and then spins a fantasy scene describing the visit of a captain from the barracks to Market Hill. Swift molds the anapestic lines to fit perfectly the rhythms of her speech: "Mrs. Harris and Mary the cook-maid distort the lines of verse in their monologues, and the effect of conversation depends somewhat on this artificial device. Swift conveys Hannah's voice within the limits of the anapestic line [and] adapts . . . [the] verse form to the variations in her tone."[15]

> And now my Dream 's out: For I was a-dream'd
> That I saw a huge Rat: O dear, how I scream'd!
> And after, me thought, I had lost my new Shoes;
> And, *Molly,* she said, I should hear some ill news.
> (*Poems* 3:868)

Even more impressive is the layering of voices in this poem, as Swift has Hannah's voice adjust to convey the inflections and character of Sir Arthur, his Lady, and the Captain. Hannah dramatizes in turn each speaker who appears in her fantasy scene. Here is the conversation between Sir Arthur and the Captain—clipped, courtly, and courteous—as Hannah imagines it would take place:

Noble *Captain,* your Servant—Sir *Arthur* your Slave;
You honour me much—the Honour is mine,—
'Twas a sad rainy Night—but the Morning is fine—
Pray, how does my Lady?—My Wife's at your Service.—
I think I have seen her Picture by *Jervis.*—
Good Morrow, good *Captain,*—I'll wait on you down,—
You shan't stir a Foot—You'll think me a Clown—
For all the World, *Captain,* not half an Inch farther—
You must be obey'd—your Servant, Sir *Arthur;*
My humble Respects to my Lady unknown.—
I hope you will use my House as your own.
(*Poems* 3:869)

The initial audience at Market Hill could enjoy the experience of hearing a humorous recreation of their own voices and personalities, exhibited in a fancied scene and situation which satirized and perhaps inverted recognizable traits and attitudes:

Dear Madam, had you but the Spirit to teaze,
You might have a *Barrack* whenever you please:
And, Madam, I always believ'd you so stout,
That for twenty Denials you would not give out.
(*Poems* 3:869)

Later readers are drawn by the voice and narrative strategies to imagine what the audience at Market Hill experienced. Imagining their experience is even more delightful for the following passage, as Hannah's voice and the voice of the Captain created by her imagination make Swift the target of his own satire:

"And Madam, says [the Captain], if such Dinners you give,
"You'll never want *Parsons* as long as you live;
. . . .
"G— d— me, they bid us reform and repent,
"But, Z—s, by their Looks, they never keep Lent:
"Mister *Curate,* for all your grave Looks, I'm afraid,
"You cast a Sheep's Eye on her Ladyship's Maid;
"I wish she wou'd lend you her pretty white Hand,
"In mending your Cassock, and smoothing your Band:
(For the *Dean* was so shabby and look'd like a *Ninny,*
That the *Captain* suppos'd he was *Curate* to *Jenny.*)
"Whenever you see a Cassock and Gown,
"A Hundred to One, but it covers a Clown.
(*Poems* 3:872)

Clive T. Probyn asserts that conversation is the "tonal, structural and ethical focus" of Swift's poetry, but the large majority of the examples he cites are from poems written during and after the Market Hill years.[16] Wonderful examples of the conversational style do appear among the earlier poems, such as "Verses wrote in a Lady's *Ivory Table-Book*" (1698), "Mrs. Harris's Petition" (1701), *An Elegy on Mr. Patrige, the Almanac-maker* (1708), *Part of the Seventh Epistle of the First Book of Horace, Imitated* (1713), "Horace, *Lib.* 2. *Sat.* 6. Part of it imitated" (1714), "Mary the Cook-Maid's Letter to Dr. Sheridan" (1718), and "Stella's Birthday. March 13, 1726/27" (1727). Nonetheless, comparing them to Swift's handling of the conversational style and of dialogue after the Market Hill years shows how much he has improved.

The importance and effectiveness of conversational techniques and the author's voice behind them can be illustrated by comparison of "The Furniture of a Woman's Mind" (1727) with *The Journal of a Modern Lady,* a year or two later. The former is a witty but impersonal list covering many of same topics as the *Journal,* but lacks the presence of the "voice" and awareness of readers and techniques for engaging them fully which developed at Market Hill. Passages of dialogue in the *Journal* capture a remarkable stylistic verve and nipping satire absent in the earlier poem:

> Lord, Madam, you have lost Codill;
> I never saw you play so ill.
> "Nay, Madam, give me leave to say
> "Twas you that threw the Game away.
>
> . . . .
>
> That's not so bad as one that rubs
> Her Chair to call the King of Clubs.
>
> . . . .
>
> "Madam, you have no Cause to flounce,
> "I swear I saw you thrice renounce.
> (*Poems* 2:452)

The direct descendent of that passage is the brilliant dialogue recorded in *Verses on the Death of Dr. Swift:*

> My female Friends, . . .
> Receive the News in *doleful Dumps,*
> "The Dean is dead, (*and what is Trumps?*)
> "Then Lord have Mercy on his Soul.
> "(Ladies I'll venture for the *Vole.*)
> "Six Deans they say must bear the Pall.
> "(I wish I knew what *King* to call.)
> (*Poems* 2:562)

Unlike anything in Swift's earlier verse, the conversational style in the poems written at Market Hill anticipates and prepares for the style not only in *Verses on the Death of Dr. Swift,* but also that to come in the years immediately following. We hear that style in such other poems as "The Day of Judgment" (1731?), "Cassinus and Peter" (1731), *The Beasts Confession to the Priest, Observing how most Men mistake their own Talents* (1732), and *On Poetry: A Rapsody* (1733).

A third convention characteristic of the poems written at Market Hill is attention to scatology. Although frequent in Swift's prose—notably *A Tale of a Tub* and *Gulliver's Travels*—it received little attention in his poetry prior to 1729. Most of the work that has given Swift notoriety was written between 1729 and 1731, but the scatology was introduced by the voice of Lady Acheson a year ealier in the conversational style of the first Market Hill poem, "My Lady's Lamentation and Complaint":

> The girls of the village
> Come flocking for pillage,
> Pull down the fine briers,
> And thorns, to make fires;
> But yet are so kind
> To leave something behind:
> No more need be said on't,
> I smell when I tread on't.
> (*Poems* 3:857)

The device returns in "A Panegyrick on the D—n," again in the Lady's voice, as she describes his prowess as architect, building "Two Temples of magnifick Size":

> Here, gentle Goddess *Cloacine*
> Receives all Off'rings at her Shrine.
> In sep'rate Cells the He's and She's
> Here pay their Vows with *bended Knees.*
> (*Poems* 3:893)

The Lady follows with eighty-nine lines, in elevated style, moralizing on the unnaturalness of confining the goddess Cloacine to cramped and smelly enclosures instead of presenting tributes to her in the open air—as, indeed, "Northern Swains" still do. The lines also reprise the earlier poem's images:

> HITHER by luckless Error led,
> The crude Consistence oft I tread.

Here, when my Shoes are out of case,
Unweeting gild the tarnish'd Lace.
(*Poems* 3:896)

The scatological motif in poems of 1729–1731 may well have had its origin in biographical details, of Lady Acheson complaining of her misadventures in country walking. It is striking that scatology enters Swift's poetry through poems clearly intended to be read by Lady Acheson, and in lines supposedly spoken by her. Since the Lady apparently was not uncomfortable with this motif, Swift may have expected the "scatological poems" to be read and accepted in part as comic and personal works.[17]

The earliest of the scatological group, "The Lady's Dressing Room," could have been written at Market Hill. The Faulkner edition of Swift's works adds "Written in the Year 1730" to the title, and the poem was originally published with "A Poem on Cutting Down the Old Thorn at Market Hill."[18] In that case Lady Acheson may have been its initial reader. At the least it was heavily influenced by the Market Hill poems. It opens in their characteristic conversational style:

Five Hours, (and who can do it less in?)
By haughty *Celia* spent in Dressing;
The Goddess from her Chamber issues,
Array'd in Lace, Brocades and Tissues.
(*Poems* 2:525)

Nothing in the poem identifies an individual initial reader. If it was written at Market Hill, it may have been read to, or passed around to, the group as a whole. There is a strong voice addressing the readers ("The Stockings, why shou'd I expose?") and including them in its choice of details ("The Virtues we must not let pass, / Of *Celia*'s magnifying Glass") (*Poems* 2:527). The poem concludes by forcing readers to assent or not assent with the speaker's dismissal of Strephon's rejection of all women because of his discovery about Celia's bowels:

I pity wretched *Strephon* blind
To all the Charms of Female Kind;
Should I the Queen of Love refuse,
Because she rose from stinking Ooze?
. . . .
When *Celia* in her Glory shows,
If *Strephon* would but stop his Nose;
. . . .
He soon would learn to think like me,
And bless his ravisht Sight to see

Such Order from Confusion sprung,
Such gaudy Tulips rais'd from Dung.
(*Poems* 2:530)

These lines build on the active involvement of readers characteristic of all the poetry written at Market Hill, as they force upon readers the choice of whether to accede or not accede to the speaker's sentiments and his reasons for holding them.

Both *The Journal of a Modern Lady* and "The Lady's Dressing Room" claim to be objective recordings of data, the one a journal transcribing "The Annals of a Female Day" (*Poems* 2:445), the other a "Survey," an "Inventory," of what Strephon found. The modern lady is "almost dress'd by Four" (2:447); Celia spends five hours dressing (2:525). The modern lady bargains over the purchase of lace (2:447); Celia issues from her chamber "Array'd in Lace" (2:525). The *Journal* concentrates on internal characteristics like compulsive gambling, senseless prattle, blatant hypocrisy, superstitious whims, and empty lives; but in attacking hypocrisy it offers a section on externals which anticipates details in the later poem:

Mopsa, who stinks her Spouse to Death,
Accuses *Chloe*'s tainted Breath;
Hircina rank with Sweat, presumes
To censure *Phillis* for Perfumes;

. . . .

And *Rufa* with her Combs of Lead,
Whispers that *Sappho*'s Hair is Red.
(*Poems* 2:449–50)

"The Lady's Dressing Room" starts from the same details: a dirty smock, besmeared armpits, various combs, sweat, dandruff, powder, lead, and stockings "Stain'd with the Marks of stinking Toes" (2:526–27). However, it greatly amplifies these unpleasant details and relates the externals to the human situation in a more sustained way than the earlier Market Hill poem attempts.

If the first half of Strephon's survey connects with Market Hill through *The Journal of a Modern Lady,* the second half has affinities with "A Panegyrick on the D—n." In both the scatology is clothed in classical garb: the "Panegyrick" contrasts the freedom in Saturn's Golden Age to deposit "Ten Thousand [smoaking] Altars" to Cloacine along purling streams and on flowery vales with the latter day confinement to "Cells and Vaults obscene" (*Poems* 3:894–95); "The Lady's Dressing Room" compares Strephon lifting the lid of Celia's "Chest" to Epimetheus opening Pandora's box (2:528). "Vapours" flew out the vent of Celia's chest (2:528); similarly, Lady Acheson bemoans the "unsav'ry Vapours" issuing from the cells and vaults (3:895). The famous allusion to *Paradise Lost* in "The Lady's Dressing Room" ("O may she better learn to keep / 'Those Secrets of the hoary deep!" [*Poems* 2:528]) links this poem to Swift's role as tutor at Market Hill: Lady Acheson in "My Lady's Lamentation and Complaint" complained that, as part of the Dean's reading program for her, she "in an ill tone, . . . murder[s] poor Milton" (3:856).[19]

Of the three other poems usually placed in the group labeled the "scatological poems," "A Beautiful Young Nymph Going to Bed" (1731) has the fewest Market Hill characteristics. Its lack of a strong "voice," conversational style, and conscious engagement of its readers aligns it with "The Progress of Beauty" (1719), rather than other poems of the 1730s. Although its date indicates that "Strephon and Chloe" (1731) was not read at Market Hill, it could well have been: its voice and the conversational style in which the narrative is related would have been well suited for reading at a country house. It requires active engagement by readers, but complicates the reading task by substituting for Lady Acheson a series of mock initial readers: parents ("NOW, *Ponder well ye Parents dear*" [2:587]); young ladies ("SAY, fair ones, must I make a Pause? / Or freely tell the secret Cause" [2:589]); men in general ("Rash Mortals, e'er you take a Wife, / Contrive your Pile to last for Life" [2:593]). Readers, having been offered a number of suggested reading strategies, are left to sort through and reject them and then search for a probably unattainable reading they can find satisfactory. "Cassinus and Peter" (1731) also builds on the Market Hill poems through its use of conversational style and comic dialogue. However, it makes no use of an initial reader and requires little of a reader except readiness to participate in the comic build-up which prepares for the anticlimactic final line.

The poems Swift wrote at Market Hill prepared him for the handling of voice, the engagement with readers, and the intensity of tone which characterize several of his best-known poems written in the following years. Williams's decision about separating some of the poems written at Market Hill from those written about Market Hill regrettably detracts from full appreciation of this interesting group of poems as a whole, and obscures their influence on Swift's development as a poet and on the impressive poems he came to write later.

NOTES

1. See Irvin Ehrenpreis, *Swift: The Man, His Works, and the Age* (Cambridge, Mass.: Harvard University Press, 1962–1983), 3:600–609, 623–27, 666–77,

685–86; and David Nokes, *Jonathan Swift, A Hypocrite Reversed: A Critical Biography* (Oxford: Oxford University Press, 1985), 340–43.

2. Jonathan Swift, *Journal to Stella,* ed. Harold Williams (Oxford: Clarendon Press, 1948), 1:119.

3. *The Correspondence of Jonathan Swift,* ed. Harold Williams (Oxford: Clarendon Press, 1963–1965), 3:311. Cited hereafter as *Corr.* The Williams text inadvertently omitted "Arthur"; it is supplied from *Letters to and from Dr. J. Swift, D. S. P. D. From the Year 1714 to 1738* (Dublin, 1741), 94. I am indebted for this correction and other valuable suggestions to the generous assistance of Professor James Woolley.

4. *The Poems of Jonathan Swift,* ed. Harold Williams, 2d ed. (Oxford: Clarendon Press, 1958), 3:866. Cited hereafter as *Poems.*

5. Joseph Horrell puts fourteen of the poems in a section called "Poems at Market Hill" and treats them as "place" poems: "His subject is the place as well as the inhabitants, and humorous glances at Cooper's Hill and Penshurst show his awareness of the component of 'local poetry' in this society verse." See *Collected Poems of Jonathan Swift,* ed. Joseph Horrell (London: Routledge and Kegan Paul, 1958), 1:161–208, 395. Pat Rogers similarly refers to "the Market Hill group, proper; other works . . . were composed whilst Swift was living with the Achesons, but have no direct link with Market Hill" (*Jonathan Swift: The Complete Poems,* ed. Pat Rogers [Harmondsworth, Middlesex: Penguin Books, 1983], 781). References to Cooper's Hill appear in "Drapier's Hill" (1729): "This Hill may keep the Name of DRAPIER . . . And DRAPIER's vye with COOPER's Hill" (*Poems* 3:875). Glances at Penshurst are more general.

6. On the Market Hill poems, see Maurice Johnson, *The Sin of Wit: Jonathan Swift as a Poet* (Syracuse, N.Y.: Syracuse University Press, 1950), 50–54; Nora Crow Jaffe, *The Poet Swift* (Hanover, N.H.: University Press of New England, 1977), 129–36; Louise K. Barnett, "Fictive Self-Portraiture in Swift's Poetry," in *Contemporary Studies of Swift's Poetry,* ed. John Irwin Fischer and Donald C. Mell, Jr. (Newark: University of Delaware Press, 1981), 101–111; Louise K. Barnett, *Swift's Poetic Worlds* (Newark: University of Delaware Press, 1981), 57–67; Jaffe, "Swift and the 'agreeable young Lady, but extremely lean,'" in *Contemporary Studies of Swift's Poetry,* 149–58; Brian A. Connery, "Self-Representation and Memorials in the Late Poetry of Swift," in *Aging and Gender in Literature: Studies in Creativity,* ed. Anne M. Wyatt-Brown and Janice Rossen (Charlottesville: University of Virginia Press, 1993), 146–49.

7. Approximately forty-six poems can be attributed to the years 1728–1730, more than in any other three year period of his life. Over twenty—and almost all of the best—were certainly or probably written at Market Hill. Two groups account for many of the ones not written at Market Hill: the six poems satirizing Richard Tighe written in 1728 before the first visit to Market Hill, and the five or six poems dealing with Delany's "Epistle to Lord Carteret" written in 1730 between the second and third visits to Market Hill.

8. An early poem which includes the addressee's voice within the work is *Part of the Seventh Epistle of the First Book of Horace Imitated: And Address'd to a Noble Peer* (1712). Harley appears as a character in the narrative Swift borrows

from Horace and speaks lines in it. Part of the pleasure of this poem, like the Market Hill poems, for subsequent readers is imagining the reaction of the initial reader actually listening to his own supposed voice as he first read the poem. "Dan Jackson's Reply" and "Another Reply by the Dean" (both ca. 1718) are written as if by Dan Jackson, but he is not, like the speakers in the Market Hill poems, the poem's primary addressee. In a few cases Swift uses an imagined speaker, as for example the table-book in "Verses Wrote in a Lady's Ivory Table-Book" (1698) or the voice of Apollo in "Apollo to Dean Swift" (1721), but usually the voice heard in the early poems is that of the author.

9. Orrery provides further evidence of Lady Acheson's response as initial reader, and of the Market Hill poems being read aloud, in this case several years later in Dublin. After reading "Death and Daphne" (in manuscript) aloud to Orrery in Swift's presence, Lady Acheson "assured me smilingly, that the portrait of DAPHNE was drawn for herself: I begged to be excused from believing it, and protested that I could not see one feature that had the least resemblance, but the Dean immediately burst into a fit of laughter. 'You fancy,' says he, 'that you are very polite, but you are much mistaken. That Lady had rather be a DAPHNE drawn by me, than a SACHARISSA by any other pencil'" (*Remarks on the Life and Writings of Dr. Jonathan Swift,* ed. João Fróes [Newark: University of Delaware Press, 2000], 168).

10. An interesting contrast to the Market Hill poems is "The Journal" (1721), written during an extended stay—June to October 1721—at Gaulstown House. The poem is about a country house gathering, and "the Dean" is among the characters described. It uses first-person narration, but the speaker is not identified. The voice, thus, seems that of the author. The poem lacks the imaginative range and satirical deftness of the Market Hill poems. For discussion of the poem, see Aubrey Williams, "Swift and the Poetry of Allusion: *The Journal,*" in *Literary Theory and Structure,* ed. Frank Brady, John Palmer, and Martin Price (New Haven, Conn.: Yale University Press, 1973), 227–43.

11. Williams says *An Epistle to a Lady* was begun during one of Swift's visits to Market Hill, then "laid aside, and completed [line 133 on], with some revision of the earlier part, in 1732–3" (*Poems* 2:629). This view has been widely accepted, as Pat Rogers notes, "although it cannot be stated with certainty that any such gap in composition occurred. . . . There is nothing in the second portion which could not have been composed during the Market Hill period" (*Complete Poems* 867).

12. On Swift's use of raillery, see Jaffe, *The Poet Swift,* 20–23, 121–43, and Clive T. Probyn, "Realism and Raillery: Augustan Conversation and the Poetry of Swift," *Durham University Journal,* n.s., 39 (1977): 7, 9–11.

13. *The Journal of a Modern Lady* is found in *Poems* 2:443–53; Horrell places it in his section of "impersonal satires" (*Collected Poems* 1:230–38).

14. See John Irwin Fischer, "Swift Writing Poetry: The Example of 'The Grand Question Debated,'" in *Swift, the Enigmatic Dean: Festschrift for Hermann Josef Real,* ed. Rudolf Freiburg, Arno Löffler, and Wolfgang Zach (Tübingen: Stauffenburg Verlag, 1998), 41–46.

15. Jaffe, *The Poet Swift,* 135.

16. Probyn, "Realism and Raillery," 2.

17. The connection with Market Hill and Lady Acheson seems to support those who argue for reading the poem as comedy. See especially Thomas B. Gilmore, "The Comedy of Swift's Scatological Poems," *PMLA* 91 (1976): 33–41.

18. *The Works of J. S., D.D., D.S.P.D.* (Dublin, 1735), 2:305; *The Lady's Dressing Room. To which is added, A poem on Cutting down the Old Thorn at Market Hill. By the Rev. Dr. S—t.* (London, 1732).

19. The allusion in "The Lady's Dressing Room" is to *Paradise Lost* 2.891. Jaffe (*The Poet Swift,* 134) notes an allusion to *Paradise Lost* 9.782–84 in "On Cutting Down the Old Thorn at Market Hill": "But from the Root a dismal Groan / First issuing, struck the Murd'rer's Ears" (*Poems* 3:850); for an additional parallel, see *Paradise Lost* 9.1001.

8

Anonymity and Authority in the Poetry of Jonathan Swift

MICHAEL J. CONLON

Edward Said's account of relations between the words *authority* and *author* provides a useful introduction to the subject of Swift's authority. The word authority, we hear, points two ways, linking the familiar meanings of power and influence to the concept of the author as one who "originates," begins, or fathers "written statements." Moreover, "*author* is tied to the past participle *auctus* of the verb *augure*." The *auctor* is an "increaser and thus a founder," and *auctoritas* means both "production" and "invention," as well as "right of possession." Finally, it means cause, "continuance, or a causing to continue." Said sums up these meanings in four concepts: "1) that of the power of an individual to initiate, institute, establish—in short to begin; 2) that this power and its product are an increase over what had been there previously; 3) that the individual wielding this power controls its issue and what is derived therefrom; 4) that authority maintains the continuity of its course."[1] Said's definition of the authority and power of the author to control and sustain a piece of writing insists that the writing *originates* with the author. This of course was not always the case. In Swift's lifetime, the idea of the author and his ownership of a work, perhaps for the first time, becomes fully "contingent upon a work's originality."[2] The subject of authority in Swift's writings, therefore, relates directly to the struggles over the nature and disposition of literary property and the creation of copyright.[3]

1.

Swift's sense of his own authority, however, poses a puzzle. He occasionally presents himself as the originator and owner of his writings, an author, he says in an "Advertisement" from 1735, who is known "never . . . in verse or prose to borrow any thought, simile, epithet, or particular manner of style; but whatever he writ, whether good, bad, or indifferent, is an original in itself."[4] It is more typical of Swift, however, either to mock his authority and originality as a writer or deliberately disguise his authorship. In the case of his poetry, we find a "bewildering array of mystifying devices—piracy, pseudo-piracy, clandestine issues, anonymous and pseudonymous works, misattributions and misreadings," which weaken the reader's confidence in Swift's authority.[5] Even in the case of poems in which Swift seems firmly in control, he shows an inclination to delimit the importance of authors, either through the use of parody, which undercuts our conception of an author's authority, or through the use of a range of casual, anonymous forms of writing which favor the ephemeral over the poetical: scribbled notes from a tablebook, edicts and epigrams, predictions, journal entries, libels, receipts, riddles, directions, confessions, verses written on the windowpanes of inns, even lines conceived—according to Swift—while he was asleep.[6] The rhetoric of the poems also shows a tendency on Swift's part either to undermine or mock his authority and creativity. In a remarkable passage in *An Epistle to a Lady* (1734), for example, he responds to the Lady's request for praise in heroic verse with an extended metaphor that compares the impotence of his muse to the premature burst of a failed rocket:

> HAVE you seen a *Rocket* fly?
> You would swear it pierc'd the Sky;
> It but reach'd the middle Air,
> Bursting into Pieces there:
> Thousand Sparkles falling down
> Light on many a Coxcomb's Crown.
> See, what Mirth the Sport creates;
> Sindges Hair, but breaks no Pates.
>
> THUS, Shou'd I attempt to climb,
> Treat you in a Stile sublime,
> Such a Rocket is my Muse,
> Shou'd I lofty Numbers chuse,
> E'er I reach'd *Parnassus* Top
> I shou'd burst, and bursting drop.
> (*Poems* 2:638)[7]

As Judith Mueller points out, in the "sexual advice literature" of Swift's age, "artillery provides a common and obvious metaphor for male virility." In the case of his *Epistle to a Lady,* Swift's "self-portrayal throughout . . . is consistent with eighteenth-century assumptions about the male impotence implied in his image of a dud."[8] The concession that his creative powers are dead recalls a similar and less rhetorical concession he makes years before in his poem "Occasioned by Sir William Temple's Late Illness and Recovery" (ca. 1693). Here, he describes his muse as first a "Malignant goddess" (*Poems* 1:53) and then as a mere delusion or "wild form dependent on the brain" (1:54).

Some years ago the late Irvin Ehrenpreis suggested that Swift avoided asserting his personal authority over his writings out of a kind of emotional impotence: "By assuming a false identity [or no identity]," Ehrenpreis writes, "Swift protects his true, weak self."[9] In this essay, I argue that Swift's ambivalent representations of his authority as a poet reflect not so much a wounded psyche but a deliberate philosophical position regarding the meaning and value of authority. He chooses to be authoritative in the style and originality of his language and chooses not to be an authority in his person. Indeed, Swift's authority often depends on a "self-vacating stance" that he achieves not only through his uses of a persona or through his irony, but also through his performances of anonymity.[10] Swift's anonymity assumes more force and significance than the "original, natural state" or simple absence or lack implied by postmodern formulations of the so-called author function. Rather, when Swift chooses anonymity, he gives it a rhetorical function similar to the function we assign to a Swiftian persona. This conception of Swift's uses of anonymity, moreover, provides an illuminating context for the study of some of Swift's more difficult and problematic satirical poems, in particular his *On Poetry: A Rapsody* (1733) and "A Character, Panegyric, and Description of the Legion Club" (1736).

2.

Several recent studies correct past misconceptions of the rhetorical uses of anonymity in the Renaissance and seventeenth century. Marcy North, in particular, notes the tendency of scholars to perpetuate the "myth that anonymity is predominantly a medieval convention" that declined in the age of print. "Contrary to traditional literary history," she writes, "anonymity did not fall out of use in this environment. [In fact,] the capabilities of the press and the intricacies of the book trade created many new and intriguing occasions for name suppression even as (and partly because) the author's name was becoming more of a commodity on the book market."[11] In Swift's time, poets like Dryden, John Oldham, and the Earl of Rochester found "subtle and important uses for anonymity."[12] Oldham deserves special notice, because he appears to have shared with Swift a contempt for what Oldham calls in the "Advertisement" to his *Poems and Translations* the "Pomp and Trappings of an Author." In "A Satyr Dissuading from Poetry," the ghost of Spenser rebukes the poet for thinking in terms of personal glory:

> *Is it not great and glorious to be known,*
> *Mark'd out, and gaz'd at thro the wond'ring Town,*
> *By all the Rabble passing up and down?*
> So *Oats* and *Bedloe* have been pointed at,
> And every busie Coxcomb of the State:
> The meanest Felons who thro *Holborn* go,
> More eyes and looks than twenty Poets draw:
> If this be all, go, have thy posted Name
> Fix'd up with Bills of Quack, and publick Sham.[13]

Oldham's withdrawal into anonymity and the identifications he makes here between the words "name," "shame," and "sham" anticipate Swift's satire on the debasement of the poet's name in his *On Poetry: A Rapsody*. This satire on the corruption of poetry under the kingship of George II shows the progressive loss of an authentic sense of literary authority. The opening movements of the poem portray a condition in which poets of true genius have no place in a culture that follows the bad example of its king. As the poem's speaker warns the poets of true genius, "*Court, City, Country* want you not" (*Poems* 2:641). The four movements of Swift's *Rapsody* explore and dramatize the complexities of originality and authorship in the kingdom of letters and the corruptions of literature and literary property in the kingdom of George II. In the final movement of the poem, Swift executes a parody of the kind of hollow panegyrics to the king published by the poet laureate, Colley Cibber, demonstrating how Cibber's debasement of the poet's calling damages the authority of all poetry.[14] As Marlon Ross explains, "the ritual of poet laureate is an extension of the state's control of the writer's authority. . . . A poet laureate is not appointed for his skill as a writer, or for his authority as an author, but for his serviceability to the crown."[15] Swift's satire in *On Poetry: A Rapsody* shows how the "rites" of laureateship have superseded the "rights of authors." This condition explains, in part, why Swift so often in his writings chooses to suppress his name and why he opposed legislation that would intrude on his right to anonymity.

In *The History of the Four Last Years of the Queen* (1713; 1758), Swift expresses his opposition to a bill that would require that the "Author's Name and Place of Abode should be set to every printed Book, Pamphlet or Paper." First, Swift objects to such a law on grounds that the "Practice of pious Men, who in publishing excellent Writings for the Service of Religion, have chosen out of an humble Christian Spirit to conceal their

Names"; and, second, he objects after the example of "all Persons of true [original] Genius or Knowledge [who] have an invincible Modesty and Suspiciousness of themselves upon their first sending their Thoughts into the World." Swift goes on to say that while poets and writers "who are Dull or Superficial, void of all Taste and Judgement" have no reservations whatsoever about sending their names into the world, writers of original genius often choose to remain anonymous.[16] These remarks recall the opening lines of *On Poetry: A Rapsody* and its description of the countless proud pretenders to poetry who litter the world with their scribbling and the few original poets who choose to live in anonymity:

ALL Human Race wou'd fain be *Wits*,
And Millions miss, for one that hits.
Young's universal Passion, *Pride*,
Was never known to spread so wide.
Say *Britain*, cou'd you ever boast,——
Three *Poets* in an Age at most?
Our chilling Climate hardly bears
A *Sprig* of Bays in Fifty Years:
While ev'ry Fool his Claim alledges,
As if it grew in common Hedges.
(*Poems* 2:640)

Given the corruptions of the author's authority, Swift, in the case of his *Rapsody* and through most of his career as a poet, suppresses his name, and after the publication of *Gulliver's Travels* (1726) his originality and emerging authority seem almost coterminous with his anonymity. We typically know Swift either by nobody named Swift, a Drapier or an Isaac Bickerstaff, or we know Swift simply by his anonymous presence in a style marked by irony, satire, ambiguity, ambivalence, and double binds. In effect, Swift's authority moves from person to works, and in the two hundred fifty odd years since his death, Ann Cline Kelly suggests, "Swift's authority as a myth grew out of his lack of authority as an author."[17]

3.

Anonymity, authority, and authorship come into sharp focus in one of Swift's last and most violent satires, "A Character, Panegyric, and Description of the Legion Club." The poem, a fantasy of retribution and judgment, expresses Swift's intense anger toward the Irish House of Commons, because its members had voted against abiding by a decision of the Court of the Exchequer in 1722 that validated a tithe of pasturage for the impoverished clergymen of Ireland. "Members of Parliament held their places because they were Church of Ireland men and not Dissenters or Roman Catholics; their own relations were often clergymen; they themselves had been educated by parsons. As Swift saw it, they were demolishing an institution on which their prosperity was founded."[18] While few would challenge the legal grounds for Swift's position, the language of the poem reaches a level of anger and invective that provokes discomfort in readers and elicits questions about the stability of the satirist's judgment and the authority behind it. Readings of "The Legion Club" commonly move immediately to the violence of the poem's language, and speculate on how deeply its expressions of personal malice undermine Swift's credibility and authority. Francis Jeffrey, writing in 1816, characterizes the animated tone of the poem as "ferocious" and occasionally "verg[ing] upon absolute insanity."[19] Years later Harold Williams, describes the poem as an "uncontrolled outburst."[20] More recently, Nora Crow Jaffe, while granting Swift some rhetorical control, argues that "despite [its] restraints and devices, the poem . . . is constantly in danger of erupting into sheer violence."[21] A. B. England agrees but finds the poem's "single mood of unremitting aggression" essential to its unity.[22]

Others insist that Swift controls the language and tone of the poem at all times and authorizes his satire by locating his representation of the Irish Parliament in a matrix of classical and Christian allusions. Swift's club of madmen takes its name from the figure of the unclean spirit in Mark 5:9 who, when asked his name by Jesus, answers, "my name is Legion: for we are many." By this opening allusion and by "his selective use of Virgil and the Bible," Peter Schakel shows, "Swift gains authority for his venomous attack on men who were, in his eyes, guilty of both impiety and injustice. [These] dual sources [classical and biblical] provide a universal standard for the condemnation of corrupt legislators."[23] John Fischer acknowledges Schakel's reading and agrees that Swift's "attack is justifiable and even necessary," but he also insists that we recognize and accept, as well, Swift's "violent excessiveness." He goes on to argue that by its "venomous" force, Swift's poem "represents for us what his long battle with a wicked world has made of him. Cursing and sneering, spurning and lashing, he has become what he portrays himself to be in his poem—the maddest of those mad whom he excoriates."[24]

One approach to the poem, then, insists on the distance between Swift and the Irish House of Commons and invites the reader to join the satirist Swift in his judgment, take the side of God against the godless, and recognize the authority of a substantial body of classical and Christian literature behind Swift's judgment. The other approach renders the poem more reflexive and argues that while Swift's "attack is justifiable and even necessary, it is also finally self-corrupting." The reader in this case is asked to recognize not only the authority behind Swift's judgment of Parliament but also the wisdom of his "painful knowledge of himself."[25] Both approaches, however, proceed from the assumption that Swift's poem embodies a conventional opposition between the satirist, speaking from an unambiguous position of moral authority, and the object of his attack. In "The Legion Club," however, the satirist's moral authority has appeared to many of the poem's readers as unstable, and in order to address that issue I urge that we consider the relationships I have described thus far between Swift's uses of anonymity and his tendency either to vacate his ownership of a work through his use of a persona or confuse his ownership by his use of anonymity.

Virtually all readings of "The Legion Club" discount the ambiguous relationship between Swift and the anonymous speaker who presents himself as a citizen of Dublin. While strolling about the city the speaker comes upon the parliament building, a lofty facade that instantly provokes his anger and resentment. He imagines the Parliament as a house of "Demoniacs" (*Poems* 3: 829) and speculates that Dean Swift may find the place perfectly suited to his plan to provide a house for "fools and mad":

> YET should *Swift* endow the Schools
> For his Lunatics and Fools,
> With a Rood or two of Land,
> I allow the Pile may stand.
> (*Poems* 3:830)

The voice of the poem is the anonymous voice of a representative of the Dublin populace, a voice apart from Swift, but familiar with Swift's reputation and plans, and like Swift, enraged by Parliament's recent actions. The ambiguity in the identity of the poet/speaker is consistent with everything we know about the poem's composition and circulation. Swift first acknowledged the poem and the severity of its language in a letter to Dr. Thomas Sheridan on 24 April 1736: "I have wrote a very masterly poem on the *Legion-Club;* which, if the Printer will be condemn'd to be Hang'd for it, you will see in a threepenny Book."[26] The poem circulated in manuscript without Swift's name, and in another letter to Sheridan on 15 May 1736, Swift pretended not to be the author: "Here is a cursed long Libel running about in Manuscript, on the *Legion-Club;* it is in Verse and the foolish Town imputes it to me."[27] Sheridan indulged Swift's disclaimer and replied some weeks later that "Surely no person can be so stupid as to imagine you wrote the panegyric on the *Legion Club.*"[28]

At least one person, however, immediately recognized Swift's hand in the poem and made marginal annotations to his copy, and in one of these annotations he suggests that Swift had not only authored the poem but also had circulated it in retribution for the actions of Sir Thomas Prendergast, who had singled out Swift's writings for censure in a session of Parliament.[29] Since the poem, in fact, describes Prendergast in such hateful terms as the "Worthy Offspring of a Shoeboy," a "vile Seducer," a perjurer, and a "brib'd Accuser" (3:831), the questions this reader raises, so close to the poem's first appearance in Dublin, challenge the validity and authority of Swift's attack on those members of Parliament he names in his satire. Swift, well aware of his vulnerability to claims of having written a "great libel" on the House of Commons, kept ambiguous his authorship of the poem, acknowledging it to friends like Sheridan, disclaiming it to others. He carries this ambiguity into his relationship to the anonymous poet/speaker of "The Legion Club," who even shares with Swift a relationship with one of the alleged lunatics in Parliament, Dr. Anthony Morgan: "BLESS us, *Morgan!* Art thou there Man?" (3:837). Swift's attitude toward Dr. Morgan before the poem appeared had not been "unfriendly," according to Harold Williams, and the speaker's immediate surprise ("Bless mine Eyes!"), again renders ambiguous the relationship between the anonymous poet and Swift.

This deliberate ambiguity in the poet's identity has a destabilizing effect on the authority behind the poem's satire and parallels the destabilizing of normal categories and differences Swift creates in the poem's opening lines:

> AS I stroll the City, oft I
> Spy a Building large and lofty,
> Not a Bow-shot from the College,
> Half the Globe from Sense and Knowledge.
> By the prudent Architect
> Plac'd against the Church direct;
> Making good my Grandames Jest,
> *Near the Church*—you know the rest.
> (3:829)

The parliament building is physically close to Trinity College, but intellectually, *close* means far away or "Half the Globe from Sense and Knowledge" (3:829). The building rests against the church, but the pun on *against* makes Parliament's closeness a moral remoteness, indeed, an opposition, in the light of Parliament's rejection of the clergy's tithes. Puns challenge settled definitions and categories, and in Swift's writing they frequently signal larger anomalies and ambiguities. The anonymous poet who consigns the members of Parliament to eternal damnation is and is not Swift; the wise Clio the speaker encounters is also disguised as a fool

(3:833). The members of Parliament go by their actual names and they move through an identifiable Dublin world, but as Fischer points out, they also occupy an "allusive landscape" that combines eighteenth-century Bedlam, "classical Hades," and a "Christian hell."[30] The men named in the poem have an existence but they are also "Phantoms, bodiless and vain, / Empty Visions of the Brain" (*Poems* 3:833). If they are the "Empty Visions" of Swift's brain or the anonymous speaker's brain, then where lies madness in the poem and where lies sanity?

"The Legion Club," in other words, creates a disturbing continuity between the madness of the members of Parliament, the anger and violence of the anonymous poet, Swift himself, and the contemporary reader who shares in Swift's anger and takes his side. This deliberate strategy on Swift's part breaks down the conventional opposition between the satirist and the object of his attack. As the poem unfolds, it becomes increasingly difficult to take sides. The authority of Swift's "The Legion Club," therefore, comes from the capacity of its language and Swift's use of anonymity to produce a certain destabilizing effect on its reader that is consistent with and a reflection of the breakdown of civil authority Swift perceived in the behavior of members of the Irish House of Commons. Swift in his anonymity chooses to be authoritative in the style and originality of his language, not in his role as satirist, and this makes it difficult for readers to locate and distinguish all the sources of the poem's violence and rage. At one moment the speaker is calling upon the Devil to take a "Poker fiery-red" and from the roof of the parliament building "Crack the Stones, and melt the Lead; / Drive them down on every Scull" (3:830). But in the poem's last lines, the speaker says rather blandly, "I have seen enough," and proceeds to take "a Pinch of Snuff" (3:839).

These wild swings of tone, together with the ambiguities in the poem's authorship and authority, strike me as perfectly suited to a political climate in which Ireland is facing a crisis of authority, because its Parliament has been "disabled by English placemen and absentee landowners," responsible, in part, for the "economic devastation of the country."[31] Swift's "The Legion Club" appears at a time in Irish affairs when legal authority—the courts had supported the position of the clergy—has given way to self-interest. On a first reading, the poem simply pronounces a curse upon this appalling abuse of authority by the members of Parliament, but in successive readings the poem's language and rhetoric keep challenging us with the difficulties of actually *taking* positions of authority in eighteenth-century Ireland.

In both *On Poetry: A Rapsody* and "The Legion Club," Swift uses anonymity as a source of authorial power. The manuscript of *On Poetry: A Rapsody,* after passing from Mary Barber to Matthew Pilkington to the publisher Motte, and finally, to Lawton Gilliver, first appeared in London on 31 December 1733. Its publication provoked the arrest of Gilliver and Mrs. Barber, but no prosecutions followed. Robert Walpole and his agents recognized Swift's hand in the poem but could not make a case against him. Swift had also instructed George Faulkner to preserve the Dean's anonymity, and in a footnote to the poem in his 1734–1735 edition of the *Works,* Faulkner says: "The following Poem was published in *London,* and *Dublin,* and having been much admired, we thought proper to insert it in this Collection: And although the Author be not known, yet we hope it will be acceptable to our Readers."[32] The people Swift cared about, of course, recognized his hand in the poem immediately, and he achieved the kind of singular authority Ehrenpreis associates with Swift's use of the persona of the Drapier: "his authorship should be ostensibly a secret but covertly told to the world. No enemy could prove he was [the author], and no friend would deny it."[33]

Swift gains another kind of power in "The Legion Club." The action of the poem involves the relocation of the Irish House of Commons from a place of authority to a place for the insane and, eventually, the damned. By narrating that action through the voice of an anonymous Dublin citizen—a citizen Parliament claims to represent—Swift extends the poem's rage from himself to the populace. A similar example of Swift's use of anonymity occurs in "A Satirical Elegy on the Death of a late Famous General" (1722; 1764). The anonymous voices of the poem, echoing from the crowds lining the route of the Duke of Marlborough's funeral procession, bear witness not only to the Duke's actual death but also to the death of his reputation and character:[34]

> Behold his funeral appears,
> Nor widow's sighs, nor orphan's tears,
> Wont at such times each heart to pierce,
> Attend the progress of his herse.
> But what of that, his friends may say,
> He had those honours in his day.
> True to his profit and his pride,
> He made them weep before he dy'd.
> (*Poems* 1:296)

The people who made the Duke's fame now unmake it. Swift uses a similar strategy in "The Legion Club." By expressing the poem's anger through an anonymous voice from Dublin's people, Swift brings a measure of popular authority to his judgment of Parliament that he could not have achieved by simply attaching his name to the poem.

In both poems, Swift takes advantage of the kind of power anonymity could claim in oral cultures. "Anonymity," Virginia Woolf suggests, "was a great possession [because] it allowed us to know nothing of the writer [and] concentrate upon his song."[35] In *On Poetry: A Rapsody* and "The Legion Club," and in other poems like his "Description of a City Shower" (1710), and *An Epistle to a Lady,* or in the great prose satires like *A Tale of a Tub* (1704) or Book 4 of *Gulliver's Travels,* our concentration inevitably focuses on a distinctive discourse that transcends the conventional opposition between the satirist and the object of his attack and draws upon the "power of the anomalous, the ambiguous, [and] the self-contradictory."[36] We have come to identify the name of Jonathan Swift with this distinctive discourse, and his performances of anonymity and pseudonymity, together with a larger body of "paratextual" strategies, are among its significant characteristics.[37] Swift's suppression of his name as the author of a piece of writing, moreover, does not prevent him from fulfilling what Michel Foucault calls the "author function." "The author's name," Foucault says, "serves to characterize a certain mode of being of discourse: the fact that the discourse has an author's name, that one can say 'this was written by so-and-so' or 'so-and-so is its author' shows that this discourse is not ordinary"; indeed, it must be accorded a measure of authority and "receive a certain status."[38] Swift shows us, however, that he can fulfill the author function by disclaiming his authorship, and in many of his finest poems, he earns the freedom of expression, which he describes to John Gay as an "infinity of Space," by vacating that finite space on the page reserved for the poet's name.[39]

NOTES

1. Edward W. Said, *Beginnings: Intention and Method* (New York: Basic Books, 1975), 83. For comment and analysis of Samuel Johnson's definitions of the words *author* and *authority,* see James Gray, "*Auctor et Auctoritas:* Dr. Johnson's Views on the Authority of Authorship," *English Studies in Canada* 12 (1986): 269–84.

2. See Martha Woodmansee, "The Genius and the Copyright: Economic and Legal Conditions of the Emergence of the 'Author,'" *Eighteenth-Century Studies* 17 (1983–84): 431.

3. See Mark Rose, *Authors and Owners: The Invention of Copyright* (Cambridge, Mass.: Harvard University Press, 1993).

4. Reprinted in *Jonathan Swift: The Complete Poems,* ed. Pat Rogers (Harmondsworth, Middlesex: Penguin Books, 1983), 577–78.

5. I take this phrasing from Pat Rogers's introduction to his edition of *The Complete Poems,* 15.

6. Neil Saccamano discusses Swift's uses of parody to undercut the "presumed singularity" and authority of the author in "Authority and Publication: The Works of 'Swift,'" *The Eighteenth Century: Theory and Interpretation* 25 (1984): 254. For Swift's memorandum on "Verses Made in Swift's Sleep," see the note by Pat Rogers in *The Complete Poems,* 879.

7. *The Poems of Jonathan Swift,* ed. Harold Williams, 2d ed. (Oxford: Clarendon Press, 1958), 2:638. Subsequent references to Swift's poetry are to this edition and will be cited hereafter in the text as *Poems* and volume number followed by a colon and page number.

8. Judith C. Mueller, "Imperfect Enjoyment at Market Hill: Impotence, Desire, and Reform in Swift's Poems to Lady Acheson," *Journal of English Literary History* 66 (1999): 53.

9. Irvin Ehrenpreis, *Swift: The Man, His Works, and the Age* (Cambridge, Mass.: Harvard University Press, 1962–1983), 2:331.

10. I take the phrase "self-vacating stance" from Marlon B. Ross, "Authority and Authenticity: Scribbling Authors and the Genius of Print in Eighteenth-Century England," in *The Construction of Authorship: Textual Appropriation in Law and Literature,* ed. Martha Woodmansee and Peter Jaszi (Durham, N.C.: Duke University Press, 1994), 240. See, as well, Brian A. Connery's comments on Swift's "self-conscious struggle with the problem of self-authorization" in "Self-Representation, Authority, and the Fear of Madness in the Works of Swift," in *Studies in Eighteenth-Century Culture,* vol. 20, ed. Leslie Ellen Brown and Patricia B. Craddock (East Lansing, Mich.: Colleagues Press, 1990), 165–82.

11. Marcy North, "Ignoto in the Age of Print: The Manipulation of Anonymity in Early Modern England," *Studies in Philology* 91 (1994): 392 n, 390–91. Robert J. Griffin, in "Anonymity and Authorship," *New Literary History* 30 (1999): 882, argues that anonymity in the eighteenth and nineteenth centuries "was at least as much a norm as signed authorship." Adrian Johns, in *The Nature of the Book: Print and Knowledge in the Making* (Chicago: University of Chicago Press, 1998), 1–57, argues that the early stages of print culture, like the present early stages of the internet, meant for writers like Swift, not consistency, accuracy, and authenticity, but inconsistency, piracy, plagiarism, and countless occasions for name suppression.

12. I take this phrasing from Paul Hammond, "Anonymity in Restoration Poetry," *The Seventeenth Century* 8 (1993): 131. I am also indebted to this essay for Hammond's insights into John Oldham's uses of anonymity.

13. John Oldham, *The Poems of John Oldham,* ed. Harold F. Brooks and Raman Selden (Oxford: Oxford University Press, 1987), 240–41 (71–79).

14. I discuss the poem in some detail in "Original Swift: Anonymity, Parody, and the Example of *On Poetry: A Rapsody* (1733)," *Swift Studies* 12 (1997): 69–79.

15. Ross, "Authority and Authenticity," 243.

16. *The History of the Four Last Years of the Queen,* intro. by Harold Wil-

liams, vol. 7 of *The Prose Works of Jonathan Swift,* ed. Herbert Davis et al. (Oxford: Basil Blackwell, 1951), 105.

17. Ann Cline Kelly, "Swift's Mythopoeic Authority" (paper presented at the Tenth International Congress on the Enlightenment, Dublin, Ireland, July, 1999), 1.

18. Ehrenpreis, *Swift: The Man, His Works, and the Age,* 3:828.

19. Francis Jeffrey, "Review," reprinted in *Swift: The Critical Heritage,* ed. Kathleen Williams (New York: Barnes and Noble, 1970), 322.

20. Harold Williams, introduction to *Poems,* 1:xvi.

21. Nora Crow Jaffe, *The Poet Swift* (Hanover, N.H.: University Press of New England, 1977), 145–46.

22. A. B. England, *Energy and Order in the Poetry of Swift* (Lewisburg, Penn.: Bucknell University Press, 1980), 114.

23. Peter J. Schakel, *The Poetry of Jonathan Swift: Allusion and the Development of a Poetic Style* (Madison: University of Wisconsin Press, 1978), 177.

24. John Irwin Fischer, *On Swift's Poetry* (Gainesville: University Presses of Florida, 1978), 201, 200.

25. Ibid., 201.

26. *The Correspondence of Jonathan Swift,* ed. Harold Williams (Oxford: Clarendon Press, 1963–1965), 4:480.

27. Ibid., 4:487.

28. Ibid., 4:495.

29. See Cyndy Hendershot, "A Contemporary Annotated Manuscript of Swift's Poem 'A Character, Panegyric, and Description of the Legion Club,'" *Notes and Queries,* n.s., 42 (1995): 455–58, and the following annotation on Sir Thomas Prendergast's resentment toward Swift for satirizing his father: "Sir Thomas asserted that the Book [in which Swift satirized his father] deserved the Censure of the House, & some days afterwards acquainted them in an explanation of his former Oration, that he would have punish'd the Author, *if he could have done it by Law*" (456).

30. Fischer, *On Swift's Poetry,* 200.

31. David Nokes, *Jonathan Swift, a Hypocrite Reversed: A Critical Biography* (Oxford: Oxford University Press, 1985), 398.

32. *The Works of J. S., D.D., D.S.P.D.* (Dublin, 1735), 2:433.

33. Ehrenpreis, *Swift: The Man, His Works, and the Age,* 3:317.

34. See the reading of this poem by Charles Peake, "Swift's 'A Satirical Elegy on the Death of a late Famous General,'" *Review of English Literature* 3.3 (1962): 80–89.

35. Virginia Woolf, "Anon," in "'Anon' and 'The Reader': Virginia Woolf's Last Essays," ed. Brenda R. Silver, *Twentieth Century Literature* 25 (1979): 397.

36. I take this phrasing from Fredric V. Bogel's "The Difference Satire Makes: Reading Swift's Poems," in *Theorizing Satire: Essays in Literary Criticism,* ed. Brian A. Connery and Kirk Combe (New York: St. Martin's Press, 1995), 50. For another perspective on the capacity of Swift's satire to move beyond the "bipolar praise and blame pattern," see Dustin Griffin, *Satire: A Critical Reintroduction* (Lexington: University Press of Kentucky, 1994), 37–46.

37. Gérard Genette discusses anonymity as a paratextual device in *Paratexts: Thresholds of Interpretation,* trans. Jane E. Lewin (Cambridge: Cambridge University Press, 1997), 37–46.

38. Michel Foucault, "What Is an Author?" trans. Josué V. Harari, in *Textual Strategies: Perspectives in Post-Structuralist Criticism,* ed. Josué V. Harari (Ithaca, N.Y.: Cornell University Press, 1979), 147.

39. On 20 November 1729, Swift writes to John Gay that "as Poets in their Greek Name are called Creators, so in one circumstance they resemble the great Creator by having an infinity of Space to work in." See *Corr.,* 3:360.

9

John Barrett, "The Whimsical Medley," and Swift's Poems

JAMES WOOLLEY

Once the great eighteenth-century editions of Swift's works effectively established the canon of his poems, additions continued to be proposed. Attributers such as Thomas Sheridan the younger, John Nichols, John Barrett, Walter Scott, William Wilde, and Elrington Ball were motivated variously by a love of the chase; by documentary discoveries; by the reasonable assumption that, particularly for years of dearth, Swift must have written poems that had not been identified; by evidence that some poems Swift wrote had been lost; by the desire to aggrandize unattributed poems; and by the desire to have every bit of Swift's writing.

John Barrett was driven by all these motives. His *Essay on the Earlier Part of the Life of Swift* was published by John Nichols in 1808, both separately and as part of Nichols's nineteen-volume edition of Swift.[1] Barrett, who printed about forty new poems putatively by or related to Swift, drew his evidence almost entirely from a three-volume manuscript miscellany that had been in the Trinity College Dublin Library for forty years.[2]

Before Barrett, "The Whimsical Medley" was neglected by Swift scholarship, but it has since been revisited many times: by scholars in quest of new documentary evidence on Swift as well as by Frank Ellis for the Yale *Poems on Affairs of State,* by Andrew Carpenter for his anthology of verse from eighteenth-century Ireland, by Robert Hogan for his edition of Thomas Sheridan's poems, and others.[3] In Swift studies, "The Whimsical Medley" has acquired something of a mystique; Harold Williams gives it pride of place in his bibliography of Swift manuscripts and calls it "extremely valuable."[4] With future researchers, Swiftian and otherwise, in mind, I wish here to set out the evidentiary value of Barrett's now seldom-read book and, more importantly, the evidentiary value of the manuscript he relied on.

1.

John Barrett is still remembered as Jacky Barrett, one of TCD's fabled eccentrics.[5] That he was not only or even primarily an eccentric, however, is suggested by his having accumulated some of TCD's highest academic distinctions and having been elected to most of the university's offices of trust and responsibility. He was at various times Archbishop King's Lecturer in Divinity, Professor of Oriental Languages, Regius Professor of Greek, Erasmus Smith Professor of Hebrew, Senior Fellow of TCD, a member of the Board, vice provost, registrar, librarian, keeper of the museum, auditor, bursar, and senior dean.[6] Recent estimates regard him as an "outstanding" librarian and the author of "scholarship [that was], if at times unbalanced, profound."[7]

He wrote an early original study in comparative religion;[8] and he recovered, from a palimpsest manuscript in the College library, an important sixth-century text of the Gospel of Matthew now known as Codex Dublinensis.[9] By the time he turned his attention to Swift, he thus had already established an impressive scholarly reputation, and in the process he had experienced the pleasure of discovering significant scholarly evidence in his own university library.

Using TCD manuscripts, Barrett hoped to demonstrate that Swift's characteristic satire had its first flowering during his college years. Barrett was energized by a letter from Samuel Richardson to Lady Bradshaigh published in 1804, in which Richardson reported having been told that Swift had been expelled from TCD.[10] The expulsion was said to be for writing a libelous tripos, a sort of academic farce in verse and prose, both Latin and English, performed as part of the 1688 commencement festivities. Its text is preserved in "The Whimsical Medley": "A Tripos or Speech Deliver'd in the University of Dublin att a Com̃encem^{t} held there The 11th of July 1688 by Mr John Jones then Batchel^{r} of Arts afterwards D:D." Although Barrett, adept in the mysteries of the TCD muniments, was able to disprove that Swift had been expelled or otherwise disciplined for the tripos in question, he found that the culprit actually punished for writing the tripos, John Jones, was Swift's close acquaintance in college. Without an independent reason to think Jones was capable of writing such a piece, and asserting "that it conveys [Swift's] own ideas clothed in his own style and language," Barrett concluded that Swift must have written it for him.[11] On that confident if dubious conjecture, Barrett found great significance in "The Whimsical Medley," from which he printed the full text of the tripos and, seemingly as an afterthought, many other poems he thought were Swift's.

By saying baldly that Swift wrote the tripos, Barrett seriously overstated his case and drew sharp criticism from reviewers and later scholars.[12] As Ball, Williams, and at greater length Mayhew judiciously explain, the tripos was a dramatic text composed and spoken by several persons, with Jones evidently presiding as the moderator or interlocutor.[13] If Swift had some role in this project—and he may have—it is now impossible to identify. Barrett, Nichols, and Scott print the complete text of the tripos; Williams includes five verse excerpts.

Barrett's book on Swift was edited for John Nichols—assembled, really—by Edmond Malone. Malone, by 1808 one of the most distinguished living Shakespeare and Dryden scholars and himself an Irishman and Trinity graduate, was probably more willing than most to take an interest in the minutiae of Swiftian inquiry.

Over a period of several months in 1808, Malone received Barrett's packets containing his biographical research findings and interpretations thereof as well as the texts of the putatively Swiftian works. As time passed, Barrett considerably expanded his first submission, a brief essay "Concerning the Censure Passed on Ion. Swift D. S. P. D.," into a forty-eight-page manuscript.[14] As requested, he also provided Malone with several supplementary bits of evidence and argumentation. From Barrett's letters to Malone, which survive in the Forster Collection at the Victoria and Albert Museum, and from the Malone papers in the Bodleian, it is not difficult to see what happened. At the prompting of his and Barrett's mutual friends Andrew Caldwell and Michael Kearney, Malone proposed and Nichols agreed that Barrett submit for publication his arguments that Swift composed the tripos. During the back-and-forth between Malone and Barrett, Barrett subsequently added the texts of other "Whimsical Medley" poems that he ventured, confidently or diffidently but—in the judgment of later scholars—almost always unpersuasively, to attribute to Swift.[15] By contrast, no one doubts the authenticity of Barrett's other addition, a substantial exchange of informal verse among Swift, Sheridan, Delany, and others.

Malone cobbled together Barrett's disconnected submissions, refined his "colloquial" style, and added various other things, including two important Swift letters and Swift's marginalia to Burnet's *History of His Own Times*.[16] For good measure, Nichols added two of his own doubtful attributions to the mix and printed the book in November 1808.[17] From a draft of a few pages, Barrett's project expanded to the 232-page book we have today.[18] Malone's strong inclination to report the detailed results of documentary research, his interest in stamping out received falsehoods (in Barrett's case, the story reported by Samuel Richardson), and his tolerance for disconnected narrative would have made him sympathetic to Barrett's methods and manner—too sympathetic for Barrett's own good.[19]

2.

Even so, Nichols seems, via Malone, to have expressed uneasiness about some of Barrett's attributions to Swift. We may infer as much from Barrett's accommodating reply to one of Malone's lost letters to him:

> I am fully satisfied that there cannot be a better Judge of what pieces are probably Swift's than is Mr Nichols: and to his and your Opinions I am always ready to yield any Ideas I might have entertained on such Subjects. The reasons why I suspected Swift to be the Author of them were these: That they were very much of a local Nature, relating to persons and transactions with which Swift was (or could have been) acquainted; and that they belonged to Times, (viz. from 1700 to 1710) in which we have scarcely any thing proceeding from Swift's Pen, altho we know how very active he was at writing and that upon very trivial Occasions.[20]

As this comment suggests, Barrett's attributions consist mainly of surmise and conjecture; one poem "is, perhaps, by Swift," but no reason is given.[21] In short, despite Barrett's own undoubted expertise in humanistic scholarship and despite the editorial supervision of Malone and Nichols, the rightness of Barrett's attributions depends less upon the reasoning of the attributer than upon the quality of the source upon which he, as sometime TCD librarian, had so ample an opportunity and so strong an inclination to draw.

To say whether Barrett's many attributions to Swift are credible, and indeed whether "The Whimsical Medley" might contain more Swift poems that he missed, we would want, ideally, as with any miscellany, to ask when, where, by whom, from what sources, and for what purposes it was compiled. Did the sources have any special authority? Was the transcription accurate? Did the collection serve any particular aesthetic or ideological purposes? Did it present any particular sort of authors or works? Systematic answers to these questions are well beyond the scope of this essay, but examination of the "Medley" texts of those poems already otherwise confidently attributed to Swift—poems, for example, that are printed in Swift's *Miscellanies in Prose and Verse* (1711) and its 1713 reprints—at least permits some hypotheses about the authority and textual accuracy of "The Whimsical Medley."

The character of the manuscript is well indicated by its full title:

The Whimsical Medley.
or
A Miscellaneous Collection
of severall Pieces in Prose & Verse
some Latin, most English, being
an Agreeable Variety of Satyr and
Elogy, Epigram & Sonnet, Fable
and Ballad, Lampoon and
Pasquinade.
To which is Added an
Appendix
of the same Nature with what
went before, Good, bad, and
Indifferent Just as it happens, to
Chime in with the Reader's
Humour and Opinion.

The "Medley" includes a generous assortment of verse riddles or "enigmas." It also features songs, toasts, political verse, epitaphs, some mildly bawdy verse, and some family poems. Though there is an interesting selection of poems from Ireland, the contents are largely English and reflect an English milieu, usually that of London but sometimes Oxford, Bath, or Tunbridge Wells. There is no organization by genre, author, or chronology, but the great majority of the pieces are from the reigns of William and Mary and of Anne, with the latest poem apparently being from 1719.[22]

Contrary to the claim in the TCD catalog of manuscripts, "The Whimsical Medley" does *not* include "most of the ephemeral poems of the period."[23] It actually includes only a fraction of the poems in Margaret Crum's bibliography of manuscript verse in the Bodleian and only a fraction of the poems listed in David Foxon's bibliography of separately published verse for the period the manuscript covers.[24] On the other hand, only about one-ninth of all poems in "The Whimsical Medley" are found in Crum, and only about one-ninth, but largely a different one-ninth, are found in Foxon. If the eighteen "Whimsical Medley" poems Frank Ellis collated for volumes 6 and 7 of the Yale *Poems on Affairs of State* are a representative sample, only about half of the "Medley" poems are taken from printed sources; the compiler must have copied the rest from manuscript sources.[25] Even if "The Whimsical Medley" preserved no poems by Swift, it would still be important as a source of poem texts from its period.

From internal evidence, "The Whimsical Medley" was formed about 1719 by Theophilus Butler, Lord Newtown Butler in the Irish peerage.[26] The manuscript, 1,272 pages in all, is a fair copy of more than 850 poems and over 30 prose selections, all written out in Newtown Butler's very characteristic hand.[27] Beyond the world of Swift studies, Newtown Butler is known, if at all, for the shelves still to be seen in St. Ann's Church, Dublin, from which, thanks to his bequest, there was a weekly distribution of loaves of bread to the poor.[28] A direct descendant of one of the Ulster planters, Theophilus Butler was the eldest son of Francis Butler, a substantial County Cavan landowner, member of Parliament, book collector, and portrait painter to whom John Dunton elaborately dedicated his *Dublin Scuffle* (1699).[29] From Theophilus's childhood, he held the profitable office of Clerk of the Pells.[30] At TCD, he and his brother Brinsley quite possibly knew Swift, but the brothers did not take degrees at Trinity, probably because the Williamite war intervened.[31]

In London, while Butler was still in his twenties, he was one of the "Persons of Quality or Gentlemen of Note" whom the Musical Society elected stewards for the year 1697 and who claimed the merit of having for £40 commissioned Dryden to write his great St. Cecilia's Day ode, "Alexander's Feast."[32] The St. Cecilia's Day feast sponsored by the Musical Society was reputed "one of the genteelest [occasions] in the world"—so said the *Gentleman's Journal;* and that the young Irishman had assumed a leadership role in such an important London event is a clue to his social standing, literary and artistic interests, and personal charm.[33]

In the *Journal to Stella,* Swift refers to Theophilus as "Ophy" Butler, a nickname that may well date from their college days together at TCD. Also from the *Journal,* we learn that Swift was in the habit of playfully (sardonically?) calling Ophy's wife Emilia "my mistress," and the use of this bantering language with Esther Johnson might suggest that she also, in her early years in Dublin, had been on familiar terms with Butler.[34] Not only that, but Emilia was a cousin of Swift's great friend Charles Ford—perhaps a better reason for Swift's and the Butlers' paths to cross. One might have supposed that they were on sufficiently friendly terms to permit Butler access to some of Swift's unpublished writings for "The Whimsical Medley."

During Swift's political heyday in London, however, it seems likely, as Ball says, that Swift and Butler were driven apart by politics.[35] After his father died in 1702, Theophilus had taken a seat in the Irish Parliament. In 1710 he was appointed as well to the Irish Privy Council, a relatively unusual distinction for a commoner and one that suggests his great value to the Whig government.[36] In fact, the "Medley" includes anti-Harley verse and anti-*Examiner* verse.[37] In a memorandum to Harley rating the Irish privy councilors for their politics, Swift called Butler "very bad, and very insignificant" and recommended that he be removed—to no avail.[38] As early as 1707, he had been thought worthy of promotion to the House of Lords, and Archbishop King recommended him for a peerage in 1715, at a time when the government found it necessary to create eleven new lords in order to assemble a working majority. King commended him for having "under[gone] the displeasure of the late [Tory] ministry, by opposing them in every Vote both in Parlmt and Council."[39] In the House of Lords, Newtown Butler attended constantly until about 1721, never taking the lead on big, controversial issues and never signing a protest.[40]

Under such conditions, Swift and Butler probably parted ways. The main sign of continuing contact between them is that the Newtown Butlers' beloved servant Ann Brent, later Ann Ridgway, was the daughter of Swift's housekeeper Jane Brent.[41] In the "The Whimsical Medley" Newtown Butler takes no particular interest in Swift: he includes only eleven of Swift's previously published poems.[42] The real question, in fact, is how, with no particular inclination to collect Swift's verse, Newtown Butler was in a position to copy into his manuscript his most interesting and salient addition to the Swift canon, the forty-four-poem section that he entitled "A Collection of several Pieces Which Occasionally Pass'd between Dan: Jackson, Tom: Sheridan[,] Pat: Delauny [=Delany], G: Rochfort, and D^{r}. Swift." These rambunctious poems are by their nature private, not designed for wide circulation. Though outside the mainstream of Newtown Butler's collecting habits, they echo some of the macaronic jollity that he chose to preserve in the 1688 tripos and some of the delight in wordplay that he also chose to preserve in copying into his miscellany nearly sixty verse riddles.

Newtown Butler may have gotten copies of the "Collection of Several Pieces" from Ann Brent, whose mother, as Swift's housekeeper, had the key to the desk where he kept his papers.[43] Another possibility is that Charles Ford and his cousin Lady Newtown Butler served as the conduits for this material. Yet another possible source is Sheridan. Although the nature and extent of ties between Sheridan and Newtown Butler are obscure, Lady Newtown Butler and Newtown Butler's younger brothers Brinsley and James are among the subscribers to Sheridan's *Ars Pun-ica* (Dublin: Carson, 1719), and "The Whimsical Medley" collects the prologue from a performance of *Julius Caesar* at Sheridan's school in 1718 as well as a prologue and epilogue from another of Sheridan's productions.[44] Be that as it may, for many of the "Several Pieces," the "Whimsical Medley" provides our only early text, and we must be grateful to Newtown Butler for having preserved this body of writing that, nearly two hundred years after Barrett, critics are still learning how to talk about and editors are still learning how to edit.

3.

Presumably all copied from the same cache of manuscripts, each poem in the "Collection of Several Pieces" was unpublished at the time Newtown Butler compiled "The Whimsical Medley." The list below shows how many of these poems would be lost to us if it were not for his compilation. Some, marked "*1735*" in the list, were later published, with others of the same sort, in *Vol. IV. of the Miscellanies Begun by Jonathan Swift, D.D. and Alexander Pope, Esq.* (Dublin: Fairbrother, 1735). John Irwin Fischer has suggested that Fairbrother's source was Thomas Sheridan.[45] Other poems, marked "*1745*" in the list, were first published in *Miscellanies. The Tenth Volume. By Dr. Swift* (London: R. Dodsley, 1745); yet others, marked "*1789*," were first published in *Miscellaneous Pieces, in Prose and Verse. By the Rev. Dr. Jonathan Swift . . . . Not Inserted in Mr. Sheridan's Edition of the Dean's Works* (London: Dilly, 1789). The *1745* and *1789* items also, Fischer suggests, derive from a manuscript collection that was formed by Thomas Sheridan (in part out of materials that Swift gave him) and that his son, Swift's biographer, released for publication.[46] Two poems first appeared in Faulkner's 18° edition of Swift's *Works*, vol. 10 ("*1762*"). From the following list, it will be evident that, unlike Barrett, later editors have found fault with Newtown Butler's, or his source's, ordering of the poems. Page references are to volume 3 of "The Whimsical Medley," with cross-references to Harold Williams ("*Poems*") and Pat Rogers, or other modern editors if Williams does not edit the poem.

page	
331	"Dan: Jackson's Picture by Pat: Delany." *1735, 1745; Poems,* 3:990–91; not in Rogers
331	"Another [picture of Dan Jackson] by Tho: Sheridan." *1735; Poems,* 3:991; not in Rogers[47]
332	"Another Picture of Dan:" ("Clarissa draws her Scissars"). *1735, 1745; Poems,* 3:992; not in Rogers
332	"Another [picture of Dan Jackson] by G: Rochfort" ("Dan's evill Genius"). *1735, 1745; Poems,* 3:992; not in Rogers
332	"Another" [picture of Dan Jackson] ("You that Gape"). *1735; Poems,* 3:994; not in Rogers
333	"The Song" ("My time O ye Grattans was happily spent"). *1735;* presumably by Sheridan; Barrett, 170; not in *Poems;* not in Rogers; see Hogan, 92–93, 292
333–34	"In Vindication of Poor Dan:'s Picture" ("Three merry Lads

with Envy stung"). *1735, 1745; Poems,* 3:994; not in Rogers

335 "Merry Dan, as tis fitting / To Sheridan sendeth greeting" [title corrected by Williams to "Answer by Dr. D——ny"]. *1735, 1745; Poems,* 3:997–98; not in Rogers

336–38 "Answer" [to "Merry Dan, as tis fitting"]. *1735, 1745; Poems,* 3:1000–1001, 998–1000; not in Rogers

338–39 "The Reply" [to the "Answer" to "Merry Dan, as tis fitting"]. *1735, 1745; Poems,* 3:1003–4; Rogers, 183–85, 684–85

340 "To Tho: Sheridan." *1735; 1745; Poems,* 3:1002; Rogers, 185, 685

340–41 [untitled] ("To You Victorious and brave"). *1735; 1745; Poems,* 3:1005; Rogers, 186–87, 685

341 [untitled] ("Poor Sherry inglorious"). *1735, 1745; Poems,* 3:1004; Rogers, 186, 685

342 "The Pardon." *1735; Poems,* 3:1006–7; not in Rogers

342–44 "The Last Speech and Dying Words of Daniel Jackson." *1735; Poems,* 3:1008–10; not in Rogers

344–45 "Dean Swift to Tho: Sheridan." *1735; Poems,* 3:987–89; Rogers, 178–79, 681–82

345 "Tho: Sheridan to Dean Swift." *1735, 1789.* First published in *A Riddle by Doctor R——fe* [Dublin, 1726?] (Foxon S899). *Poems,* 3:971–72; not in Rogers

346 "Dean Swift to Tho: Sheridan." *1735, 1789.* First published in *A Riddle by Doctor R——fe* [Dublin, 1726?] (Foxon S899). *Poems,* 3:972–73; Rogers, 171, 676

346–47 "To the Dean of St Patricks." *1789; Poems,* 3:973–74; not in Rogers

347–48 "The Dean of St Patrick's to Tho: Sheridan." Barrett, 148–49; *Poems,* 3:975–77; Rogers, 171–73, 676–77

349 "To the Dean of St. Patricks" [address at end used as a title]. Barrett, 150–51; *Poems,* 3:977–78; not in Rogers

350–51 "The Dean to Tho: Sheridan." Barrett, 151–53; *Poems,* 3:978–79; Rogers, 174–75, 678–79

351–52 [untitled] ("Delany reports, and he has a shrewd Tongue"). Seemingly first published in Faulkner's 18° edition of Swift's *Works,* vol. 8 (1762). Listed by Barrett (153) but not printed, since it had already been incorporated into Nichols's edition. *Poems,* 3:966–68; Rogers, 173–74, 677–78

352–53 “To the Dean of St. Patrick’s.” Barrett, 153–54; *Poems,* 3:969; not in Rogers

353 [untitled] (“Oft have I been by Poets told”). Barrett, 154; *Poems,* 3:970; not in Rogers

354–55 [untitled] (“Deliciae Sheridan, Musarum dulcis Amice”). First published in Faulkner’s 8° edition of Swift’s *Works,* vol. 2 (1735); reprinted in *1735.* Listed by Barrett (155) but not printed, since it had already been incorporated into Nichols’s edition. The “Whimsical Medley” text differs significantly from Faulkner’s. *Poems,* 1:211–14; Rogers, 569, 905

355 [untitled] (“Ad Te, doctissime Delany”). Barrett, 155–57; not in *Poems;* not in Rogers; see Hogan, 71–72, 274–76

356–57 [untitled] (“Vivitur parvo male, sed canebat”). Barrett, 157; not in *Poems;* not in Rogers; see Hogan, 69–71, 274–76

359 “To the Dean of St. Patrick’s.” Barrett, 158; not in *Poems;* not in Rogers; see Hogan, 78–79, 281

360–61 “Palinodia Horat: Od: 16: Lib: 1.” First published in Faulkner’s vol. 16 of Swift’s *Works* (8°, 12°, and 18°, 1767). Not in Barrett (previously included in Swift’s works); not in *Poems;* not in Rogers; see Hogan, 88–90, 288–90

361–62 “To the Dean of St. Patrick’s.” Barrett, 159; not in *Poems;* not in Rogers; see Horrell, 1:298[48]

362 “To Tho: Sheridan.” Barrett, 160; not in *Poems;* not in Rogers; see Horrell, 1:298–99

363 [untitled] (“I Like Your Collyrium”). Barrett, 161; not in *Poems;* not in Rogers; see Hogan, 75–76, 277–78

363–64 [untitled] (“My Pedagogue Dear I read with surprise”). Barrett, 162; not in *Poems;* not in Rogers; see Horrell, 2:299–300

364–65 “To Tho: Sheridan.” Barrett, 162–63; *Poems,* 3:980–81; Rogers, 175–76, 697 (as presented in “The Whimsical Medley,” the English and Latin parts seem to be two separate poems).

366 [untitled] (“Perlegi Versus versos, Jonathan bone, tersos”). Barrett, 164; *Poems,* 3:981–82; not in Rogers

366–67 “To the Revd. Mr. Daniel Jackson[,] to be humbly presented by Mr. Sheridan in Person, with Respect, care and Speed[.] To be deliver’d by and with Mr. Sheridan.” *1762.* Listed by Barrett (164) but not printed, since it had already been incorporated into Swift’s works. *Poems,* 3:1010–12; not in Rogers

367 P:S: ("Lean Tom: when I saw him last week on his horse a-wry"). *1762*. Listed by Barrett (165) but not printed, since it had already been incorporated into Swift's works. *Poems,* 3:1012; not in Rogers

367–68 [untitled] ("A highlander once fought a Frenchman at Margate"). Barrett, 165–66; *Poems,* 3:983–84; not in Rogers

368–69 [untitled] ("Tom for a Goose You keep but base Quills"). Barrett, 166–67; *Poems,* 3:982–83; Rogers, 176–77, 679–80

369–70 [untitled] ("I can't but wonder Mr. Dean"). Barrett, 167; *Poems,* 3:1018–19; not in Rogers

370 [untitled] ("Poor Tom wilt thou never accept a defiance"). Barrett, 168; *Poems,* 3:1019; Rogers, 200, 692

370–71 "A Prologue to a Play perform'd at Mr. Sheridan's School Spoke by One of his Schollars." Barrett, 168–69; not in *Poems;* not in Rogers; see Hogan, 105, 298–99

371 "The Epilogue [to a Play perform'd at Mr. Sheridan's School]." Barrett, 169–70; not in *Poems;* not in Rogers; see Hogan, 105, 298–99

Unlike this "Collection of Several Pieces," most "Whimsical Medley" verse is on public (political or social) topics and without authorial attribution. Newtown Butler draws this material from a wide range of sources, as can be seen from the following listing of the previously published Swift poems that he included. He seldom mentions that these poems are by Swift, whether because he did not know, did not care, or thought that it went without saying. The list also shows that for this material, he almost never drew on manuscript sources, perhaps out of a sense that if one had a printed text, there was no particular point in getting and keeping a manuscript. From the evidence of paper and of the compilation of the manuscript table of contents inserted into volume 1, I believe that Newtown Butler compiled the "Whimsical Medley" in this order: volume 1, volume 2, appendix to volume 1, appendix to volume 2, volume 3, and appendix to volume 3. I therefore present the following listing in the same order, showing that he gathered the Swift materials at different points (whimsically?) in his compiling effort.

1:102 "On a Celebrated Beauty. Mrs. Lloyd" [="On Mrs. Biddy Floyd"]: One of Swift's most popular poems in his own lifetime, many times reprinted and with many manuscript copies. Newtown Butler's text probably has a manuscript source, closely related to

	the text in *The Works of the Right Honourable the Earls of Rochester, and Roscommon. . . . The Third Edition. To Which Is Added, A Collection of Miscellany Poems. By the Most Eminent Hands* (London: Curll, 1709), vol. 2. ESTC T95392. *Poems,* 1:117–18
1:238–42	"The Seavent[h] Epistle of the First Book of Horace Imitated and Address'd to a Noble Lord." Text from the Dublin edition, Foxon S894. *Poems,* 1:170–75
2:323–24	"The Description of a Citty Shower." Probably taken from *Tatler* 238, either from one of the editions of the original halfsheet (17 October 1710) or from any of several reprinted collections. *Poems,* 1:136–39
2:368–69	"To Their Excellencies &—The Humble Petition of Frances Harris, / Who must Starve, and die a Maid if it miscarries." Taken from *The Works of the Right Honourable the Earls of Rochester, and Roscommon* (1709), vol. 2. ESTC T95392. Newtown Butler adds a note to "Chaplain" in line 49: "Doc^{tr} Jonath^{n} Swift then Chaplain to Ld Berkly (one of y^{e} L$^{d's}$ Justices) and suppos'd Author of this whimsical and humorous Petition." *Poems,* 1:68–73
1, App: 31–33	"An Excellent New Song being the Intended Speech of a Famous Orator against Peace." Text from Foxon S844 or S845. Discussed by Barrett (87–88n) in one of his strongest attributional arguments, but not printed, since the poem had already been incorporated into Nichols's edition. *Poems,* 1:141–45
1, App: 42–44	"The Description of a Salamander. Anno 1705." *Poems,* 1:82–85
1, App: 44–46	"The Virtues of Sid Hamet the Magician's Rod. 1703." Newtown Butler adds a note on "Sid": "The Earl of Godolphin. but may indiff'rently be apply'd to most Treasurers." *Poems,* 1:131–35
1, App: 47–50	"A Grubstreet Elegy on the Supposed Death of Patrige the Almanack-Maker. 1708." *Poems,* 1:97–101
1, App: 50	"A Description of the Morning. Ap: 1709." *Poems,* 1:123–25
1, App: 51	"Lady Betty Berkley finding in the Author's Room some Verses unfinish'd, underwrit a Stanza of her own, with Raillery upon him whi[c]h gave Occasion to This Ballad. Aug: 1704." *Poems,* 1:76–77

The previous five are taken from [Swift's] *Miscellanies in Prose and Verse. The Second Edition* (London, 1713), the ESTC T39455 edition. Newtown Butler's erroneous date for "The Virtues of Sid Hamet the Magician's Rod," which Williams calls attention to (1:132), in fact comes directly from an error in the 1713 *Miscellanies*. The following two are also probably taken from the same 1713 edition of the *Miscellanies*, or possibly from the other 1713 edition, ESTC T170386:

1, App: 61–62 "The History of Mr. Vanbrug's House." *Poems*, 1:85–88

1, App: 73–77 "Vanbrugg's House Built from the Ruins of Whitehall That was Burnt. Written 1703." *Poems*, 1:105–10, not noting the "Whimsical Medley" text

After this point in "The Whimsical Medley," Newtown Butler includes no other poems from the group that Swift collected in *Miscellanies in Prose and Verse* (1711, 1713). That is, he excludes "Verses Wrote in a Lady's Ivory Table-Book," "The Metamorphosis of Baucis and Philemon, Burlesqu'd" (Swift's most popular poem in his own era, to judge by the frequency of reprinting and inclusion in manuscript collections), "A Famous Prediction of Merlin, the British Wizard," and "Apollo Outwitted. To the Honourable Mrs. Finch." These omissions in themselves sufficiently show that he is a less than ardent collector of Swift's writings.

3:288–89 Another copy, more conventionally titled, of "On M^{rs}. Biddy Floyd," along with the Latin translation "In Lydiam" (cf. "On a Celebrated Beauty" above). These are probably taken from *Poetical Miscellanies: The Sixth Part. Containing a Collection of Original Poems, with Several New Translations. By the Most Eminent Hands* (London, 1709). Newtown Butler remarks, "N. B. not haveing the lattin Version att the time I Wrote the English Coppy in Page 102^{d}. Voll: 1st. of These Miscellanys I have again Transcrib'd the English Opposit to the Lattin Translation on the other side" (3:288). *Poems*, 1:117–18

A collation of these texts with their probable sources shows clearly enough that Newtown Butler was capable of leaving out or misreading words; on at least one occasion, he left out an entire line. The importance of the compilation notwithstanding, scholars using texts from "The Whimsical Medley" must therefore be alert to possible textual corruption.[49]

4.

It was only a few years before his death in 1724 that Newtown Butler, drawing on a lifetime's accumulation of favorite poems, compiled his manuscript, presumably for his personal convenience. When or by what means "The Whimsical Medley" came to Trinity is not clear, though as we have seen, Barrett suggests that it arrived about 1768, well before the rest of his library.[50] In his will, Newtown Butler refers to his library, which came to TCD, though apparently not until the early 1790s.[51] Then, as James Malton's watercolor of 1794 shows, Newtown Butler's books could be found—as they still can—at the western end of the Long Room in a bay inscribed "BIBLIOTH^A BUTLERIANA" in gilt lettering.[52] Altogether the Butler Library is a collection of about a thousand volumes, preserving a diverse range of printed matter, including political and poetical pamphlets, newspapers, plays, history, philosophy, and theology. Although most of the books seem to have been rebacked in the nineteenth century, many of them preserve Theophilus Butler's bookplate and occasionally his annotations.

It seems to have escaped notice that some and perhaps much of "The Whimsical Medley" is compiled from precisely these volumes.[53] An interesting chapter in the history of the book could be written if some scholar were to connect the poem texts in this important compilation to their sources in the poem texts on the shelves of Bibliotheca Butleriana in the Long Room.[54] Then a much more comprehensive and useful analysis of Newtown Butler's accuracy as a scribe and tastes as an anthologist would be possible. What did he include and what did he exclude? Did he typically improve upon his sources? Did he annotate them or in some other way clarify them? Armed with an understanding of how he handled his printed sources, one could then better evaluate the remaining "Medley" texts that apparently derive from manuscript sources.

For an inkling of what such research might reveal, consider that among the "Whimsical Medley" poems that Williams edits, or lists among poems "attributed to Swift," four also were published in Peter Anthony Motteux's London periodical the *Gentleman's Journal* (1692–1694):

"Ode to King William, on His Successes in Ireland" (*Poems* 1:11; first attributed to Swift by John Nichols in 1780, citing the *Gentleman's Journal* text)[55]
"There's scarce a well-drest coxcomb" (*Poems* 3:1056)
"The Story of Orpheus, Burlesqued" (*Poems* 3:1073)
"Actaeon; or The Original of Horn Fair" (*Poems* 3:1073)

Newtown Butler's copy of the *Gentleman's Journal* survives today in the Long Room, evidence sufficient to raise the possibility that that periodical served him as a source not only for these four poems but for others as well.

If we compare the *Gentleman's Journal* with "The Whimsical Medley," we find that to all appearances about one of every four "Medley" poems is silently copied from the *Gentleman's Journal*.[56] Indeed, Newtown Butler borrowed at least one poem from each number of the *Gentleman's Journal*. He copied more or less faithfully, sometimes composing a new title and often ignoring information about authorship, though in two instances, he adapted a poem so that it praised his wife Emilia.[57] He shared Motteux's fondness for enigmas, so much so that Motteux was Newtown Butler's chief source for these bits of verse.

Newtown Butler probably borrowed three of the four poems mentioned above—all doubtful attributions to Swift—from the *Gentleman's Journal*. Motteux took the fourth, the tripos poem beginning "There's scarce a well-drest coxcomb," from a Dublin source other than the tripos text Newtown Butler used.[58] Two poems that Hogan doubtfully attributes to Sheridan from "The Whimsical Medley" can safely be crossed off Sheridan's list, since Newtown Butler took them from a periodical published in London when Sheridan was only a child in Ireland.[59]

Such information not only makes it more treacherous to use "The Whimsical Medley" as a source for new attributions to Swift, in the absence of any reason to believe that Swift published in the *Gentleman's Journal*; it also narrows the search for "Whimsical Medley" items that derive from manuscript sources.

So far as I know, Butler's file of manuscript material has not survived. Not improbably he discarded a rag-tag collection once he transcribed what he wanted to save. But by comparing the relevant "Medley" texts with those that could be found in printed miscellanies as well as in the great collections of manuscript verse from his period, such as those in the British Library, the Bodleian Library, the Osborn Collection at Yale, and the Brotherton Collection at Leeds, one might at last reliably assess Newtown Butler's value as a collector of poem manuscripts, even though the actual manuscripts he was transcribing have disappeared.[60]

As for John Barrett, although in using "The Whimsical Medley" he thought his main achievement was to antedate the extant evidence of Swift's development as a satirist and a poet, the evidentiary value of Barrett's book lies elsewhere. First, he negotiated the tricky biographical complexities of the TCD muniments, which no Swiftian except possibly Irvin Ehrenpreis has understood so well. Second, he introduced to eighteenth-century studies a comprehensive verse miscellany whose importance awaits a full assessment. In so doing, he presented a substantial body of authentic informal verse exchanged among Swift, Sheridan, and others about 1718 and 1719, just prior to Newtown Butler's completion of the "The Whimsical Medley."[61] Except for this body of verse, Barrett offered no credible new Swift attributions. Although Scott and Ball each tried his hand at extracting more Swift verse from the "Medley," their attributions are no more credible than Barrett's—indeed perhaps less so.[62] There are good reasons for continued study of "The Whimsical Medley," but the unending search for new attributions to Swift is probably not one of them.[63]

NOTES

1. *An Essay on the Earlier Part of the Life of Swift. By the Rev. John Barrett, D.D. and Vice-Provost of Trinity College, Dublin. To Which Are Subjoined Several Pieces Ascribed to Swift; Two of His Original Letters; and Extracts from His Remarks on Bishop Burnet's History* (London, 1808), hereafter cited as Barrett; *The Works of the Rev. Jonathan Swift, D.D. Dean of St. Patrick's, Dublin.* Arranged by Thomas Sheridan, A.M.; corrected and revised by John Nichols (London, [1808]). See both volumes 1 and 17 of Nichols's 1808 edition of Swift's works; that some of the Barrett material appears in volume 17 has been overlooked by earlier scholars. In the present article, Barrett is always cited from the separately-published *Essay,* which is differently paginated from the *Works* issue of the same pages.

2. "The Whimsical Medley" (hereafter WM), TCD MS 879, vols. 1–3; for permission to quote from this manuscript, I am indebted to the Board of Trinity College Dublin (hereafter TCD). "The MSS [i.e., the WM volumes] . . . have been in the College Library these 40 years." Barrett to Edmond Malone, 14 April 1808, Forster MS 571, Victoria and Albert Museum, filmed in *Britain's Literary Heritage: The Forster and Dyce Collections from the National Art Library at the Victoria and Albert Museum, London* (Brighton: Harvester Microforms, 1987), reel 19, item 53 (hereafter cited as Forster-Dyce films).

3. "Neglected" is Williams's accurate judgment; see *The Poems of Jonathan Swift,* ed. Harold Williams, 2d ed. (Oxford: Clarendon Press, 1958), 1:xlii–xliii; hereafter cited as *Poems.* The manuscript was obviously examined by Barrett and by someone on Walter Scott's behalf if not by Scott himself. It was also closely examined by F. Elrington Ball for *Swift's Verse: An Essay* (London: John Murray, 1929) and by Harold Williams for *Poems* (see 1:xlii–xliii and 1:xlviii). Other uses of the manuscript include Paul Vern Thompson, "The Canon of Swift," *Review of English Studies* 14 (1938): 182–89; George Mayhew, "Swift and the Tripos Tradition," *Philological Quarterly* 45 (1966): 85–101; Frank H. Ellis, ed., *Poems*

on Affairs of State: Augustan Satirical Verse, 1660–1714, vols. 6–7 (New Haven, Conn.: Yale University Press, 1970, 1975); and Andrew Carpenter, ed., *Verse in English from Eighteenth-Century Ireland* (Cork: Cork University Press, 1998), 606. Pat Rogers, ed., *Jonathan Swift: The Complete Poems* (New Haven, Conn.: Yale University Press, 1983), cites the WM occasionally as a copy text (e.g., 676, 678, 679, 681, 684). Robert Hogan, ed., *The Poems of Thomas Sheridan* (Newark: University of Delaware Press, 1994; hereafter cited as Hogan) "made much use of the third volume" of the WM (20).

4. *Poems,* 1:xlviii; 1:xliii.

5. The stories are well exemplified in the *Dictionary of National Biography* entry on Barrett by P. B[ruce] A[ustin]. See also "Authentic Anecdotes of the Late Rev. Dr. Barrett, Vice-Provost of Trinity-College, Dublin," *London Magazine* 5 (1822): 53–60; "Doctor Barrett, Late Senior Fellow and Vice-Provost of Trinity College, Dublin," *Dublin University Magazine* 18 (1841): 350–58; Courtenay Moore, "Jacky Barrett," *Journal of the Cork Historical and Archaeological Society,* 2d ser., 6 (1900): 47–54; and Wyse Jackson, "Jacky Barrett," *Bell* 6 (1943): 503–8. For a more balanced estimate, see R. B. McDowell and D. A. Webb, *Trinity College Dublin, 1592–1952: An Academic History* (Cambridge: Cambridge University Press, 1982), 82.

6. *The Dublin University Calendar, M.DCCC.XXXIII. Corrected to November 20, 1832* (Dublin, 1833), 102, 103, 108, 114, 116, 124, 143, 172, 194. Barrett's own list, with some divergences from the official record, is in TCD MS 2370, p. 254.

7. Charles Benson, "Trinity College: A Bibliographical Essay," in *Trinity College Dublin and the Idea of a University,* ed. C. H. Holland (Dublin: Trinity College Dublin Press, 1991), 365; McDowell and Webb, *Trinity College Dublin,* 82. See also William Bedell Stanford, "Classical Studies in Trinity College, Dublin, since the Foundation," *Hermathena* 57 (1941): 16; and J. E. L. Oulton, "The Study of Divinity in Trinity College, Dublin, since the Foundation," *Hermathena* 58 (1941): 13.

8. Barrett, *An Enquiry into the Origin of the Constellations that Compose the Zodiac, and the Uses They Were Intended to Promote* (Dublin, 1800); I am indebted to McDowell and Webb for their estimate of the book (82).

9. Barrett, "Account of a Greek Manuscript of Saint Matthew's Gospel, in the Library of Trinity College, Dublin," *Transactions of the Royal Irish Academy* 1 (1787): Antiquities section, 121–38; *Evangelium Secundum Matthaeum ex Codice Rescripto in Bibliotheca Collegii SSae. Trinitatis juxta Dublin.* Descriptum opera et studio Johannis Barrett (Dublin, 1801).

10. Richardson to Lady Bradshaigh, 22 April 1752, in *The Correspondence of Samuel Richardson,* ed. Anna Laetitia Barbauld (London, 1804), 6:171–72.

11. Barrett, 1–84; the quotation is from 81.

12. [Walter Scott], review of Barrett, *Quarterly Review* 1 (April 1809): 162–77, esp. 168–71—a review of doubtful propriety, inasmuch as Scott was at work on a competing edition of Swift and in his role as a Dryden biographer and editor was already a competitor of Malone's. For Scott's authorship, see, among other sources, Hill Shine and Helen Chadwick Shine, *The Quarterly Review under Gif-*

ford: Identification of Contributors, 1809–1824 (Chapel Hill: University of North Carolina Press, 1949), 4. For the chronology of Scott's work on his edition, see Lee H. Potter, "The Text of Scott's Edition of Swift," *Studies in Bibliography* 22 (1969): 240, 249; and William B. Todd and Ann Bowden, *Sir Walter Scott: A Bibliographical History, 1796–1832* (New Castle, Del.: Oak Knoll, 1998), 144–45, 327. A critique of Barrett much like Scott's is found in a review in the *British Critic* 35 (March 1810): 230–40. Barrett's attribution of the tripos was treated more tolerantly in the *Critical Review* 18.2 (October 1809): 151–59; and by [Thomas Denman, later Lord Denman] in the *Monthly Review,* 2d ser., 62 (1810): 138–45. For the attribution to Denman, see Benjamin Christie Nangle, *The Monthly Review, Second Series, 1790–1815: Indexes of Contributors and Articles* (Oxford: Clarendon Press, 1955), 17–18, 84. In the life of Swift, Scott delicately expresses his skepticism over Barrett's account: *The Works of Jonathan Swift,* 2d ed. (Edinburgh, 1824), 1:20–25. John Forster ridicules Barrett in *The Life of Jonathan Swift,* vol. "1" (London, 1875), 32–40.

13. Ball, *Swift's Verse,* 7–8; Harold Williams, "The Canon of Swift," *Review of English Studies* 14 (1938): 326–27; *Poems,* 3:1056; Mayhew, "Swift and the Tripos Tradition." Mayhew indicates (86) that he hoped to develop more fully elsewhere an argument that the seeds of Swift's early art were sown in the tripos, but this hope does not seem to have been realized.

14. Barrett to Malone, 14 April 1808, Forster-Dyce films, reel 19, item 53; Bodleian MS Malone 37, ff. 68–69, 70–91.

15. Barrett, 88–105, 132–141, 144.

16. For Barrett's acquiescence in Malone's stylistic adjustments, see Barrett's letters of 2 July 1808 and 27 July 1808, Forster-Dyce films, reel 19, items 57 and 59. The letters Malone added were Swift to Henry Jenney, 8 June 1732, and Swift to John Brandreth, 30 June 1732 (Barrett, 171–81).

17. "The Swan Tripe Club in Dublin" and "The Famous Speech-Maker of England." Nichols had already included both poems in his *Supplement* to Swift's works (London, 1776); see *Poems,* 3:1077–78, 1083; D. F. Foxon, *English Verse, 1701–1750: A Catalogue of Separately Printed Poems with Notes on Contemporary Collected Editions* (London: Cambridge University Press, 1975), T495. For the November printing, see Barrett to Malone, 22 November 1808, Forster-Dyce films, reel 19, item 60. The publication date of Barrett's *Essay* is not clear, though Potter concludes that Nichols's edition of the *Works* was not published until the last week of December 1808 or the first week of January 1809 (249).

18. Twelve letters from Barrett to Malone, 14 April 1808 to 7 April 1809, Forster MS 571, Forster-Dyce films, reel 19, items 53–64; Andrew Caldwell to Malone, 9 April 1808, Bodleian MS Eng. lett. c.15, ff. 129–32; Bodleian MS Malone 41, f. 68 (an amendment, evidently, to proofs of Barrett's *Essay*); Michael Kearney to Malone, 20 August 1808, 25 November 1808, 9 December 1808, 23 December 1808, Bodleian MS Malone 39, ff. 81–87; Nichols's "Advertisement" to Barrett, dated 31 October 1808: "In the summer of 1808 . . . , the Proprietors were favoured (through the friendly exertions of Mr. MALONE, a name respected by every literary man) with an elaborate and valuable Essay on the early part of the Dean's Life; an Essay which had been, with much labour, research, and atten-

tion, some time before composed by the learned writer of it, the Rev. Dr. BARRETT, Vice-Provost of Trinity College; accompanied with several Pieces ascribed to Swift on Authorities which carry with them their own conviction" (v; the latter remark may embody calculated ambiguity). For a later recounting of Malone's role, see Nichols, *Illustrations of the Literary History of the Eighteenth Century,* vol. 5 (London, 1828), 396; for the account by Malone's modern biographer, see Peter Martin, *Edmond Malone, Shakespearean Scholar: A Literary Biography* (Cambridge: Cambridge University Press, 1995), 259, 261–62. The preliminary matter in volume 1 of Nichols's 1808 edition of Swift—a volume whose dedication is dated June 1808 but whose "Advertisement" and table of contents contain no reference to Barrett's treatise—includes a note, p. [lxxiv], explaining that Malone procured Barrett's essay "after the Title-pages, Preface, and a part of the Index, were actually printed off; which must be our apology for its not being more regularly and earlier noticed." Throughout the process, Barrett seemed to derive considerable gratification from his association with scholars of the stature of Malone and Nichols, and in a flourish of gratitude, he donated his copyright to Nichols and the other members of Nichols's conger (Barrett to Malone, 24 January 1809, 7 April 1809, Forster-Dyce films, reel 19, items 62, 64).

19. See, e.g., Martin, *Edmond Malone,* 231–32, 234, 241–42.

20. Barrett to Malone, 27 July 1808, Forster-Dyce films, reel 19, item 59.

21. Barrett, 88; see also 141.

22. Toward the very end of the last volume, there is a reference from 1719 to "this summer"—evidently looking forward (3, appendix: 31).

23. T. K. Abbott, *Catalogue of the Manuscripts in the Library of Trinity College, Dublin* (Dublin: Hodges Figgis, 1900), MS 879.

24. Margaret Crum, ed., *First-Line Index of English Poetry, 1500–1800, in Manuscripts of the Bodleian Library, Oxford* (New York: Modern Language Association of America, 1969).

25. *Poems on Affairs of State,* 6:714–15, 718, 720–21, 755–56, 757, 780–83, 786–87, 791, 792–94; 7:642, 654–55, 656, 657–59, 661–62, 671, 674–75, 677–81. The proportion is higher for volume 6 (1697–1704) than for volume 7 (1704–1714). Ellis cites WM as "TCD MS. I.5," using an old shelfmark.

26. Newtown Butler seems to have called himself simply "Newtown," though in his period the full title was given as "Newtown Butler," or yet more formally, "Baron Butler of Newtown Butler."

27. The handwriting has been identified by comparison with Newtown Butler's signature on a deed among Lanesborough deeds in the National Library of Ireland (Theophilus Lord Newtown to Matthew French, 3 August 1723, filed among D.8896–8926) and with handwriting found in the Butler Library books in TCD. One poem is not in Newtown Butler's hand but appears to be in that of his brother James Butler. Barrett's own discussion of the handwriting is on pp. 85–86 of his essay.

28. Theophilus Butler, Baron Butler of Newtown Butler's will, dated 20 February 1721[?/2], Registry of Deeds, Dublin, memorial 25645; text confirmed in certified transcript 41-245-25645 (registered 16 March 1723[/4]); S. G. Poyntz, *St. Ann's: The Church in the Heart of the City* (Dublin, [1976]), 13.

29. John Dunton, *The Dublin Scuffle* (London, 1699), a2^{v}–a4^{v}, 135–36, 417, 536. The identification of Dunton's dedicatee with Theophilus's father Francis is only inferential. Dunton's Butler is a member of the House of Commons; the only Butler in the Irish Commons at this time (1698) who was not a knight was Francis Butler. (See *Journals of the House of Commons of the Kingdom of Ireland,* vol. 2 [Dublin, 1796], covering the years 1692–1713.) Dunton places this Butler's house in St. Stephen's Green; the Dublin house of Theophilus Butler's family was there, in approximately the present location of the Shelburne Hotel annex (*The Georgian Society Records of Eighteenth-Century Domestic Architecture and Decoration in Dublin* [Dublin: Ponsonby and Gibbs, 1910; reprint, Shannon: Irish University Press, 1969], 2:52–53, 60; this compilation errs, p. 52, in identifying Dunton's dedicatee as Theophilus Butler). On the other hand, Dunton calls his man "the Honourable Colonel Butler," and it is not clear how Francis was entitled to be called Honourable; Dunton may have misunderstood him to be a nobleman's son or a member of the Privy Council. The title "Colonel" may have been his as colonel of a County Cavan militia company; militia records do not go back before 1708, but Francis's heirs Theophilus and Brinsley both served as colonel of a County Cavan troop of horse, suggesting that this may have been a quasi-hereditary post: H. B. Swanzy, "Militia Commissions, Co. Cavan," *Notes and Queries* 146 (1924): 164.

30. Jointly with a maternal uncle and I presume as a gift from his maternal grandfather Theophilus Jones. Swift says that the reversion of Newtown Butler's office of Clerk of the Pells sold for £2500 (*The Drapier's Letters to the People of Ireland,* ed. Herbert Davis [Oxford: Clarendon Press, 1935, 1965], 73).

31. The brothers entered Trinity together 27 September 1686 (George Dames Burtchaell and Thomas Ulick Sadleir, *Alumni Dublinenses* [London: Williams and Norgate, 1924]), so that they were undergraduates while Swift was an MA candidate. The LL.D. degrees which Burtchaell and Sadleir record the brothers as having received from TCD in March 1718 have no special significance, the same degree being conferred on thirty-five others on the same occasion. "Every member of the Irish parliament, learned or unlearned, has, by custom, a right to have an honorary degree in law" from TCD, according to Patrick Duigenan, *Lachrymae Academicae: or, The Present Deplorable State of the College of the Holy and Undivided Trinity, of Queen Elizabeth, near Dublin* (Dublin, 1777), 56–57; Board's register, 1661–1739, TCD MUN/V/2, p. 489.

32. The stewards are listed in the first edition, *Alexander's Feast; or The Power of Musique. An Ode, in Honour of St. Cecilia's Day. By Mr. Dryden* (London, 1697), the probable source for the poem's text in the WM, 3:10 ff., where Newtown Butler carefully transcribes the stewards' names. See also Peter Anthony Motteux's *Gentleman's Journal: or The Monthly Miscellany* (Jan. 1691/2): 5; William Henry Husk, *An Account of the Musical Celebrations on St. Cecilia's Day in the Sixteenth, Seventeenth and Eighteenth Centuries* (London, 1857), 38–39; Samuel Derrick's prefatory life of Dryden in *The Miscellaneous Works of John Dryden, Esq;* (London, 1760), 1:xxviii. I owe the Derrick reference to Scott's life of Dryden.

33. *Gentleman's Journal* (Jan. 1691/2): 5.

34. *Journal to Stella,* ed. Harold Williams (Oxford: Clarendon Press, 1948), 1:12, 199, 348; D. Nichol Smith, ed., *The Letters of Jonathan Swift to Charles Ford* (Oxford: Clarendon Press, 1935), 92 n. Others besides Swift used the nickname "Ophy"; see Sir Richard Cox to Edward Southwell, 5 September 1713, British Library MS Add. 38157, f. 9 (for this reference I am grateful to David Hayton). Emilia's name is sometimes given as Emily or Aemilia.

35. Ball, *Swift's Verse,* 6–7.

36. David W. Hayton, "Ireland and the English Ministers, 1707–16" (D.Phil. thesis, University of Oxford, 1975), 192, 266, 312–14, and 320, and on the procedure of the Irish Privy Council, 43–45; I thank David Hayton for permission to cite his thesis. See also *Index to Irish Privy Councillors 1711–1910 (and Partially from 1660)* ([Dublin], n.d.), 2 (photocopy: National Library of Ireland Ir 35 i 4).

37. WM, 1:261; 2:88–91, 177, 206; 2 Appendix:14–15; 3:169–70, 174–76, 178–79.

38. Swift, "Observations on the Privy Council of Ireland" [19 December 1713] in Swift, *The Correspondence of Jonathan Swift, D.D.,* ed. F. Elrington Ball (London: G. Bell and Sons, 1910–1914), 6:243; cf. *The Correspondence of Jonathan Swift, D.D.,* ed. David Woolley (Frankfurt am Main: Lang, 1999–), 1:575, n. 4.

39. Historical Manuscripts Commission 36, *Calendar of the Manuscripts of the Marquess of Ormonde,* n. s., vol. 8 (London: HMSO, 1920): 296; for this reference and for noticing that "Theodore Butler" is an error for "Theophilus Butler" I thank David Hayton. William King to Earl of Sunderland, 7 April 1715, TCD MS 750/4, f. 250^{v}; quoted by permission of the Board of Trinity College Dublin. Patrick McNally, *Parties, Patriots and Undertakers: Parliamentary Politics in Early Hanoverian Ireland* (Dublin: Four Courts, 1997), 74–76. Cox to Southwell, 5 September 1713, offers an additional glimpse of Butler's role in the Irish Privy Council.

40. *Journals of the House of Lords* [*of Ireland*], vol. 2, covering 1703–1725 (Dublin, 1780). In his will (20 February 1721[?/2], Newtown Butler describes himself as "Weake in Body but of Perfect Mind and Memory."

41. *The Correspondence of Jonathan Swift,* ed. Harold Williams (Oxford: Clarendon Press, 1963–1972), 3:286 n, 297, 473–74; Swift, *Correspondence,* ed. Woolley, 1:613. When Theophilus died in 1724, Swift told Ford that his cousin was a "Fool" who had made a "wise will," presumably for the bequest to St. Ann's but also for a £20 life annuity he left to Ann Brent "for her Fidellity and Care of my Dear Wife Deceased and of my Selfe" (Swift, *Correspondence,* ed. Williams, 3:11; Newtown Butler's will). In time, as a way of giving money to Ann, Swift bought the annuity from her but continued to pay it to her himself, and in his will he returns to her Lord Newtown's annuity (*Directions to Servants and Miscellaneous Pieces 1733–1742,* ed. Herbert Davis, vol. 13 of *The Prose Works of Jonathan Swift,* ed. Herbert Davis et al. [Oxford: Basil Blackwell, 1964], 158; see also 154 and 200). Mrs. Brent's first name is preserved in the record of her will, proved in 1735: see Appendix to *Twenty-Sixth Report of the Deputy Keeper of the Public Records of Ireland* (Dublin, 1895).

42. Nine that had been collected in Swift's 1711 *Miscellanies in Prose and Verse* and its derivatives, plus *An Excellent New Song, Being the Intended Speech of a*

Famous Orator Against Peace (an attribution in which Barrett had been anticipated by Nichols) and *Part of the Seventh Epistle of the First Book of Horace Imitated.*

43. Barrett himself thought as much: Barrett to Malone, 7 April 1709, Forster-Dyce films, reel 19, item 64. Jane Brent, as a printer's widow, would have been well aware of the potential interest of Swift's manuscripts; John Lyon says that the daughter Ann Ridgway asked Swift for a copy of a poem on at least one occasion, and she seems to have given or sold the poem to Dublin newspapers (*Poems,* 2:673; George P. Mayhew, *Rage or Raillery: The Swift Manuscripts at the Huntington Library* [San Marino, Calif.: Huntington Library, 1967], 121–25).

44. WM, 3:273–74, 370–71. Perhaps significantly, the latter prologue and epilogue immediately follow the "Collection of Several Pieces" by Swift and his friends in the WM and may have been part of the same manuscript source. One could speculate that Newtown Butler's son and heir James, who died 10 January 1721[?/2], aged fourteen, was a student of Sheridan's. See John Lodge, *The Peerage of Ireland,* rev. and enl. Mervyn Archdall (Dublin, 1789), 2:397.

45. John Irwin Fischer, "Swift's Early Odes, Dan Jackson's Nose, and 'The Character of Sir Robert Walpole,'" in *Reading Swift: Papers from the Second Münster Symposium on Jonathan Swift,* ed. Richard H. Rodino and Hermann J. Real (München: Wilhelm Fink, 1993), 226–29.

46. Fischer, "Swift's Early Odes," 227–28, 231–35. Whether the texts of poems printed in more than one of these Sheridan-derived sources in all cases descend from the same archetype remains to be analyzed; see Williams's note in *Poems,* 3:990. Malone (or Nichols), editing for publication Barrett's vague reference to "the English editor" of *1789,* identifies that person as "Mr. Sheridan" (Barrett to Malone, 27 July 1808, Forster-Dyce films, reel 19, item 59; Barrett, 84).

47. Untypically of items printed in *1735,* this one was reprinted in Barrett (145).

48. Joseph Horrell, ed., *Collected Poems of Jonathan Swift* (London: Routledge and Kegan Paul, 1958); hereafter cited as Horrell.

49. Particularly in the foregoing section, this paper draws upon the resources of the Swift Poems Project, an edition and electronic archive in progress, of which John Irwin Fischer and I are editors.

50. From early nineteenth-century references to the WM as the "Lanesborough MSS" (Barrett, 106 n, 142, 143, 144; William Monck Mason, *The History and Antiquities of the Collegiate and Cathedral Church of St. Patrick, near Dublin* [Dublin, 1820], 288 n), we may speculate that at that time there was on the flyleaf of this MS (removed during rebacking in the mid-nineteenth century) or the endpaper (overlaid with a new endpaper on the same occasion) some reference to its having been presented to the Library by or in the name of one of the earls of Lanesborough ca. 1768. This is consistent with the supposition that the manuscript descended to Theophilus's successor, his brother Brinsley Butler, second Baron Newtown Butler and first Lord Lanesborough, and his heirs, unlike the library of printed books, which Theophilus in his will leaves to his brother James. James Malton reported that the library was "lately" presented to TCD by "a Mr.

BUTLER": *A Picturesque & Descriptive View of the City of Dublin in a Series of the Most Interesting Scenes Taken in the Year 1791* (1799; facsimile with introduction by the Knight of Glin, Dublin: Dolmen, 1978), letterpress description facing the engraving of the Trinity College library, what is now known as the Long Room. Although at this period the TCD Board's registers (minutes) often record significant gifts to the library, I have been unable to find either of these. The Library has no systematic accession records covering the period when the books and the manuscript could have been acquired. The original early eighteenth-century bindings have been rebacked twice—once in the mid-nineteenth century and once in 1909; at some point in the late twentieth century, volume 1 split into two text blocks, around one part of which the TCD conservation laboratory has placed temporary boards and a temporary canvas back. For an analysis of the history of the manuscript's binding and rebacking, I am indebted to the technical director of the Trinity College Library's conservation laboratory, Anthony Cains.

51. He ordained "that my Books now in my Study be by my Brother Collonell James Butler Carefully preserved and Neither to be sold or lent to any P[er]son Whatsoever[,] but those of my Family may at Convenient times and in the day have Liberty to peruse Books in the study only[,] Placeing such books againe Regularly." Quite probably some of these were books he had inherited from his father, but it will be found that a number of the Bibliotheca Butleriana imprints come from what would have been his own book-buying years.

52. For Malton's watercolor—currently (1999) available as a poster and in other formats, not excluding a mouse pad, from the library shop at Trinity College Dublin—see Anne Crookshank and David Webb, *Paintings and Sculptures in Trinity College Dublin* (Dublin: Trinity College Dublin Press, 1990), 178, recording a note on the back of the picture: "View of the Inside of the College Library Dublin Drawn March 30th 1794 by James Malton." Crookshank and Webb say, "The date on the back of the drawing appears to be inaccurate, as the engraving after it was dated July 1793." Yet in his article "Who Was Malton?" P. J. Raftery notes that "Malton, *after* he finished the engravings, did a series of watercolor-and-india ink versions which were exhibited in the Royal Academy, and the picture of the College Library was so exhibited in 1795" (*Dublin Historical Record* 19 [1964]: 110–11; emphasis mine). In the collection in which the "1793" engraving was published, Malton notes that "all of the views were taken in the year 1791, yet, as the work was in hand till the year 1797, such alterations as occurred in each subject, between the taking and publishing any view of it, have been attended to" (*A Picturesque & Descriptive View* [1799]). The engraved version of the picture does not show any inscription over the bay holding the Butler Library, though the facing letterpress states, "On the left, as you enter, is one case full [of books], lately given by a Mr. BUTLER." The case is evidently the V/W bay where the Butler Library still stands. The inscriptions above the bays do not appear in the engraved version of the picture, whether because the inscriptions had not been painted as early as 1793 or because such detail was simply omitted in the engraving. It seems reasonable to conclude that the Butler Library had arrived at TCD by 1794 ("lately").

53. As Henry J. Monck Mason first noted in his calendar of TCD manuscripts compiled for the Irish Record Commission in the early nineteenth century but never published: TCD MS 1708, vol. 5, f. 197^{r-v}.

54. A spot check suggests that the printed books sometimes have X marks on pages with WM poems or sometimes have such pages dog-eared. Most often, however, there is no tell-tale.

55. *A Select Collection of Poems,* vol. 4 (London: J. Nichols, 1780; reprint New York, 1969), 303 n.

56. In this comparison, I have used the British Library copy of the *Gentleman's Journal* (hereafter *GJ*) as filmed in the English Literary Periodicals series (University Microfilms), though I am grateful to Charles Benson for examining Newtown Butler's copy on my behalf (TCD V.ff.31–32).

57. See *GJ* 1 (June 1692): 13 and WM, 3:98; *GJ* 2 (April 1693): 115 and WM, 2:394. I suppose his use is an adaptation since he and Emilia did not marry until 1701.

58. *Poems,* 3:1056–57; *GJ* 3 (August-September 1694): 228–29. The *GJ* text, "sent me from Dublin by an unknown hand," begins, "There's scarce a dressing coquett but will own" and is entitled "The Fop."

59. These poems are the enigma beginning "I never did eat, yet I'm still at a feast" (*GJ* 3 [May 1694]: 131; WM, 3:372; Hogan, 236) and the solution to it, beginning "Your riddle does feed though it never could eat" (*GJ* 3 [June 1694]: 177; WM, 3:372; Hogan, 236–37; and Hogan, 382–83).

60. The best point of access to verse in published miscellanies is the Boys-Mizener index to the miscellanies listed in Arthur E. Case, *A Bibliography of English Poetical Miscellanies, 1521–1750* (Oxford: Oxford University Press, for the Bibliographical Society, 1935). The index, on slips, is in the Spencer Research Library of the University of Kansas.

61. The Swift-Sheridan material occurs late in volume 3, the last volume to be compiled.

62. Scott attributed six WM items to Swift: see *Poems,* 3:1057, 1099. For attributions added by Ball in which the WM seems to have played some role, see *Poems,* 3:1084, 1087 and Ball, *Swift's Verse,* 111, 114, 122. Ball also asserted that "On Humphrey Duke of Gloucester's Tomb," another WM poem, was "inspired, if not written by" Swift (113).

63. For various kinds of assistance in the preparation of this article, I am indebted to Charles Benson, Susanna Boylston, Anthony Cains, Tom Desmond, A. C. Elias, Jr., Dennis Glew, David Hayton, Jane Maxwell, Felicity O'Mahony, Alexandra Mason, and Stuart O Seanóir.

10

The Editing of Pope's Dunciad *from Scriblerus to* * * *

DAVID L. VANDER MEULEN

As its title conspicuously announces, Alexander Pope's satire *The Dunciad Variorum* (1729) claims among its realms the intellectual enterprises of textual criticism and scholarly editing. Its typographical layout reiterates that interest: the volume's physical characteristics imitate well-known editions of ancient and modern classics.[1] But the attention to textual matters shines through most clearly in a feature that is a staple of learned editions, the editorial notes. Their ubiquity—they appear on every page of the poetic text—marks the concern with editorial matters implicitly, but these "Remarks" also comment on textual affairs directly. Not surprisingly in a work devoted to exposing folly across the range of human activity, the evaluations often are unfavorable—again, both implicitly and explicitly. The commentary exaggerates and parodies itself, but it also attacks straightforwardly: one note, for instance, characterizes the "verbal Critick" responsible for such productions as being "to his Author as a Quack is to his Patients, the more they suffer and complain, the better he is pleas'd. . . . Some-body said well of these men, that their heads were *Libraries out of order*."[2]

Most of the direct observations on editing occur in the two dozen notes in the 1729 quarto edition (the first with extensive annotation) that are attributed to a specific commentator, Martinus Scriblerus.[3] Although his observations and practices are *ad hoc* and do not constitute a systematic presentation of editorial theory, taken together they reflect a coherent approach to important questions that serious editorial thinkers of any era must address.[4] Simultaneously they also point most usefully to the kinds of editions that are possible. In what follows I would like to use his remarks as a way of surveying the fundamental approaches available to scholarly editors and then to illustrate those possibilities by drawing on the ways in which the several *Dunciad*s have been or might be edited.[5] Although the examples are not intended to comprise an exhaustive survey of the hundreds of appearances of the work during the past three centuries, they do incidentally provide a conspectus of major and interesting forms of what Pope considered his "Chef d'œuvre."[6]

1.

The foundation of all that Scriblerus says about the text is his belief that the *Dunciad* edition must have an historical orientation; nearly all of his comments honor that point of reference. This commitment means a number of things to him, but above all it entails establishing a text based on historical evidence rather than on his own taste. Before exploring the ramifications of that approach, it is worth considering the implied alternative, an edition based on non-historical factors.

Forms of non-historical editing include that in which modern publishing house editors engage or that which contemporaries saw Richard Bentley as having undertaken in his 1732 edition of *Paradise Lost.*[7] Such work may be scholarly, but its purpose is not to preserve or reconstruct a text expressed or intended at a particular historical moment; rather, it is to honor some other goal, probably aesthetic, possibly in the form of a house style. Though such an approach is difficult to implement in an edition that purports to present the work of a standard author, with Pope it happens especially in editions for use in schools. To take a couple of examples: the 1963 Dell paperback, with its contents "selected" by John Wain and in a series edited by Richard Wilbur, becomes uncomfortable with eighteenth-century punctuation and adjusts to modern standards such features as commas before closing parentheses or speech not surrounded by quotation marks. Robin Sowerby's 1988 edition of Pope includes what the back cover identifies as an "abridged version of *The Dunciad*"—in its "entirety." That text modernizes capitalization, spelling, and punctuation, and it expands contractions—in the process making Pope a master of anapestic pentameter. The most bizarre example of a non-historical edition, or perhaps of any edition of Pope, is one edited by Peter Stryker and published in 1978. Created well into the age of photocopying, this volume is a 490-page bound typescript—mostly of carbon copies, on which typos have been corrected—of Pope's poetry derived from the Twickenham Edition, but with the initial capital of each line reduced to lower case. *The Dunciad* presented here is the four-book version of 1743, now divided into four "chapters."[8]

Bowdlerization is another form of nonhistorical editing, and it too is represented among *Dunciad* editions. In 1849 the actor William Charles Macready privately published a volume of Pope's works "For the Use of Young People," according to the title page. Sometimes large sections are deleted—portions of the games in book 2, for instance. At some points only a few words are changed: "Bawdry" (B1.307) is altered to "Lewdness" (342) and "Whore" (B4.272) softened to "Wench" (381), for example, while "And now had Fame's posterior Trumpet blown" (B4.71) becomes "And now again had Fame's loud trumpet blown" (374). On other occasions the beginning of one verse is grafted to the close of a later one. Thus,

> Why should I sing what bards the nightly Muse
> Did slumb'ring visit, and convey to stews;
> Who prouder march'd, with magistrates in state,
> To some fam'd round-house, ever open gate!
> (B2.421–24)

becomes:

> Why should I sing what bards were marched in state
> To some famed round-house' ever open gate!
> (357)

In the dedicatory letter "To My Children" prefacing this scarce book, Macready explained that the volume was prepared to assist in achieving "that first duty of your lives—self-improvement" (vi). The *Times* reviewer on 15 August 1849 sympathized with Macready's aims: objections would come, he predicted, from "purists as to text, not decorum," and "scarcely any one but a literary fanatic would be particularly edified at finding his daughter absorbed in the perusal of uncastigated works of Pope and Dryden." The writer unwittingly showed how the new edition misunderstood or at least misrepresented Pope's characteristically suggestive approach: "Mr. Macready has left no blanks, considering them as so many temptations to pry into unclean places" (8).

The most prominent example of nonhistorical editing is the Pope edition that has been perhaps the most influential of all: William Warburton's, of 1751. Published seven years after Pope's death, it held sway for the rest of the eighteenth century and cast its spell long after, serving in 1966 as the basis for much of the Oxford Standard Authors volume by Herbert Davis. The special circumstance for Warburton was that he served two roles, with competing objectives: as editor he was committed to historical fidelity, but as Pope's literary executor he was interested in polishing Pope's public image. A third factor added further complications. Warburton has been widely seen as exploiting Pope's confidence for his own purposes. Indeed, the frontispiece of the 1751 edition pictures a bust of Warburton at its center, with Pope's own bust, near the top edge, receiving light that emanates from the editor. Warburton's treatment of the verbal text confirms the assessment of his self-interest. At line B4.568, for instance, he added a long note that he signed with the name Scriblerus rather than with the initial "W" that he used elsewhere to indicate his own contributions. He there attacked Thomas Edwards for a book that had appeared four years after Pope's death, *A Supplement to Mr. Warburton's Edition of Shakespear. Being the Canons of Criticism, and Glossary, Collected from the Notes in That Celebrated Work* . . . (1748).

In contrast, Scriblerus intends to be rigorously historical, but having chosen that goal he faces a second question: does he reproduce a particular documentary text, without alteration, or does he introduce modifications into an existing text? The issue arises from his recognition that no extant text—even a manuscript—might faithfully represent the intended readings. He chooses to make emendations, within the guidelines he sets out, though in his appendices he also includes various unemended texts. Both editorial traditions have found expression in the subsequent history of *The Dunciad.*

The simplest form of a text reproduced without alteration has been the photofacsimile. The 1729 quarto *Variorum,* for instance, has been published twice this way: on its bicentennial, by Robert Kilburn Root and the Princeton University Press, and in 1966 by the Scolar Press. The 1728 edition has likewise been reprinted photographically, in an edition I prepared in 1991. A related but quite different production is the type-facsimile of the 1728 edition that the Oxford University Press published on that version's two hundredth anniversary. Still a third form of unemended reproduction is the literal or diplomatic transcription, represented in Pope scholarship by Maynard Mack's *The Last and Greatest Art,* where he publishes manuscript readings of *The Dunciad* that Jonathan Richardson copied at Pope's request. Surprisingly, there seems as yet to be no complete facsimile or transcription of *The Dunciad* (including its notes and other attendant prose) available electronically.

These documentary editions may seem the easiest to produce in that although they need careful thought they do not require critical judgment about the elements of the text itself. Yet often the questions such editions raise are not addressed carefully. At some point the editor must determine which copy to photograph. This decision, in turn, rests on an assessment of whether there are any differences between related copies; more than twelve dozen variants occur in the 1728 printings, for instance. The editor must guarantee that the documentary reproduction is accurate and also needs to describe the physical features of the original and clarify any readings that might be ambiguous. The two reproductions of the 1729 quarto demonstrate that strict accuracy cannot be taken for granted: each lacks the signature "a" at the foot of the table of contents, even though the mark is present in the copies at Princeton and the British Library that were photographed for these printings. The Scolar publication also differs from the copy it claims to reproduce by moving an errata leaf, by silently inserting blank leaves to mark divisions, and by enlarging slightly the pages bearing ornaments or plates, thereby revealing that these may have been produced at a different time or by a different process. In addition, the first and second Scolar printings differ from each other. On pages 14 and 15 in the "Testimonies of Authors," the footnote superscripts "o" and "r" disappear in the later impression of 1968, probably removed accidentally as marginal spots were cleaned up. Bewilderingly, the superscript "r" is missing in the Princeton facsimile as well, though it is present in the copy that was photographed.[9]

Diplomatic transcriptions likewise are fraught with challenge. With obvious smugness Joseph Warton reprinted the 1728 *Dunciad* in his 1797 edition of Pope to show, he said, "how much it suffered, and was disfigured, by a fourth book" (331). But what he actually published was not the 1728 version but the *Variorum* of 1729 simply shorn of its notes, and the edition of the *Variorum* he reprinted was for some reason from the second 1736 octavo edition of Pope's *Works*. In the nineteenth century, Whitwell Elwin and William John Courthope also printed what they called the 1728 edition. They mostly got it right, making 120 minor changes and silently emending on a larger scale at four other places. Herbert Davis's 1966 Oxford edition also includes the 1728 text, with only four dozen minor changes. The version of the prose introduction that he prints with it, however, is one that Pope did not publish until fifteen years later.

Scriblerus's decision to present a text that introduces editorial emendations has largely been followed by later editors. The extent to which they have intervened, however, has varied widely. Scriblerus suggests the range that is possible: the editor might simply correct typos, the "accidental Faults escaped the press" (81 ["M. Scriblerus Lectori"] in the 1729 quarto), or go so far as to incorporate words that are not found in any extant document but that on the basis of other evidence are judged to be part of the historically intended form of the work that the edition attempts to present. Given the role that the issue of emendation had played in scholarly debates for centuries, it is surprising that three of the four major collections appearing between Warburton's in the eighteenth century and the Twickenham in the twentieth give very little attention to the text itself. They agree with one important historical goal of Scriblerus, to make the author's meaning clear, and they are also like him in the degree of their partisanship—except that most of them are against Pope. Their emphasis, however, is on the commentary, for they are satisfied with earlier editions of the text itself. As a self-described "Scholiast," Scriblerus avoids judgments "purely of the Poetical kind" (A1.10n), whereas the later editors specifically aim to provide evaluations of the work and the man.

The first of those four editions was the nine-volume one by Joseph Warton in 1797. In it he incorporated as notes much of his earlier study, *An Essay on the Genius and Writings of Pope,* first published in 1756 with a second volume added upon publication of its fourth edition in 1782. Warton's former pupil, the poet William Lisle Bowles, published a ten-volume edition in 1806, thereby extending the commentary but not the canon and precipitating a virulent debate over Pope's poetic merits that drew Byron as a participant.[10] One of the contestants, William Roscoe, determined "to stem this inundation of modern Vandalism" by Warton, Bowles, and the "great herd of modern critics" and to produce an edition of his own, which he published in 1824.[11] "One of the principal objects of the new edition," according to his son, "was to give a fuller and more accurate [and more favorable] life of the poet than had yet appeared";[12] his attempt to do so was aided by the two editions of Joseph Spence's *Anecdotes* that had been published on the same day in 1820.[13] This intense interest in Pope prompted John Wilson Croker in 1831 to collect materials for still another attempt, which he planned to finish in a year.[14] Unfortunately, though he worked on the edition over a quarter of a century until literally his dying day, he did not complete it; his materials passed in 1857 to Whitwell Elwin, who "declared that he knew every line of Pope by heart, and that to complete the edition would be an easy and pleasant task which he could carry out in his hours of leisure."[15] Fourteen years later Elwin published his first volumes. In all, he produced five of them, with his successor William John Courthope bringing the ten-volume set to completion in 1889.

In a letter of 1831 Croker offered an interesting explanation of why fresh editing was called for:

> None of our poets has been so often and so badly edited. Notes upon notes, commentaries on commentaries, tell you *all,* except just what one wants to know. Warburton has given us razor-edged disquisitions, fine and false, in the Divine Legation style, which are much more difficult to be understood than the text itself. Joe Warton has emptied into his notes all his classical commonplace books, and tells us a great deal about the literature and manners of every age except just Pope's own. Bowles has done little but scent out the taints of Pope's private char-

acter; and Roscoe tells nothing, because he knows nothing, beyond what he found before his eyes in former editions. But towards making the author as intelligible to posterity as he was to contemporaries, and putting the reader of 1831 into anything like the position of the reader of 1731—*that,* none of them have done, nor (what I complain of) even *attempted* to do.[16]

The edition that developed from Croker's dreams treated textual matters with greater care than any editor had for a century, in part by taking into account newly resurrected manuscripts. But as with the others, the emphasis was on elucidating the meaning of the poetry and the character of the poet.

Once Scriblerus decides that his edition will be historical, and, moreover, one that will introduce alterations into documentary texts, he is confronted with a third issue: what specific historical goal to pursue. His aim is to capture the historical intent of the writer—"the true sense of the Poet" (A3.28n) or "the meaning of our author" (A1.109n). He immediately confronts a difficulty, however, for he recognizes that the publication process has been a collaborative effort involving people whose contributions may be at cross-purposes with the author's. Citing misrepresentations of the author's intention by copyists (A1.28n), printers, and correctors (the latter two both noted in "M. Scriblerus Lectori"), he reserves his most plaintive cry for the work of editors, by whose "shameful ignorance," he says, "Our own specimen of *Virgil* [in the Appendix to the *Variorum*] hath been mangled in such miserable manner, that scarce without tears can we behold it" (Addenda list on Y1^r inserted into some copies of the quarto).

Scriblerus develops ways of sorting the author's intention from the contributions of others, but he then faces still another question: which intention of the author? He notes, for instance, how Pope's intentions changed: the author added a name because of provocation since earlier editions (A3.159n), but he also removed a former target in response to the victim's protestation of innocence (A3.146n). *The Dunciad,* with its many forms, provides superb occasions for editions that represent final intentions at different stages, but these have been possibilities not often seized. One editor who has taken excellent advantage of the opportunity is Valerie Rumbold, in her 1999 edition of the fourth major version of the poem, the 1743 *Dunciad in Four Books.* Her thoughtful attempt to honor Pope's intentions includes arranging the preliminary prose sections in the order she believes Pope had in mind (the sequence varies considerably among copies of the 1743 quarto). For another example of the form an edition of a particular version might take, one might consider the *Variorum.* Work there could start as the Twickenham Edition does, with the first 1729 quarto, though if one were seeking the author's final intentions for this version one would not join the Twickenham editors in stopping there to base the new edition exclusively on a text that is "best" overall but not in each particular. Rather, an editor might incorporate whatever variants in substantives or accidentals seemed attributable to Pope in later editions of that version. An editor could also focus even more narrowly, trying to establish the text that Pope intended at an intermediate point in the history of a version—in, say, 1735, the year of a major collection of his works and about midway between the first and last *Variorum* editions.

Scriblerus's own editorial goals, then, gradually become clear, but one historical approach he implicitly rejects, editing the work as a collaborative social product, could also be pursued. It might be that an editor would want to reconstruct the text intended by a participant other than the author. If one were interested in the printers of *The Dunciad* such as John Wright or William Bowyer, for instance, and were able to ascertain the characteristics of their house style, one could emend *The Dunciad* to make manifestations of the style consistent. If one were interested in the work as shaped by its editor Warburton, one could produce an edition of his edition, possibly emending the first 1751 text by variants from his later editions. To estimate properly Warburton's contribution, one would still need to know how much of the text represented the original author's intention, however, if only to subtract the author's influence from that of the editor.

A different goal of an historical editor wishing to emphasize a text as a social product might be to reconstruct the text available to a given audience at a certain time. Because the intentions of any of the producers would in such cases be irrelevant, it is hard to conceive of a format more efficiently suited than a photographic or electronic facsimile, whose presentation would include errors untouched or unretouched by editorial intervention. Such an edition would, of course, be subject to the usual standards for facsimiles, particularly the need to justify reproducing that particular copy of that particular edition.

Finally, vaguely hinted at in Scriblerus's work is the suggestion that either emended or unemended texts that are generated by one or more of the methods already discussed might be presented simultaneously. The suggestion implicitly arises from the fact that the *Variorum* contains not only the materials immediately essential to its own rhetorical development but also (in the Appendix) parallel ones from the 1728 edition. Several classes of textual materials call out for comparative presentation: alterations within a manuscript; or the editions, impressions, and states of a single version; or the texts of several versions. Depending on the complexity of the material, different solutions are possible. Transcriptions may suffice, either inclusive ones with all elements present in the main text, or a clear text with the alterations recorded elsewhere. A traditional historical collation report, placed at the foot of the page or at the back of the edition, often is an efficient means of comparing forms. The Twickenham Edition demonstrates this treatment to some extent, though it does not record all variants in the poetry, and it reports almost none for the notes.[17] For large-scale variation, presentation as parallel texts might be appropriate. The Twickenham Edition provides an incipient form of this with its A (three-book) and B (four-book) versions of *The Dunciad,* but their display in separate sections makes comparison difficult.

What seems inevitable is a hypertext version of *The Dunciad,* not simply one in which editorial notes can be consulted by appropriate clicking but one in which any combination of texts might be compared. *The Dunciad* would seem to be the intertextual hypertextual project par excellence, the one for which the technology was created; but as yet not even a full machine-readable transcript of *The Dunciad* seems available. Chadwyck-Healey's *English Poetry Database* (1992) provides a 1743 *Dunciad,* but with "Preliminaries and introductory matter omitted." The latest version of the University of Toronto's *Representative Poetry On-Line* provides the text of *The New Dunciad,* book 4, of 1742, but nothing of books 1–3, and none of Pope's prose except for a few of the notes from book 4. In 1995 a University of Maryland student, Wendy J. Carter, began work on a web project named *The Hyper-Dunciad: Another Variorum,* but that website is no longer accessible.[18]

Hypertext may seem a great distance from our starting point, the remarks and practices of a fictional scholiast in an eighteenth-century satire. But while the technology for implementing editorial decisions may change, the fundamental issues to be dealt with remain those that Scriblerus encountered. The literary work he inhabits is, in its many manifestations over nearly three centuries, itself a showcase of the editorial possibilities that editors of any work have available for going about their task.

APPENDIX: *DUNCIAD* EDITIONS CITED

The Dunciad in Four Books. Vol. 5, *The Works of Alexander Pope Esq.* Edited by William Warburton. London: J. and P. Knapton, 1751.

The Works of Alexander Pope. Edited by Joseph Warton. Vol. 5. London: B. Law et al., 1797. New ed., 1822.

The Works of Alexander Pope, Esq. in Verse and Prose. Edited by William Lisle Bowles. Vol. 5. London: J. Johnson et al., 1806.

The Works of Alexander Pope, Esq. Edited by William Roscoe. Vol. 4. London: C. and J. Rivington et al., 1824. New ed., vol. 3, 1847.

The Poetical Works of Alexander Pope. Revised and Arranged

Expressly for the Use of Young People. Edited by William Charles Macready. London: Bradbury and Evans, 1849.

The Works of Alexander Pope. With introductions and notes by Whitwell Elwin and William John Courthope. Vol. 4. London: John Murray, 1882.

The Dunciad. An Heroic Poem. In Three Books. 1728. Facsimile reprint, Oxford: Clarendon Press, 1928.

The Dunciad Variorum with the Prolegomena of Scriblerus by Alexander Pope Reproduced in Facsimile from the First Issue of the Original Edition of 1729. With an introductory essay by Robert Kilburn Root. Princeton, N.J.: Princeton University Press, 1929.

The Dunciad. Edited by James Sutherland. Vol. 5, *The Twickenham Edition of the Poems of Alexander Pope,* edited by John Butt et al. London: Methuen; New York: Oxford University Press, 1943. 2d ed., rev., 1953. 3d ed., rev., 1963.

Pope. Selected, with an introduction and notes, by John Wain. The Laurel Poetry Series, edited by Richard Wilbur. New York: Dell, 1963.

The Dunciad Variorum. 1729. Facsimile reprint, Menston, U.K.: Scolar Press, 1966. 2d prtg., 1968.

Poetical Works. Edited by Herbert Davis. Oxford Standard Authors. London: Oxford University Press, 1966.

Alexander Pope's Poems. Edited by Peter Stryker. Peter Stryker's Zig-Zag Books. New York: Presto, 1978.

The Last and Greatest Art: Some Unpublished Poetical Manuscripts of Alexander Pope. Transcribed and edited by Maynard Mack. Newark: University of Delaware Press, 1984.

Alexander Pope: Selected Poetry and Prose. Edited by Robin Sowerby. London and New York: Routledge, 1988.

Pope's Dunciad of 1728: A History and Facsimile. Edited by David L. Vander Meulen. Charlottesville: University Press of Virginia for the Bibliographical Society of the University of Virginia and the New York Public Library, 1991.

The Dunciad in Four Books. Edited by Valerie Rumbold. Longman Annotated Texts. Harlow: Longman, 1999.

NOTES

1. James McLaverty discusses and illustrates these in "The Mode of Existence of Literary Works of Art: The Case of the *Dunciad Variorum*," *Studies in Bibliography* 37 (1984): 82–105. David Foxon suggests a similar phenomenon for the

1728 *Dunciad,* whose physical design he believes is indebted to Pope's association of the "Elzevier style with books of fame" (*Pope and the Early Eighteenth-Century Book Trade,* rev. and ed. James McLaverty [Oxford: Clarendon Press, 1991], 31).

2. Note to book 3, line 188, in the 1729 quarto and in the "A" version of the Twickenham Edition. Subsequent references, incorporated in the text, will be to this conveniently available modern source and will be preceded by an "A" or "B," in reference to the two versions it presents. Fuller information about the editions cited appears in the Appendix to this essay.

3. The 1729 version of the work, named *The Dunciad Variorum,* was the second of four major manifestations of a project that occupied Pope for nearly two decades and that appeared in five dozen editions, impressions, and issues by the time of William Warburton's posthumous collection of Pope's writings in 1751. *The Dunciad in Three Books* had been published as a small pamphlet in 1728; in the 1729 *Variorum,* the poem of the previous year was wrapped in elaborate prose apparatus and laden with footnotes. Pope published a fourth section, *The New Dunciad,* in 1742, and the next year he combined the *Variorum* and *New Dunciad,* in the process revising both parts, replacing the earlier hero Lewis Theobald with the current poet laureate, Colley Cibber, and calling the result *The Dunciad in Four Books.*

4. I consider Scriblerus's policies more fully in an article complementary to the present one, "The Editorial Principles of Martinus Scriblerus," in *The Culture of the Book: Essays from Two Hemispheres in Honour of Wallace Kirsop* (Melbourne: Bibliographical Society of Australia and New Zealand, 1999), 173–81.

5. In pondering the possibilities that Scriblerus suggests, I am especially indebted to the introductory article in a recent collection of essays on editorial traditions: G. Thomas Tanselle's "The Varieties of Scholarly Editing," in *Scholarly Editing: A Guide to Research,* ed. D. C. Greetham (New York: Modern Language Association, 1995), 9–32.

6. See Pope to Swift, January 1727/28 in *The Correspondence of Alexander Pope,* ed. George Sherburn (Oxford: Clarendon Press, 1956), 2:468.

7. Marcus Walsh deals lucidly with Bentley's work on Milton, and with contemporary responses to it, in *Shakespeare, Milton, and Eighteenth-Century Literary Editing: The Beginnings of Interpretive Scholarship* (Cambridge: Cambridge University Press, 1997), particularly on pages 62–94 of his chapter "Making Sense of Milton: The Editing of *Paradise Lost.*"

8. My own copy is stamped "Duplicate" and "Surplus" by the Library of Congress Copyright Office. I have been unable to locate any record of a copy the library may have kept—or of another copy anywhere.

9. The theoretical and practical problems raised by facsimiles are perceptively surveyed by G. Thomas Tanselle in "Reproductions and Scholarship," *Studies in Bibliography* 42 (1989): 25–54, reprinted in his *Literature and Artifacts* (Charlottesville: Bibliographical Society of the University of Virginia, 1998), 59–88.

10. Andrew Nicholson outlines the controversy and lists its publications in his edition *Lord Byron: The Complete Miscellaneous Prose* (Oxford: Clarendon Press, 1991), 399–409.

11. Letter to Thomas James Mathias on 2 October 1822, quoted in Henry Roscoe, *The Life of William Roscoe* (London, 1833), 2:334.

12. Roscoe, *The Life of William Roscoe,* 2:334.

13. *Anecdotes, Observations, and Characters, of Books and Men,* ed. Samuel Weller Singer (London: W. H. Carpenter, 1820), and *Observations, Anecdotes, and Characters, of Books and Men,* ed. Edmond Malone (London: John Murray, 1820).

14. Myron F. Brightfield, *John Wilson Croker* (Berkeley: University of California Press, 1940), 311.

15. George Paston, *At John Murray's: Records of a Literary Circle, 1843–1892* (London: John Murray, 1932), 155.

16. *The Croker Papers: The Correspondence and Diaries of the Late Right Honourable John Wilson Croker,* ed. Louis J. Jennings (New York, 1884), 1:533–34.

17. Critics have recognized increasingly that the text of *The Dunciad* consists of far more than its verse. For an example of Pope tinkering with its prose—in this case, a footnote—over several editions, see my "Pope's Revisions during Printing: A Variant Section in *The Dunciad,*" *Modern Philology* 78 (1981): 393–98.

18. I have consulted *English Poetry* through the website of the University of Virginia Library's Electronic Text Center, <etext.lib.virginia.edu> (22 November 2000). *Representative Poetry On-Line,* version 2.07, is available at <www.library.utoronto.ca/utel/rp/intro.html> (22 November 2000). *The Hyper-Dunciad* originally appeared at <www.wam.umd.edu/%7Ewendyjc/pope/popehp.html>.

11

"What Must the World Think of Me?"

Pope, Madame Dacier, and Homer—The Anatomy of a Quarrel

HOWARD D. WEINBROT

"I was first translated ignorantly, and then read partially."[1] That pained speaker is not the beleaguered Alexander Pope in the *Dunciad* but the presumably confident Alexander Pope at the end of his "Postscript to the Odyssey" in April of 1725. He had just finished the most publicly successful period of his career. Whatever the storm clouds already rising, Homer and then Shakespeare had made Pope financially independent, provided his squirarchic home at Twickenham, and elevated him in the European world of letters. Homer also provided sufficient poetic status for him to transcend both crude and subtle attacks by men like Dennis and Addison. Pope's subsequent responses make plain that these attacks angered him; but they were the blows a veteran in early eighteenth-century literary combat anticipated. For the time being he remained defensive rather than aggressive.

Even in 1725 Pope responds rather than provokes. He does so not to a living English enemy but to a recently dead French ally—to Madame Anne le Fevre Dacier, part of the most deservedly respected family of classicists in contemporary Europe. Her distinguished husband André edited, translated, or commented on several major classical authors including Aristotle, Plutarch, and Horace. His edition of Horace (1681–1689) indeed was the most influential vernacular eighteenth-century version and included a vigorous defence of the classics as bastions of civilization.[2] André was a member of the Académie Française and then its Secrétaire

Perpétuel, a member of the Académie des Inscriptions et Belles Lettres, and Garde des Livres du Cabinet du Roi. Madame Dacier herself was a preeminent editor, translator, and commentator. She had provided several Greek and Latin texts and in 1711 a major highly annotated prose version of the *Iliad* that also would become a European vernacular landmark. The Daciers' name was a compelling argument on authority.

Pope read Madame Dacier's translation of the *Iliad* and used many of her notes, which he generally admired, though he sometimes disagreed with her excessive praise of Homer and his age. Indeed, as a team the Daciers were such fierce defenders of the "Ancients" that they even regarded Boileau as "presque . . . un héretique" because he withheld praise from "la scandaleuse Sapho" and suggested that Socrates was sexually attracted to Alcibiades.[3] Pope's remark regarding Madame Dacier's misrepresentation of him is in fact a skirmish in the Anglo-French battle between the Ancients and the Moderns. She was an unyielding combatant and in her way as bellicose towards presumed Dulness in Paris of 1714 as Pope would be in London of 1728. It had not occurred to Pope, though, that he could be the Modern Dunce that Madame Dacier claimed he was. The story begins on the French side of the channel.

1.

In 1716 the *Journal literaire* reports that the dispute concerning Homer had moderated, since "la Paix s'est fait entre les deux grands Antagonists M. [Houdar] *de la Motte* & *Mad. Dacier,* par la mediation de quelques amis communes." As Madame De Staal Delaunay records it, Madame de Lambert and Jean-Baptiste de Valincour had arranged "un repas . . . pour réunir les *Anciens* avec les *Modernes.*" This earlier French version of the Johnson-Wilkes dinner negotiated an armistice sealed with a toast "à la santé d'Homére, et tout passa bien." Houdar stops writing the fourth part of his *Reflexions sur la critique* in answer to Madame Dacier's *Des Causes de la corruption du goust* (Paris, 1714) and upon her death celebrates her in a laudatory ode "dans une seance publique de l'Académie."[4]

As the Marquise de Lambert knew, and as the Duke of Buckingham warned Pope, no one who appeared to doubt Madame Dacier's vision of a sanctified Homer in a sanctified age was safe from her anger, however briefly suppressed. Madame de Lambert writes two confidential letters to le Père Bussier in which she clearly sides with Houdar and the Moderns and concludes with a plea for the reverend father's secrecy, the need for which Alexander Pope would well have understood: "Je vous prie de ne pas montrer ma Lettre à Mad. DACIER, & de n'en donner copie à personne."[5]

Madame Dacier's battles were scarcely over. In 1716 she also attacked le Père Jean Hardouin, whose generally pro-Ancient *Apologie d'Homere* (1716) she nonetheless feared would sap the basis of ancient authority.[6] She thus would have been especially interested when in that same year the *Journal literaire* glowingly reviews the first installment of Pope's *Iliad* and makes plain that even its front matter and preface announce an event of international importance: the book's eight pages of subscribers are headed by his royal highness the Prince of Wales ("Son Altesse Royale le Prince de Galles"). Pope's brilliant and faithful poetry already has earned him more than £5,000. One wonders, the *Journal* says, whether this more honors M. Pope or the English nation ("fait le plus d'honneur ou à M. *Pope,* ou à la Nation Angloise," 8:1). Madame Dacier herself thought that anyone who genuinely had read and understood Homer must translate him into prose faithful to his morality, rather than misrepresent him in poetry merely designed to please.[7] Here, in contrast, an eloquent French voice praised the sort of version that she regarded as undesirable.

The *Journal literaire* adds two more points regarding Pope that Madame Dacier would have found disturbing. The first is that in spite of general fidelity, "bien souvent il corrige *Homere* sans l'altérer, & en exprimant avec politesse, ce qui dans son modele est taxé justement de grossiéreté" (8:1). The second point is consistent with such incipient modernism—namely, that Pope generally agrees with Houdar—and implicitly corrects Madame Dacier for her heated attacks upon him: "Voilà comme bien souvent des gens paroissent se combattre, lors qu'étant réelement de la même opinion" (8:41).[8]

By 1717 this favorable response probably encouraged four francophone literary journals, including the *Journal literaire* and the *Journal des sçavans,* to review the translated *Essai sur la critique; imité de l'Anglois de Mr. Pope* (1717). Emile Audra long ago speculated that while in France Pope's Catholic Jacobite older friend John Caryll helped to spread Pope's reputation: it would seem, Audra says, that Pope owed his first fame in France to the friendship of Caryll, that is, in the last analysis because he was Catholic.[9] Audra understandably may be confusing John Caryll the Jacobite Secretary of State to James II at St. Germain, with his nephew John Caryll also educated in France. Nonetheless Pope knew the Carylls at least as early as 1703; John Caryll and his family were abroad, presumably in France, in 1714 and were familiar with Pope's work on Homer. Certainly by the midpoint of Pope's career he was indeed known, as the Abbé du Resnel put it in 1737, as "Né, & élevé dans le sein de la Religion Catholique." The Abbé Yart later adds that Pope was the offspring of parents "vertueux & Catholiques." Given the small world of Anglo-French literary relations, Audra's sound hypothesis suggests one reason the French were attracted to Pope, whom they preferred as a ratiocinative rather than imaginative or satiric poet. In 1753, for example, the Abbé Yart describes "l'Essai sur la Critique" as the "Ouvrage qui immortelisera M. Pope." The highly specific *Dunciad,* "si vanté dans son pays, a perdu tout son mérite en passant la mer."[10]

Whether or not Madame Dacier was concerned regarding favorable response to Pope's *Iliad* and its Preface, by 1717 she almost certainly knew that a foreign Catholic interloper was mapping her land already under attack by traitors from within. As Audra again says, unfortunately a new corrupter of taste was about to appear, one who sprang from the fogs of Albion. Those English fogs were propelled by André Robert Perelle who in 1718 translated portions of Pope's Preface into French. Had Madame Dacier seen the favorable review of Pope in the *Journal des sçavans* for March of 1719 she surely would have been troubled. The "habile Ecrivain" seems to engage the Moderns and argue on Homer's behalf; but he also agrees with several of the Moderns' views regarding Homer: "M. de la Motte *admire l'Ouvrier* plus que l'Ouvrage; il est en cela d'accord avec M. Pope." This was heresy for Madame Dacier who would regard Pope's praise of Homer as duplicitous "faux éloges." She thus transfers her recorded anger from Houdar to Pope, about whom she appends a severe attack in the second edition of her *Iliad* translation in 1719.[11] The title page of her first volume even includes a phrase announcing to Europe that this edition was *Avec Quelques Reflexions sur la Preface Anglois de M. Pope.*

These "Reflexions" provide evidence that she already knew of Pope's translation, to which she offers grudging and tentative respect: "As I do not understand that [English] Language, I cannot form any Judgment of his Performance, tho' I have heard much of it. I am indeed willing to believe, that the Praises it has met with are not unmerited, because whatever Work is approved by the *English* Nation, cannot be bad."[12] She soon contradicts this judgment and soon includes larger denigration. Pope, she ironically claims, "had done us a great Piece of Service" if he had demonstrated what he thought were the asymmetrical branches that should have been lopped from Homer's perfect plot-tree: "it would be very happy for the present Age, and glorious to *England,* to have produced so perfect a Critick" (8).[13]

On 8 February 1724 Edmund Curll printed her "Reflexions" as *Madame Dacier's Remarks upon Mr. Pope's Account of Homer, Prefixed to His Translation of the Iliad,* nominally translated by one of Curll's ghosts, a phantom Thomas Parnell. H. Stanhope (William Bond) later reissued the pamphlet in *The Popiad* (1728); it appears again in *Mr. Pope's Literary Correspondence, Volume the Fifth* (1737); and again in William

Ayre's (Edmund Curll's?) *Memoirs of . . . Pope* (1745). Such circulation allowed the "Reflexions" to be noted at home and abroad. The *Journal des sçavans'* éloge for Madame Dacier in January of 1721 notes her attack on Pope and her ability to smite the alien hip and thigh: "Ces reflexions tendent à relever quelques méprises & quelques contradictions de ce nouveau Traducteur, au sujet des divers jugemens qu'il porte sur le mérite d'Homere." The first number of the vocally Hanoverian *St. James's Journal,* 3 May 1722, adapts this remark as, "her Reflections tend to discover some Absurdities and Contradictions in that young Translator."[14] The éloge for Madame Dacier in the *Mémoires de Trévoux* provides yet sterner insults that are both unanswerable in such a context and make plain that the dead French woman easily polished off the living English man:

> on lui communiqua une partie de la Préface de M. Pope sçavant Anglois qui a traduit Homere en vers. Elle fut choquée des faux éloges que cet Auteur donne à ce Poëte, & elle crût qu'il étoit encore plus important de faire voir la fauseté de ces éloges, qu'il ne l'avoït été de refuter les fausses critiques qu'on en avoit faites. C'est ce qu'elle fit dans une petite reponse qu'elle a ajoûté à cette nouvelle édition, & c'est son dernier ouvrage.[15]

No wonder that Pope's domestic detractors could exploit such material. *The Curliad* (1729) complains that Pope's nominal *Dunciad* ally William Cleland "says not one word of Madame *Dacier*'s Character of his Version of *Homer;* which is now translated and inserted, in the POPIAD, p. 26." John Dennis sounds as if he knows her reflections on Pope when he says that Pope "blindly says more infamous Things of him [Homer], than either *Terrasson, Le Motte,* or *Perrault.*" No wonder also that the hostile *Popiad* adds that "Dacier *and* Dennis *in* one Cause *unite, / And prove that* Pope *can nor* Translate, *nor* Write." After reading Madame Dacier and Dennis even Pope's "most partial" friends must allow "that, the present Residence of the *Goddess* of *Dullness* is at *Twickenham.*"[16] In 1745 William Ayre apparently invents an exchange of letters in which Pope says *mea maxima culpa* to Madame Dacier and she says *tant mieux* and *pax vobiscum.*[17] She had given Pope's enemies yet another stick with which to beat him and from which, however ineffectually, he needed to protect himself if he also was to protect his own professional integrity, the integrity of his translation, and the continuance of its sales. Samuel Johnson alludes to the tenuous nature of the literary marketplace when he observes: "To those who censured his politicks were added enemies yet more dangerous, who called in question his knowledge of Greek, and his qualifications for a translator of Homer."[18]

Madame Dacier's "Reflexions" are indeed dangerous. They censure

Pope for apparently saying that the *Iliad* lacks order and should be retrenched, that the moderns have improved morally upon the ancients, that Virgil had better judgment than Homer, and that the Homeric heroes were not like Old Testament patriarchs. They also charge that he borrowed from her without acknowledgment, that he did not understand the Aristotle he cited, and that he spoke incomprehensible nonsense when he referred to Homer's moving world ("monde mouvant"). In spite of all her battles "against the Cavils of so many ignorant Censors" she again must defend Homer "against the Reproaches of one of greater Penetration, and [who] may therefore do him more Injury in the Minds of unlearned Readers, tho' at the same time he pretends to have a great Veneration for him" (4–5).[19]

Madame Dacier makes her response to Pope a family affair by invoking her husband as a formidable ally—as well she might, since both in private and in public the Daciers were regarded as a virtual team of distinguished Ancients.[20] She insists that Pope misunderstands the Aristotelian poetics he invokes when discussing Homer: "Nothing can be more repugnant to the Doctrine of that Philosopher" (15).[21] She thus implicitly reminds her readers that André Dacier's translation and commentary on the poetics (1692), with English translations in 1705, 1709, and 1713, is the French and thus by assumption the font of proper Aristotelian wisdom. According to André's subtitle his book contains "*les règles les plus exactes pour juger du poëme héroique*," to which Pope clearly had not attended: "It is astonishing, that Mr. Pope has not understood a thing which is so clearly explained in Aristotle's *Art of Poetry,* and in my *Preface* to the *Odysseys.* I refer that learned Man to these *two Works*" (16).[22] Moreover, when scolding becomes insult she invokes an episode from Plutarch's life of Alcibiades that was known in England and also translated by André Dacier:

> When he was past his Childhood, he went once to a Grammar-School, and ask'd the Master for one of *Homer*'s Books; and he making Answer, that he had nothing of *Homer*'s, *Alcibiades* gave him a Blow with his Fist, and went away. Another School-master telling him that he had *Homer* corrected by himself; *How,* said *Alcibiades, and do you imploy your Time in Teaching Children to read? You, who are able to amend* Homer, *may well undertake to instruct Men.*[23]

Madame Dacier's version of this episode is even harsher than it appears in English. As both she and André translate it, Alcibiades uses the here patronizing *tu-toi* with the arrogantly dim-witted schoolmaster: "*Eh mon ami,* luy dit-il, *tu es capable de corriger Homere, & tu t'amuses à enseigner des enfants, que ne t'appliques-tu à former des hommes?*"[24] After quoting this second episode Madame Dacier exclaims, in the French version: "Voilà une grande ressource pour un Estat!" (3:sig. *8^v in 1719). As Pope's English translator expands it, "Of what infinite Consequence, then will Mr. POPE be to a State, since he can reform HOMER?" (18). She associates Pope with a Homer-deprived schoolmaster—for the Daciers a "Grammairien"—who deserves a beating. This arrogant and dim upstart should not be inflicted on children who, as her *Des Causes de la corruption du goust* made plain, are the precious seeds of a civilized "Ancient" future. By analogy, like Houdar, Pope is dangerous enough to sap the foundations of received wisdom.[25] On 19 October 1709 Pope told Henry Cromwell: "if I have any Taste, [Plutarch] is the greatest of Moral Philosophers."[26] He could not have missed the hostility in Madame Dacier's allusion and quotation.

By 1719 Pope had come to expect savaging by real or fancied enemies, but here probably for the first time he was savaged by a presumed ally. He could regard attacks by Dennis or Gildon as attacks by venomous insects. He could not so regard Madame Dacier's attacks and in spite of his growing reputation was professionally threatened at home and abroad. The respected colleague of the notes to his *Iliad* has become a bitter antagonist; the translator who excoriated Houdar for reading Homer in translation now excoriates Pope whom she read in a bad and partial translation. Yet worse, in lines Madame Dacier designed to be offensive, she attacks "this *new Poet*" who thinks he can reform Homer. Surely, she sneers while adapting Plutarch's Alcibiades, such a man will shift from poetry to politics and attempt to reform the state as he attempts to reform Homer: "he'll perfect the *Art of Politicks,* much more valuable and more important than that of *Epick Poesy*" (17).[27] Pope's reply in 1725 softens her remarks to, I suspect, soften the political attack for his large readership. Such a man thinks himself "capable of 'correcting *Homer,* and consequently of reforming mankind, and amending this Constitution'" (*TE* 10:397).[28]

Concern with dangerous literary and political decline long had characterized the Ancients' fear of instability—questioning classical supremacy is a dangerous step off the straight and narrow. For Roger Ascham in *The Scholemaster* (1570), prideful reservations regarding Aristotle or Cicero lead "to the misliking of greater matters"—like dissent in religion "or in the common wealth, to haue a factious hart."[29] Swift's *Tale of a Tub* (1704) exploits a comparable assumption, in which enemies of Homer and enemies of the established Church and state share a disruptive attitude toward the past. In Madame Dacier's own *Des Causes de la corruption du goust* letters are the source of good taste, of politeness, and of good government, as Socrates knew and taught "pour former de bons sujets à la Republique."[30]

Madame Dacier also well understood the dangers and pressures of being a visible exemplar of a putative alien treasonous religion. Pierre Bayle reports that when she was a Protestant only her patron the powerful Duc de Montausier dared to present Louis XIV with her book dedicated to him. He at first rejected the offer, threatened to seize the entire edition, and relented when shamed by the brave duke himself.[31] In September of 1685 she and André renounced Protestantism for French Catholicism and were indeed later attacked by some as unprincipled literary mercenaries. Bayle and then Chaufepié repeat the *Bibliothèque Francoise*'s charge that the Daciers converted themselves and then others in their native Castres in order to gain ample pensions.[32] However welcome the pension, it was perhaps not more important than the ultimate desire for such prominent French scholars. As D'Alembert later says, "L'Académie Françoise est l'objet de l'ambition, secrete ou avouée, de presque tous les Gens de Lettres." Here is the crown that is "une récompense flatteuse pour les Ecrivains distingués."[33]

Like almost all of the French intellectual and aristocratic elite, the Académie itself warmly supported the 18 October 1685 Revocation of the Edict of Nantes and its abolition of lingering Huguenot civil and religious liberty. That learned body even sponsored a poetry contest whose subject was the Revocation and whose prize Fontenelle won. Geoffrey Adams thus accurately observes that the Académie was "bound to become involved in the campaign to uproot and destroy heresy."[34] Perhaps that also is one reason why in 1695 André's "Discours . . . lorsqu'il fut reçu" so emphasized Louis XIV's achievement as religious unifier of France.[35] This emphasis was all the more appropriate because Dacier replaced the late Francis de Harlay, Archbishop of Paris, whose theology he praised. Dacier also was initiated into the Académie by the Abbé de Clérambault. André was so prudent because he was the first Catholic convert to be received into the Académie since the Revocation ten years earlier. As Jules Chavannes said in 1856, this discours de reception amounted to Dacier's formal renewal of his Protestant abjuration, without which he could not have acquired his royal and academic honors.[36] In 1708 André may have had such political and religious tokens in mind when he sternly responds to Jean Masson's attack upon his *Horace* and observes that Masson is a *Ministre refugié en Angleterre*.[37] The memorial éloge for André also makes much of religion. He was born into the Protestant church as "la Religion prétendue Reformeé"; the Daciers' conversion to Catholicism was "l'édifiant spectacle de leur réunion au sein de l'Eglise dont leurs peres étoient sortis"; and André's painful death from throat cancer required a written confession after which he received "les autres Sacremens de l'Eglise avec . . . zèle & . . . ferveur."[38]

As a French Protestant Madame Dacier of course knew about the dragonnades that forced conversions through physical threat. By 1719 she also well knew that some 400,000 of her once co-religionists had fled France for England, Holland, and Brandenburg, among other places. On 5 October 1713 she thus wrote to a senior authority in the French Catholic Church asking that her Anglican-priest brother Tanneguy le Fevre be allowed to return to France from England. She observes that he angered the Whigs, always swore loyalty to the French king, and will become a Catholic and a model for other dispersed French Protestants who may convert and return home.[39] By suggesting Pope's disloyalty to his own crown Madame Dacier was being consciously hurtful and Pope was consciously hurt.

2.

Pope read Madame Dacier's remarks in February of 1723. Sir Luke Schaub, the British ambassador to France, then asked the government printer Samuel Buckley to deliver the gift of Madame Dacier's second edition of the *Iliad* translation.[40] On 17 February 1717, under the emblem of the House of Hanover, Buckley published firm evidence of a Jacobite plot to engage the goth Charles XII of Sweden with "the design of raising a Rebellion in His MAJESTY's Dominions, to be supported by a Force from *Sweden*."[41] Buckley also printed the government's *London Gazette*, sought out seditious publications, and arrested their printers. Whatever Schaub's and Buckley's motives, they alerted Pope to Madame Dacier's attack upon him at a delicate time—shortly after he was associated with the Duke of Buckingham's putatively Jacobite *Works* in January of 1723, and shortly before Bishop Atterbury left the Tower to be tried as a Jacobite traitor in May. Pope long had been attacked as part of a Catholic-Jacobite literary fifth column preparing England for the Pretender as, for such readers, much of Pope's early poetry and the *Iliad* translation itself seemed to make plain. John Dennis, for example, argues that the *Essay on Criticism* is a Jacobite poem by a Catholic poet written for rewards from the Pretender. Here is a slanderous poet, Dennis also claims, who "has Libell'd two Monarchs and two Nations." William Bond accuses Pope of inventing a Homer who speaks "like a *Papist*."[42] The later *Dunciad* clearly amplifies anger against Pope and doubts regarding his loyalty to the Protestant Hanoverian monarch. In 1723 troubled, defensive, and aware that Madame Dacier's inferences could be used against him, Pope in turn uses Buckley as a conduit to the Whig administration:

> What indeed most concerns me is her last period, in which she seems both angry & merry (so far I like it very well) but she concludes, that because I some-

times own Homer not to be the Pope, that is not to be infallible; therefore I must think myself wiser, & so correct him. And consequently that I must be qualify'd to Reform all mankind, and be at the Head of the Government. . . . This truly Sir I do not like, & think proper (to you, who are a sort of a Minister, and to all my Friends of the Office) to enter my Protest against such suggestions; especially at this time, when I am told People blame me for having Seen a Book [Buckingham's *Works*]. And such a Book (God knows) as I had no more thoughts of Correcting, than of Homer himself—

Pope wonders whether Tickell might be the better translator of the *Odyssey* "for the honour & safety of the Protestant Religion & Establishment, which otherwise (according to M. Dacier) a Papist may do much damage to. I did not think I had such Talents in Politicks." He concludes with a mock request that reveals genuine concern: "Pray assure all our Friends of the Office, of my Services & good intentions toward them all, when I am Premiere Ministre."[43]

Pope's next three letters demonstrate his fear concerning the Buckingham and Atterbury affairs and the toll his government's disapprobation could take on his pending translation of the *Odyssey.* On 13 February 1723 he asks Harley if "our Governors are displeas'd at me" (*Corr.* 2:159); on 16 February he tells Carteret that he does not want to be "(however innocently) under the least displeasure of the Government. . . . Indeed my Lord I love my Country, better than any Personal friend I have" (2:160); and on 20 February he similarly tells Harcourt that he fears he is "under . . . displeasure of my Governours, (however innocently)" (2:161).

Pope learned that he could not limit awareness of so tempting an insult, for his old adversary Edmund Curll soon published *Madam Dacier's Remarks.* He had been biding his time at least since 1716 when Pope's *A Full and True Account of a Horrible and Barbarous Revenge by Poison, On the Body of Mr. Edmund Curll, Bookseller* recounted the punitive emetic inflicted on that unscrupulous man. Madame Dacier's "Reflexions" provided splendid cover, an opportunity to even the score behind a great name and, perhaps, to ingratiate himself with the court's foreign office which may have alerted Curll to the attack.[44] An alarmed and frightened Alexander Pope thus needed not only to refute Madame Dacier's charges in private correspondence with Samuel Buckley. He also needed a public campaign to exonerate himself from her charges of incompetence and from the implications of treason that her "Reflexions" encouraged in France and England. After all, as Pope says, "Had these reflections fallen from the pen of an ordinary Critick, I should not have apprehended their effect, and should therefore have been silent concerning them: but since they are Madam *Dacier*'s, I imagine that they must be of weight. . . . What must the world think of me, after such a judgment pass'd by so great a Critick?" (*TE* 10:392). In April of 1725 Pope's final pages of his "Postscript to the Odyssey" moderately but sternly nullify so weighty a judgment. He uses four different but overlapping approaches.

The first is to grant her authority regarding Homer while undermining her authority regarding Pope. He acknowledges her role as general in Homer's army and laments her abuse of the soldier at her side. "I have fought under Madam *Dacier*'s banner, and have wag'd war in defence of the divine *Homer* against all the Hereticks of the age. And yet it is Madame *Dacier* who accuses me of nothing less than betraying our common Cause." She even claims that Homer's "most declar'd enemies . . . have never said anything against him more injurious or more unjust than I" (10:392). This also is a virtual holy war. Madame Dacier as martial high priestess both wrongly excommunicates her loyal priest and confuses analysis of poetry with religious dogma: "I am as orthodox as Madame *Dacier* herself in those articles in which she treats me like an Heretick." Pope offers "*opinions*, and she delivers *doctrines*." Pope thinks Homer "the greatest of human Poets"; she thinks him "exalted above humanity; infallibility and impeccability were two of his attributes" (10:394). As for stealing her sentiments without acknowledgment, Pope says, "I used them on purpose, being then professedly citing from her"—but, he makes plain, they also are her own unacknowledged borrowings from Eustathius and are commonplaces (10:394).

His second approach is both to grant and to diminish some of her complaints. She did not object to his general or essential points, but only to a few of his similes. Pope the mature poet knows "that to combate a Simile is no more than to fight with a shadow, since a Simile is no better than the shadow of an Argument" (10:393). She has confused poetic with logical argument, ornament with substance, and the inconsequential with the substantial. "She lays much weight where I lay'd but little, and examines with more scrupulosity than I writ, or than perhaps the matter requires" (10:393). He also grants that his language regarding Aristotle was imprecise, as indeed was Madame Dacier's. Moreover, she mistranslated Eustathius' Cratisthenes the Philasian as Callisthenes the Physician and she insulted Houdar de la Motte for "omitting a material passage in the speech of *Helen* to *Hector, Il.* 6" when "there was no such passage in *Homer*" (10:396).[45]

Pope's third mode of defence is to offer related theories of causation. One is based on Madame Dacier's known zeal and temperament and the other on her unwitting fall into the error for which she skewers her French adversaries. She wrote too quickly, too severely, and too easily paraphrased Pope's words which she so misrepresented that they say "the very contrary to what I have said in the passages themselves" (10:394).[46] She compounds inadequate conceptualizing with inadequate moderation. Madame Dacier was innocent of English and so did not know that her anger was based on a mistranslation of part of his Preface to the *Iliad.* In so depending on this version she has committed "the very same error, from which so many false criticisms of her countrymen upon *Homer* have flow'd, and which she has so justly and so severely reprov'd: . . . the error of depending on injurious and unskilful *translations*" (10:392). Pope urges "that no translation ought to be the ground of *Criticism,* because no man ought to be condemn'd upon another man's explanation of his meaning" (10:393). In this respect Madame Dacier is all too like her great adversary Houdar de la Motte and Homer's other Greekless critics "whom she styles *blind Censurers,* and blames for condemning what they did not understand" (10:393).

Pope justifiably lamented that Madame Dacier knew little "of my true sense from that faulty translation" (10:393). Specifically, here is an example of why the puzzled Alexander Pope was outraged by Madame Dacier's outrage. He had written that Homer "open'd a new and boundless Walk for his Imagination, and created a World for himself in the Invention of *Fable*" (*TE* 7:5). In Perelle's translation and Madame Dacier's "Reflexions," however, that appeared as "*Homere . . . crea pour son usage un monde mouvant en inventant la fable,*" about which a perplexed Madame Dacier rightly asks: "Qu'est ce que cela signifie!" (*Iliad* 3:sig. *vi^{r}). Neither she nor Pope could then have seen the Avertissement to the 1728 reprint of Perelle's translation that responds either to Madame Dacier's consternation, to Pope's anger, or to both: "il y a avoit dans cet endroit une faut d'impression; car au lieu de *monde mouvant,* il faut lire *monde nouveau;* & un moins habile homme que le Traducteur ne s'y seroit pas mépris."[47]

Finally, Pope makes plain that there are indeed substantive issues on which he and Madame Dacier disagree and that on these issues related to national character his own view is superior to hers. Pope's *Windsor Forest* (1713) long ago included an impassioned celebration of commercial peace and prosperity that improve civilization. He thus sings Modern progress rather than Madame Dacier's Ancient sense of decline. She insists that classical times were the better "the less they were like ours." Pope rejects such pagan manners "as the custom of putting whole nations to the sword, condemning Kings and their families to perpetual slavery, and a few others. Madam *Dacier* judges otherwise in this" (*TE* 10:394).

Similarly, though Madame Dacier was far the better at classical scholarship, Pope was far the better at poetic understanding. She scolds him for ignorance of the Daciers' version of Aristotle: read André's commentary and my Preface to the *Odyssey,* we recall that she says. Rather than take such instruction Pope flaunts his British independence and, as in Johnson's definition of "saucy," his contempt for superiors: "I am sawcy enough to think that one may sometime differ from *Aristotle* without blundering, and . . . I am sure one may sometimes fall into an error by following him servilely" (10:395).[48] As usual, though, she fails to understand what Pope actually wrote regarding epic poetry in action. For him, Homer's variety requires a variety of speeches: "Every thing in it has manners, as *Aristotle* expresses it; That is, every thing is acted or spoken: very little passes in narration." She claims that the mere act or speech "has not necessarily manners," to which he asks "whether any thing can have manners which is neither acted nor spoken?" Pope instinctively understands Homer's genius at characterization. Whatever Aristotle said or the Daciers interpreted, Homer "excell'd in drawing Characters and painting Manners"—which Pope regards as functions of speech and action (10:395).

Pope begins his peroration by repositioning himself as he shifts his role from Madame Dacier's subaltern to her equal in Homeric combat: "Our concern, zeal, and even jealousy, for our great Author's honour were mutual, our endeavours to advance it were equal." He then returns to national distinctions with, not surprisingly, relative British toleration. Pope here says covertly what he soon will say overtly: Madame Dacier's absolutist version of Homer is consistent with her absolutist French political and religious system. In contrast, Pope's fluidity of praise is consistent with British freedom: "as different people have different ways of expressing their Belief, some purely by public and general acts of worship, others by a reverend sort of reasoning and enquiry about the grounds of it; 'tis the same in Admiration, some prove it by exclamations, others by respect." Pope himself prefers "the more moderate, and I hope, more rational method" (10:396–97).

Pope's British via media in religion and in literary praise is a function of the British constitution to which he is loyal and which she wrongly thinks he could wish to change. He concludes the Postscript by directly refuting Madame Dacier's attack upon his loyalty or, at the least, political tergiversation. Here is a triumphant confrontation well prepared for in his earlier uses of a defining national aesthetic. In so doing, he resorts to familiar language of British liberty and constitutional balance so different from that in France. He also implicitly grants the Ancients' notion that there is a direct correlation between literary and political stability: Britain not France, Pope optimistically claims, is the true place for Homeric adulation that politically free English Alexander Pope represents. In reading this portion of the Postscript we remember that in *A Tale of a Tub* Swift had linked respect for Homer with support for the established Church and the stable English state:

I am far from thinking my self that Genius, upon whom at the end of these remarks Madam *Dacier* congratulates my country: One capable of 'correcting *Homer,* and consequently of reforming mankind, and amending this Constitution.' It was not to *Great Britain* this ought to have been apply'd, since our nation has one happiness for which she might have preferr'd it to her own, that as much as we abound in other miserable misguided Sects, we have at least none of the blasphemers of *Homer.* We stedfastly and unanimously believe, both his Poem, and our Constitution, to be the best that ever human wit invented: That the one is not more incapable of amendment than the other; and (old as they both are) we despise any *French* or *English* man whatever, who shall presume to retrench, to innovate, or to make the least alteration in either. Far therefore from the Genius for which Madam *Dacier* mistook me, my whole desire is but to preserve the humble character of a faithful Translator, and a quiet Subject.[49] (*TE* 10:397)

Pope's manuscript draft of the Postscript was yet more obvious in its mingled fear and resentment of her political slur. He originally had written "one capable of correcting ye faults of Homer & consequently of reforming our State," rather than "mankind." He also originally had hoped to preserve his "honest"—as opposed to the printed "humble character of a . . . quiet Subject" (*TE* 10:456).[50]

Pope begins his *Iliad* notes with collegial respect, normal disagreement with an admired predecessor, and consistent efforts to avoid the cross-channel heat and abuse that so poisoned literary exchange in battles of books and personalities. He ends his *Odyssey* Postscript with an admission of failure, with the unlovely realization that now he was being attacked by an apparent ally who had made herself a real enemy. Pope begins to write the *Peri Bathous,* his portion of the *Miscellanies* (1727), shortly after he finishes his Homer and its unforeseen concluding rancor. The *Miscellanies* in turn are designed to evoke yet more negative response so that Pope could claim to write the 1728 and 1729 *Dunciad* poems to defend himself. He naively thought himself able to mock Theobald and other dunces as securely and successfully as Dryden had mocked Shadwell in *Mac Flecknoe.* Instead, of course, those years increased attacks upon him and gave his enemies new ammunition, some of which was imported from France. It was one thing for John Dennis to label him an ignorant translator and offensive traitor; it was another for Madame Anne le Fevre Dacier to do so.

Pope felt himself obliged to write troubled and supplicating letters to powerful aristocrats as well as to a midlevel government bureaucrat. To Pope's credit, when defending himself he also defends his printer and responds to Madame Dacier with anger tempered by dignity, concern, and learning. It is all the sadder that this unfortunate misunderstanding stemmed from an erroneous translation, read by a brilliant classical scholar bereft of English. Madame Dacier feared that an alien Houdar de la Motte was now rising to threaten her cherished "Ancient" world and was being praised at home and abroad. Pope feared that he was being vilified for something he had neither done nor written. Each could have said, as Pope did, "This truly Sir I do not like." Each would have been right and each must have been sorry that so unhappy an event ever occurred.

NOTES

1. "Postscript to the Odyssey," in *The Odyssey of Homer Books XII–XXIV,* ed. Maynard Mack et al., vol. 10 of *The Twickenham Edition of the Poems of Alexander Pope,* ed. John Butt et al. (London: Methuen; New Haven, Conn.: Yale University Press, 1967), 395–96. Subsequent quotations are from this edition and are cited in the text as *TE* 10, or merely the volume and page number when the context is clear.

2. The classical authors were "Genies Divins" and their Modern detractors "odieux." Even the gothic barbarians "ont . . . jamais rien fait plus horrible." See André Dacier, *Oeuvres d'Horace en Latin et en François, avec des remarques critiques et historiques. Par Monsieur Dacier, garde des livres du cabinet du roy,* 3d ed. rev. (Paris, 1709), 6:xxx (Genies), xxxij (horrible), xxxiij (odieux). These remarks would have been especially well known since they conclude the important and often translated "Préface sur les satires d'Horace" in which Dacier elegantly popularizes Isaac Casaubon's 1605 theory of the derivation of satire from *satura lanx.* The volume's dedicatory Epistre to Louis XIV also carries a hagiographic message similar to Dacier's later discours before the Académie Française. See note 35 below.

3. For Sapho and "héretique" see *Eloges lus dans les seances publiques de l'Académie Françoise,* ed. Jean le Rond D'Alembert (Paris, 1779), 72. For the remark regarding Socrates as "très-équivoque ami de jeune Alcibiade" in satire 12, *L'Equivoque* (1705–1711), see [M. de Vigneul-Marville, pseudonym for Noël Bonaventure d'Argonne], *Mélanges d'histoire et de litérature,* 4th ed. (Paris, 1725), 3:289–91. The episode is reported and translated in, among other places, Pierre Bayle, *A General Dictionary, Historical and Critical,* ed. and trans. John Peter Bernard, Thomas Birch, John Lockman et al. (London, 1736), 4:497 n. D., "Andrew Dacier." Bayle's discussion makes plain that the Daciers shared all essential values regarding the Ancients and their enemies the Moderns.

4. *Journal literaire* 8 (1716): 473; Fern Farnham, *Madame Dacier Scholar and Humanist* (Monterey, Calif.: Angel Press, 1976), 178–79; the event is in *Mémoirs*

de Mme *De Staal Delaunay,* ed. François Barrière, Bibliothèque des Mémoirs relatifs à l'histoire de France pendant le 18e siècle, (Paris, 1888), 1:211; the episode also is in *Mémoires de Madame de Staal* (Londres [for Paris?], 1755), 2:191–92 with grammatical variations. Farnham's *Madame Dacier* remains the standard biography in English, but students of the period should see Giovanni Saverio Santangello, *Madame Dacier, una filologa nella 'crisi' (1672–1720),* Biblioteca di Cultura 255 (Rome: Bulzoni editore, 1984). Santangello discusses Pope and Madame Dacier on 216–23 and 464–68. Houdar's poem was "Ode à la louange de Madame Dacier, Prononcée à l'Académie dans une séance publique." See *Oeuvres de Monsieur Houdar de la Motte* (Paris, 1754), 2:508–13. It is a generous act of postmortem conciliation in which Houdar praises both Daciers, urges that she is worthy of the Académie Française which wrongly excludes women, and says that heroic zeal in literary combat is less important than conquest by truth. Houdar also had written odes praising her edition of Anacreon (1, part 2:195–96), and André's Horace (2:473–76). He must have felt his politesse rudely reciprocated. For the remark concerning Houdar's ode, see *Histoire des membres de L'Académie Françoise,* ed. Jean Antoine Nicolas Caritat, Marquis de Condorcet (Amsterdam, 1787), 4:493. Houdar's pacific dinner engagement with Madame Dacier did not change his opinion of the Ancients. The eulogist slyly observes of Houdar's ode: "Les louanges qu'il donne à cette Savante, ne sont guere moins ingenieuses que les Epigrammes douces qu'il avoit faites contre elle" (4:493).

5. *Oeuvres de Madame la Marquise de Lambert,* [ed. Marc-Michel Bousquet], (Amsterdam, 1748), 389. The letters later were translated as part of *The Works of the Marchioness de Lambert. A New Edition from the French* (London, 1769), 2:49–53, 53–62. Madame de Lambert also wrote a "Portrait de M. de la Motte" in which she says: "Avec quelle dignité & quelle bienséance n'a-t-il pas répondu à la Critique amere de Madame Dacier?" See *Oeuvres . . . de la Motte,* 1:v–vi. This originally appeared in the *Mercure de France* 1 (1751): 6–11. In August of 1718 Buckingham responds to Pope's request for "my opinion as to the late dispute in *France* concerning *Homer.*" See *The Correspondence of Alexander Pope,* ed. George Sherburn (Oxford: Clarendon Press, 1956), 1:485, 1:485–87 for the letter. Pope responds on 1 September 1718, *Correspondence,* 1:492–93. This is referred to hereafter as *Corr.* Pope prints Buckingham's letter in *The Works of John Sheffield, Earl of Mulgrave, Marquis of Normanby, and Duke of Buckingham* (London, 1723), 2:288–95. Buckingham approximately reverses Pope's respect for Houdar and for Madame Dacier. Such relative praise by an eminent peer and man of letters might further have put Pope on the defensive, especially since Pope did not print his own respectfully corrective reply to Buckingham. Emile Audra, followed by Santangello, claims that Pope fabricated Buckingham's letter in order to refute and denigrate Madame Dacier; but he offers no evidence other than supposition and Sherburn accepts the letter as Buckingham's. See Audra, *L'Influence Française dans l'oeuvre de Pope,* Bibliothèque de la revue de littérature comparée Tome 72, (Paris: Honoré Champion, 1931), 253–57 and Santangello, 218–19 and 219 n. 442.

6. *Homere défendu contre l'apologie du R. P. Hardouin. Ou suite des causes de la corruption du goust* (Paris, 1716), 19.

7. The English translation is *The Iliad of Homer, Translated from the Greek into Blank Verse, By Mr. Ozell, Mr. Broom, and Mr. Oldisworth To which are added a Preface, the Life of Homer, and Notes by Madame Dacier.* The first volume of the set here used is from the second edition of 1714; the other volumes are from the first edition of 1712. See 1:xxxii for this remark.

8. This does not diminish the *Journal*'s high opinion of Madame Dacier, whom it elsewhere calls "L'Illustre Madame *Dacier,* qui fait tant d'honneur à son Sexe, & en même tems à notre Siècle": (3 [1714]: 232). See also Farnham, 21–25. This association of Pope's and Houdar's values remained clear later in the eighteenth century as well. In writing about Houdar, Condorcet refers to Pope as "un de ses amis le célebre Pope, un des plus illustres modernes": Condorcet, *Histoire des membres,* 4:487.

9. Audra, *L'Influence,* 59. For the other reviews see Audra, *Les Traductions Françaises de Pope (1717–1825)* (Paris: Honoré Champion, 1931), 1.

10. For Caryll, see Howard Erskine-Hill, *The Social Milieu of Alexander Pope: Lives, Examples and the Poetic Response* (New Haven, Conn., and London: Yale University Press, 1975), 58; for Caryll in France, see Pope, *Corr.*, 1:265–66 and 265 n. 1. Erskine-Hill's chapter concerning the Carylls remains the best such discussion. He also mentions Max de Trenqualeon, *West-Grinstead et les Carylls: étude historique et religieuse sur le Comte de Sussex en Angleterre* (Paris and London, 1893), see 2:157–80 for the Carylls and Pope; Jean François du Bellay du Resnel, *Les Principes de la morale et du goût. En deux poëmes. Traduites de l'Anglais de M. Pope* (Paris, 1737), x; Antoine Yart, *Idée de la poësie Angloise, ou traduction des meilleurs poëtes Anglois* (Paris, 1753), 3:9. Yart gets much of his information from William Ayre's often erroneous life of Pope, which also calls his parents nobles and apparently invents Pope's letter of apology to Madame Dacier for his presumed abuse of Homer. See Ayre, *Memoirs of the Life and Writings of Alexander Pope, Esq.*, (London, 1745), 1:245, and Yart, *Idée,* 3:49. Yart discusses the Homer quarrels on 3:41–49; Yart on the *Essay on Criticism, Idée,* 3:17; Yart on the *Dunciad, Idée,* 3:51 n.

11. Pope, *Corr.*, 2:158; Audra, *L'Influence,* 60; for "habile Ecrivain" see *Journal des sçavans* 65 (1719): 167, and for "M. de la Motte" see 171. Madame Dacier may have been a prisoner of her own concept of translation: for her, French prose always give the most accurate versions. For the text she read, see Perelle, *Traduction de la premiere partie de la préface de l'Homere anglais de M. Pope* (Paris, 1718). This was reissued in a larger volume: *Remarques sur Homère avec la traduction de la préface de l'Homère Anglais de M. Pope* (Paris, 1728). The British Library catalogue calls him Antoine; the Bibliothèque Nationale calls him André, which I have accepted. Madame Dacier titles her remarks "Reflexions Sur la premiere Partie de la Preface de M. Pope," as quoted in *L'Iliade d'Homere, traduite en François, avec des remarques par Madame Dacier. Seconde edition revüe, corrigée & augmentée. Avec quelques reflexions sur la preface Angloise de M. Pope* (Paris, 1719), from which I quote her French with references cited in the text or in the notes as appropriate. "Reflection" still carried the older association of "censure," as in John Dennis's severe *Reflections Critical and Satyrical, Upon A Late Rhapsody, Call'd An Essay Upon Criticism* (1711). See also Johnson's

fifth and sixth definitions of the verb "To Reflect" and his seventh definition of the noun "Reflection" in *A Dictionary of the English Language* (London, 1755). Pope may have been aware of both the 1718 and 1728 versions of his Preface. A note to William Cleland's—that is, Pope's—"Letter to the Publisher" before the *Dunciad* of 1743 observes in Pope's favor that "His Essays and Dissertations on Homer [were] several times translated in French." Pope's sensitivity to European disapprobation, however, is made plain in his subsequent quotation from the 1716 *A True Character of Mr. Pope:* the censures Boileau passed on bad authors "have been confirmed by all Europe." See the nominal William Cleland's "A Letter to the Publisher" in *The Dunciad,* ed. James Sutherland, vol. 5 of *The Twickenham Edition of the Poems of Alexander Pope,* 3d ed., ed. John Butt et al. (London: Methuen; New Haven, Conn.: Yale University Press, 1963), 20; cited hereafter as *TE* 5. The Irish exile Jacobite M. Keating (d. 4 November 1748), later translated "La Préface de l'Homére Anglois" and commented on Perelle's inadequate version. The earliest Keating text I have been able to see is in *Oeuvres diverses de Pope. Traduites de l'Anglois. Nouvelle édition, considerablement augmentée* (Amsterdam and Leipzig, 1754–1758), 3 (1754): 283–96 (Avertissement), 297–332 (Préface).

12. Quotations are from *Madame Dacier's Remarks upon Mr. Pope's Account of Homer, Prefixed To his Translation of the Iliad. Made English from the French, By Mr. Parnell* (London, 1724), here 2, with subsequent citations given in the text. The version in volume 2 of "Ayre's" *Memoirs of . . . Pope* has some slight variations. I will include her French in the notes from volume 3 of the 1719 second edition, *L'Iliade:* "Comme je ne sçay pas cette langue, je n'ay pu juger de son poëme dont j'ay beacoup entendu parler. Je veux croire qu'il merite les loüanges qu'on luy a données, un ouvrage que l'Angleterre a approuvé aprés l'impression ne sçauroit estre mauvais" (3:sig. *1^{r}).

13. "Il seroit heureux pour notre siécle & glorieux pour l'Angleterre, d'avoir produit un critique si parfait" (*L'Iliade* 3:sig. *iiij^{r}).

14. *Journal des sçvavans* 69 (1721): 40; "Abstract of the Life of Madam Dacier," Number 1, 3 May 1722, as in *A Compleat Set of St. James's Journals From May 3. 1722; to May 18. 1723* (London, 1732), 5. Thomas Robe's dedication to Queen Caroline praised "the most Illustrious House of HANOVER" and abused Atterbury and other "Instruments of Rebellion": sigs. a2^{r-v}, with the title page as a1. It seems possible that drawing attention to these reflections on Pope also had political implications. This is demonstrably true in an English abstract from Henri Philippe de Limier's *Histoire de Suede sous la regne de Charles XII* (Amsterdam, 1721), the French *History of Sweden under the Reign of Charles XII* (1721) in the second number, 10 May 1722. His death abolished absolute power in Sweden. As a martial monarch Charles was impetuous, imprudent, and so immoderate that "the *Swedish* Nation can never pardon him." He was quixotic at Pultowa; he was a bad Christian and insane for invading Norway and then, he hoped, England. Finally, "to ruin his Country for nothing and drain it entirely of Men and Money, were the Actions of a Man without Compassion or Religion, and which no Exterior Devotion can atone for": *A Compleat Set,* 9–10. For the fuller context of so severe and widespread a view, see note 41 below.

15. The familiar *Mémoires de Trévoux,* sometimes called the *Journal de Trév-*

oux, are officially called *Mémoires pour l'histoire des sciences & des beaux arts, recuëillis par l'ordre de son altesse serenissime Monseigneur Prince Souveraïn de Dombes.* See January 1721, "Article VI. Eloge de Madame *Dacier*," 106.

16. See *The Popiad* (London, 1728), 26–32 for "Madame Dacier's Reflections upon Mr. Pope's Account of Homer, in his Preface to the Iliad"; *The Curliad. A Hypercritic upon the Dunciad Variorum* (London, 1729), 3; Dennis, *Remarks upon Several Passages in the Preliminaries to the Dunciad* (1729) as in *The Critical Works of John Dennis,* ed. Edward Niles Hooker (Baltimore, Md.: The Johns Hopkins Press, 1939, 1943), 2:363; the *Popiad* on Dacier and Dennis, 26; the *Popiad* on partial friends, 32. See also *Sawney and Colley. A Poetical Dialogue . . . To the Homer of Twickenham* (London, 1742), where Pope is accused of translating "from DACIER'S *Translation*" (13); and John Lord Hervey, *An Epistle from a Nobleman to a Doctor of Divinity* (London, 1733), where Pope "is call'd Poet, 'cause in Rhyme he wrote / What *Dacier* construed, and what *Homer* thought" (6).

17. Ayre, *Memoirs of . . . Pope,* 1:245. The Abbé Yart accepts Ayre's story and is amused at English Pope's civility and politesse: "ainsi un Anglois surpassa en politesse une Françoise, & un homme fut plus doux qu' une femme, ce qui n'est pas absolument rare" (*Idée* 3:49).

18. "Pope" in *Lives of the English Poets by Samuel Johnson, LL.D.,* ed. George Birkbeck Hill (Oxford: Clarendon Press, 1905), 3:113. The Abbé Yart also observes and laments "La haine des ennemis de Pope": "de quels excès la jalousie n'est-elle point capable, quand elle est jointe à l'opiniâtré des Anglois? Ils traiterent Pope d'ignorant, d'âne, de fou, de monstre, d'homicide, d'empoisonneur, de traître, uniquement parce qu'il avoit fait l'Iliade" (*Idée* 3:49–50).

19. "Aprés l'avoir assez heureusement defendu contre les critiques de tant de censeurs aveugles, qui l'ont condamné sans le connoistre, je me sens obligée de le defendre encore contre les reproches d'un homme plus esclairé & qui seroient d'autant plus capables de luy nuire dans l'esprit des lecteurs peu instruits, que l'auteur paroist rempli pour lui d'une admiration plus grande" (*L'Iliade* 3:sigs. *ij$^{r\text{-}v}$).

20. For example, the official "Eloge de M. Dacier" read in 1723 spends nearly as much time praising and discussing Madame Dacier as André Dacier and suggests their collaboration on Plutarch and their gratifying mutual support in a life of dedicated and preeminent classical scholarship. See the éloge by François de Boze in *Histoire de l'Académie Royale des Inscriptions et Belles-Lettres* (Amsterdam, 1731), 3:619–33.

21. "Rien n'est plus opposé à la doctrine d'Aristote" (*L'Iliade* 3:sig. *vii^{r}).

22. "Il est estonnant que M. Pope n'ait pas compris une chose qui a esté si clairement expliquée dans la poëtique d'Aristote & dans ma Preface sur l'Odyssée. Je renvoye ce sçavant homme à ces deux ouvrages où il pourra s'en esclaircir" (*L'Iliade* 3:sigs. *vii^{v}–viii^{r}).

The title of Dacier's Paris 1692 12° was *La Poetique d'Aristote, contenant les règles les plus exactes pour juger du poëme heroïque, & des pieces de theatre. . . . Traduites en François, avec des remarques critiques . . . par Mr. Dacier.* The Daciers commonly were regarded as a team. See Boileau's concerns in D'Alembert, *Eloges lus,* 72–73, and Condorcet, *Histoire des membres,* 3:134. See also *Histoire des membres,* 4:493, where Houdar is said to be reconciled "avec M. Dacier & sa femme." Common sense and the Académie's bylaws required civility among members. Given the severe exchanges between Madame Dacier and Houdar and the frequent academic contacts between André and Houdar politesse must have been sorely strained. For the rules of the Académie see "Statuts et Règlements de l'Académie Françoise: 22 février 1635," in L'Institut de France, *Lois, statuts et règlements concernant les anciennes académies et l'institut, de 1635 à 1889,* ed. M. Léon Aucoc (Paris, 1889), xxxiv–xliii. Note especially rules 11, in which opinions are to be exchanged without interruption or jealousy, and 13: "Si un des académiciens fait quelque action indigne d'un homme d'honneur, il sera interdit ou destitué selon l'importance de sa faute" (xxxvi). For the many meetings at which Houdar and André were present, see L'Institut de France, *Les Registres de L'Académie Française 1672–1793* (Paris, 1895), 1:517–608, 2:1–137.

23. *Plutarch's Lives in Eight Volumes. Translated from the Greek. With Notes Historical and Critical from M. Dacier* (London, 1727), 2:268. See also the earlier *Plutarch's Lives. Translated from the the Greek By Several Hands. To which is prefixt the Life of Plutarch* (London, 1683–1686); the life is by Dryden (1683). See 2 (1684): 11–12 for the relevant quotation.

24. For André's version see *Les Vies des hommes illustres de Plutarque, revues sur les mss. et traduites en François, avec des remarques historiques et critiques,* ed. and trans. André Dacier (Paris, 1721), 2:380. He does not include the yet more patronizing "*Eh mon ami.*" André's gloss on the first part of the anecdote also carries heavy baggage: "Alcibiade trouvoit donc qu'il estoit honteux à un Grammairien de n'avoir aucune partie des ouvrages de cet homme divin, qui excelloit dans tous les parties de l'Eloquence. Certainement un Grammairien qui ne connoist pas Homere, ne sçauroit estre capable de bien instruire les enfants" (2:380n). The word "divin" well glosses the Daciers' attitude towards Homer, Alcibiades, and the ancients in general. For the Daciers, Pope would be shamefully ignorant of the poet he presumably was translating. This was a familiar charge among Pope's English enemies; he could not have been pleased to see it both cross the channel and make its way back home in Curll's version. Fortunately for Pope in 1728 three different French texts praise him and his translation of Homer. See Voltaire, *Essay sur la poësie epique. Traduite de l'Anglois de M. de Voltaire,* trans. Pierre-François Guyot Desfontaines (Paris, 1728), 21; Paolo Antonio Rolli, *Examen de l'essai de M. de Voltaire sur la poësie epique. Par M. Paul Rolli,* trans. Annibale Antonini (Paris, 1728), sig. avi^{r}; *La Boucle de cheveux enlevée. Poëme hériocomique de monsieur Pope,* trans. Desfontaines (Paris, 1728), where Pope is "le premier Poëte moderne de l'Angleterre" and his Homer was "si justement louée par Monsieur de Voltaire dans son *Essai sur la Poësie Epique. . . .* 'On vient aussi de traduire & de publier les discours sensez & ingenieux, dont Monsieur Pope a accompagné sa traduction de l'Iliade; & on est obligé d'avoüer qu'on n'a jamais rien écrit de plus judicieux en faveur d'Homere'" (sigs. avii^{r-v}). Both Voltaire and the Abbé Desfontaines took "Modern" stands regarding Homer. See also the remark in *Traités divers traduits de l'Anglois du Dr. Jonathan Swift* (Amsterdam, 1732) that refers to Pope as a great man whose translation of

Homer together with several other pieces established a reputation that long "a passé les Mers, & . . . sont connus . . . particulierement en France" (i).

25. In 1683 Dryden called Plutarch "a great Philosopher and Historian"; in 1695 André Dacier called him "le plus utile des tous les Historiens, & qui possede parfaitement tous les talens necessaires pour corriger & pour instruire." For these see, respectively, *Plutarch's Lives,* 1:3; Dacier, *Les Vies des hommes illustres de Plutarque,* 2:380. In 1697 the compiler of *Verdict of the Learned concerning Virgil and Homer's Heroic Poems* (London) includes this observation: "*Alicbiades* . . . was in the right to Box that Master, in whose School he found not *Homer*'s Works" (27).

26. Pope, *Corr.*, 1:75. Sherburn observes that Pope omits this remark in the printed texts of this letter. The term "Grammairien" also could have had negative connotations, as in Warburton's note to the *Dunciad* 4.175. When Greece and Rome lost their liberties they were "overspread" with "a great cloud of Scholiasts and Grammarians" (*TE* 5:358 n. 175).

27. "Les fautes que je luy reproche sont si legeres, qu'elles ne doivent pas empescher l'Angleterre d'attendre de ce nouveau poëte les grands avantages qu'uon doit esperer d'un reformateur d'Homere. Un homme si habile ne se bornera pas à perfectionner l'art du poëme Epique; ce seroit peu de chose, il perfectionnera l'art de la politique, bien plus estimable & plus important que celuy de l'Epopée; un homme capable de corriger Homere, sera capable de former des hommes. . . . [the episode with Alcibiades follows] Voilà une grande ressource pour un Estat!" (*L'Iliade* sigs. *viii$^{\text{r-v}}$).

28. Later in the 1730s Pope indeed tries to reform the state, but by correcting Horace rather than Homer. Like other members of the political opposition to Walpole, however, Pope did not think of himself as amending the constitution. Rather, he hoped to return it to the balance and integrity that Walpole apparently threatened.

29. Roger Ascham, *English Works,* ed. William Aldis Wright (Cambridge: Cambridge University Press, 1904; reprint 1970), 244.

30. *Des Causes de la corruption du goust,* 9–10.

31. The episode is reported in the *Bibliothèque Françoise ou histoire litteraire de la France,* 2d ed. (Amsterdam, 1725), 1:11–12 n. 1, in "Memoires sur la Vie & les Ouvrages de *Mr. Dacier* . . . mort à Paris le *18* de Septembre *1722*." This forms the basis of Bayle's *Dictionnaire* and then of Chaufepié's *Nouveau Dictionnaire* articles on Dacier. See note 32 below. The *Bibliothèque Françoise* cites *Histoire du tems sous Charles II. & Jacques II. Roys d'Angleterre* (London and then Amsterdam, 1691) as its source. In the translation of Bayle this appears as *History of the Times during the Reigns of Charles II and James II, Kings of England.* I have not been able to locate such a title in English, Dutch, or French sources and suspect that it is a section of another work rather than a separately published title. Nor have I found the book putatively dedicated to Louis XIV. The closest chronological possibility is Anne le Fevre's *Les Poësies d'Anacreon et de Sapho* (Paris, 1681), but that is dedicated to "Monseigneur le Duc de Montausier."

32. For the reported story, see *Bibliothèque Françoise,* 1:9–10, and in French,

Jacques George de Chaufepié *Nouveau dictionnaire historique et critique, pour servir de supplement ou de continuation au dictionnaire de M*r. *Pierre Bayle* (Amsterdam and the Hague, 1750), 2:5 n. G. As an example in English, see Bayle, *A General Dictionary,* 4:499 n. G; see note 3 above. Fern Farnham discusses the abjuration and conversion in *Madame Dacier,* 88–96; see note 4 above.

33. D'Alembert, *Eloges lus,* xiv–xv.

34. For the poetry contest, see Jules Chavannes, "Le Protestantisme Français et L'Académie Française," *Bulletin de la sociéte de l'histoire Protestantisme Français* 4 (1856): 607; Adams, *The Huguenots and French Opinion, 1685–1787: The Enlightenment Debate on Toleration* (Waterloo, Ontario: Wilfred Laurier University Press, 1991), 19; 19–33 are especially helpful. He sums up his findings: "for established writers and artists, the Revocation offered an occasion to celebrate an act which they genuinely welcomed and to consolidate their standing at court. For the ambitious and for those out of favour, it was an opportunity to flatter the prince and to launch or restore a career" (30). Houdar de la Motte's own "Eloge Funebre de Louis Le Grand, Protecteur de l'Académie Françoise" (1715) praises Louis for crushing the monster from Hell and reclaiming the Church's authority. See Houdar's *Reflexions sur la critique. . . . Avec plusieurs autres ouvrages,* 2d ed. (Paris, 1716), xxx of new pagination after the *Reflexions.*

35. For André's discours, see *Recueil des harangues prononcés par messieurs de l'Académie Française dans leurs receptions . . . depuis l'establissement de l'Académie jusqu' à présent* (Paris, 1698), 732–40. For example, Louis XIV "qui est proprement le Ministre de Dieu pour rendre heureux ses Peuples, a brisé les chaisnes d'une erreur hereditaire qui lioient une grande partie de ses Sujets, & a fait tomber une rosée de lumiere sur ceux qui estoient couchez dans les tenebres" (738).

36. Harlay, however, was an ecclesiastic of no literary distinction and dubious virtue. He used St. Augustine as an authority to support Louis XIV's removal of heresy through the Revocation of the Edict of Nantes. Harlay also personally welcomed the newly converted Daciers back to Paris from Castres and established them in his suburban home at Mesnil-Montant. There they translated and commented on Marcus Aurelius, dedicated to Harlay in 1691 (Farnham, *Madame Dacier,* 95–97). For the list of those reçu in the Académie Française between 1685 and 1695, see Albert Rouxel, *Chroniques des élections à l'Académie Française (1634–1870),* 2d ed. (Paris, 1888), 426. Most of the ten were connected to the Church in some way; they ranged from abbé (Clérambault) to bishop (Clermont-Tonnere). For the remark concerning André's discours, see Chavannes, "Le Protestantisme Français et L'Académie Française," 609. Marc Fumaroli offers an excellent overview of the intellectual changes in the Académie Française from its inception to the twentieth century. See his "La Coupole," in *Les Lieux de mémoire,* ed. Pierre Nora (Paris: Gallimard, 1986), 2:321–88. Note especially 334, 345, and 351.

37. The full title is *Nouveux eclaircissemens sur les oeuvres d'Horace. Avec la réponse à la critique de M. Masson, ministre refugié en Angleterre. Par M. Dacier, garde des livres du cabinet du roy* (Paris, 1708). The contrast between the refugee Masson in England who published his book in Leyden (Lugdunum Batavorum) and the loyal scholar who published in Paris is clear. Dacier also defends his fa-

ther-in-law Tanneguy le Fevre. As for Masson, he lacks "la moindre idée de le bonne & veritable critique" (152). Like his wife, André clearly did not suffer disagreement lightly. Masson criticized Dacier and his father-in-law in *Q. Horatii Flacci vita ordine chronologico sic delineata, ut vice sit commentarii historico-critici inplurima & praecipua poetae Carmina* (Leyden, 1708).

38. *Histoire de l'Académie Royale,* 3:619 (Protestant), 623 (conversion), 633 (sacraments).

39. The letter apparently is one of Madame Dacier's few letters to have survived. See Farnham, *Madame Dacier,* 187–88 and 214 n. 12. The petition was granted and on 4 October 1713, with Anne and André present, le Fevre abjured "l'hérésie dans laquelle il a vécu." See *Bulletin de la societé de l'histoire Protestantisme Française* 12 (1863): 309.

40. I can only offer reasonable but at least plausible conjectures regarding Schaub's and Buckley's motives. Unpublished diplomatic letters in the British Library and the Public Record Office suggest the following: Carteret, Secretary of State for the Southern District, tells Schaub to send Buckley all materials with a political impulse for Buckley to publish in the *Gazette;* perhaps upon a hint from the Cardinal Premier Ministre Guillaume Dubois who was familiar with English, French, and classical literature, Schaub reads Madame Dacier's "Reflexions" and sends them to Buckley; he too reads them and sees them as harmless literary slanging; but since he also was a Hanoverian operative, he and the Court want Pope to know that they are aware of such attacks upon his loyalty during the Buckingham-Atterbury tensions. Pope's response indicates his awareness of such motivation. For further discussion, see my "Alexander Pope and Madame Dacier's *Homer:* Conjectures Concerning Cardinal Dubois, Sir Luke Schaub, and Samuel Buckley," *Huntington Library Quarterly* 62 (1999): 1–23.

41. The pamphlet was published in English and in French. Its English title is *Letters which passed Between Count Gyllenborg, the Barons Gortz, Sparre, And others; Relating to the Design of Raising a Rebellion in His Majesty's Dominions, To be Supported by a Force from Sweden. Published by Authority* (London, 1717). The front matter includes the royal seal with "DIEU ET MON DROIT." For the full context of the Jacobites' Swedish gambit, see my "Who Said He Was a Jacobite Hero? The Political Genealogy of Johnson's Charles of Sweden," *Philological Quarterly* 75 (1996): 411–50.

42. Dennis on the *Essay on Criticism, Reflections Critical and Satyrical upon a Late Rhapsody, call'd An Essay upon Criticism* (1711) in Hooker, *Critical Works of John Dennis,* 1:415, see note 16 above; Dennis on royal slander in "To the Author of the Dunciad," as in *A Complete Collection of All the Verses, Essays, etc.* (London, 1728), vi; Bond on the papist, *The Popiad,* 15. For further discussion of some political elements and response to *The Dunciad* see my "The *Dunciad,* Nursing Mothers, and Isaiah," *Philological Quarterly* 71 (1992): 479–94.

43. Pope, *Corr.*, 2:157–58.

44. For the Curll-Walpole connection see Ralph Straus, *The Unspeakable Curll: Being Some Account of Edmund Curll, Bookseller; To Which Is Added, a Full List of His Books* (London: Chapman and Hall, 1927), 93–97. Straus was not aware of Public Record Office State Papers Domestic 35/31/39, in which Curll

writes to Townshend or Carteret expressing delight at having suppressed an anti-government libel, giving information regarding a pending seditious *Freeholder,* and offering to seize all such libels with government "messengers'" help.

45. Pope had already pointed this out in his commentary on Homer. See *The Iliad of Homer Translated by Alexander Pope,* ed. Steven Shankman (London: The Penguin Group, 1996), 291, regarding Book 5.1101 in Pope's translation. Unlike the Twickenham editors, Shankman uses the 1743 Homer as his copy-text.

46. This is consistent with Houdar's complaints regarding Madame Dacier's arguments, her "petites ruses de guerre," in her *Des Causes:* "On choisit un passage de son adversaire, qui raissonable avec ce qui le précede, ou ce qui le suit, devient ridicule quand il est isolé." See Houdar's *Reflexions sur la critique,* 131.

47. "Avertissment" in *Remarques sur Homére,* 50; see note 11 above, italics and roman type inverted.

48. In the same year Pope also dismissed Aristotle as an infallible guide regarding Shakespeare: "To judge therefore of *Shakespear* by *Aristotle*'s rules, is like trying a man by the Laws of one Country, who acted under those of another." See his Preface to *Shakespeare* (1725) in *Eighteenth-Century Essays on Shakespeare,* ed. D. Nichol Smith, 2d ed. (Oxford: Clarendon Press, 1963), 47.

49. Warburton, presumably with Pope's approval, adds a note to the fourth book of the *Dunciad* associating the Académie Française with arbitrary government and the decline of all arts except the verbal: "It is unsafe under such Governments to cultivate the studies of things of importance" (*TE* 5:358 n. 175).

50. Pope remained sensitive to attacks upon his loyalty. See, among other places, *The Dunciad Variorum* 3.322, where he resents Ambrose Philips' "constant cry . . . that Mr. *P.* was an Enemy to the government" (*TE* 5:188 n. 322). Note also that in the *Dunciad* 4.189–94 Pope criticizes Aristotle as the Dunces' favorite philosopher. In the note Pope further associates him with Dulness and arbitrary government: Aristotle's friends "come out like Confessors, and make an open profession of the ancient faith in the *ipse dixit* of their Master" (*TE* 5:360 n. 192). Pope and Warburton together penned another attack upon arbitrary government in general and French absolutism and its creation the Académie Française: "when Cardinal Richelieu had destroyed the poor remains of his Country's liberties, and made the supreme Court of Parliament merely *ministerial,* he instituted the *French Academy*" (*TE* 5:358 n. 175).

12

Desdemona's Strawberries and Clementina's Ark

Text, Textile, and Scripture in *Sir Charles Grandison*

PATRICIA C. BRÜCKMANN

In an essay on the famous textile collection at the Victoria and Albert, Donald King, formerly Keeper of Textiles and the foremost textile historian of his time, gives an overview of the holdings in this department of the museum. His title, "Magic in the Web," comes from *Othello,* from the hero's comments in act 3, at the center of the play, on Desdemona's handkerchief, that critical piece of linen Iago manipulates to confirm Othello's jealousy.[1] The loss and relocation of the handkerchief with Cassio, Desdemona's presumed lover, further distorts Othello's view of his wife and leads decisively to her death. The magic is, in the end, compounded of the machinations of Iago, the innocence of Desdemona, the insecurities of Othello, and the wishes of Emilia and Cassio to have the embroidery of this first token of love "taken out" for a copy.

Shakespeare, says King, would have made a good textile historian. He gives us not just a description of the handkerchief "spotted with strawberries" (3.3.434), but its provenance as well. Given to Othello's mother by an Egyptian, the work was sewed by a sibyl, "the worms were hallowed that did breed the silk" (3.4.71–75). Readers of Shakespeare will recollect strawberries from other places—*Henry V* (1600; 1.1.60–62), *Richard III* (1597; 3.4.46–59), and from Shakespeare's source for his play, Thomas More's *Historie of Richard III* (1513). Somewhat mysteriously, Richard sends the Bishop of Ely out for strawberries, apparently out of season.

King does not, however, explain why there should be so much emphasis on strawberries, even though the fruit was a favorite figure for Elizabethan and Stuart embroiderers. As Lawrence J. Ross showed long ago, they can have a distinctly sinister implication, made clear in texts like Geffrey Whitney's *A Choice of Emblemes* (1586), a widely-known late sixteenth-century emblem book. The twenty-fourth emblem shows us a strawberry plant, with a serpent twining round it. Beware, says Virgil in the third eclogue, of low growing strawberries because a snake lurks in the grass.[2]

Clearly this piece of iconography is critical to our understanding of Shakespeare's "magic web"; yet while readers and commentators on *Othello* know the part played by Desdemona's handkerchief, nearly none comment on the subtleties of its device. We no longer live in a world where significant handwork is part of our daily life. Writers like Daniel Miller have made us aware of the importance of material culture, why "some things matter."[3] In ways which were often the same as in the Stuart age, for Shakespeare and his contemporaries, material objects—cushions, carpets, hangings, dress, tapestry, decorated boxes—signaled richly in the eighteenth century.

1.

Samuel Richardson, giver of beans and cucumbers to the heroine of his first novel and creator of telling devices for the coffin of the heroine of his second, was also vividly aware of the ways in which ladies looked to, worked with, and were defined by their linen. When we meet Pamela, for example, three years after she has entered the B— household in Bedfordshire, she occupies an ambiguous status. She is a servant, but Mrs. B has taught her to be expert at her needle, an art inappropriate for one of her station, notably since she is clearly expert enough to be set to work on one of Mr. B's waistcoats.[4] This is a project more suitable for a spouse than for a waiting maid, like the task he assigns her of taking care of his linen.[5] Given the association of fine needlework with ladies of the upper classes, we are not surprised to find that Clarissa, so considerable a reader and writer, is also a "worker." She apologizes to the women around her when they look at the emblems on her coffin, hourglass, and ouroboros. The extravagance, she says, should be attributed to the "drawing she is accustomed to do for her needleworks."[6] Her observation not only links her to other women of her talent and class; it also marks out her independence. Most women worked from patterns.[7]

In Richardson's last novel, however, we find perhaps the richest of his allusions to women's work, an allusion which draws out his knowledge of scriptural text, theology, painting, gesture and stage, and finally, the difference between the ways in which men and women "work." The central choice for the eponymous hero of *The History of Sir Charles Grandison* is, as it would be for a rich and cultivated member of the English upper class, a suitable marriage partner, one who will help to carry on his line and extend his English and Protestant values.[8] But the "Names of the Principal Persons" in the novel list "Men, Women, and Italians."[9] By the time Sir Charles rescues Harriet Byron from the abduction she courted by going to a masquerade, he has also, in his very long Grand Tour, established a relationship with a beautiful Italian Catholic from Bologna.[10] He has been prepared to marry Clementina, although he is not prepared to convert to Catholicism, as she, her relatives, and her clerical advisors wish.[11] In addition to being her suitor, he has also been her tutor. Not quite so dramatically as Paolo and Francesca, they fall in love, in fact, as they read. Their text is properly Protestant—Milton's *Paradise Lost* (1667).[12] It is also the story of a marriage, and by many allusions, of families.

By the fifth volume of the novel, it is clear that Sir Charles must choose Harriet, English and Protestant, as part of the political destiny which will bring him back to the peaceful rationalism of the garden at the end of the novel. Clementina, who prefers a religious vocation to a second-best marriage she rejects, has lost her wits, apparently the effect of the pull between her love of Sir Charles and fidelity to her religious convictions (2:4.18.355).[13] Sir Charles (his voice reports the episode) comes to the palace of Porretta in response to an invitation for a "conversation-visit." Having spent half an hour with his friend Jeronymo, he is "admitted to the presence of Lady Clementina" with her father, mother, and the bishop. Clementina is eager, her mother says, "to recover her English."[14] Her health and self-protection make Sir Charles doubtful, but Clementina wants to be happy. "Well, madam [he says], let us begin now. What English book have you at hand? I don't know [she says]. But I will fetch one." Sir Charles adds, "poor Lady, forgetting her purpose, brought down some of her own work, the first thing that came to hand, out of a drawer that she pulled out, in her dressing-room; instead of looking into her book-case. It is an unfinished piece of Noah's ark, and the rising deluge; the execution admirable. And, coming to me, I wonder where it has lain all this time. Are you a judge of womens works, Chevalier?" She beckons, including her parents:

> Come hither, and sit down by me . . . . She spread it [the work] on the table, and, in an attentive posture, her elbow on the table, her head on one hand, pointing with the finger of the other—Now tell me your opinion of this work.
>
> I praised, as it deserved, the admirable finger of the workwoman. Do you know, that's *mine,* Sir? said she: But tell me; every-body can praise; Do you see no

fault?—I think *that* is one, said I; and pointed to a disproportion that was pretty obvious—Why so it is. I never knew you to be a flatterer.

Men, who can find faults more gracefully, said the Bishop, than others praise, need not flatter. Why that's true, said she. She sighed; I was happy when I was about this work. And the drawing was my own too, after—after—I forget the painter. (2:5.5.488–89)

The first thing we note about the passage—apart from the fact that Sir Charles speaks, reports, comments—is that Clementina, as a step to "recovering" her English and her tutor, has gone to fetch a book, an unspecified printed text, and returned with a figured textile with a title.[15] Johnson remarked that he who read Richardson for the plot would hang himself. We read for the sentiments, here those of a highly strung young woman who offers an image as a comment on the scene, on the overall situation. Apart from her own comment on the source of the image, however, the discussion rapidly becomes one of connoisseurship. If one detail, never specified, were put right, says the hero, the work would be a masterpiece.

But we do have an object, an event, and a name. Here, as elsewhere, Richardson invites us, as Naomi Schor suggests that women do, to read in detail.[16] Many eighteenth-century women stitched what Xanthe Brooke calls "tales in thread," characteristically using contemporary prints as models. In one or two striking cases, they drew from contemporary events, but more often they rendered biblical stories, of which one was the familiar story of Noah.[17]

2.

God admonishes a faithless generation which pays no attention. He determines to destroy most of his Creation, with the exception of a single good man and his family. Noah, who "walked with God," is directed to build an ark. His labor takes a hundred years. The rest of that world is faithless, takes no heed of God's word, and ridicules Noah for his preparation so that he is one of the first to suffer for faithfully adhering to divine dictate. We know the rest of the story: Noah gathers two of each kind, and embarks with his family. The familial part of the scene is not usually emphasized, although it is remembered in those baptismal fonts whose eight sides recall the small number of eight who were saved.[18] The faithless perish in the rising deluge, although the chief emphasis in the biblical story falls on the saving of Noah and his family and the reconstitution of the world. When the waters recede and the dove brings a branch which certifies that the land is indeed dry, God sends a rainbow as a promise that he will never again destroy the world by water. No more water, says the spiritual: the fire next time.[19]

Although we think of the Noah story chiefly in Genesis, its hero appears elsewhere in the Old and New Testaments and in three of the non-Pauline epistles. In Isaiah 54 we are told that Noah's waters will not come again: this is part of Isaiah's preamble to his account of the New Jerusalem. The next apocalypse, will burn away the old, as the waters of the deluge swept out the first wickedness. In Ezekiel 14 we hear of God's power again. Even as the Almighty can save Daniel and Job, so he saved Noah. In Matthew 24 this trope is converted into a parallel for the coming of the Son of Man. It is echoed as such in Luke 17:29.

These last two belong to the discourse of eschatology. As the commentator in the *Jerusalem Bible* puts it, this is a two-level discourse concerning the destruction of Jerusalem in 70 A. D. and the end of the world:

> Their fusion . . . is a theological expression of truth: though separated in time, these two are inseparable in the sense that the first is the inevitable forerunner and prefiguration of the second. The destruction of Jerusalem marks the end of the Old Covenant. . . . Such a decisive intervention in the history of salvation will not occur again until the end of time when God will judge the whole human race, now chosen in Christ, with the same judgement he pronounced (in 70 A.D.) upon the first chosen people.

Moreover, he continues, "as the days of Noe were, so shall also the coming of the Son of Man be. For as in the days that were before the flood they were eating and drinking, marrying and giving in marriage, until the day that Noe entered into the ark, and knew not until the flood came, and took them all away; so shall also the coming of the Son of Man be . . . . 'Therefore be ye also ready; for in such an hour as ye think not, the Son of man cometh.'"[20]

In 1 Peter, Noah reappears, as the writer, addressing those "strangers scattered" (1:1), urges them to accept suffering in the body so as to survive in the spirit, as Christ did himself. "Once the long-suffering of God waited in the days of Noah, while the ark was preparing, wherein few, that is, eight souls were saved by water. The like figure whereunto even baptism doth also now save us, (not the putting away of the filth of the flesh, but the answer of a good conscience toward God,) by the resurrection of Jesus Christ: who is gone into heaven, and is on the right hand of God; angels and authorities and powers being made subject unto him" (3:20–22).

In 2 Peter, in a particularly powerful passage, we hear of Noah once more, again in the context of the saving of a few: God "spared not the old world, but saved Noah the eighth person, a preacher of righteousness, bringing in the flood upon the world of the ungodly" (2:5). Those addressed are "them that have obtained like precious faith with us" (1:1);

the concern is that they should be led astray by false prophets "who privily shall bring in damnable heresies, even denying the Lord that bought them, and bring upon themselves swift destruction" (2:1).

In the Epistle to the Hebrews, the author writes to a Jewish Christian community that is discouraged by persecution, even tempted to return to an old way.[21] He underlines the value of the new cult as distinguished from and superior to the old. In the summary part of the letter the author emphasizes the superiority of the sacrifice of Christ to the sacrifices of the Mosaic law. He also stresses the importance of the Christian community or family, and the need for remaining faithful, whatever the hardships. "By faith Abel offered unto God a more excellent sacrifice than Cain, by which he obtained witness that he was righteous, God testifying of his gifts: and by it he being dead yet speaketh" (11:4). There follows a series of others who merited salvation through faith: Enoch, taken up because his faith had pleased God; Abraham, who obeyed and set out, not knowing where he was going, for a foreign country; Sarah, who believed that she would give birth despite her age because of God's promise; and Noah, who "being warned of God of things not seen as yet, moved with fear, prepared an ark to the saving of his house; by which he condemned the world, and became heir of the righteousness which is by faith" (11:7). I emphasize the dramatic context. Paul speaks to an audience of disparate cult, urging choice, as a demonstration of faith, in the added context of scriptural history and scriptural promise. The saving of Noah and his family is a continuing touchstone: faithlessness has unhappy precedents. Apostates may expect punishment—the fire next time, for those of no faith and for their connections, friends, and family.

In centuries before Richardson's, the ark and its builder were frequently glossed on the basis of the commentaries offered by later references to Noah in Scripture itself. Arnold Williams sums up the chief places of correspondence in his study of the commentaries on Genesis, in which Noah figures Christ and the flood figures baptism: "As Noah by an ark made of wood preserved the eight persons from bodily death, so Christ by a cross of wood redeemed mankind from spiritual death. The ark is a figure of the Church, and the waves in which the ark pitched and tossed during the flood are the persecutions by which the Church is assailed. The ark was a long time in the building, so was the Church. The wood of which the ark was constructed was incorruptible, so must the Church be incorruptible."[22]

Even for those whose theological opinion did not stretch the allegory quite so far, the ark was not simply the ark. It was a richly metaphorical vessel which emphasized the relation of the testaments and emphasized them from a doctrinal point of view, as scripture itself encourages by the cross-referencing which makes up its fabric and is itself a testimony to the single message scriptural text gives, for those who read it carefully and read it whole.

Although, as Williams says, "Renaissance commentary on Genesis came to an end some time in the first half of the seventeenth century," the major equivalences and interpretations hung on in epitomes and compilations.[23] For England he cites John Pearson's *Critici Sacri* (1660) and Matthew Poole's *Synopsis Criticorum* (1669). The image of the good man, strong in faith and saved by faith, was still powerful and readers of Genesis would always have the rest of Scripture to tell them what the event in the first book meant to those who read it and wrote the rest of the canon.

Faith is the central virtue for the salvation of Noah and his human and animal family from the deluge; it is the central virtue, in perhaps an obvious way, for the salvation of those who come under the new covenant established by Christ, himself an instance of faith at the time of the crucifixion. The stark examples underline the fact that the truest faith is that which is tried by appalling catastrophe. There are rewards for endurance, as the Epistle for Easter Even tells us. The text is 1 Peter 3:17–21:

> It is better, if the will of God be so, that ye suffer for well doing, than for evildoing. For Christ also hath once suffered for sins, the just for the unjust, that he might bring us to God, being put to death in the flesh, but quickened by the Spirit: by which also he went and preached unto the spirits in prison; which sometime were disobedient, when once the long-suffering of God waited in the days of Noah, while the ark was a preparing; wherein few, that is, eight souls was saved by water. The like figure whereunto even baptism doth also now save us, (not the putting away of the filth of the flesh, but the answer of a good conscience toward God,) by the resurrection of Jesus Christ.[24]

3.

What happened to Noah as the Renaissance commentaries declined? We need to return to Clementina's textile and to her account, as it were, of its provenance. She says that the drawing was her own, too "after—after—I forget the painter." Her hesitation and forgetting give us Richardson's brilliant representation of her state, but we are not hindered by her forgetting the painter. It would have been hard for a young Italian, or any young European, not to see a painting of Noah and the rising deluge. And all the painters Clementina would have seen, from Michelangelo onwards, had no cheerful view of Noah's ark and the rising deluge.[25] Michelangelo's decoration for the Sistine Chapel evidently began a new tradition in representations of the ark and the rising deluge. The emphasis goes to the suffering souls who perish—not to the salvific ark. "This," says Don Cameron Allen, in his classic study of the legend of Noah in the Renaissance, "is a humanization of the story which is in keeping with the [later] rational abandonment of the Genesis text. If there was a Flood, one might say, the fearful death of the unfavored is for a rationalist a greater and more important fact than that a patriarch and his children were saved."[26] Allen's comment extends Williams's sense of a changing tradition in reading Scripture. To this one might also add the sharpness lent by contemporary religious division. This newly represents that disparity of cult which Paul, or the author of the Epistle to the Hebrews, addresses as he speaks of perseverance in faith and, necessarily, adherence to the Church. In this theological universe, God is vigilant about deviance and quick to punish those outside the pale.

In Richardson's own century, this view is strongly represented in texts like Samuel Wesley the Elder's *History of the Old and New Testament* (1716).[27] The only illustration for Genesis 6 is the image of perishing souls (fig. 1). As he draws this, the illustrator responds to the emphasis of Wesley's text. The saving of Noah is reported, but drowned, as it were, by his long account of the perishing wicked. Matthew Poole's commentary grows in enthusiasm when he comments on what happens to those not included in the ark. The flood, he says, overflowed "Men, and Houses, and Trees, where possibly they did or thought to secure themselves." The flood itself rose to fifteen cubits, "which was sufficient for the destruction of the highest men or other Creatures, though perched upon the highest Mountains." Pausing over "destroyed" in 7:20, he says that "This is so often repeated that it may be more deeply ingrafted into the dull minds and hard hearts of men, to teach men that they might again and again to consider this dreadful instance, of God's justice against sin and incorrigible sinners."[28]

That this was the view inscribed in popular consciousness is illustrated not only by a later Noah quilt, with the damned climbing trees, rejoicing in their good places, but especially by biblical accounts for children in the period contemporaneous with Richardson.[29] In *An Introduction to the Reading of the Holy Bible* (1716) we find: "Water rose up to the Tops of the Houses and of the Trees on the highest Mountains, so that the Men, Women, and Children were every one of them drown'd."[30] Thereafter, another author makes the parallel of Old and New: "And as there was no place of safety then but the ark, neither will there be any hiding-place in the great conflagration but Christ, of whom the ark may be considered a striking type; but as sure as Noah and his family were safe in the ark, during the whole of the deluge, so sure will all who are found in Christ, the living ark, be safe, not only when the world is in flames, but at the last great judgment-day."[31] Some of these texts for children are reinforced with vivid woodcuts of the perished souls (fig. 2). That the "del-

Figure 1. From *History of the Old and New Testament,* Library of Trinity College, Toronto

uge" has been thus literalized, even materialized, helps to tell us about the distance we have come since the earlier days—not just from the friendly ark, encompasser of family, but also from metaphoric ways of reading Noah's adventure.[32]

By the time we come to Nicolas Poussin's *The Deluge* (1660–1664), part of his four paintings of the seasons, the sense of tragedy in the story

Figure 2. From *Introduction to the Reading of the Holy Bible,* Osborne Collection of Early Children's Books, Toronto

Figure 3. Nicolas Poussin, *The Deluge,* The Louvre, Paris

comes to what was regarded as an instance of the apocalyptic sublime (fig. 3). In addition to putting the ark so far in the background that it could be ignored by a viewer unfamiliar with the biblical scene, Poussin "also introduced a motif that was to be widely imitated: the inundated family group spanning three generations."[33] While the figures of the victims are clear, the light in the picture is dim, anticipating Burke's later dictum that obscurity is a source of the sublime. Indeed, just as Joseph Addison discovered that *Paradise Lost* was a sublime poem, so did later art critics find Poussin's *Deluge* a sublime painting. As Morton D. Paley says, it

> was also . . . important to British artists and critics that *The Deluge* represented a scene from sacred history, as emphasized by the Ark floating off in the background and by the enormous serpent . . . slithering away at the left. These images of salvation and Fall, along with general associations with the most "sublime" of books, take Poussin's *Deluge* to a threshold beyond the natural sublime . . . [it becomes], as may be seen from its subsequent influence on British art, . . . the forerunner of the apocalyptic sublime.

Poussin's painting was, of course, exhibited in France, but as Paley observes it was known in England through engravings and drawings.[34]

The theology of the passages from Wesley and from the texts for children may seem fierce, like the painting tradition which represents them, but it is no more so than certain official theological positions about salvation and about how it is gained and lost. Though there were movements to end or to modify the divisions in the Christian church as early as the sixteenth century, these were not successful, despite the pacific efforts of theological statesmen in many parts of Christendom. In an effort to emphasize the positive initiatives of the Roman Church, we now speak not of the Counter-Reformation, but of the Catholic Reformation.[35] It would, however, gravely misrepresent the climate to suggest that even the most liberal in any camp regarded members of the others as spiritual equals, whatever their moral virtue. Certainly the Roman position was clear and strongly felt. We cannot understand Clementina's apparent hysteria without reflecting further on the disparity of cult and its implication on the official position of the Church of Rome about those who are and are not saved.

Section I of the Code of Canon Law, on "persons in general" (Canon 87), runs as follows:

> A person in a juridical sense means a subject of rights; correlatively a person will also be the subject of duties. Rights and duties belong to persons as members of a society. By creation all human beings are made members of human society, and have at least radically all the *natural rights* of human persons. . . . They are . . . capable of becoming members of other societies, and of acquiring thus a new juridical personality, that is, new rights and duties as members of these other societies. The Church is a society established by Jesus Christ with divine authority for all mankind. Hence human beings can become members of the Church, and as such they acquire a new juridical personality. Baptism of water has been established by Christ as the external sign and effective cause of membership in His Church. It is therefore the title by which a human person, already endowed by creation with natural rights, acquires a new personality juridically, that is, becomes the subject of new rights, and correspondingly also of new duties, as a member of the Church.[36]

I quote at length to stress the tight language of the Code and its insistence on "society." By extension, this word means family.

Among obstacles to unity with the Church are voluntary withdrawal, that is, effectively cutting off ecclesiastical communion, a state which is heresy or schism or censure. This results in exclusion from external communion with the Church. By what may seem a paradox, these obstacles do not free the party (a baptized heretic) from the duties exacted of the baptized. The implications of the canon will be clear: personhood in the Church is achieved by baptism and lived in ecclesiastical communion. Being excommunicate means that those who are rendered legally so are deprived of sacramental communion in the Church and, at least theoretically, of the society of communicating Christians.

Other canons are very clear about the dangers of association with those who are, for whatever reason, outside the communion, or society, or family of the Church. The most extreme statement of this position, that salvation cannot be found, in effect, outside the Church, was classically stated in Boniface VIII's bull, *Unam Sanctam,* 18 November 1302: "Unam sanctam Ecclesiam, catholicam et ipsam apostolicam urgente fide credere cogimur et tenere, nosque hanc firmiter credimus et simpliciter confitemur, extra quam nec salus est, nec remissio peccatorum." Boniface's metaphorical expansion of the doctrine comes by way of scriptural citations—the dove in Canticles—and, not surprisingly, Noah: "Una nempe fuit diluvii tempore arca Noe, unam Ecclesiam praefigurans, quae in uno cubito consummata unum, Noe videlicet, gubernatorem habet et rectorem, extra quam omnia substentia super terram legimus fuisse delete."[37] The method of exegesis may strike us as fanciful. Certainly Boniface writes from the standard point of view of a medieval commentator, but these views and analogies were very long-lived. It would be a mistake to read modern liberality back into the canonical positions of earlier centuries. For the literal and pious mind, persons outside the church were in a compromised position.

If single persons were thus at risk from their failure to be in communion with Rome, we should not be surprised to find that canonical views of marriage were equally clear in their insistence upon the union of baptized Christians. Mixed marriage does not permit full nuptial rites. In days gone by nearly everything was done to make it evident that a marriage between a Catholic and a non-Catholic might be permitted, but was not encouraged. The Catholic party was supposed, in addition to being sure that the children of the union were raised as Roman Catholics, to attempt to secure the conversion of the non-Catholic party. The practice may seem restrictive, but it made theological sense. If exclusion from the body of the Church (that is what excommunication means) is a matter of uttermost importance, it is evident that the person who attempts to persuade is acting in charity for the good of the persuaded. Mixed marriage is discouraged precisely because of the potential danger to the faith and morals of the Catholic party and of the children, the family, which may result from the union.

While there is no specific Tridentine legislation about mixed marriage, these marriages were prohibited by the decree *Tametsi,* which demanded under pain of invalidity that marriages be celebrated before the proper pastor or his or the Ordinary's delegate, and at least two witnesses. Only

Catholic pastors could be *parochi proprii* and since they were forbidden to assist at marriages between Catholics and non-Catholics unless an abjuration preceded or a Papal dispensation had been given, all avenues to mixed marriage seemed to be closed.[38]

As history tells us, dispensations were given.[39] There were instances of royal houses and mixed marriage.[40] Since by the eighteenth century there were many mixed marriages in the Low Countries, without fulfillment of the canonical regulations spelled out in *Tametsi,* Benedict XIV (pope 1740–1758) decreed in 1741 that these marriages were no longer subject to the Tridentine rule. This ruling, the Benedictine privilege or *Benedictina,* was extended to other regions by later popes. Benedict condemned, however, those who applied for dispensation without indicating clearly that one of the parties was in heresy. In Richardson's time, then, in some regions, mixed marriage could be tolerated, if it is clear that tolerated means precisely that. It was not regarded lightly, and the Tridentine decree of *Tametsi* would certainly have applied in Italy, even to, and perhaps especially for, an Italian family of rank, however acceptable a suitor might be.

Benedict XIV is relevant to Richardson's story. His other achievements will present him in a rather different light than his relatively firm position on marriage. Before he ascended to the papal throne, he was the Cardinal Archbishop of Bologna, the city of the Della Porrettas. An early life by Louis-Antoine Caraccioli sums up the response Benedict elicited: "Pontifice caro al Protestanti ed ai Cattolici, al populo ed al Re."[41] This evaluation was echoed outside the Italian world. Voltaire wrote a distich in praise of Benedict: "Lambertinus hic est, Romae decus, et pater orbis / Qui mundum scriptis docuit, virtutibus ornat."[42] He also dedicated his drama *Mahomet* (1742) to the Pope.

Benedict was known in England as well. Horace Walpole wrote to Sir Horace Mann with an inscription for the Pope not long before Benedict's death in 1758. Among other observations, Walpole says that Benedict "restored the lustre of the Tiara by those arts alone, by which alone He obtained it, his Virtues. Beloved by Papists esteemed by Protestants: a Priest without insolence or interest; A Prince without favourites; A Pope without nepotism; an Author without vanity; in short a Man whom neither Wit nor Power could spoil." Walpole is part of this: as the "Son of a favourite Minister . . . who never courted a Prince nor worshipped a Churchman, offers in a free Protestant Country, this deserved Incense to the Best of Roman Pontiffs."[43] Thomas Gray also met him on the Grand Tour and admired his wit, as well as his retrenchment in expense.[44]

A man of great learning, in the sciences as well as in the arts, Benedict was also a reformer—of clerical practice, of procedures for canonization—and, in some ways, an enlightened liberal whose attitude towards the situation of the Jews was humane and sensible—as it was towards native peoples subject, often in violent ways, to missionaries. What he could not change he managed to tolerate and make less bad. His comic comments from his observations on who should be pope, after the six-month conclave could apparently produce no decision, make it clear why he would be praised by persons of all sects and sympathetically regarded by Enlightenment writers.[45] He was responsible for helping two women scholars obtain positions at the University of Bologna. I know of no reference to Benedict in Richardson, but given the admiration of others for him, I cannot think that he did not know of his humanism and relative toleration. The latter is not unlike his own, as this is described in Eaves and Kimpel's biography.[46]

Although Benedict issued the privilege that bears his name, the privilege that permitted marriage between Protestants and Catholics, with the provisos noted above—absence of the usual rite, a requirement of official petition and sanction—he was not, in the end, what we might now describe as a liberal in matters of marriage. The extension of the *Benedictina* came gradually and later than his pontificate. Although, after a very long process, persons of royal rank might still be permitted to marry, it would not have been possible for "res publicam"—for all Benedict's accommodating instincts—to sanction a marriage, notably in Italy, of a Roman Catholic and a Protestant. The danger to the faith of the Catholic party would, given the circumstances in England, be even greater than in continental Europe. The heyday of the hide, or priesthole, was over, but some were in use even in the later eighteenth century.[47]

Although, to use the example in *Grandison,* Catholic clergy consulting on an issue of marriage might be sympathetic to a Protestant who is, to use the phrase all use when speaking of Sir Charles, "a good man," the issue was a serious one, for from the Roman point of view, he is also a heretic, one whose soul, as Clementina says in an anguished late letter "is allied to perdition" (2:5.24.564). As she reflects on what might have been she says:

> How can I be sure, that, were I thine, thou wouldst not draw me after thee, by Love, by sweetness of Manners, by condescending Goodness? I, who once thought a Heretic the worst of beings, have been already led, by the amiableness of thy piety, by the universality of thy charity to all thy fellow-creatures, to think more favourably of all Heretics, for thy sake? Of what force would be the admonitions of the most pious Confessor, were thy condescending goodness, and sweet persuasion, to be exerted to melt a heart wholly thine! I know that I should not forbear

arguing with thee, in hopes to convince thee: Yet, sensible of thy superior powers, and of my duty, might I not be entangled? (2:5.24.564–65)

When the Marquis says that "All we have now to do . . . is to gain his Holiness's permission. That has not been refused in such cases, where either the sons or daughters of the marriage are to be brought up Catholics" (2:5.17.536), of course he alludes to the possibility of papal dispensation for "res publicam." Father Marescotti, however, goes "into history" upon this question and cites the "unhappy consequences which followed the marriage between our Charles I. and the Princess Henrietta of France" (2:3.28.219).[48] He elaborates on the problems occasioned by disparity of cult. A similar compromise would be worse in Italy, although not for political reasons and, given papal views of marriage, to my mind quite impossible. If Sir Charles does not become a Roman Catholic, there can be no marriage. And, at least in Clementina's mind, Charles can look forward to perdition. "You will call to mind, Chevalier, said the Bishop, that your church allows of a possibility of salvation out of its pale—Ours does not" (2:3.26.182).

4.

This content informs the dramatic scene of the unfinished textile, with its speaking image. We recall that Clementina used a piece of decorative art which shows her situation, rather than a book, to recover her English. She thinks of her early days, when Milton is "one good man," Noah, was Sir Charles. Clementina then stages the final actions of the scene, in the story of the deluge, one of whose meanings is that recovery of those early days is simply not possible. Sir Charles has been her tutor; she becomes, or attempts to become, his.

Richardson, as we know, thought theatrically. Aaron Hill's letter "To the Editor of Pamela," says: "One of the best judg'd peculiars, of the plan, is, that these instructions being convey'd, as in a Kind of dramatical representation, by those beautiful *scenes,* her own letters and journals, who acts the most moving and suffering *part,* we feel the force in a threefold effect,—from the motive, the act, and the consequence."[49] Hill pays special attention to gestures in his treatise on the art of acting. Richardson's own feeling observation on Hill's treatise is recorded in a letter to Hill on 29 October 1746.

Last Sunday I attempted to read it not as a Printer; and, was not aware, that I should be so mechanically, as I may truly say, affected by it; I endeavoured to follow you in your wonderful Description of the Force of Acting, in the Passion of Joy, Sorrow, Fear, Anger &c. And my whole Frame, so nervously affected before, was shaken by it; I found, in short, such Tremors, such Startings that I was unable to go thro' it; and must reserve the Attempting it again, till your *Oak Tincture* . . . has fortify'd the too relaxed, unmuscled Muscles.[50]

Clementina gives an image of the central conflict in her "work" of Noah's ark and the rising deluge. Her physical pointing, in itself highlighted by Richardson's description of the position of her arm and hands, emphasizes, in another way, that she works without book, with her hands, here extending meaning with a hand. As earlier commentators emphasized individual genius by stressing the life of the hand "as though it were a kind of second, or alternative self," so here Richardson unites work and worker.[51] That we, part of the audience, are made to look, comes from gesture—that critical feature of eighteenth-century acting, commented upon extensively by Hill and others. From Quintilian forward, gesture is elemental, in both senses of the term, more so than speech. Clementina has left language as it is usually understood and had recourse to women's work and to the body gesturing. Her wordless pointing to her picture has a name in the language of painting. It is a gesture of indication. These provide "an important means by which artists [may] tell a story in visual terms."[52] These gestures were part of the language of the theater and the language of painting.

The stage is part of Clementina's nature and of her religion, as it is not of the English ladies in the cedar parlor at home at Grandison Hall. They write and speak, but they are, in the distinction Richardson himself encourages us to make, women, not Italians. Jocelyn Harris's splendid discussion of the novel draws telling parallels between the relation of Sir Charles and Clementina and, on the one hand, the story of Eloisa and Abelard and, on the other, the equally erotic scenes and tones of the Song of Songs, as she argues for the more compelling qualities of the Italian scenes and distinguishes them sharply from the English scenes.[53] The medieval hero and heroine are prevented from their love by religious vows. After a distraction that is nearly madness, by the end of the poem, Eloisa comes to acceptance. Clementina's distraction is complete, but it is rooted not in her fidelity to Sir Charles, but in her painful fidelity to her church.

The story of Noah is about faith, firm in catastrophe; faith is the condition for his own and for his family's salvation; his story is deepened by the cross references provided to it later in the Old and New Testaments and in some of the non-Pauline epistles. It is holy fear, and wholly fear which governs Clementina as she chooses, in the language of Canon 87, a specific society, a family with its unrelenting responsibilities. As she does so, she achieves a certain grandeur, even a sublimity, which is not accessible to the ladies of England, certainly not to Harriet Byron whose opening disaster comes from a brief flirtation with a costumed world of romance. Harriet recovers, as it were, her English, as she laments the folly of her masquerade, not least the effect it has doubtless had on that good man who rescues her. She will be completely at home in the gardens of Grandison Hall. Clementina, in danger of a marriage she does not want, prefers to opt as Eloisa necessarily did for that favorite gothic place, the convent. While Richardson, who does not read nunneries as some of his contemporaries did and would, leaves us at the end of the novel not knowing whether the marriage the della Porrettas want will be achieved, on the evidence of the rest of the narrative, their daughter Clementina still lives in the agony of her choice for her church. Sir Charles has taught her the "language of England," but she has not been able to teach him what she takes to be the "language of Heaven!—No heretic [she says] can learn that" (2:3.28.212).

Clementina cannot recover the happy days when she read a sublime epic with her lover and embroidered a biblical scene with another "good man" she would have met, among others, in the eleventh book of *Paradise Lost.* She can, under great stress, recover her sense of what her religion requires and act upon it. Although I have documented those requirements in part through books, the Italian heroine does so through a woman's work, a woman's wordless gesture, all the more powerful for not being in words.

She makes her choice and Richardson makes his. Remarkably sympathetic to the Roman Church, in ways that, as I have implied, should be further explored, he has Sir Charles speak favorably of the notion of "*Protestant Nunneries,*" here in *Grandison* (2:4.18.355) where Father Marescotti, at least, is a positive character. Clarissa's desire for a single life, especially since she is a dedicated reader of John Norris, suggests a sympathy (as with the nunnery) for women, like nuns, who seek a life of virtue and independence in a single state. He is, as he said he tried to be, even-handed: he was, he says, "as zealous a Catholic when I was to personate the Lady, and her Catholic Friends, as a Protestant, when I was the Gentleman, and have done Credit to the Clergy of both Religions, who are good Men . . . a very eminent Clergyman told me, on seeing some Parts of this Management, that I should be thought by some, to be more of a Catholic than a Protestant."[54]

But in the end, although he knows and is drawn towards the language of the sublime as it comes to us in handwork, in painting, and in dramatic speech and gesture—even in masquerade, and even in the Church of Rome—Richardson opts with his hero for Protestant England. He also opts for a sensible, recovered bride who, in an early exchange with one of her correspondents, speaking of the "early descendants" of the first man, notes their building of "that surprising naval structure the Ark" (1:1.13.54).[55]

NOTES

1. Donald King, "Magic in the Web," *Hali* 107 (1999): 70–85. William Shakespeare, *Othello*, ed. E. A. J. Honigman (1622; Walton-on-Thames: Thomas Nelson and Sons, 1997), 3.4.67. All quotations are from this edition and will be cited in text.

2. Lawrence J. Ross, "The Meaning of Strawberries in Shakespeare," *Studies in the Renaissance* 7 (1960): 229. There is also a countertopos. Strawberries are associated with the Virgin because of her humility. The context dictates our reading. More's and Shakespeare's Richard send us to Virgil's snake in the grass. The allusion in *Othello* is double: Desdemona is pure; Iago a dissimulator. I have seen two other instances of this topos in Stuart decorative art. A cushion cover at the Cooper-Hewitt Museum in New York represents the five senses. There is a sinister subtext in the ambiguous devices—like the mirror for a lady and the strawberry and worm at the bottom. In a lecture on the Hardwick textiles (Folger Library, January 1999), Santina Levey, the expert on these fabrics found persuasive my suggestion that the strawberry-worm image in one hanging was an instance of this topos. Ross lists some of the most important studies of early embroidery in notes 3, 4, and 5. For an extensive bibliography, see Levey, *Elizabethan Treasures: The Hardwick Hall Textiles* (New York: Abrams, 1998), 107–8. My point is that to read these early texts, we need many disciplines.

3. See *Material Cultures: Why Some Things Matter*, ed. Daniel Miller (Chicago: University of Chicago Press, 1998), especially the essays on the domestic sphere in part 2, 25–73, and Neil Jarman, "Material of Culture, Fabric of Identity," 121–46.

4. This is a considerable project. Unlike modern waistcoats, most eighteenth-century ones were long. The shorter ones I have seen are more thickly embroidered.

5. Samuel Richardson, *Pamela; or, Virtue Rewarded*, ed. T. C. Duncan Eaves and Ben D. Kimpel (Boston: Houghton Mifflin, 1971), 25.

6. Samuel Richardson, *Clarissa; or, The History of a Young Lady*, ed. Angus Ross (New York: Penguin, 1985), 1306. These emblems are important in the eighteenth-century imagination. In the later abridgement of the novel, the heroine gives "directions about some emblems, of which she had made drawings, and chose to have them placed on the lid." See *Clarissa; or, The History of a Young Lady. Abridged* (London, ca. 1780), 139.

7. For a list, see F. Lotz, *Bibliographie der Modelbuecher* (Leipzig, 1933). For examples of Richard Shorleyker's patterns, see Donald King and Santina Levey, *The Victoria and Albert Museum's Textile Collection: Embroidery in Britain from 1200–1750* (New York: Canopy Books, 1993), 66.

8. Richardson is particularly preoccupied with this matter. Mr. B's family, heir to considerable property in three counties across England, will lose this to strangers if he does not marry; in the second part of the novel, Pamela provides him rapidly with seven children, five of them boys. In *Clarissa* the family is discomposed by the grandfather's unusual disposition of property and their desire to marry the heroine to an unsuitable but wealthy man. We finish with the heroine dead, her sister and brother unmarried, and Lovelace, the end of his line, dead in a foreign country. See Richardson's "A Collection of the Moral and Instructive Sentiments Contained in the History of Sir C. Grandison," in *Samuel Richardson's Published Commentary on Clarissa 1747–65*, ed. Thomas Keymer (London: Pickering and Chatto, 1998), 3:326–35: "FAMILIES are little communities. There are but few solid friendships out of them. They make up worthily, and help to secure, the great community of which they are so many miniatures." This quotation appears on 3:326.

9. See Samuel Richardson, *The History of Sir Charles Grandison,* ed. Jocelyn Harris (1753–1754; Oxford: Oxford University Press, 1986). References will be to this edition and cited in my text in parentheses as volume number then book, chapter, and page.

10. See note 41 below for speculation about a reason for choosing Bologna as the Italian heroine's family's home. It might be argued that Sir Charles's relation to Clementina della Porretta and with her family is, given the standard Protestant view of the practice of the Catholic church, his own involvement with the world of masquerade. See Jonas Barish's "Puritanism, Popery, and Parade" in his *The Antitheatrical Prejudice* (Berkeley: University of California Press, 1981), 155–90; and for the attractions of disguise and masquerade and metamorphosis, Terry Castle, *Masquerade and Civilization: The Carnivalesque in Eighteenth-Century English Culture and Fiction* (Stanford, Calif.: Stanford University Press, 1986). The hints of the Jacobites belong with this possibility. See notes 43 and 48 below.

11. Sir Charles is prepared to raise the daughters of a union with Clementina as Roman Catholics, but the sons as Protestants (2:3.20.130). This arrangement ostensibly allows Clementina's allegiance to be carried on with some of her offspring, but not those who will inherit the Grandison title and estates. This may answer to Sir Charles, but it does not answer to Clementina.

12. The Italian translation, by Paolo Rolli, was placed on the *Index* in 1732. See *Index Librorum Prohibitorum* (Rome, 1758), 181. The Congregation's reason for placing the poem among forbidden books would have been theological. For the relevance of Milton to the temptations offered to Sir Charles by Clementina, read as Eve, see Susan K. Lamb, "Transformations: The Culture of Tourism and Novelistic Literature in the Eighteenth Century" (Ph.D. diss., University of Toronto, 1997), 260.

13. Through Sir Charles, Richardson reflects on the advantages of "*Protestant Nunneries.*" Although his hero, when confronted with a character who describes himself as a Catholic, is quick to emend to "Roman Catholic," both Sir Charles and his creator are remarkably sympathetic to the church of Rome, as Clementina's family and ecclesiastical advisors are to Sir Charles. Clarissa's strong at-

traction to the single life, supported by her reading in texts like the *Imitation of Christ* and especially in John Norris, also reflects this sympathy and attraction.

14. "Recover" occurs four times within the page. It has the obvious meaning, the meaning of "recovery" as in illness, and, possibly, a theological implication.

15. Biblical scenes were familiar subjects in the embroidered pictures of the Stuart and Georgian periods, and were often so finely worked that they looked as if they were painted. See Margaret Swain, *Embroidered Stuart Pictures* (Haverford West: Shire Publications, 1990), 1, 14–19, and *Embroidered Georgian Pictures* (Princes Risborough: Shire Publications, 1994), 6, 13 (see the "needle painting," 18–20); Katharine B. Brett, *English Embroidery* (Toronto: Royal Ontario Museum, 1972), 31, 59; Yvonne Hackenbroch, *English and Other Needlework . . . in the Irwin Untermyer Collection* (London: Thames and Hudson, 1960), figures 98–101, 156, 161, 162; John L. Nevinson, *Catalogue of English Domestic Embroidery* (London: Victoria and Albert Museum, 1950), plates 15, 31, 33 (*Eikon Basilike*); Patricia Wardle, *Guide to English Embroidery* (London: Her Majesty's Stationery Office, 1981), 47.

16. Naomi Schor, *Reading in Detail: Aesthetics and the Feminine* (New York: Methuen, 1987), 11–22.

17. Xanthe Brooke, "Tales in Thread," *Antique Collector* 61 (1990): 118–24. Brooke discusses some of the biblical and two of the contemporary subjects worked which are in the Lady Lever Collection. See also Roszika Parker, *The Subversive Stitch: Embroidery and the Making of the Feminine* (London: The Women's Press, 1984) and Margaret Swain, *Historical Needlework* (London: Barrie and Jenkins, 1970). For prints as a source of textile patterns, see Anthony Wells-Cole, *Art and Decoration in Elizabethan and Jacobean England: The Influence of Continental Prints, 1558–1625* (New Haven, Conn.: Yale University Press, 1997).

18. I am grateful to my colleague, the Rev. William Craig, for calling this detail to my attention.

19. Chaucer renders this promise comical in his "Miller's Tale." The foolish old carpenter, a figure of Noah (Genesis 6), believes in the coming flood, having forgotten the divine promise. The trickster, however, is burned in the end, in both senses.

20. *The Jerusalem Bible* (New York, 1966), explanatory note for Matthew 24:37–42. All following quotations from the Bible are from the King James version. See also Luke 17:26–31.

21. See Harold W. Attridge, *The Epistle to the Hebrews: A Commentary on the Epistle to the Hebrews* (Philadelphia: Fortress Press, 1989), 319. See also Donald A. Hagner, *Hebrews* (San Francisco: Harper and Row, 1983), 167.

22. Arnold Williams, *The Common Expositor: An Account of the Commentaries on Genesis, 1527–1633* (Chapel Hill: University of North Carolina Press, 1948), 236. This passage comes from Benedictus Perrerius. There was a Cologne edition of this work as late as 1685. Nicolas de Lyra's *Biblia Sacra* (Paris, 1590) was known by all with a taste for commentary. Nicolas supplies, in quotations from all the fathers he can muster, what is, in his subtitle, the "glossa ordinaria," passages for

nearly every line of scripture. For a recent summary, see H. S. Benjamin, "Noah, the Ark, and the Flood in Early Christian Theology: The Ship of the Church in the Making," in *Interpretations of the Flood,* ed. Florentino García Martínez and Gerard P. Luttikhuizen (Leiden: Brill, 1998), 134–49. A late fifteenth-century Dutch woodcut, "The Early History of Man and the Baptism of Christ," puts images from the fall of the angels to the fall of man to the routing of Pharoah to the baptism of Christ into a single place. See figure 329 in Arthur M. Hind, *An Introduction to a History of Woodcut* (Boston: Houghton Mifflin, 1931), 2:575. See also "Das Schiff der Kirche" in Ewald M. Vetter, *Die Kupferstiche Zur Psalmodia Eucaristica Des Melchor Prieto von 1622* (Münster: Ascherdorff, 1972) especially 4, 108–9, 165, 171. Further attention needs to be paid to the ark and the church in the visual rhetoric of the Catholic Reformation. I am grateful to my colleague, Jeffrey Hamburger, for calling this volume to my attention.

23. Williams, *The Common Expositor,* 258.

24. *The Book of Common Prayer* (Oxford, 1765). The Noah texts appear elsewhere in the lessons of morning and evening prayer: Genesis 6, Sunday, Sexagesima, 4 and 7 January; Ezekiel 14, seventeenth Sunday after Trinity, 17 August; Isaiah 54, 20 December; Matthew 24, 27 January, 26 May, 23 September; Luke 17, 6 March, 5 May, 31 October; Heb. 11, 15 April, 8 August, 5 December; 1 Peter 3, Good Friday, 19 April, 8 August, 15 December; 2 Peter 3, 24 April, 23 August.

25. For a list of Dutch, French, Italian, German, and Spanish painters of the scene see Andor Pigler, *Barockthemen: eine Auswahl von Verzeichnissen zur Ikonographie des 17. und 18. Jahrhunderts,* 2d ed. (Budapest: Akademiai Kiado, 1974), 1:24–27. For two striking images see 3:24, plates 4 and 5, for the *Sintflut* done by Carracci (Paris) and by Cossiers (Brussels).

26. Don Cameron Allen, *The Legend of Noah: Renaissance Rationalism in Art, Science, and Letters* (Urbana: University of Illinois Press, 1963), 166.

27. Samuel Wesley, *History of the Old and New Testament* (London, 1716), 16.

28. Matthew Poole, *Annotations upon the Holy Bible* (London, 1683–1685), notes, seriatim, on Genesis 6:8–17, 7:20, 23. Pearson's method is different. For each of the verses annotated, he provides the views of important commentators like Grotius and Scaliger. See *Critici Sacri, sive, Doctissimorum virorum in ss. Biblio annotationes, & tractatus* (London, 1660). The passages given for the relevant text in Genesis provide the later scriptural allusions in Matthew, Luke, and 1 Peter.

29. See Sandi Fox, *Wrapped in Glory: Figurative Quilts and Bedcovers, 1700–1900* (New York: Thames and Hudson, 1990), 84–87.

30. [Lady Frances Mayne?], *An Introduction to the Reading of the Holy Bible* (London, 1716), 17.

31. B. Miller, *Scripture History for the Improvement of Youth Embellished with Upwards of 200 Illustrations* (London, 1822), 10.

32. See also *The History of Genesis,* 2d ed. (London, 1701), 25; Mark Anthony Meilan, *Holy Writ Familiarized to Juvenile Conceptions in a Series of Pathetic Stories and Affecting Dialogues* (London, 1791), 47; *The Holy Bible Abridg'd: or the History of the Old and New Testament. Illustrated with Notes and Adorned*

with Cuts for the Use of Children (London, 1791), 14; and *An Abridgement of Scripture History designed for the Amusement and Improvement of Children: wherein the most Striking actions in the Old Testament are made plain for the youngest Capacities* (London, 1765), 7. This has a headpiece of lost souls climbing trees, trying for dry land. The ark is far in the distance and the emphasis of the text is on the corruption of mankind. Thomas Towne's *Automatical Camera-Obscura* (London, 1821) presents such awful scenes of swimming, scrambling, and running folk that the young lady viewers are quite overcome and have to take time out. See 52–54. These are selections from a rich supply of improving works for children at the Osborne Collection of Early Children's Books, Toronto. I am indebted to Elizabeth Derbecker and Leslie McGrath for their kind assistance.

33. Morton D. Paley, *The Apocalyptic Sublime* (New Haven, Conn.: Yale University Press, 1986), 8. See also Walter Friedlaender, *Nicolas Poussin: A New Approach* (New York: Abrams, 1978), 87, 196. Friedlaender emphasizes the horror of the painting and speaks of the possible ecclesiastical influence on Poussin for the cycle of these paintings.

34. See Paley, *Apocalyptic Sublime,* 10–17. See also Anthony Blunt, "Poussin and the British Collectors," *The Connoisseur* 208 (1981): 118–21; Richard Verdi, "Poussin's 'Deluge': the Aftermath," *Burlington Magazine* 123 (1981): 388–400; and Joseph Burke, *English Art, 1714–1800* (Oxford: Clarendon Press, 1976), 71, 207, 224, 275. James Thomson refers to the "learned Poussin" in *The Castle of Indolence* (London, 1748) just after an account of "black tempests" and "flashing torrents" (1.38), but this reference is not specific to the *Deluge* and there is, in my reading, no place in his *Winter* which is related to the painting. The illustrations are classical, not biblical.

35. See R. Po-Chia Hsia, *The World of Catholic Renewal, 1540–1770* (Cambridge: Cambridge University Press, 1998). For additional titles on this subject, see Hsia's bibliography.

36. T. Lincoln Bouscaren and Adam C. Ellis, *Canon Law: A Text and Commentary,* 3d ed. (Milwaukee, Wis.: Bruce Publishing, 1957), 75–76.

37. Heinrich Denzinger, *Enchiridion Symbolorum Definitionum et Declarationum de Rebus Fidei et Morum,* ed. Karl Rahner (Friburg: Herder, 1952), 218: "Prompted by faith, we are compelled to believe and to hold that there is one, holy, catholic, and apostolic church, and we believe firmly and confess simply that outside this Church there is neither salvation nor remission of sins. . . . Certainly at the time of the flood Noah had but one ark, prefiguring one church which . . . had but one guide and governor, that is to say, Noah. Outside the ark, we read, all others on the earth were destroyed" (translation mine).

38. Francis J. Schenk, *The Matrimonial Impediments of Mixed Religion and Disparity of Cult* (Washington, D.C.: Catholic University of America, 1929), 48–49.

39. For a discussion of this topic in terms of the dissolution of marriage, a discussion which elegantly outlines the Catholic Church's positions on marriage, see John T. Noonan, Jr., *Power to Dissolve: Lawyers and Marriages in the Roman Curia* (Cambridge, Mass.: Harvard University Press, 1972); on Benedict XIV, see 123, 128.

40. Compare Schenk on royal marriages, 51–56.

41. "A pope dear to Protestants and to Catholics, to the King and to the people" (my translation). Louis-Antoine Caraccioli, *Vita dei Papa Benedetto XIV, Prospero Lambertini* (Venice, 1783), 26. Given Richardson's flirtation with names in *Grandison* (see note 48 below for references to Harris and Lamb on names) it is hard not to wonder about the name of the principal priest in the narrative, as well as about the future pope's earlier appointment to the see of Bologna when he was still Prospero Lambertini. His first biographer (I have not been able to locate a copy) was Marescotti. For the most detailed study of Benedict, see Ludwig Pastor, *The History of the Popes,* trans. E. F. Peeler (London: Routledge and Kegan Paul, 1961), all of vol. 35 and 36:1–142. According to Pastor, Marescotti was a considerable student of Roman antiquities (35:185–86).

42. "Here is Lambertini, ornament of Rome, father of the world, who teaches all by his writing and adorns all by his virtues" (my translation). For an account of Voltaire's correspondence with the Pope, see Pastor, *The History of the Popes,* 35:205–8. The correspondence between them is printed in an appendix, 486–89.

43. *Horace Walpole's Correspondence,* ed. W. S. Lewis (New Haven, Conn.: Yale University Press, 1937–1983), 21:105 (to Mann). Benedict appears frequently in the Mann letters. See 44:185–88. He was inevitably involved with the Stuarts in Rome. See his *Correspondance de Benoît XIV,* ed. Emile de Heeckeren (Paris: Plon-Nourrit, 1912), passim.

44. See *Correspondence of Thomas Gray,* ed. Paget Toynbee and Leonard Whibley (Oxford: Clarendon Press, 1935), 1:174, 175.

45. Benedict's comment on the right man for the job is as mildly translated in Gray as it is by others. Gray cites the Italian: "Si vi piace un Santo, c' el'Gotti; si volete una testa scaltra, e Politica, c' el Aldrovande, se un Coglione, eccomi!" (1:174). (If you want a saint, choose Gotti; if you want a politician, choose Aldrovando, if you want someone tough, choose me [translation mine].)

46. T. C. Duncan Eaves and Ben D. Kimpel, *Samuel Richardson, A Biography* (Oxford: Clarendon Press, 1971), 550–56. See especially 552–53, on *Grandison.*

47. Michael Hodgetts, *Secret Hiding Places* (Dublin: Veritas, 1989), 232.

48. In the explanatory notes to *Grandison,* Jocelyn Harris observes that "many details of the proposed compromise between Sir Charles and Clementina correspond to arrangements between Charles and his Queen" and that these were "discussed in a book that Richardson both edited and printed, Sir Thomas Roe's *Embassy to the Ottoman Porte* (1740)" (2:674). See also Lamb, "Transformations," 251–60. Lamb's notes refer to others who have commented upon the Jacobite possibilities—Harris, John Dussinger, Margaret Anne Doody, Morris Golden, and Paul Monod, as well as William Merritt Sale, Jr. and Eaves and Kimpel. For an essay on other "romantic" dimensions of the Italian action, viewed in terms of Clementina, see Albert J. Rivero, "Representing Clementina: 'Unnatural' Romance and the Ending of *Sir Charles Grandison,*" in *New Essays on Samuel Richardson,* ed. Albert J. Rivero (New York: St. Martin's Press, 1996), 209–25.

49. Aaron Hill, *Works,* 2d ed. (London, 1754), 2:116–17. The letter is dated 17 December 1740. Richardson subscribed for six sets of this edition.

50. *Samuel Richardson, Selected Letters,* ed. John Carroll (Oxford: Clarendon Press, 1964), 74–75.

51. See Michael Neill, "'Amphitheatres in the Body': Playing with Hands on the Shakespearean Stage," *Shakespeare Survey* 48 (1995): 29. Neill cites the classic study, John Bulwer's *Chirologia: or the Natural Language of the Hand and Chironomia: or the Art of Manual Rhetoric,* ed. James W. Cleary (Carbondale: Southern Illinois University Press, 1974). See also David Bevington, *Action Is Eloquence: Shakespeare's Language of Gesture* (Cambridge, Mass.: Harvard University Press, 1984) and Alastair Smart, "Dramatic Gesture and Expression in the Age of Hogarth and Reynolds," *Apollo* 82 (1965): 90–97.

52. Fritz Laupichler, "Pointing," in *Encyclopedia of Comparative Iconography,* ed. Helene E. Roberts (Chicago: Fitzroy Dearborn, 1998), 2:743.

53. Jocelyn Harris, *Samuel Richardson* (Cambridge: Cambridge University Press, 1987), 158–62. For a different reading of the textile, see Janet E. Aikins, "Richardson's 'Speaking Pictures,'" in *Samuel Richardson: Tercentenary Essays,* ed. Margaret Anne Doody and Peter Sabor (Cambridge: Cambridge University Press, 1989), 164–65. Commenting upon the "disproportion" Sir Charles observes in the unfinished piece, Aikins says that "Richardson depicts Clementina as an amateur artist of the school attacked by Hogarth, for she draws after the Old Masters rather than from life and what she produced is not only incomplete but exhibits a failure in perspective . . . [he] hints at both her distorted mind and her misplaced faith" (164). I admire this study of Richardson and art, but I do not concur with this reading of the Noah textile.

54. Carroll, *Selected Letters,* 238.

55. In addition to those I have thanked in the notes, I should like to acknowledge the help of F. Donald Logan; the librarians at the Royal Ontario Museum, the Department of Fine Art at the University of Toronto, the Art Institute of Chicago, Trinity College and the Fisher Rare Book Library in Toronto, and St. John's Seminary in Brighton, Massachusetts; and the textile curators at the Museum of Fine Arts in Boston, the Royal Ontario Museum in Toronto, and the Cooper-Hewitt Museum and the Ratti Center at the Metropolitan Museum of Art in New York. I am also grateful to those who listened and offered help in early stages at the meetings of the Aphra Behn Society and the Eighteenth-Century Group at the University of Toronto. I owe a special debt to Susan Lamb, once my graduate student, now my colleague. I meant to write more generally on Richardson and textiles. At the beginning I asked her if there was a textile in *Grandison.* She thought there was.

13

Early Women Novelists, the Canon, and the History of the British Novel

BRIAN CORMAN

The history of the English novel is a Regency invention, and the tastes and values of the Regency historians set the tone for all subsequent study. This is the time of the first serious attempts at canon making, and the canon established by the critics of the Romantic period became the canon to be modified thereafter. It is a period of ever-increasing anthologies and collections of novels, reviews of novels, and general novel criticism and theory. The three most important Regency novel critics, Anna Laetitia Barbauld, John Colin Dunlop, and Sir Walter Scott, merit special and fuller attention. A number of others, some more famous and important in other contexts, also deserve serious, if less full, discussion.[1]

In 1931, Byron Hall Gibson praised Barbauld for producing the "most complete and the most accurate history of prose fiction to appear during the years intervening between the publication of John Moore's *A View of the Commencement and Progress of Romance* (1797) and John Colin Dunlop's *History of Fiction* (1814)."[2] This was no doubt intended as high praise, notwithstanding the lack of competition from other novel critics between Moore and Dunlop, but it does not begin to do justice to Barbauld as critic-historian of the novel. "On the Origin and Progress of Novel-Writing," the essay prefixed to her fifty-volume collection, *The British Novelists* (1810), is a quantum leap beyond the limited and narrow history offered by Moore. Barbauld is less well-informed about the novel before Cervantes, but as soon as she reaches post-medieval prose fiction, her greater gifts as a novel critic become evident.

Barbauld had rehearsed the early history of the novel in her "Life of

Richardson," the introduction to her edition of Samuel Richardson's *Correspondence* (1804).[3] In "On the Origin" she fleshes out the earlier version, without altering her earlier judgments, while bringing the narrative up to date. It here introduces a collection of twenty-eight novels by twenty-one writers rather than the letters of the "father of the modern novel of the serious or pathetic kind."[4] The Richardson edition had already shown that though Barbauld herself was not a novelist, she had given much productive thought to the novel's formal qualities. In the "Life of Richardson" she begins by making a case for the lumping of epic, dramatic, didactic, and satiric with romantic narratives under the general class of "*fictitious adventures*" (vii). She then asks why it is that writers of romance alone among adventure writers have such a low reputation. This is followed by a division of novels into three kinds based on mode of narration: the "narrative or epic," the "most common way" and also Barbauld's favorite because of the flexibility it enables (xxiii–xxiv); the mode of "memoirs," that is, the first-person narrative, Barbauld's least favorite because of the limitations imposed by the single voice and perspective (xxiv–xxvi); and the mode of Richardson, the "*epistolary correspondence*," able to capture the moment dramatically with the variety allowed by as many voices as the author chooses, but nonetheless "the least probable way of telling a story" (xxvi–xxviii). A critic who has already written so attentively and thoughtfully about the art of the novel is well-prepared to provide a more sophisticated history than Moore's.

"On the Origin and Progress of Novel-Writing" focuses on different critical issues, a shift made evident by its opening sentence: "A Collection of Novels has a better chance of giving pleasure than of commanding respect."[5] The expected defense of the novel with a full literary pedigree does follow, but it is accompanied by a repeated insistence on the value of pleasure—though, of course, pleasure that is not at odds with morality—in a work of literature:

> To measure the dignity of a writer by the pleasure he affords his readers is not perhaps using an accurate criterion; but the invention of a story, the choice of proper incidents, the ordonnance of the plan, occasional beauties of description, and above all, the power exercised over the reader's heart by filling it with the successive emotions of love, pity, joy, anguish, transport, or indignation, together with the grave impressive moral resulting from the whole, imply talents of the highest order, and ought to be appretiated accordingly. (1:2–3)

The following sentence introduces the other central concept to be developed throughout the essay, that realism is the defining characteristic of the modern novel: "A good novel is an epic in prose, with more of character and less (indeed in modern novels nothing) of the supernatural machinery" (1:3). Although the emphases on pleasure and on realism are already present, at least implicitly, in Barbauld's earlier novel criticism, they now loom large in determining which novels are most worthy of inclusion in an English canon.

Well into her essay, Barbauld declares in language anticipating critics like E. M. Forster, that "It is sufficient therefore as an end, that these writings add to the innocent pleasures of life; and if they do no harm, the entertainment they give is sufficient good. . . . The unpardonable sin in a novel is dullness: however grave or wise it may be, if its author possesses no powers of amusing, he has no business to write novels" (1:48). Barbauld's discussions of novels always take into account their power to give pleasure.

The rise of the novel, for Barbauld, is tied closely to the development of realism. "If the stage is a mirror of life, so is the novel, and perhaps a more accurate one, as less is sacrificed to effect and representation." Novels are thus in the best position to present the world as it is in order to prepare young readers for what they will find when they enter it. That preparation also requires, however, some protection from the most vicious realities, and considerable discretion in presenting vice triumphant: in "good novels," vice always leads to "infamy and ruin" (1:51). Barbauld calls attention to the varieties of prose fiction that make up the history of the novel, but she gives special attention to those like Cervantes, who attacked the old romances, and Lafayette, whose works "are esteemed to be the first which approach the modern novel of the serious kind" (1:18). She runs through English fiction from Chaucer to Behn in a couple of pages before reaching the "first author amongst us who distinguished himself by natural painting . . . that truly original genius De Foe" (1:37). The next generation brings Richardson, "the first English author who has given celebrity to the modern novel" (1:i).

Women play a prominent role in Barbauld's history. She holds the French novel in very high esteem, and of the twenty-five French novelists she names, nine are women. Of the twenty-eight British novels in her history, six are by women. Of greater importance, of the twenty-one novelists whose works are reprinted in the subsequent volumes, eight are women, accounting for twelve of the twenty-eight titles.[6] It is of course true that Barbauld was not entirely free to choose which novels to anthologize. They are, however, some of the "most approved novels," though of "very different degrees of merit," selected in part to insure variety, in part in response to the "taste and preference of the public," and in part by the constraints of copyright (1:61). Barbauld acknowledges the place and the importance of personal taste in the selection process. She thus ends "On the Origin" with a claim that might very well have seemed extravagant at the time: "It was said by Fletcher of Saltoun, 'Let me make the ballads of a nation, and I care not who makes the laws.' Might it not be said with as much propriety, Let me make the novels of a country, and let who will make the systems?" (1:62).

As Elizabeth Kraft has pointed out, the list of titles and authors covered in "On the Origin" far exceeds the number in the collection, and "is notable for the few titles it shares."[7] Barbauld's history is far more inclusive, covering novels from other countries and earlier periods. The anthology, on the other hand, accurately named *The British Novelists,* begins with Richardson. The area that interests her least is the British novel before 1740. Aside from two sentences of high praise for Defoe, Barbauld has little good to say about the early British novelists: her discussion totals under two pages, and nearly half of it is devoted to a relatively extensive treatment of *Gaudentio di Lucca* (1737). The only women Barbauld mentions before 1740 are Margaret Cavendish, Duchess of Newcastle, and the long-notorious "Female Wits," Aphra Behn, Delarivier Manley, and Eliza Haywood. Newcastle is dismissed as an "indefatigable writer" of "ponderous performances." Because "Behn's novels were licentious," they have "fallen." Manley provided her readers with nothing more than "fashionable scandal"; she is remembered only because of her place in *The Dunciad.* Haywood was able to profit from Pope's just chastisement; "her later works are by no means void of merit" (1:35–37). In short, Barbauld has no desire to revive interest in the earliest women novelists.

Barbauld is scarcely more impressed by the first generation of women novelists to appear after the publication of *Pamela* (1740). She mentions only two in "On the Origin," Sarah Fielding and Frances Sheridan, in the context of a discussion of novels "which are, or have been popular, though not of high celebrity." Fielding was "a woman of good sense and cultivation; and if she did not equal her brother in talent, she did not, like him, lay herself open to moral censure" (1:43). Sheridan, "an ingenious and amiable woman," nonetheless produced in *Sidney Biddulph* (1761) a work that heaps "distress upon virtue and innocence, merely to prove, what no one will deny, that the best dispositions are not always sufficient to ward off the evils of life" (1:44). She is concerned about excessive melancholy in the novel and suggests that for reasons she does not understand, women novelists are especially vulnerable to what she considers sentimental weaknesses.[8] Three other women of the earlier generation are discussed in the introductions Barbauld provides within the collection proper. Clara Reeve has "but a moderate degree of merit," though she has always been "a great favorite." "Subsequent publications of more elegance and invention" have caused *The Old English Baron* (1777) "to slide from the place it once held" (22:i). Its plot is too easy to predict, though it remains a good, moral tale for young readers. Charlotte Lennox was "a diligent and successful author," and *The Female Quixote* (1752) "an agreeable and ingenious satire" (24:i) (Romantic critics' adjectives of praise are as telling as ours), but Lennox did not know how to end her novel: "the grave moralizing of a clergyman is not the means by which the heroine should have been cured of her reveries" (24:iii). Though "the style of Mrs. Lennox is easy," it "does not rise to the elegance attained by many more modern female writers" (24:iv). Finally, Frances Brooke, an "elegant and accomplished woman," was "perhaps the first novel-writer who attained a perfect purity and polish of style" (27:i). Her greatest strength is as a descriptive writer, especially of the climate, landscape, and people of Canada.

This is not to suggest that Barbauld held earlier women novelists in contempt. On the contrary, she takes those she mentions seriously enough to engage in thoughtful criticism of their work. She does not choose to recover or include neglected women writers, in part, no doubt, because she was not persuaded of their worth, but also in part (the more compelling part in my view) because of her greater enthusiasm for more recent fiction, especially fiction by women. She accepts a number of the earlier historical commonplaces, especially those that see a decline in the novel after Richardson and Fielding, aided and abetted by the circulating libraries which encourage "a great deal of trash" to be published year after year (1:58). Yet despite the "many paltry books" that continue to appear, "it may safely be affirmed that we have more good writers in this walk living at the present time, than at any period since the days of Richardson and Fielding" (1:58–59). She argues that the decline is over and that progress has been restored, largely thanks to the efforts of the current generation of women: "A very great proportion of these [good writers] are ladies: and surely it will not be said that either taste or morals have been losers by their taking the pen in hand. The names of D'Arblay, Edgeworth, Inchbald, Radcliffe, and a number more, will vindicate this assertion" (1:59).

Additional vindication comes in the introductions to the novels of Inchbald, Burney, Radcliffe, and Edgeworth in the collection proper. A sample of Barbauld's superlatives should be sufficient: "To readers of taste it would be superfluous to point out the beauties of Mrs. Inchbald's novels" (28:i); "Scarcely any name, if any, stands higher in the history of novel-writers than that of Miss Burney, now Mrs. D'Arblay" (38:i); "A greater distinction is due to those which stand at the head of a class; and such are undoubtedly the novels of Mrs. Radcliffe,—which exhibit a genius of no common stamp" (43:i); "The editor feels it would be superfluous to indulge her feelings in dwelling on the excellencies of an author

[Edgeworth] so fully in possession of the esteem and admiration of the public" (49:i). Even after discounting for the tact required in treating authors still living, and personal friends at that, there can be little doubt about Barbauld's critical agenda. *The British Novelists* offers a forum for furthering the reputations of contemporary novelists, the best of whom are women. In reflecting and voicing the taste of her time as well as her personal taste, Barbauld is doing what most critics have always done. What makes her effort unusually significant is that it is one of the formative attempts at canon making for the British novel. Once there is a canon in place, subsequent critics must address it as their starting point. That the first canons of the British novel are the products of early nineteenth-century critics is enormously important to eighteenth-century women novelists' critical histories.

With the appearance of *The British Novelists,* it becomes possible to talk about a fully realized canon of the novel. A fully realized history of the novel in English, John Dunlop's *The History of Fiction,* appeared a mere four years later, perhaps just a coincidence, but one which helped cement the nineteenth-century base upon which subsequent structures had to be built. Dunlop's plan is encyclopedic, an historical account of all prose fiction from earliest times, though very little non-European fiction is, in fact, included. Acknowledging the contributions of few of his predecessors—Percy and Warton, but not Reeve, Moore, or Barbauld—Dunlop considers his work the first "attempt towards a general History of Fiction."[9] In terms of comprehensive coverage, his claim is warranted. Of his fourteen chapters, only the final two cover "the novel." The first two are on ancient prose fiction; the remaining ten are on medieval and Renaissance "romance." All these works share a number of things in common: "fictitious narrative[s]" (7) are as ubiquitous as Barbauld's "fictitious adventures."

Dunlop's general theory of fiction, a phrase he would disdain since he considers the "establishment of a theory" generally in conflict with the "investigation of truth" (11), is traditional and inclusive. He follows Bacon's lead in preferring fiction to history because fiction "presents us with the fates and fortunes of persons rewarded or punished according to merit. And as real history disgusts us with a familiar and constant similitude of things, *Fiction* relieves us by unexpected turns and changes, and thus not only delights, but inculcates morality and nobleness of soul. It raises the mind by accommodating the images of things to our desires, and not, like history and reason, subjecting the mind to things" (8).

Dunlop continues in this vein, arguing that prose fiction is superior to poetry, since it "can discriminate without impropriety, and enter into detail without meanness." And even if the "utility" of "Fiction were less than it is, how much are we indebted to it for pleasure and enjoyment!" (8). Fiction is thus unique among human products as a "powerful instrument of virtue and happiness." Like Barbauld, he thinks it has been too long "despised." His own project is part of a wider and timely effort to see fiction "more justly appreciated" (9). A history of fiction is another important sign that it has come of age.

Dunlop's discussion of the Greek romances provides an interesting introduction of some of the characteristics he values most in the novel. He criticizes all early fiction for consisting largely of "a succession of strange, and often improbable adventures." What distinguishes the Greek from the other early romances, and as a result makes them "extremely pleasing," is that they are "almost the first productions in which woman is in any degree represented as assuming her proper station of the friend and companion of man." Dunlop is unequivocal in his privileging of "manners and character" over "adventure" as the most important and valuable constituents of the best novels (46).

Dunlop recognizes that literary forms develop and change over time, "that one species of fable has scarcely disappeared, when it has been succeeded by another," a consequence of the constant need of fiction to satisfy the requirements of "the human mind" for "amusement and relaxation" (360). He credits the French with the most important recent changes in the kinds of fictions that now attempt to satisfy these basic human desires. Recent French fiction is divided into four "classes," fictionalized history, romances describing European manners through foreign eyes, fairy tales (including Oriental tales and *voyages imaginaires*), and "novels . . . of which the incidents, whether serious or comical, are altogether imaginary" (361).

The last class, which is the most important in the history of fiction, is given the most thorough treatment. Dunlop uses Johnsonian language to consider *La princesse de Clèves* (1678), "the earliest of those agreeable and purely fictitious productions, whose province it is to bring about natural events by natural means, and which preserve curiosity alive without the help of wonder—in which human life is exhibited in its true state, diversified only by accidents that daily happen in the world, and influenced only by passions which are actually to be found in our intercourse with mankind" (362). *La princesse de Clèves* and Lafayette's other novel, *Zaïde* (1670), "may justly be regarded as forming a new æra in fiction, and as effecting the most fortunate revolution we have witnessed in the course of our survey." Since that time, novels "no longer attempted to please by unnatural or exaggerated representations, but emulated each other in the genuine exhibition of human character, and the manners of real life" (366). Dunlop welcomes the new demands for realism, though his judgments of specific works point to a very different standard of realism from those made familiar by more recent, higher-profile critics. The other French novelists Dunlop extensively treats are Marivaux, Prévost, Riccoboni, Rousseau, Le Sage, Crébillon, and Voltaire. Three of the seven writers of historical romance Dunlop mentions are women, and Grafigny is one of the five writers of fictions examining manners from the perspective of a foreigner.

Dunlop shares Barbauld's preference of French to British fiction, though his canon is far more selective than hers. His discussion of French fiction is twice the length of his discussion of British fiction, the final chapter of the *History.* He apologizes for the "compression" of his discussion of "modern French tales and novels" (400); his rationale is that these works are more familiar to his readers than the earlier romances. That is still more the case for modern British novels, so he limits himself to "a very short and general survey" (401), though not without acknowledging that a proper analysis of British novels "would require some volumes" (413). One of the more interesting reasons Dunlop offers for the difficulty in covering modern novels is that the recent explosion in number has also multiplied the kinds of fiction being written: "In former periods, when readers were few, and when only one species of fiction was written at a time, it was easy to judge what were the circumstances which gave birth to it, and to which it gave birth in turn." It is no longer the case that novels are clearly "expressive of the taste and feelings of the period of their composition" (400–401), a view at odds with most of his predecessors, and one that Dunlop's many readers would increasingly reject.

English prose fiction of the middle ages and romances of the Renaissance are covered in earlier chapters. Dunlop begins his final chapter with the other kinds of Renaissance fictions, especially those of Lyly, Lodge, and Greene. There is little of importance between them and the Restoration, when the demand for prose fiction was restored with the monarchy. He mentions Newcastle and Orrery as worthy of notice, though without influence. They are followed by the "Female Wits," and here Dunlop repeats the familiar tale. Manley was popular because she provided her readers with the "fashionable scandal" they craved; her popularity could not last. Behn is clearly a far greater writer, but "her writings have not escaped the moral contagion which infected the literature of that age." *Oroonoko* (1688) is the least indecent of her novels and the only one still worthy of mention. Haywood's early novels are too corrupt for a more refined age, but *Betsy Thoughtless* (1751), "though not free in every passage from the objections that may be charged against her former compositions, is deserving of notice, both on account of its merit, and of having apparently suggested the plan of Miss Burney's Evelina" (409).

There are so many novels by midcentury that it is useful to subdivide them, and Dunlop chooses to consider them in three groups, "the *serious*, the *comic*, and the *romantic*." "At the head of the first class" (410) is Richardson, who is joined by Sheridan and Godwin. The only comic novelists noticed are Fielding and Smollett; the British comic novelists are no more successful than the French in commanding Dunlop's respect. The romantic novel, "which seems in a great measure peculiar to the English" (413), excites Dunlop's greatest interest and enthusiasm. Here the examples are again limited: to the pioneers, Walpole and Reeve, and to the master, Radcliffe, "this justly celebrated woman" (415), who is treated at greater length than any other British novelist with more than double the space given to Richardson, her nearest rival. Dunlop concludes his account of the British novel with brief discussions of the important fiction from the other three categories he established in his discussion of French fiction. Fictionalized history has produced nothing worth noting in English—this in 1814. *The Citizen of the World* (1762) is the only romance of manners through foreign eyes of genuine merit. Fairy tales and Oriental tales have produced nothing of value. But the *voyage imaginaire* is a form in which British writers are unsurpassed; *Robinson Crusoe* (1719), *Gulliver's Travels* (1726), and *Gaudentio di Lucca* provide conclusive evidence, and *Peter Wilkins* (1751), *William Bingfield* (1753), and *John Daniel* (1751) show that the tradition Defoe established continued to thrive for at least another generation.

Dunlop's *History* is important as the first comprehensive history of the novel in English. It was frequently reprinted throughout the nineteenth century and remained the standard work in the field until Ernest Baker's eleven-volume *History of the English Novel* over a hundred years later. As a standard reference work, even its brief discussion of the British novel had considerable influence. Dunlop was clearly an elitist in his tastes with a strong preference for serious fiction; he had little patience for humor or immorality, though he took great pleasure in the gothic. His canon is small and exclusive, but it is gender neutral. It includes only eight of the twenty-one authors in Barbauld's collection; even in 1814, there is no single canon. Especially significant for this study is Dunlop's reinforcement of Barbauld's treatment of the women novelists before the generation of Burney: only Frances Sheridan survives.

Barbauld edited an important collection of novels; Dunlop provided a history. A third monument to the growing status of the novel is the writing of a series of "Biographical and Critical Sketches," on the model of Johnson's *Lives of the Poets* (1779–1781), by Sir Walter Scott. His essays were originally written as prefaces to *Ballantyne's Novelist's Library,* a project that was neither successful nor completed; but like Johnson's, they were later collected, first in a pirated edition by the French publisher, Galignani, subsequently as part of Scott's collected *Miscellaneous Prose Works* (1827), and later in a single volume as *Lives of the Novelists,* the title they are best known by today. When taken together with Scott's occasional essays and reviews, they form one of the most important bodies of novel criticism in English. It is surprising that such a statement is necessary, but Scott is remarkably underrated as a critic. René Wellek devotes a mere two paragraphs to him in *A History of Modern Criticism,* asserting that he is not "an important critic." The highest praise he offers is to note that "there is some rudimentary criticism in the *Lives of the Novelists* (1821 [*sic*])." He also observes that "Scott preferred Smollett to Fielding and praised Jane Austen, as he should. But he praised almost everyone of whom he wrote," and he "lacked discernment, and even critical pretensions and principles."[10]

Scott's extended comparison of Fielding and Smollett in the "Memoir of Tobias Smollett," modeled on Johnson's comparison of Dryden and Pope in "The Life of Pope," argues for granting Smollett "an equal rank with his great rival Fielding," as the conclusion to an essay that places both novelists "far above any of their successors in the same line of fictitious composition."[11] Scott indeed praised Austen long before most others, and his approach to criticism is one that looks for the best. Like Johnson, though, Scott always offers a balanced view of the strengths and weaknesses of his subjects, however much his presentation accentuates the positive. Perhaps most unforgivable for Wellek is Scott's indifference to principles and his complete lack of pretension. Peter Morgan accurately captures Scott's values as a critic with the following adjectives: "untheoretic, sincere, careless, modest, generous, good-tempered, judicious, gentlemanly."[12] These are not qualities highly prized in critics in the late twentieth century, but their presence should not hide the fact that in quantity, quality, range, and insight, Scott's criticism earns him a high place in any study of the criticism of the novel.[13]

Ballantyne's Novelist's Library consists of novels by fourteen writers, of whom but two are women, Clara Reeve and Ann Radcliffe. With the exception of Le Sage, all are British. None were still active in 1821; most were dead. Scott's choices of recent novelists, if they were his, were limited by copyright; his choice of earlier writers was more clearly an expression of his taste. When Galignani issued his piracy and the *Lives* came to the attention of Scott's friend Lady Louisa Stuart, she wrote him to urge him to publish a British edition and to inquire about omissions from his canon:

Either Galignani has not printed all, or many are wanting whom you certainly do not mean to pass by: Moore's "Zeluco," Godwin's "Caleb Williams" and "St. Leon," Charlotte Smith, Miss Burney, Miss Hamilton, Miss Edgeworth, Miss Austen, and may I petition a word in favour of Charlotte Lennox, Dr. Johnson's favourite, whose female Quixote delighted my childhood so much that I cannot tell whether the liking I still have for it is from taste or memory.[14]

Lady Louisa's list of recent novels seems to her beyond dispute, but her case for Lennox is far less assured. She recognizes that tastes change, and that books that once pleased do not necessarily continue to do so. She includes the following anecdote with reflections in her letter:

I am lately returned from a friend's house where these prefaces have been *devoured* by man, woman, and child. One evening after they were finished, a book was wanting to be read aloud, and what you said of Mackenzie made the company choose the "Man of Feeling," though some apprehended it would prove too affecting. However, we began. I, who was the reader, had not seen it for several years, the rest did not know it at all. I am afraid I perceived a sad change in it, or myself, which was worse, and the effect altogether failed. Nobody cried, and at some of the passages, the touches that I used to think so exquisite—oh dear! they laughed. (234–35)

It is an anecdote worthy of attention for its own sake, revealing as it does the always unstable nature of any literary canon, and it is additionally important for the reply it provoked from Scott, a reply that only indirectly deals with Lady Louisa's excluded favorites, but one which reveals Scott's complete agreement with her about the effect of changing tastes on the canon:

It is very difficult to resolve your Ladyships curious question concerning change of taste but whether in young or old it takes place insensibly without the parties being aware of it. A grand aunt of mine old Mrs. Keith of Ravelstone . . . lived with unabated vigour of intellect to a very advanced age. She was very fond of reading and enjoyd it to the last of a long life. One day she asked me when we happend to be alone together whether I had ever seen Mrs Behns novels—I confessd the charge.—Whether I could get her a sight of them—I said with some hesitation I believed I could but that I did not think she would like either the manners or the language which approachd too near that of Charle[s] IIds time to be quite proper reading. Nevertheless said the good old Lady I remember them so much admired & recollect being so much interested in them myself that I wish to look at them again. To hear was to obey. So I sent Mrs. Afra Behn curiously seald up with "private & confidential" on the pacquet to my gay old grand aunt. The next time I saw her afterwards she gave me back Afra wrapd up with nearly these [words] "Take back your bonny Mrs Behn and if you will take my advice you will put her in the fire for I found it impossible to get through the very first of the novels—But is it not she said a very odd thing that I an old woman of eighty and upwards sitting alone feel myself ashamd to read a book which sixty years ago I have heard read aloud for the amusement of large circles consisting of the first and most creditable society in London."[15]

The optimistic Scott's nod to progress aside, these passages document the changing responses to the first several generations of women novelists by two generous and unusually well-informed readers, themselves of different generations, in the 1820s.

Scott's choice of recent writers, he explains, has been limited by factors other than taste: "I thought of Charlotte Smith whom I admire very much. Miss Edgeworths novels & Miss Austens are inimitable but being both copy-rights could not come within my plan" (10:95–96). Smith had been included in the original plan, but the series failed before it reached her; Scott's "Memoir" of her is included in the *Miscellaneous Prose Works*. The only other "Memoir" not part of the original collection is of Defoe; any other additional authors part of Scott's original plan remain unrecorded. But he does record a number of other recent women novelists he considers important in the "Memoir" of Smith:

> We cannot but remark the number of highly-talented women, who have, within our time of novel-reading, distinguished themselves advantageously in this department of literature. Besides the living excellence of Mrs D'Arblay, and of Maria Edgeworth, of the Authoress of *Marriage* and the *Inheritance,* and of Mrs Opie, the names arise on us of Miss Austen, the faithful chronicler of English manners, and English society of the middling, or what is called the genteel class; besides also Mrs Radcliffe, Miss Reeves, and others, to whom we have endeavoured to do some justice in these sheets. We have to thank Mrs Inchbald, the authoress of *Frankenstein,* Mrs Bennett, too, and many other women of talents, for the amusement which their works have afforded; and we must add, that we think it would be impossible to match against these names the same number of masculine competitors, arising within the same space of time. (4:69)

Scott's list is remarkably inclusive, ranging from popular favorites like Burney and Edgeworth to writers without strong critical reputations like Austen and Shelley. Like Barbauld and Dunlop, he recognized the novel as an international form with a long tradition and a wide range of species under the umbrella of prose fiction. The passage above testifies to the inclusiveness of his taste: unlike most of his predecessors and still more of the critics of the next generations, he was receptive to good writing regardless of form. He recognized faults within individual writers as well as the inevitable shortcomings of the various novelistic genres, but no writer is dismissed for choice of form and no form dismissed because of weak practitioners.

Scott accepts the basic distinction between "novel" and "romance," but happily embraces both. He condemns coarseness, crudeness, and indecency, but forgives Defoe, Smollett, and Sterne when they are guilty. He thinks it misguided to provide rational explanations for the supernatural, but finds Radcliffe's fertile imagination and poetic gifts, particularly of natural description, more than sufficient compensation. He claims that Mackenzie's originality in portraying human feeling excuses his neglect of plot and character.

In two important areas, Scott anticipates critical trends that will later be developed by far less tolerant writers. Though Scott recognized that the novel was an international form, he had a much stronger predilection for the British novel than most of his predecessors. He credits Fielding with retrieving the novel from "the disgrace in which he found it," and rendering it "a classical department of British literature" (3:93). He even wonders whether Fielding's novels, quintessentially English as they are, "can be fully understood, or relished to the highest extent, by such natives of Scotland and Ireland, as are not habitually and intimately acquainted with the characters and manners of Old England" (3:77). For Scott, Fielding's Englishness is an essential quality of his writing, but not an honorific. Later critics would build upon such observations as part of a nationalistic agenda for the novel.

Nor does Scott use his admiration for Fielding to denigrate Richardson, whom he recognizes as a great innovator, and as the author of the "most affecting and sublime" *Clarissa* (1748) (3:41), the writer of a "classic" whose "fame" is guaranteed "for ever" (3:38). The "gentleness of [Richardson's] mind was almost feminine" (3:13); yet "his manly and virtuous application of his talents [has] been of service to morality, and to human nature in general" (3:76). Richardson remains for Scott what he was for Johnson, a great novelist through mastery of the affective and instructive powers of fiction, powers undiminished by Scott's recognition of Fielding's different but equivalent excellence. Scott will not condemn Richardson any more than Radcliffe for not possessing the "excellence proper to a style of composition totally different from that which she has attempted" (3:363). Yet Scott is writing at a time when the Fielding versus Richardson dialectic had long been established, and the balance had clearly shifted in favor of Fielding.[16] The increasingly feminized Richardson continued to be out of favor with most critics for well over a century. It is no coincidence that most eighteenth-century women novelists shared his fate.

Scott is never unaware of gender issues in his criticism, but his evaluations are notable for their gender neutrality. Susan Buchan is right to argue that "Walter Scott had no vanity of sex, and he never condescended."[17] Others responded quite differently to a literary form with an enormous readership and increasing respectability (as evidenced by the critical work of Barbauld, Dunlop, and Scott) dominated, almost controlled, by women writers. This is not the place to repeat Scott's critical history, but it is a history not without consequences for the women novelists who preceded him. It is ironic that Scott the novelist was welcomed by so many of his contemporaries and for some time thereafter as "a robust and manly writer," a novelist free of the influence of women writers, "a novelist without origins except in the legends and traditions of oral culture,"[18] and one who finally "validates novel reading as a male practice."[19] Scott's criticism, as well as his novels, continued to provide a powerful influence on his successors; no critic of the novel is cited more frequently throughout the nineteenth century. Though few of those successors shared his enthusiasm and respect for Georgian novels written by women, they nevertheless had inherited a Georgian canon—the canon of Barbauld, Dunlop, and Scott. The critical history of the novel in English, the history we continue to build upon, is the history that emerged in the first two decades of the nineteenth century. Its impact on early women novelists was especially great and long-lasting; it has taken nearly two hundred years to question and reconsider the judgments and tastes of this formative period for novel criticism.

NOTES

1. This essay is part of a book-length study of the critical history of British women novelists before Jane Austen. In the full-length version I discuss many other critics of the novel from this period, most notably William Hazlitt, Francis Jeffrey, John Wilson Croker, and Eaton Stannard Barrett.

2. Quoted in Catherine E. Moore, "'Ladies . . . Taking the Pen in Hand': Mrs. Barbauld's Criticism of Eighteenth-Century Women Novelists," in *Fetter'd or Free? British Women Novelists, 1670–1815,* ed. Mary Anne Schofield and Cecilia Macheski (Athens: Ohio University Press, 1986), 384.

3. Her interest in the novel goes back at least as far as her youthful "On Romances, an Imitation" [of Samuel Johnson], in J. and A. L. Aikin, *Miscellaneous Pieces, in Prose* (London, 1773).

4. Anna Laetitia Barbauld, "Life of Richardson," in *The Correspondence of Samuel Richardson,* ed. Anna Laetitia Barbauld (London, 1804), 1:xi. All references are to this edition.

5. Anna Laetitia Barbauld, "On the Origin and Progress of Novel-Writing," in *The British Novelists,* ed. Anna Laetitia Barbauld (London, 1810), 1:1. All references are to this edition.

6. *The British Novelists* consists of the following novels: Richardson, *Clarissa,*

Sir Charles Grandison; Defoe, *Robinson Crusoe;* Fielding, *Joseph Andrews, Tom Jones;* Reeve, *The Old English Baron;* Walpole, *The Castle of Otranto;* Coventry, *Pompey the Little;* Goldsmith, *The Vicar of Wakefield;* Lennox, *The Female Quixote;* Johnson, *Rasselas;* Hawkesworth, *Almoran and Hamet;* Brooke, *Lady Julia Mandeville;* Inchbald, *Nature and Art, A Simple Story;* Mackenzie, *The Man of Feeling, Julia de Roubigné;* Smollett, *Humphry Clinker;* Graves, *The Spiritual Quixote;* Moore, *Zeluco;* Smith, *The Old Manor House;* Burney, *Evelina, Cecilia;* Radcliffe, *The Romance of the Forest, The Mysteries of Udolpho;* Bage, *Hermsprong;* Edgeworth, *Belinda, The Modern Griselda.*

7. Elizabeth Kraft, "Anna Barbauld's Edition of the British Novelists and the Making of a Canon" (paper delivered at the Ninth International Congress on the Enlightenment, Münster, Westphalia, 25 July 1995), 5.

8. This concern is related causally to another of Barbauld's concerns, that the novel be mistaken for real life. See Kraft, 9–11.

9. John Dunlop, *The History of Fiction: Being a Critical Account of the Most Celebrated Prose Works of Fiction from the Earliest Greek Romances to the Novels of the Present Age,* 3d ed. (London, 1845), 11. All references are to this one-volume reprint which includes Dunlop's additions of 1816 (the second edition), but not the later additions of Henry Wilson (1888).

10. René Wellek, *The Romantic Age,* vol. 2 of *A History of Modern Criticism* (New Haven, Conn.: Yale University Press, 1955), 122.

11. Sir Walter Scott, *Biographical Memoirs of Eminent Novelists, and Other Distinguished Persons,* in *Miscellaneous Prose Works,* rev. ed. (Edinburgh, 1834), 3:181. The fourteen novelists in the original series are: Richardson, Fielding, Smollett, Cumberland, Goldsmith, Johnson, Sterne, Walpole, Reeve, Radcliffe, Le Sage, Johnstone, Bage, and Mackenzie.

12. Peter Morgan, "Scott as Critic," *Studies in Scottish Literature* 7 (1969): 91.

13. Fiona Robertson observes that "Scott's reputation for generosity has undermined his claims to be taken seriously as a literary critic"; see *Legitimate Histories: Scott, Gothic, and the Authorities of Fiction* (Oxford: Clarendon Press, 1994), 57.

14. Lady Louisa Stuart, *Selections from Her Manuscripts,* ed. James Home (New York, 1899), 234. All references are to this edition.

15. *The Letters of Sir Walter Scott,* ed. H. J. C. Grierson (London: Constable, 1936), 10:96. All references are to this edition.

16. For a detailed, if extremely partisan account, see Frederic T. Blanchard, *Fielding the Novelist: A Study in Historical Criticism* (New Haven, Conn.: Yale University Press, 1926).

17. Susan Buchan, *Lady Louisa Stuart: Her Memories and Portraits* (London: Hodder and Stoughton, 1932), 208.

18. Robertson, *Legitimate Histories,* 21, 14.

19. Ina Ferris, *The Achievement of Literary Authority: Gender, History, and the Waverley Novels* (Ithaca, N.Y.: Cornell University Press, 1991), 10.

14

Talk into Text

The Shaping of Conversation in Boswell's *Life of Johnson*

BRUCE REDFORD

In the beginning was Samuel Johnson. The first paragraph of Phillip Harth's first book launches itself by quoting the *Preface to Shakespeare:* "Curiosity is always busy to discover the instruments, as well as to survey the workmanship, to know how much is to be ascribed to original powers, and how much to casual and adventitious help." The young scholar then provides a magisterial gloss on the master: "To the extent that any work is the product of both these sets of circumstances, neither can be ignored if we would form a just estimate of the author's achievement."[1] All three of Harth's books, while concentrating on "background," also attend to the emergence of texts out of contexts. To honor such a richly divided allegiance, my pen joins this party, my *Schrift* this *Fest,* by surveying "workmanship" as well as discovering "instruments." The workmanship in question is James Boswell's, as it manifests itself in the manuscript of his *Life of Johnson*—a complex assemblage of some two thousand leaves that served not only as biographer's laboratory but also as printer's copy. To traverse this textual labyrinth is to emerge with a keen awareness of Boswell's procedures and paradigms.

As Boswell begins to collect materials for his magnum opus, he gives little thought to principles of biographical design. Nonetheless, his friendship with Sir Joshua Reynolds and his lifelong fascination with the stage guide him toward two powerful models—the portrait and the theater-piece. Before the first of these has taken decisive shape, however, Boswell announces his decision to "write Dr. Johnson's *Life* in Scenes."[2] After beginning to compose the biography, he expands upon this idea in a letter to Thomas Percy: "It appears to me that mine is the best plan of Biography that can be conceived; for my Readers will as near as may be accompany Johnson in his progress, and as it were see each scene as it happened."[3] This statement adumbrates the introduction to the *Life,* which Boswell composed after he had completed the body of the text:

> Indeed I cannot conceive a more perfect mode of writing any man's life, than not only relating all the most important events of it in their order, but interweaving what he privately wrote, and said, and thought, by which Mankind are enabled as it were to see him live and to "live o'er each scene" with him. . . . What I consider as the peculiar value of the following Work, is the quantity that it contains of Johnson's conversation. . . . That the conversation of a celebrated man, if his talents have been exerted in conversation, will best display his character, is I trust too well established in the judgement of mankind to be at all shaken by a sneering observation of Mr. Mason in his Memoirs of Mr. William Whitehead, in which there is literally no *Life,* but a mere dry narrative of facts.[4]

Boswell "displays" Johnson's "character" and causes us to "see him live" by dramatizing, by setting his protagonist in motion within a sequence of carefully scripted playlets. He signals his intention by quoting part of a couplet from Pope's prologue to Addison's *Cato:* "To make mankind, in conscious virtue bold, / Live o'er each scene, and be what they behold."[5] This couplet not only exhorts the audience to emulate the worthy protagonist; it also suggests that the key to the didactic exercise, as in "to make mankind, in conscious virtue bold," is the absorption of spectator into spectacle, as in "live o'er each scene, and be what they behold."

Boswell understood that Johnson, for all his strictures against players and playacting, was himself a consummate performer. He practiced, perfected, and strove to institutionalize through the Literary Club a highly theatrical kind of conversation. As on so many other topics, Johnson had thought carefully about the theory behind his practice:

> Of conversation he said, "There must, in the first place be knowledge; there must be materials. In the second place, there must be a command of words. In the third place, there must be imagination to place things in such views as they are not commonly seen. And in the fourth place, there must be presence of mind and a resolution which is not to be overcome by failures."[6]

The greatest conversational set pieces in the *Life* are precisely those that fulfil these Johnsonian prerequisites. The talk is substantive, fluent, and competitive; it exhibits a conscious virtuosity that never lapses into preciosity. In order to recreate the aura as well as the substance of such talk,

Boswell shapes his raw materials into a succession of scenic arcs. As the quotation from Pope suggests, these arcs are designed to turn beholding into being, as the essential (and inspirational) Johnson imprints himself upon the reader.

1.

The raw materials for the *Life* confirm and enhance the testimony of the manuscript: Boswell devoted his primary efforts to recording not isolated sayings but sayings-in-context. These efforts begin immediately after the initial encounter at Tom Davies', when he "preserved the following short minute without marking the [connecting *del*] questions and observations by which it was [produced/drawn out] produced" (*Life MS* 1:270). It is ironic that the words Boswell discards, "connecting" and "drawn out," should help us to grasp the importance of conversation as a vital explanatory matrix for Johnsonian *mots*. This function emerges even more strongly from a revealing aside that Boswell plants midway through the narrative for 1773: "Much pleasant conversation passed which Johnson [relished/seemed to relish>] relished with great good humour. But [his conversation alone/only his sayings>] his conversation alone or what led to [it/them] it or was interwoven with it [that *del*] is the business of this [record>] work."[7]

In order to win the trust of the potentially skeptical reader, Boswell describes what amounts to a biographical apprenticeship, during which he masters his craft as a reporter of conversation:

> Let me here once for all [lament how imperfectly I have preserved the remembrance/how defective my record is of such conversation, as if completely recollected would be the richest treasure. But I hope I shall be allowed credit for the diligence which has preserved so much of it.>] apologise for the imperfect manner in which I am obliged to exhibit his conversation at this period. In the early [part/period>] part of my acquaintance with Johnson, I was so rapt in admiration of his extraordinary colloquial talents, and so little accustomed to his peculiar mode of expression that I found it [very difficult to write down with its genuine flavour what I had heard him say>] extremely difficult to recollect and record his conversation with its genuine vigour and vivacity. (*Life MS* 1:291)

Boswell's first version of this passage is abject in tone: it "lament[s]" his inadequacy and mourns his impartial recovery of "the richest treasure." The revisions temper these keen regrets into an apology for what is not so much radically inadequate as regrettably "imperfect." Within months of the first meeting, moreover, Boswell is not only remembering, he is confidently shaping what he remembers:

> We staid so long at Greenwich that our sail up the river in our return to London was by no means so pleasant as in the morning . . . the night air was so cold that [I shivered in the boat>] it made me shiver. ^I [was the more sensible of it/felt it the more that I had sat/been up all the former night recollecting and recording in my Journal the scenes and conversations of the foregoing/preceding day>] was the more sensible of it from having sat up all the night before recollecting and writing in my Journal what I thought worthy of preservation. . . .^ (*Life MS* 1:323–24)

The original version of this passage quietly forecasts the mode that will soon be dominating the biography: "scenes and conversations."

The sources of life in the *Life* are various: they include the massive "Flemish picture" of the protagonist, a gallery of subsidiary portraits, and an eloquent array of letters.[8] But no feature of the biography is more *vital,* in more senses than one, than the conversation pieces. In fact we tend to remember the biography, especially on first reading, as a glorious anthology of scenes. Boswell elicits this response by lavishing all his arts on sustained exercises in conversational polyphony—the most ambitious of which repay the closest attention.[9] Yet there are scores of less intricate conversations that do almost as much to make us "live o'er each scene." To create these chamber pieces, most of which originate in his journal, Boswell makes expert use of two basic moves: deletion and interpolation. Only the *Life* manuscript can reveal what he changes and why he changes it. Before moving on to the virtuosic ensembles, let us consider several examples of Boswell at work on a small scale.

2.

When Boswell and Johnson meet on 27 March 1768, they engage in a short-lived but intense dispute. The point at issue concerns "the pleasing system of brutes existing in the other world," a system that Boswell "wanted much to defend."[10] With characteristic doubleness, he splits into an actor who struggles and a narrator who stands apart, observing his own "serious, metaphysical, pensive face" as he "venture[s] to say, 'But really, Sir, when we see a very sensible dog, we know not what to think of him.'"[11] In the original account, Johnson behaves like *Ursa Major*—a bear who, "growling with joy," "bounced along . . . laughing and exulting over me": "No, Sir; and when we see a very foolish fellow, we don't know what to think of him." But it is Boswell who has the last word: "I took it to myself and had only to say, 'Well, but you do not know what to think of a very sensible dog.'"

As Boswell begins to incorporate this episode into the biography, he decides to conceal his identity behind the mask of "a Gentleman . . . who seemed fond of curious speculation" (*Life MS* 2:28). He tempers Johnson's aggressively physical reaction by turning "growling with joy" into "rowling with joy," and "bounced" into "strided"; moreover, Johnson's "joy" is now said to "beam in his eye." As a consequence of these changes, benevolence and a sense of the ludicrous peek through the bearish behavior. But the decisive alteration occurs when Boswell deletes his final retort: [The Gentleman did not shrink; but when the merriment was/had abated gravely persevered saying '^Well^ But you Sir do not know what to think of a very sensible dog.' *del*] (*Life MS* 2:28). This deletion keeps the exchange from degenerating into petulance, allows Johnson to have the last word, and sustains the seriocomic tone of the episode.

Johnson the talker-for-victory likewise emerges undimmed from a reshaped conversation at Streatham Park:

> Mrs. Thrale disputed with him on the merit of Prior. He attacked him powerfully, said he wrote of love like a man who had never felt it. His love verses were College verses. And he repeated the Song Alexis shunned his fellow swains [so ludicrously>] . . . in so ludicrous a manner [that he made us laugh very heartily, and wonder>] as to make us all wonder how any body could have been [seriously *del*] pleased with such fantastical stuff. Mrs. Thrale stood to her gun with great courage in defence of amorous ditties which Johnson despised till he at last silenced her by saying, 'My Dear Lady talk no more of this. Nonsense can be defended but by nonsense.' [This was in a great measure/degree a sportive attack; for in his Life of Prior he has given him deserved praise. *del*] (*Life MS* 2:41)

Had Boswell retained his original ending, he would have complicated, and thereby diffused, the effect of the dispute by quoting Johnson against himself. The vividness of the account depends upon the reader's ability to remain within the scene: to experience the push and pull, the unqualified force of Johnson's pronouncements, and the silencing of Hester Thrale. The final deletion helps us to understand anew that Boswell will always subordinate Johnson the writer, and the complex sense of the author that emerges from his work, to Johnson the social performer.

Deletions in the middle of a conversational block occur less frequently than those at the end of a paragraph, but their effect is no less pronounced. As Boswell drafts the account of a breakfast meeting at William Strahan's, his first thought is to inset two conversations within the scene: as the three men talk, Johnson mentions an encounter with Mrs. Abington, which Boswell then links to similar speeches before moving back to the primary conversation:

> He told us that he was engaged to go [at night/that evening>] that evening to Mrs. Abington's benefit. 'She was visiting some Ladies whom I was visiting, and begged that I would come to her benefit. I told her I could not hear. But she insisted so much on my coming, that it would have been brutal to have refused her.' This was a speech quite characteristical. [He did not mention the Ladies whom he was visiting. He loved to be mysterious in little matters. He used to say 'I am to dine at the other end of the town. I am to dine near Grosvenor Square,' so that we might suppose that it was with a Duke. And he was vain of a fine actress's solicitations. He said the Play was to be the Hypocrite, altered from Cibber's Nonjuror. He said>] (*Life MS* 2:137)

In the course of revision, Boswell retains the first inset conversation but eliminates the second, replacing it with an indulgent comment on Johnson's social behavior: "He loved to bring forward his having been in the gay circles of life. And he was perhaps a little vain of the solicitations of this elegant and fashionable actress" (*Life MS* 2:137). In making this change Boswell not only avoids the imputation to Johnson of Goldsmithian strutting and snobbery; he also sustains the momentum of the primary conversation, which might have been disrupted by too much interpolation. The result is a clear gain in dramatic focus and control of sympathy.

As part of his reshaping of small-scale conversations, Boswell not only deletes, he also conflates. An occasional brief aside alerts the reader to this practice: "^Sometimes^ short notes of different days shall be blended together and sometimes a day may seem important enough to be separately distinguished" (*Life MS* 2:37). Such bland remarks, however, do almost nothing to tip Boswell's hand; in fact, I would argue, they are intended to cover him as he boldly "blend[s] together" his raw materials. The governing purpose is usually to create or sustain a unified conversation—but scenic biography can sometimes shade into tacit polemic, as in Boswell's handling of remarks about Edward Gibbon. On their trip to Oxford in 1776, the topic of the newly published *Decline and Fall* surfaces repeatedly. In the manuscript Boswell creates one scene out of two by silently folding his rejoinder to John Smith, a don "who indecently talks as an unbeliever," into a conversation with Johnson that took place after the meeting with Smith.[12] As Boswell quarries the journal, moreover, he changes his warning against the *Decline and Fall* from "Springs and traps set here" to "Spring-guns and mantraps set here" (*Life MS* 2:196). He also adds a sentence to Johnson's sardonic commentary on Gibbon's religious history: "It is said that his range has been more [varied>] extensive, and that he has once been Mahometan" (*Life MS* 2:196). The combined effect of these moves is to unite biographer and protagonist even more strongly in opposition to Gibbon's "Bolus . . . of infidelity."[13]

3.

As a moralist, Johnson was keenly aware of the gap between ideal code and actual conduct; as a practicing critic, he constantly violated, complicated, or undercut his own theoretical pronouncements. So too his talk about talk can seem almost disingenuously wide of the mark:

> He [said>] was pleased to say "If you come to settle here, we will have one day in the week on which we will meet by ourselves. That is the happiest conversation where there is no competition no vanity, but a [quiet/calm/fair>] calm quiet interchange of sentiments." (*Life MS* 2:159)

Boswell may well have decided to discard "fair" because he wished to eliminate a potentially misleading ambiguity: conversations with Johnson, however "gentle," could not also be described as "equal."[14] But if any can be accurately judged free of "competition" and "vanity," it is the intimate exchanges we have just been considering. The polyphonic conversations, by contrast, are always marked by virtuosic combat. We can locate such conversations in "that semi-private world of talk which is located between the fully public scene of oratory and the totally private scene of reading."[15] At the same time, we must grant that they move much closer than the duets and trios to the "fully public scene of oratory"—witness their length, complexity, and sophistication.

Our ability to make meaningful comparisons across the rhetorical spectrum is a direct result of Boswell's ability to adjust means to mode. As we juxtapose notes and journal entries to the manuscript we come to suspect Paul Korshin's sweeping claim: "A thorough comparison of the longer conversations in the *Life* with their earlier form . . . reveals that Boswell almost always transfers the earlier long form of a conversation to the *Life* without significant changes."[16] Far from transferring "without significant changes," Boswell pulls out all the stops, demonstrating in text that very "imagination" and "command" that Johnson had called for in talk.

For his account of a dinner at Allan Ramsay's, Boswell devises a sophisticated tripartite format which frames the central conversation with two scenes: the first prepares for the entrance of Johnson, the second offers a postmortem that clinches the principal point at issue. In the preliminary scene, Boswell, Ramsay, William Robertson, and Joshua Reynolds behave like courtiers who are debating the character and conduct of their Prince. Each testifies out of his own experience:

> Before Dr. Johnson came, we talked of him. Ramsay said he had always found him a very polite man, and he treated him with great respect, which he did very sincerely. I said I worshipped him. Robertson said, "But some of you spoil him. You should not worship him. You should worship no man." Said I, "I cannot help worshipping him. He is so much superior to other men." (Let Robertson take this.)[17]

As Boswell recasts his journal entry, he softens the asperity of Robertson's remark by inserting a speech that describes the historian's first meeting with Johnson:

> *Robertson* he and I have been allways very gracious. The first time I met him was one evening at Strahan's, when he had just had an unlucky altercation with Adam Smith to whom he had been so rough that Strahan after Smith was gone had remonstrated with him, and told him that I was coming soon and that he was uneasy to think that he might behave in the same manner to me. No no Sir said Johnson. I warrant you Robertson and I shall do very well. Accordingly he was gentle and good humoured and courteous with me the whole evening; and he has been so upon every occasion that we have met since. (MS 733)[18]

Robertson's testimony not only tempers his initial objection to "spoiling" Johnson, it also prepares for the issue that will dominate the entire episode: what is the relationship, if any, between Johnson's social and his literary conduct?

Shortly before Johnson arrives, Boswell and Reynolds discuss his powers as a verbal portraitist:

> *Boswell.* His power of reasoning is very strong, and he has a peculiar art of drawing characters which is as rare as good portrait painting. *Sir Joshua Reynolds.* He is undoubtedly admirable in this; but in order to mark the characters which he draws he over=charges them, and gives people more than they really have, whether of good or bad. (MS 733)

And so the introductory scene ends as it has begun, in polite but provocative disagreement. The consequence is that, even seven hundred pages into the biography, our curiosity is piqued afresh: whose assessment will Johnson's behavior, as actor and as analyst, go on to confirm? Boswell enlists us as witnesses and interpreters, who will "mark" Johnson marking character.

Boswell introduces the central scene with a comparison that clinches our understanding of what has gone before and creates the atmosphere for what is to follow: "[When the great Man arrived>] No sooner did he of whom we had been thus talking so easily arrive, then we were all as quiet as a school upon the entrance of the Head=Master" (MS 734). The comparison strikes home, in part because Johnson duly proceeds to behave like a schoolmaster in a classroom. His pupils are accomplished, but they remain pupils nonetheless. The headmaster contradicts, he qualifies, he admonishes, he discourses on multiple topics: Pope's poetry, modern literature, antiquarianism, abstinence, Robert Adam, Lord Clive. Boswell heightens the *ex cathedra* quality of these dicta by balancing Johnson's clauses and making his diction less colloquial:

> We must read what the World reads [for the time>] at the moment. It has been maintained that this superfoetation this teeming of the press [in modern times/in our day>] in modern times [hurts>] is prejudicial to good literature because it [makes us have>] obliges us to read so much of ^what is of^ inferiour value [to read from fashion>] in order to be in the fashion so that better works are neglected for want of time because a man will have more ^gratification of his^ vanity in conversation [who has>] from having read modern books than [who has>] from having read [better>] the best works of antiquity. (MS 734–35)

At a late stage of revision, this speech is rounded off with the most incisive of epigrams: "Greece appears to me to be the fountain of knowledge Rome of elegance" (MS 735).

When the conversation turns to Robert Adam and Lord Clive, Robertson offers "characters" of both. Johnson's responses to these portraits demonstrate his superior powers by adding to the historian's command of fact the moralist's ability to generalize from the particular:

> Dr. Robertson expatiated on the character of [an eminent man>] [a great general>] a certain great general—that he was one of the strongest-minded men that ever lived; that he would sit in [a *del*] company quite sluggish, while there was nothing to call [forth/out>] forth his vigour of mind; but the moment that any important subject was started, for instance how this country is to be defended against a french invasion he would rouse himself and shew his [great>] extraordinary talents with the [utmost>] most powerful ability and animation. *Johnson.* Yet this man cut his own throat. The true strong and sound mind is the mind that can [equally embrace>] embrace equally great things and small. . . . [An ingenious gentleman/Mr Robert Adam architect>] An ingenious gentleman was mentioned [as to whom>] concerning whom both Robertson and Ramsay agreed that he had a constant firmness of mind; for, after a laborious day and amidst a multiplicity of cares and anxieties he could sit down with his sisters and be quite cheerful and good=humoured. Such a disposition it was observed was a happy gift of nature. *Johnson.* I do not think so. A man has from nature/naturally a certain portion of mind; the use he makes of [which depends upon his will>] it depends upon his own free will.[19] (MS 736–37)

Boswell invites us to understand that Johnson exemplifies both generalizations, that his mind as it manifests itself in such talk is "true," "strong," "sound," and "free." Our admiration is clinched by the following day's postmortem, when Johnson delivers a concise "character" of their host: "Well Sir Ramsay gave us a splendid dinner. [Ramsay is a fine fellow>] I love Ramsay. You will not find a man in whose conversation there is more instruction more information and more elegance than in Ramsays" (MS 738). This declaration, which sends us back to the opening scene, completes Boswell's enterprise in three ways: it supports his opinion about Johnson's "peculiar art of drawing characters"; it shows Johnson to be more judicious than Robertson; and it unites acuity of judgment with generosity of spirit, thereby confirming the "character" of Johnson himself that was sketched before his arrival.

Johnson plays the role of schoolmaster to somewhat different effect at a dinner given by Eva Maria Garrick—the first time she had entertained since her husband's death, Boswell is careful to tell us. Though his notes provide the scaffolding, he turns to Shakespeare for help in recreating "one of the most agreable days that I can remember to have enjoyed in the whole course of my life" (MS 828). Boswell sets the stage for this *ne plus ultra* of evenings by quoting from Johnson's tribute to David Garrick in his "Life of Edmund Smith": "We found ourselves very elegantly entertained at [Mrs. Garrick's] house in the Adelphi where I have [enjoyed>] passed many a pleasing hour with him 'who gladdened life'" (MS 828).[20] He then makes special mention of two portraits—one that dominates Eva Maria Garrick's drawing room and one that belongs to Topham Beauclerk:

> She . . . talked of her husband with complacency, and while she cast her eye on [the>] his portrait which hung over the chimneypiece said that "death was now the most agreable [thought>] [idea>] object to her. The very [appearance>] semblance of David Garrick was cheering. Mr. Beauclerk with happy propriety inscribed under [that/his>] that fine portrait of him which by Lady Diana's kindness is now the property of my friend ^Mr.^ Langton the following passage from his [divine>] [favourite>] [immortal>] beloved Shakespeare
>
> A merrier man
> (three lines) (MS 828–29)

The lines in question come from Rosaline's speech at the beginning of act 2 of *Love's Labour's Lost:* "but a merrier man, / Within the limit of becoming mirth, / I never spent an hour's talk withal."[21] By the time of revised proof, Boswell had decided to include the rest of the speech, which praises the "sweet and voluble . . . discourse" of Berowne. By conjuring up the two images of the dead actor, and supplying the full Shakespearean quotation, Boswell helps to convey the emotionally complex atmosphere of the evening, whose conversational buoyancy, like that of *Love's Labour's Lost,* is tinged with sadness. Even before it begins, talk has come to figure as the vehicle both for joyful celebration and for elegiac commemoration.

As Boswell cuts, expands, and reorders, he shapes a conversational sequence that emphasizes Johnson's Garrick-like wit and assimilates itself to the "sweet and voluble . . . discourse" of Rosaline's encomium. The sequence begins with a toast consolidating the link between Garrick and Johnson:

In addition to a splendid entertainment we were regaled with Lichfield ale which had a peculiar appropriated value. Sir Joshua and Dr. Burney and I drank cordially of it to Dr. Johnson's health, and though he would not join us he as cordially answered "Gentlemen I wish you all as well as you do me." (MS 829)

This cordial atmosphere prevails in the face of several potentially divisive topics. When the conversation turns to Thomas Hollis, a radical and irreligious democrat, Johnson's usual anxieties, hostilities, and dogmatisms are suspended. He moderates Elizabeth Carter's condemnation of Hollis's atheism, and even indulges in genial wordplay:

Mrs Carter . . . I doubt he was an Atheist. *Johnson* [(smiling) *del*] I dont know that. He might perhaps have become one if he had had time to ripen ^(smiling)^ He might have *exuberated* into an Atheist. (MS 830)

The same amused tolerance governs his commentary on Hugh Blair's sermons:

Though the dog is a Scotchman and a presbyterian and every thing he should not be, I was the first to praise them. Such was my candour ^(smiling)^ *Mrs Boscawen.* Such his great merit to get the better of all [this>] your prejudices. *Johnson.* Why Madam ^let us compound the matter. Let us ascribe it to^ my candour and his merit. (MS 830)

In both his comments on Hollis and on Blair, Johnson relaxes into something that approaches self-parody: the move from "ripen" to "exuberate" mocks his penchant for polysyllabic Latinate diction, and the "compounding" his Ramblerian taste for doublets.

Yet the schoolmaster, however benign he may be, is always on duty: later in the conversation, when a daring or a forgetful "somebody" declares that "the Life of a mere literary man could not be very entertaining," Johnson is swift to correct:

But it certainly may. This is a remark which has been made and repeated without justice. Why should the life of a literary man be less entertaining than the life of any other man. Are there not as interesting varieties in such a life? As a literary life it may be very entertaining. (MS 831)

Absent from this rejoinder is any direct reference to Johnson's *Lives of the Poets*, the second installment of which was about to appear. Yet Boswell works hard to make it tactfully clear how to construe Johnson's corrective. As his handling of the notes attests, he invites us to understand how the speech contributes to the scene while pointing beyond it: first we register the fact of Johnson's social self-command; then we go on to apply his remarks both to the *Lives* and to the *Life*. In their separate but complementary ways, Boswell suggests, both are brimming with "interesting varieties."

In the manuscript the gathering at Mrs. Garrick's ends with a serio-comic reassertion of the authority that Johnson had been content to suspend, mute, and even parody. The tone of this final episode depends in large part on the stage directions that Boswell adds as he shapes the scene. The episode begins when Johnson tells the company of the printer's devil who married John Campbell.

(Then looking very serious and very earnest). And she did not disgrace him. The Woman had a bottom of good sense. The word *bottom* thus introduced was so ludicrous [in contrast to>] when contrasted with his gravity, that most of us could not forbear tittering and laughing, though I recollect that the Bishop of Kilaloe kept his countenance with perfect steadiness, [and>] while Miss Hannah More slyly hid her face behind a Lady's back who sat on the same settee with her. (MS 831–32)

The version in Boswell's notes supplies a minimum of interpretation:

He . . . cried, "Where's the merriment?" Then, I believe wilfully, choosing a still more ludicrous word, and looking awful to show his power of restraint over us, he added, "I say the woman was *fundamentally* sensible"—as if he had said, "Hear this and laugh if you dare." We were all close.[22]

The manuscript account, by contrast, attends closely to motivation and reception—to what is happening inside Johnson and around him:

His pride could not bear that any expression of his should excite ridicule when he did not intend it [^but meant to be serious^ *del*]. He therefore resolved to assume and exercise despotick power, [looked>] glanced sternly [arround/round upon us>] arround and [called out>] asked in a strong tone "Where's the merriment?" Then collecting himself, and looking aweful to make us feel how he could impose restraint, and as it were searching his mind for a still more ludicrous word he slowly pronounced "I say the *Woman* was *fundamentally* sensible" as if he had said hear this now and laugh if you dare. We all sat [in full composure>] composed as at a funeral. (MS 832)

These telling adjustments continue into the stage of proof: having chosen "asked" in preference to "called out" ("He . . . asked in a strong tone"), Boswell reverts to "called out" as a way of dramatizing Johnson's vehement response. The final comparison ("as at a funeral") is a stroke of genius, for it ends the entire scene on the note of serious comedy with which it had begun. From start to finish, Boswell succeeds in holding opposites in delicate suspension: the grave and the ludicrous, the profound and the playful, the lively and the mournful. His labor of love is far from being lost.

Reporting to Edmond Malone on his progress with "the first draught," Boswell noted that "the Conversation with the King is to be formed into a complete scene out of the various minutes."[23] Though this royal "interview" testifies eloquently to Boswell's powers of selection and synthesis, no "scene" in the *Life* is more "complete" than the account of Johnson's first meeting with John Wilkes. Here Boswell contrives a perfect fit between the arts of social management that create the encounter and the arts of biographical management that do it full justice. In this instance, the original notes, which are quite cryptic, generate the narrative in the manuscript, which Boswell then revised several times over. The physical evidence suggests that, at an early stage of revision, Boswell detached the relevant leaves and circulated them among his friends, Wilkes perhaps among them: the leaves are folded and docketed on the outside, "First Conversation Between Dr. Johnson and Mr. Wilkes, 1776." Below this docket is a note: "It is prefaced in the book with a full Account of the *negociation* by which I led Johnson to affirm that meeting Mr. Wilkes would be nothing to him (affecting perfect ease of manners) so that when I brought them together he was *obliged* not to find fa<ult.>" (MS 607). This evidence helps to confer upon the Wilkes-Dilly episode the status of a highly polished, semi-autonomous artefact—a display piece that would function, like the Chesterfield letter, to epitomize and advertise the riches of the biography as a whole.

Boswell's notes, his cake of "portable soup," preserve the core of the dialogue but little in the way of vivid or circumstantial detail.[24] When he expands these dehydrated pellets into biographical broth, he translates theatrical metaphor into structural practice more fully than anywhere else in the *Life*. The result is a miniature play, complete with prologue, rising action, blocking action, climax, and epilogue.[25]

The prologue emphasizes the difficulty of Boswell's self-appointed enterprise: "to bring . . . together" men "more different" than could be imagined. The two key verbs are "negotiate" and "manage." Boswell tells Edward Dilly, his prospective host, "if you'll let me negotiate for you I will be answerable that all shall go well." Yet "how to manage" this negotiation is "a nice and difficult matter" (MS 592–93). Boswell emphasizes the difficulty of the undertaking by describing Johnson and Wilkes as aggressive enemies locked in combat:

They had even attacked [one another/each other>] one another [keenly/violently>] keenly in [their writings/print>] their writings; yet I lived in [very good habits>] habits of friendship with both, [and their arrows were shot over my head and past my sides but never through me *del*] (MS 592)

The version that Boswell settled on in proof tones down the violence of this image: "They had even attacked one another with some asperity in their writings; yet I lived in habits of friendship with both." It thereby diminishes the resonance of the phrase, "bond of union," with which Boswell marks the reconciliation of the two antagonists.

The playlet's blocking action begins when Boswell discovers on the afternoon of the dinner that Johnson has completely forgotten, or says that he has forgotten, the engagement at Dilly's. The first edition reads, "I found him buffeting his books, as upon a former occasion, covered with dust, and making no preparation for going abroad." The celebrated verb "buffeting" poses a special challenge to editor and critic alike, for it emerges from an unconscious collaboration between author and compositor. Boswell's original choice was "battling with"—a choice that derives from his journal entry for 3 April 1776:

I called on Dr. Johnson; found him putting his books in order. He had gloves on, and was all dusty. He was quite in the character which Dr. Boswell drew of him: "A robust genius! born to grapple with whole libraries!"[26]

As he revised his first draft, Boswell changed "battling with" to "bustling among" (MS 595). However, the compositor misread "bustling among" as "buffeting among." Because Boswell did not read proof against printer's copy, he did not catch the error, and settled for deleting "among." The result is an editorial crux that might well occasion a latter-day grappling/battling/buffeting, as Johnsonian upholders of an author's first intentions contend with Wilkite proponents of a "socialized" text.[27]

The blocking action continues when Johnson refuses to go to Dilly's unless Anna Williams can be persuaded to release him. The first draft captures the full measure of Boswell's frustration: "Here was a sad dilemma. . . . He stood in some degree of awe of Mrs. Williams and if she should be obstinate he would not stir" (MS 596). In order to emphasize that Johnson was governed not by female caprice but by his own code of courtesy, Boswell then makes a significant alteration: "He had accustomed himself to shew Mrs. Williams such a degree of humane attention as sometimes imposed some restraint upon him, and I knew that if she should be obstinate he would not stir."

This phase of the playlet makes especially effective use of Boswell's theatrical paradigm. Out of the briefest of notes, "She peevish," he creates a scene of social seduction that owes its dynamics to Restoration comedy.

By inviting us to imagine first the blind poet and then the Great Cham as objects of desire, Boswell narrowly skirts the grotesque. But his pair of implied comparisons—of Mrs. Williams to an ingenue who "softened to my solicitations," and of Johnson to an heiress who is spirited off to Gretna Green—brilliantly serves the purpose of making us "live o'er each scene." At the same time, Boswell signals his structural debt to neoclassical drama by heightening an allusion to *Cato*. When he has persuaded Mrs. Williams to release Dr. Johnson, Boswell returns to the study and finds him, in the original reading, "indifferent in his choice, Dilly's or home" (MS 597). The quotation floats to the surface when the phrase becomes, "indiff'rent in his choice to go or stay"—a direct parallel to Addison's line, "indiff'rent in his choice to sleep or die."[28]

Boswell's notes suggest that the conversation at Dilly's did not progress in a sustained arc, but moved instead by fits and starts. As Boswell expands the notes, he repositions blocks of dialogue, creating a growing sense of cordiality as Johnson and Wilkes discover common ground. Perhaps the single most striking moment in the entire *Life* occurs when they turn the tables on their tormentor:

> I claimed a superiority for Scotland over England in one respect, that no man can be arrested there for a debt . . . [unless] his creditor should swear that he is . . . *in meditatione fugae*. WILKES. 'That, I should think, may be safely sworn of all the Scotch nation.' JOHNSON. (to Mr. Wilkes) 'You must know, Sir, I lately took my friend Boswell and shewed him genuine civilised life in an English provincial town. I turned him loose at Lichfield, my native city, that he might see for once real civility: for you know he lives among savages in Scotland, and among rakes in London.' WILKES. 'Except when he is with grave, sober, decent people like you and me.' JOHNSON. (smiling) 'And we ashamed of him.' (*Life* 3:77)

Boswell fashions this climax, which feels inevitable in its every nuance, out of inchoate materials:

> Talk of swearing a debt. I mentioned not in Scotland but in meditat fugae. *Wilkes* Then it may be of all the Scotch. Arch Duke of Argyll quite a household God, the best Landlord—had got into his Anecdotage. *Johns* I took Bo to see civilised life in an english provinc town. I turned him loose at Litchfield to see civility for you know he lives among savages at home and among rakes in London. *Wilkes* Except when he is with sober people like you and me. *Johns* (laughing) And we ashamed of him. *Wilkes* Bos you have kept a great deal of bad company.

Boswell's first decision is to cut the reference to the Duke of Argyll, so that Wilkes's "That I think" becomes more clearly what might be described as a feeder line. He then adds to Johnson's speech the stage direction "to Mr. Wilkes," the introductory "You must know, Sir," the adjectives "genuine" and "real," and the epithet "my native city." Taken together, these changes make of the speech a pointed challenge to Wilkes and a sly criticism of Boswell; they also inject a faint but unmistakable note of self-directed irony, as Johnson plays up the status of Lichfield as a school for rakish savages and savage rakes.

Boswell's additions continue with the adjectives "grave" and "sober": these make Wilkes's response an antiphonal exercise in recognition and deflection. The stage direction "laughing" disappears at first but resurfaces as "smiling"—a sign that Boswell has decided to retain a tonal marker but to inflect it as subtly as possible. Finally, he cuts Wilkes's blunt criticism ("you have kept a great deal of bad company"), which undercuts the impact of the sly collaboration between Johnson and Wilkes.

The dramatic structure of the whole is completed by the addition, at a later stage of revision, of a one-sentence epilogue: "Mr. Burke gave me much credit for this successful *negociation* and pleasantly said that there was nothing to equal it in the whole history of the *Corps Diplomatique*" (MS 606). This verdict reintroduces the idea of negotiation and crowns Boswell's achievement with the accolade of a brilliant and highly theatrical politician.

Theatricality, in sum, pervades every aspect of the biography's scenic construction. Though Boswell plays other roles in the *Life,* we have been concentrating here on his operations as playwright, who creates conversational performance-pieces of many genres and sizes. To make us "live o'er each scene," Boswell tries to make himself fully absent *as biographical craftsman.* That is the danger of our analytic enterprise: attending to technique, we run the risk of obscuring or even dispelling the dramatic illusion of transparency. It is a price worth paying, however, if it allows the playwright to take a long-postponed bow.

NOTES

1. Phillip Harth, *Swift and Anglican Rationalism: The Religious Background of "A Tale of a Tub"* (Chicago: University of Chicago Press, 1961), 1.

2. Journal entry dated 12 October 1780; see *Boswell, Laird of Auchinleck, 1778–1782,* ed. Joseph W. Reed and Frederick A. Pottle (New York: McGraw-Hill, 1977), 260.

3. Letter to Percy dated 9 February 1788; see *The Correspondence of James Boswell with Certain Members of The Club,* ed. Charles N. Fifer (New York: McGraw-Hill, 1976), 258.

4. *James Boswell's Life of Johnson: An Edition of the Original Manuscript,* ed. Marshall Waingrow, vol. 1 (Edinburgh: Edinburgh University Press; New Haven,

Conn.: Yale University Press, 1994), 10–11. Henceforth cited as *Life MS* 1. For a full explanation of the editorial sigla used in the transcription, see xvi–xxvii.

5. "Prologue to Mr. Addison's Tragedy of *Cato*," in *Minor Poems*, ed. Norman Ault, vol. 6 of *The Twickenham Edition of the Poems of Alexander Pope*, ed. John Butt et al. (New Haven, Conn.: Yale University Press, 1954), 96.

6. Journal entry dated 21 March 1783; see *Boswell, The Applause of the Jury, 1782–1785*, ed. Irma S. Lustig and Frederick A. Pottle (New York: McGraw-Hill, 1981), 75.

7. *James Boswell's Life of Johnson: An Edition of the Original Manuscript*, ed. Bruce Redford, with Elizabeth Goldring, vol. 2 (Edinburgh: Edinburgh University Press; New Haven, Conn.: Yale University Press, 1998), 104. Henceforth cited as *Life MS* 2.

8. "This may be laughed at as too trifling to record; but it is a small characteristick trait in the Flemish picture which I give of my friend, and in which, therefore, I mark the most minute particulars." See *Boswell's Life of Johnson*, ed. G. B. Hill, rev. L. F. Powell (Oxford: Clarendon Press, 1934–1950), 3:191.

9. My musical terminology acknowledges Boswell's own wish to notate Johnson's talk: "His tone in speaking was indeed very impressive, and I wish it could be preserved as musick is written, according to the very ingenious method of Mr. Steele in his 'System of intonation as applied to language' in which that of Mr. Garrick and other eminent speakers is if I may use the expression put *in score*" (*Life MS* 2:140–41).

10. Journal entry dated 27 March 1768; see *Boswell in Search of a Wife, 1766–1769*, ed. Frank Brady and Frederick A. Pottle (London: Heinemann, 1957), 164.

11. The classic study of this split is Bertrand H. Bronson's essay, "Boswell's Boswell," in *"Johnson Agonistes" and Other Essays* (Berkeley: University of California Press, 1965), 53–99.

12. See *Boswell, The Ominous Years, 1774–1776*, ed. Charles Ryskamp and Frederick A. Pottle (New York: McGraw-Hill, 1963), 282–83.

13. This reading does not survive the final round of revision.

14. These are definitions 12 and 8 respectively in Johnson's *Dictionary of the English Language*, 4th ed. (London, 1773).

15. Alvin Kernan, *Printing Technology, Letters, and Samuel Johnson* (Princeton, N.J.: Princeton University Press, 1987), 206.

16. Paul J. Korshin, "Johnson's Conversation in Boswell's *Life of Johnson*," in *New Light on Boswell*, ed. Greg Clingham (Cambridge: Cambridge University Press, 1991), 178.

17. Journal entry dated 29 April 1778; see *Boswell in Extremes, 1776–1778*, ed. Charles McC. Weis and Frederick A. Pottle (New York: McGraw-Hill, 1970), 322.

18. "MS" refers to the unpublished portion of the "Life" manuscript; this portion is divided between the Beinecke Library and the Houghton Library.

19. The alternative phrasing of "from nature/naturally" is not resolved in the MS. By the time of revises, "from nature" had been selected.

20. The phrase in question comes from a paragraph that may have guided Boswell as he strove to combine gaiety and pathos in this conversation: "At this man's

table I enjoyed many chearful and instructive hours, with companions such as are not often found: with one who has lengthened and one who has gladdened life; with Dr. James, whose skill in physick will be long remembered; and with David Garrick, whom I hoped to have gratified with this character of our common friend: but what are the hopes of man! I am disappointed by that stroke of death, which has eclipsed the gaiety of nations, and impoverished the publick stock of harmless pleasure." See "Edmund Smith," in *Lives of the English Poets,* ed. G. B. Hill (Oxford: Clarendon Press, 1905), 2:21.

21. *Love's Labour's Lost,* in *The Complete Works,* ed. Alfred Harbage (Baltimore, Md.: Penguin Books, 1969), 2.1.66–68.

22. Journal entry dated 20 April 1781; Reed and Pottle, *Boswell, Laird of Auchinleck,* 328–29.

23. Letter to Malone dated 17 November 1788; *The Correspondence of James Boswell with David Garrick, Edmund Burke, and Edmond Malone,* ed. Peter S. Baker et al. (London: Heinemann, 1986), 360.

24. "I have thought my notes like portable soup, of which a little bit by being dissolved in water will make a good large dish." See "On Diaries," in *The Hypochondriack,* ed. Margery Bailey (Stanford, Calif.: Stanford University Press, 1928), 259.

25. See Sven Eric Molin, "Boswell's Account of the Johnson-Wilkes Meeting," *Studies in English Literature* 3 (1963): 307–22. Molin's attempt to diagram the episode as a five-act neoclassical drama is overly schematic, but his underlying insight is fully supported by close study of the manuscripts: "Boswell so clearly manages the whole and the transitions between the parts that . . . he could hardly have been unconscious of what Dryden calls the 'design'" (315).

26. Ryskamp and Pottle, *Boswell, The Ominous Years,* 310.

27. Is a "bond of union" possible? I myself prefer to live "in habits of friendship with both."

28. Joseph Addison, *Cato,* in *Eighteenth-Century Plays,* intro. Ricardo Quintana (New York: Modern Library, 1952), 51.

15

On Rerouting the History of British Literary Theory, 1650–1800

ERIC ROTHSTEIN

My title adapts "On Writing the History of Criticism in England, 1650–1800" (1953), one of two synoptic articles in which R. S. Crane gave what have remained the best short accounts of British criticism over its first century and a half of flourishing.[1] After these acute, learned, and clear accounts were in print, excuses vanished for using cant to sort and bale eighteenth-century critics' production. To some degree I'll follow what has been frequent practice since Crane, merely adapting Crane's work, expanding and descanting on the types and examples he offers. I'd like, though, also to reroute the history he offers and those offered since, by addressing the problem of change. Unable to find an adequate, embraceable account of change, literary historians have often flirted with or even wed terms of easy virtue, isms that stroll the red-light districts that a reliance on rubrics defines. Crane made this practice as innocuous as it can be, but he did assume that an Aristotelian ordering, like a biological phylum, could represent the "single dominant and unified conception" of criticism that ran "from Dryden to the death of Johnson." As a "common intellectual scheme," the "neoclassical" phylum divides subjects into six groups having four primary frames of reference, and developing along three axes. For Crane "even the more seemingly revolutionary changes in the latter part of the period" appear "as so many shifts of emphasis" within a selectively followed, hence "neoclassical," Roman rhetorical tradition.[2] Whatever this structure's virtues, it can only inventory similarity and difference. It can't address history, how one got from "whence" to "whither."

Nor can chronicles, the one-damn-thing-after-another alternative to phyla. Chronicles, however humane, subtle, revelatory, and learned they may be, won't show how or why eighteenth-century literary theory remains central to historiographical debate over continuity and change.[3] By what energy did it mediate tradition and modernity, or in the cartoon version, did it liven the cold dry hand of "neoclassicists" with the damp throb of "Romantics"? Reasonably, too, one would expect eighteenth-century criticism to have great entrepreneurial breadth. After all, between 1650 and 1800 authors employed every form that occurs in the pre-Joycean novel as well as every new form that modern popular drama has adopted, including the musical, satiric fantasy, the sitcom, and prose tragedy. How odd if literary theory, so new and prolific, hadn't done as much! How odd if it hadn't shaped and responded to the profound contemporary disruption of the intellectual and social status quo! Thinkers from Descartes to Kant gave us the disciplines of epistemology, ethics, and aesthetics, our conceptual foundations for the true, the good, and the beautiful—literary theory draws on all three. Shouldn't it have developed its own disciplinary logic accordingly?

Immanent principles and logic preserve the individuality of texts, writers, and situations, but propel a truer, more flexible, more credible narrative of historical change than does an inherited momentum or random reactions to ambient contingencies. An immanent model for a changing practice might include a "research program," a set of premisses and a logic whose first aim is a descriptive understanding of a designated part of its environment. For critical practice and theory the premisses and logic tell what counts as literary criticism and licit modes of procedure within it. Premisses and logic have a feedback and feedforward relationship to the environment that literary production and use, and more indirectly printers and booksellers, create for literary theory.[4] Such a model and research program embody principles of continuity in that the logic ceaselessly aligns what is said with what has been said. They embody principles of change, for feedback allows literature to accord with new theory, and feedforward prompts theory to respond to new literature and new social demands.

The first half of my argument presents a pair of ideal types as bases for such programs. The second half inquires into what they explain when deployed through time. I use coherent ideal types, not actual patterns of social causation, so as never to pretend that the facts of history are a legible text. One can gauge facts, though, against a model, an artifact. To do so frees them from a set schema, allowing them to be contingent. It recognizes that on the aggregate, though, people choose freely only within the broad and the particular constraints set by a discipline, a situation, a kind of problem, and a kind of audience. Ideal types can gauge these. I'll suggest two that provide a simple, anticanonical way of redescribing the history of literary theory from the mid-seventeenth century to well after the end of the eighteenth. I'd go further: we in the early twenty-first century still write in accord with the generative logic increasingly behind changes in literary theory 1650–1800. If I'm right, a good account of eighteenth-century literary theory informs us about the most profound shift in theory between Aristotle's time and our own. Whereas a history using the imaginary literary "periods" dangles like a string of fat sausages, the comprehensible, narratable continuity I propose has the tensile strength of principle.

My account adopts, with caveats, two of Crane's choices of method. I've advanced a rational description of behavior, not calculations and motives. Critics' doings, like anyone's, made sense in terms of a history about which critics varied in knowledge, awareness, beliefs, information, and intentions. They practiced programs with Darwinian survival value, but their reasons for adopting those programs were often altruistic, philosophical, or habitual. These reasons also form part of the causal, social, and directional history of literary theory. Nonetheless, I'm bypassing contingent reasons in favor of a perspicuous narrative. Like Crane too, I'm writing about literary theory, not literature. Making art and talking about it are loosely yoked. Only literary historians, longing to clinch something, fret about gaps between Chaucer's or Spenser's conceptual complexity, say, and critical means and goals of 1400 or 1600. Nor can one infer what readers perceived, just what appeared relevant for the analytic address of criticism. Many works would be beneath the critic; almost all would present issues outside critics' purview. Doubtless, to find criticism of mode X raises the probability of finding X-like elements in contemporary artworks. People living at the same time in the same country share enough so that critics' work has a lot in common with writers' and each contributes to the other's prestige. Still, I am unsure how well one can construct a narrative that coordinates critics and writers. The disciplinary conventions and the market for each differ widely and alter unpredictably at different tempi. A coordinating narrative therefore runs the risk of harping on similarities and of slighting differences in the course of argument.

Numbers of useful logics exist to model literary theory 1650–1800, my own nominalism assures me. But because the social legitimation of literature is integral to literary theory, I'll describe my logics through sociopolitical ideals that I'll name "Civic" and "Personal." Everyone will recognize them as "community" and "society," or "traditional" and "modern." Their generative logic for literary theory is less familiar. A Civic program defines literary works as public things, held in common and devoted to common goods. By contrast, Personal theory legitimates art and artworks as they serve individuals. Different forms of the Civic assumption entered Western tradition from some ancient literary theory, with strong patriotic, often political biases. They thrived where artworks presumed a public employer representing a "general will," whether the government or its effective proxies, like exemplary dedicatees. While *noblesse* obligates patronage, writers' own roles bind them too. In form, literary works are public forms of speech, subsumed under rhetoric, as in classical criticism. One sees artistic problems from universal or social, never individual, points of view.[5]

Such Civic logic, I propose, underlies nearly all postclassical literary theory until Dryden. Personal logic, however, underlies virtually all *innovations* in literary theory after Dryden until 1800. A robust Civic tradition greatly thins out during this process but it never disappears as a presence. Meanwhile, the possibilities inherent in Personal logic expand, stimulated by its feedback/feedforward relation with its environment. The weight shifts more easily from one toward the other because they share some premisses. Personal logic, like Civil, wreathes value throughout literary theory. Both logics suppose that theory and criticism have more than simply cognitive goals. Both require social formations that guide actions and provide norms. Yet a Personal structure of artistic value becomes immanent and individual, always to readers and often, as in "self-expressive" art, to authors. Older notions of priority, apprenticeship, and emulation burgeon into rights based on private ownership for private ends. Unlike Civic theory, Personal theory and its logic do not assign writers a duty, from without as in older societies or from inner moral law as in Kant's ethics. (Writers may feel a duty, of course, as they try to live up to the ideal image Personal theory affords them.) Whereas the Civic model regards artworks, like people, as good or bad citizens in a social domain, the Personal model casts them as members in a market of goods and appraisals, quasi-persons with selves of a sort.

1. THE LOGIC OF THE IDEAL TYPE "CIVIC THEORY"

In most English literature before 1650, the Civic assumption supports direct or implied theological values, hierarchical politics, and obedience-grounded ethics.[6] Civic theory also allots artworks paradoxical self-assertion and self-effacement. An icon or Gothic church asserts itself as an object, glorifying and communicative, while it effaces itself by pointing only to an unseen beyond itself. We need to fish out the unseen, the *fabula* that inhabits a feigned history, by knowing the proper angle to do so. If all citizens, including the artist or writer, had rectified souls, spirits, and minds, Civic arts would not differ from crafts. We would already apprehend the current measure of difference, which is moral truth, the golden world, political rectitude, or a proper scorn for knaves. When truth blazes, who needs its mimetic glimmer, the endeavors of art? Civic theory, then, grants artists the public role of employed artisans otherwise like their audiences. Civic authorship envisions "a situation in which an author can write while . . . at the same time . . . being able to substitute himself for his own reader, and to judge . . . what he has accomplished from the point of view of the reader that he also is. The writer knows the solicitation that is addressed to him; he shares it in his capacity as reader; he answers it in his capacity as writer."[7] Within the commonly held aesthetic world of language and genre, literary form, like literary content, again repeats what one should already know. Its beauties grease the gullet for the gilded pill.

Civic theory therefore normally values clarity in style and ideas, transparently proffering doctrine and author, related as principle to practice. As to truth-value, Civic art yearns for the condition of the proverb, what has oft been thought but ne'er so mnemonically expressed. "True wit" optimally expresses iterable truth: wit is true (= genuine) just because it is true (= veridical). When author and receiver are merely two instances of the common audience, one has an "absolute subject," the subject of phrases such as "the Navajo believe" or "the eighteenth century tried."[8] Civic theory has little to say about real authors, audiences, or works, except as they serve for examples. Similarly, within these communal terms, truthful mimesis means an iterable, persuasive, and often highly decorated predication about reality, oft thought because it is "nature," repeatedly seen as true. By indexing plots, characters, ideas, and images to the norm, the "should," Civic artworks lend themselves to lumping. Such constructions express a sharp-focused band of aspirations, sometimes attainable in this world (as in much satire) and sometimes more utopian (as in much religious writing). Only within this proper spectrum, valued good/bad, devout/impious, zealous/lukewarm, do real people's reactions have systemically significant meaning.

Most elements of this ideal logic—clarity, normativity, reference to civic tradition—have been tagged "neoclassical" and referred to the varieties of "rules" criticism, with their public standards and Civic legitimating of art. Classical and seventeenth-century "rules" critics talk systematically about the content of individual works only by taking the works as instances of types with inherited status, therefore invitations to allegory, abstraction, and canonical pregnancy by *droit de seigneur*. Particulars dissipate. While in principle one can perform minute rhetorical analysis to show how audiences are affected, Civic critics tend not to. Only through canon membership, therefore, do individual works or persons play important roles in legitimating artistic practice. Civic theorists crown artworks with a communal appeal free from contingencies of time and place, as proved by having pleased many and pleased long. For seventeenth-and eighteenth-century criticism, a Civic model might draw on communal public terms from "the ancients," "nature," and "reason," respectively a shared past, a set of shared assumptions about how to read the world, and a shared set of criteria to mediate differences of judgment. Typified and out of history, these three courts of appeal collude. Since at least the latter two occur in many different social contexts, with different kinds of force behind them, various critical arguments emerged as critics chose which to heed. No Civic criticism, however, can do without all three or proxies for them. In the later seventeenth century, for example, an obvious such proxy for an old shared past was a local, contemporary one. "Moderns" supplemented or substituted for "ancients."

My ideal Civic aesthetic, in sum, stresses that to produce an artwork is first of all a public act, hence to be aligned with analogous public acts. Its success or failure turns on a proper alignment of values among audiences who relearn lessons that they forget at their peril, of life's uncertainties, sin's misery, and *areté*'s reward. Maxims and examples show how to extract implications or to reason in familiar precincts. For Civic theory and its preferred genres, the mnemonics and exposition of governance remains art's essential goal. Here I include governance at every level, from God, through politics, the arts, objects of civic praise and blame, and the self. Whether these adhere to the supposed order of nature or simply keep the *res publica* running least riskily, "we" should concur, we civic beings within nature, supplied with history (the past) and reason (the present and future). Such a theory is rational, coherent, and based on a rational, coherent political ideal. In principle, often in practice, it is neither foolishly authoritarian nor foolishly dogmatic.

The most sneered-at part of seventeenth-century Civic theory, the "rules," are also reasonable. They tally with the speech-act analysis that J. L. Austin, and differently Wittgenstein, inaugurated in the 1940s and 1950s. Like Civic readings, speech acts require "socially defined, publicly visible embodied being[s], endowed with all kinds of powers and capacities for public, meaningful action."[9] Neither they nor Civic readings require the intuited, unified, existential self. At times, one invokes the private category of intentions for judging a speech-act's "felicity," the conditions under which saying something does what it's supposed to. Promises, for example, don't work when speakers are deceitful, ironic, or joking, or mutter in delirium. In Civic theory, readings change along the same lines, as for example with visible irony. Still, both Civic and speech-act theory deliberately draw on only a shallow idea of intention and hardly at all on subjectivity. Since the "rules" take writers to be simply citizens who happen qua citizens to write, a Civic system links responsible artists, audiences, and works.

Communicative protocols, not formalist pedantry, the "rules" in Civic aesthetics share three foci with Austin's speech acts. These are the *illocution* of the speech act (statement, question, order, promise, performative), its *locution* (referential and predicative content), and its *perlocution,* or communicative result. Each of these foci is public. Illocutions are always conventional, locutions call for competence in the language of their utterance, and perlocutions make sense in terms of the other two, embedded in correctly executed conventional procedures. In Civic literary theory, the genres are illocutory. Each has conditions, spelled out by the "rules," under which a polite society might consider a work epic, tragedy, comedy, and so forth. Some form of mimesis or predication, the locution (content) of the work, adheres to these felicity conditions. Finally, perlocutory norms, effects, derive from the public functions of artworks. By the "rules," for instance, a tragedy has a set, public form that competent persons know, and its content has a set, public kind of purpose, the health of the person ("catharsis"), *polis,* and often nation.

One can define some genres as redeeming felicity violations. No established literary illocution (genre) fits a locution about Flecknoe and Shadwell with real world referents. Only imaginary referents, the men's self-images, might. *Mac Flecknoe* (1682) restores felicity by employing a parasitic genre, mock-heroic, to imitate those delusions of grandeur, parasitic on true grandeur. Typically such parasitic genres reaffirm the "serious" ones, extending the genre system by dividing unruly goats from worthy sheep who properly align genre, content, and response. The more the traditional genres codify norms, the more useful it is to have mock-epics, pseudo-tragedies, and works such as Pope's *Peri Bathous* (1728), where parasitism tests criteria for both critical ideas and poetic texts. Parasitic forms don't so much silently use the standard genres as implicitly or openly mention them so as to spotlight internal infelicities between what's referred to and the way it's referred to.

The leitmotifs of a dominant program of literary theory in the latter half of the seventeenth century approach my ideal type "Civic theory." Readers can test that assertion against English figures such as Rymer and influential French imports into England—d'Aubignac for drama, Rapin for poetics, Le Bossu for the epic. As an ideal-type model shows, these different, sometime differing critics don't simply share sacred touchstones. They have a comprehensive, logical program with interdependent, adjustable elements. Undoubtedly their Civic logic had stability from being circular: it told one how to read the past from which it drew its own credentials. Nonetheless, it wasn't a Gibraltar of dogma. In authorizing his own kind of drama and satire, Dryden, for example, stretched Civic theory to explain altered forms of old genres. Some limited flexibility in fulfilling the logic behind the Civic program gives a better reason than mass, inertia, docility, or equally improbable, superstitious worship of the ancients for its survival and decline. Its strength allowed some of its logic, touchstones, and leitmotifs to survive its heyday.

With time it revealed built-in instability on at least two fronts. First, Civic theory had to take value judgments as self-evident, in keeping with reason and nature. By elevating taste, Personal theory finessed that issue, but Civic theory could not, since it relied on general, exemplified standards. When taste and standards conflicted, when new standards of legitimation arose, Civic theory had a bad choice, bluster or blunder. The blunder was to shift the base of Civic principles to "reason" and "nature." Secured that way, the theory lay open to dissent, for an increased historical sense showed those seemingly fixed criteria to be rolling. Far worse for Civic critics, "reason" and "nature," co-opted, provided springboards for Personal theory. A second instability was similar: Civic theory ran thin because it usually neglected the details of individual works. Successful artistic details barely need explaining—Civic theory urges clarity—or they're too particular for the Civic critic to explain. Once one has set out the felicity conditions for a successful speech act, description dries up. With its base in fixed, timeless values and authority/obedience, Civic theory lends itself badly to an empirical, falsifiable research program. Like an administrative code within a bureaucracy, it is largely normative and often focused on something other than its ostensible subject. Too much, besides, lies outside its purview as a program that is a function of civic government. When research programs and modernization became *desideranda,* Civic theory ran thin at a task it was not designed for.

As people increasingly pursued interests in the new, they deserted the full range of Civic precepts. Civic logic remains, however, in a shrunken form. Although today's Civic theorists often oppose "hegemonic" values, they have kept Civic injunctions and shibboleths, a love of lumping, a relative indifference to aesthetic merit, a focus on rhetoric, and a zeal to convert all things to a higher good. Their work treats people as tokens of social types, such as the right-thinking, right-acting hero[ine]; the martyr; the corrupted conformist. Popular critics, like journalists and "public intellectuals," rely on Civic truths to handle restricted, useful tasks. Their audience is the leftover of an obedience-oriented, "impressionable" Civic populace. Once that meant women and the lower classes. It now means children, citizens at crisis times, and groups to be rallied in favor of some *Volk* or mass judgment upon what is proclaimed as saintliness and sin.

From what I've said, one may infer a few proposals:

1. If the terms and theses of Civic theory had long dominated criticism, the newcomer Personal theory had to address them, most easily by co-optation.
2. If Civic theory has lasted till now, the co-optation was incomplete. Literary theory after 1650 was a hybrid of Civic theses and those of the developing Personal theory. Johnson's criticism from the 1760s on wonderfully illustrates such a hybrid.[10]
3. If Civic theory lost power to push further, Personal theory drove change. As I have said, what's new in literary theory after 1650 develops from Personal logic.
4. Finally, people who desired new insights into new matters were rational, not arbitrary or fashionable, in shifting towards Personal theory from a Civic theory that ran thin on such matters.

2. THE LOGIC OF THE IDEAL TYPE "PERSONAL THEORY"

Civic theory assumes that one will value artworks for how well they play their assigned civic role, recalling common civic information, maybe as parceled into precepts. In economic terms, I suggest, Civic theory has a supply-side logic. Like most traditional stores of truth, it regulates production and expects its good product to sell. My ideal type Personal theory, with a different, variable system of value, has a demand-side logic. Raise demand by raising perceived value and you spur consumer-chosen supply. Just as I have used the one-way flow of a speech-act model to help define Civic theory, I will use a market-strategy model to suggest an ideal Personal logic, with eighteenth-century particularization.

For raising value and consumer demand, there is a rule of marginal utility: among goods for which one has commensurable needs, scarcity raises value. Literary theory that moves from Civic toward Personal forms should make scarce, new, and personalized information gain value relative to common, recalled, and civic information. To maintain scarcity, artworks should turn from communal property to property in which given persons hold rights.[11] Eighteenth-century Personal theory exemplifies this turn. Accepting Locke's ideas of property rights through labor, it gave property value to the labor of value-generating genius and taste. Critical innovations jibed with this logic: interest in reader response and sensibilities attuned to novelty, unity and variety, and suspense. Maybe readers in 1500 engaged with texts this way; but if so, silently. Civic theory neglects it except as mnemonic help, a haberdasher to Truth. Aesthetic experience, an eighteenth-century notion, ennobled itself as its own form of truth in a Personal program.

In supply-and-demand markets value accrues to property the more that others desire it, especially others of various interests. As a corollary, a market continues to exist for long-term investments. By upping the utility of literature for individual readers and upping its socially assessed value, Personal theory grounds the merits of literature without requiring broad social consensus on macrocosmic issues. Its structure is again such as Locke's principles of private property might occasion. Personal theory describes one's property, the artwork in relation to the self and its capacities, as fully as possible; it objectifies this property; and it values the property as highly as possible, for richness, uniqueness, privileged access to truth, lovability—extend this list of assets as you like. Most literary critics perform these market adjustments. From before Johnson's *Lives of the Poets* (1779–1781) to the present, critics have had as a main task the study of artworks' provenance and artistic counterparts, and annotating inventories of their worth. They help assure possible readers who work for a living, and for whom time is therefore money, that literature generally, and select works within it, have worth. The worth becomes spiritual capital despite any literate, mildly well-heeled person's having access to literary works. Capital worth follows from greater emphasis on emulable but rare marks of the *esprit de finesse:* taste, distinction, and sensibility. These qualities, as Personal criteria, parallel speech-act felicity conditions. In that sense, taste replaces "rules," as connoisseurs set criteria and get accredited through them. The new English word "connoisseur" and the new discipline "aesthetics" defined a realm of principled taste from early in the eighteenth century.

In elaborating the idea of art as private property, bearing distinctive information and high cultural capital, I am referring to a *way* art is a social, consumer commodity. The *fact* of its being a commodity, a topic for Bernard Mandeville or Thorstein Veblen, has held since before Praxiteles. Whether commissioned, sold, or bought in an aftermarket, Western artworks have always been purchased at least by or for the moneyed. They've always transmitted power and bestowed cultural capital on individual or corporate entities such as the church, the state, and the nobility, often as embodied by their dutiful representatives. Every buyer lives in a system of exchange, so that art as commodity always refers to the buyer's social role; but it's the flux of social roles that changes, not the position of artworks as commodities. As "natural" legitimacy dribbled from the old corporate entities, and as the property value of artworks went up, shifts of course occurred in allotting cultural capital. Furthermore, the idea of art as private, individuated property hides the social role by stressing selfhood and inner worth, as betokened by secular effects of the "soul." What is striking in Personal theory is the conceptual place that its scheme of value supposes for art as property, a value less like flashing diadems than like love, an inner, participatory enrichment.

As the variety of these public, private, self-reflexive, and market needs entails, the ideal type "Personal program" works less single-mindedly than its Civic counterpart. It relies, as market economies do, on a useful equipoise among forces. From these comes its dynamism, as against the grudging shifts of Civic theory over time. Apparent paradoxes in Personal theory loom when one goes outside the theory's own logic to look for consistency rather than for a changing balance among confederated elements. During the eighteenth century for instance, James Engell notes, "an increasing suspicion of traditional, didactic rules governing artistic creativity and the formal or generic characteristics of literature was paradoxically yoked to a growing mandate for more exact 'systematic' and methodical principles of criticism. We are still living with this paradox."[12] In another "paradox," also still with us, by the mid-to-late eighteenth century the cult of genius partnered the autonomy of the artwork. The "paradoxes" inhere in the multiple, interdependent criteria for value in Personal theory. To raise general market value, Personal theory should assign considerable autonomy to literary texts—that way they keep their permanence and flexibility—while simultaneously it honors the private labor needed to produce and consume them. Just so, market strategies use multiple, logically antagonistic principles to make artworks more desirable, therefore valuable. One raises their price by discussing and evaluating them carefully, because everyone knows you don't lavish intellectual attention on disposable trivia. One raises their price by declaring their rights to selfhood, rights not to be hampered by too many rules. One raises art's price, too, by honoring its creator because of it, and by ascribing to it a "depth" that compels readers to commune with it or contemplate it, not simply to get a message from it and relish its style. As the literary text apes divine creation in its "organic" self-sufficiency, it also soars on the market. It is a created object and an autonomous one, the object of both "deep" communion and solicitous analysis. Over time, the memory of various kinds of equipoise accumulates, as a profitable fund of tested, workable, and motley loci for understanding artworks. Consequently, Personal theory draws upon its own historical swerves and momentum while squaring various kinds of utility and measures of value.

3. REAL WORLD EIGHTEENTH-CENTURY INITIATIVES

In a Personal program, critics should begin by first, exploring what rights authors and readers have in individual works; second, objectifying artworks as things in the world; and third, boosting market values. The distinctive initiatives of eighteenth-century criticism, bar none, enjoy legitimacy from this triple, convergent agenda. Let me rapidly sketch what I mean. To insure I haven't chosen or omitted facts for my convenience, I will draw on Crane's summary, replete with examples, in "English Neoclassical Criticism." Among eighteenth-century critical initiatives or "pronounce[d] shifts of emphasis," Crane lists the growth of psychological aesthetics as a discipline ("the natural principles on which . . . the rules of art in general and of all particular arts are founded"); affective reader-response criticism (the exalting of "an inquirer into the operations of the mind" as "the expert best qualified to determine the rules of art"); and historical criticism ("critical argument or appraisal based on the dictum that it is unfair to judge works by rules of which their authors were ignorant or which they did not intend to observe"). Other, more internal initiatives he lists are systematic emphases on genius, taste, imagination, originality, and revamping or bypassing traditional genres.[13] All these follow Personal logic, some entailed and some encouraged by it.

Inferences to proprietorship, which are rarely the explicit stuff of literary theory, are mine. To illustrate other issues as to authors, readers, and artworks, I will recur nonexclusively to Hugh Blair's *Lectures on Rhetoric and Belles Lettres* (1783).[14] Anyone who wishes to see the contexts for most of my uprooted quotations, then, can locate them in that one book. Blair, regius professor of rhetoric and belles lettres at Edinburgh University, informed and trained students over many years (1759–1783) through these thoughtful, judicious, and learned, though seldom original, lectures.

Authors. Everybody always knew that "all the Rules in the World will never enable a Writer to distinguish himself" without "Genius or Spirit."[15] No Civic critic, though, could deploy that knowledge beyond invoking some celestial flatus, such as "inspiration." By embracing "genius" and "spirit," Personal critics derive cachet for art. They explore taste, imagination, sensibility, and "that delicate contexture in writing, by which the colours, as in the rainbow, grow out of one another, and every beauty owes its lustre to a former, and gives beauty to a succeeding one."[16] Authors became individual proprietors the more that critics admired individuated *esprits de finesse*. Individuated too were originality and personal genius. By the mid-eighteenth century, bardolatry for Shakespeare, Milton, Homer, or Ossian had swept into British criticism. If writers depict their own souls and if sublimity catches power, vastness, and speed, then sublime writers, especially when cleansed by historical criticism, take on the grandeur they convey.[17] To preserve great past authors from growing ever more deficient by modern standards, historical critics exculpated them through charitable reconstruction. One can then pare accident from substance, imputing Shakespeare's strengths to him, his flaws "to the grossness of the age in which he lived"; so too with Homer (Blair 1:46, L3; 3:241, L43).

Here genius transcends the moment through canonization, "the historical form that most denies historicity."[18] Timeless genius and continuing tradition brought Personal theory the benefits that timeless truths brought to Civic theory. Additionally, doubling "originality"—"*originality as novelty* and *originality as historicity*," emergent genius and causal lineage—doubly individuates the author's labor, increasing proprietorship.[19] Authors' doubled originality, in turn, countered and thus enfeebled an imperious genre criticism that feted the non-proprietary and non-original. When prime normative force seeped from genre distinctions, the reading protocol for a specific work became more immanent in that work itself, enlarging the author's creative, inventive role. This author/work symbiosis exemplifies Crane's categories of genius, imagination, originality, and revamped genres.

Readers. To apply the same logic to readers, one has only to substitute "taste" for "genius." Genius being scarcer than taste, the proprietary reader's rights and powers tracked the author's at a lower level. Just as the author's person stood behind a given illocution, readers stood behind given perlocutions and diversified them by individual appropriations of texts. "Truth, which is the object of reason, is one; Beauty, which is the object of Taste, is manifold," said Blair. "Though all differ, yet all pitch upon some one beauty which peculiarly suits their turn of mind" (1:32, L2). Taste became the readerly faculty corresponding to authorial imagination—"two concepts once considered different . . . [but] increasingly treated as synonyms or indispensable partners."[20] Blair agrees that "Genius cannot be found without including Taste," though since creating differs from judging, he distinguishes these "two words frequently joined together" (1:46, L3). To supplement the written text, or emotionally invest in it, gave readers a property share in it, earned by their labor of taste, reading for and to the moment as Richardson spoke of "writing to the moment." Temporalized, the reader's private experience of the work replaced the search for public, discursive truth outfitted in rhetoric.

The highest Civic genres, tragedy and epic, show this pattern. By the 1670s critics began veering from moral fables towards the affective strengths of tragedy, raising pity, fear, and admiration, and melting hearts into compassion. Later, Le Bossu's Civic advice to epic poets, to build a work around a fable, came to seem "frigid, and absurd" (Blair 3:192, L42). As to descriptive and narrative poetry, including the epic, eighteenth-century critics increasingly stressed the sensibility of reading to the moment. "Description is the great test of a poet's imagination; and always distinguishes an original from a second-rate genius"; a "true Poet," this "original," describes an object so that "we see it before our eyes" (Blair 3:149, L40). When "the *World* is seen" passing "before the *Readers* Eyes" in "inchanted Motion," readers supplement texts with their own imagination. "Artful *Silence* more than Words explains" as one fills out "unfinish'd . . . Sense."[21] Reading also occasions reveries that spin out "a thousand Thoughts, which perhaps never enter'd into the Imagination of the Artist."[22] Similarly by the mid-eighteenth century the sublime had passed into the reader. Poetic practice in James Thomson, David Mallet, or Edward Young, glossed by critics, located the effect in readers' sensitive, striving, passionate rather than reasoning attempt to grasp the ungraspable, utter what couldn't be said—"the imagination is awakened, and put upon the stretch" (Blair 1:82, L4). As they read, readers experience their own labor.[23]

The aesthetic. If in Personal theory authors became illocutors of a different sort, and readers appraised perlocutions differently, so locutions took on changed social functions with the corporeality and privacy of aesthetic response. Private feelings within artworks had always served discursive truth, as stimulus-response reactions for public purposes. To elevate the private, as in Personal theory, reverses that hierarchy. Truth or its emblematic representations—a heroine, say, or a self-sacrificial act—could be shown for the sake of their affect, as I have suggested happened in eighteenth-century tragedy. Often truth itself might be less an end than a means, the source for an emotional kick. "The Ruins of an old Castle properly dispos'd, or the Simplicity of a rough-hewn Hermitage in a Rock," John Gilbert Cooper thought, "enliven a Prospect, by recalling the Moral Images of *Valor* and *Wisdom*," thus yielding "by Analogy, some pleasurable Image."[24] Truth and virtue might be cosmeticians for pleasure or beauty. Eighteenth-century terms of praise for Shakespeare make me suspect that Cooper's view governed literary moral fables and poetic justice, which exhilarated or weepily delighted readers. Where pleasure and beauty arose through sympathy, the Personal program elevated a form of truth that would give access to the private. This included truth *about* things, such as truths about the human heart we get as privileged eavesdroppers and voyeurs of psychological novels (*Clarissa*) or many lyric poems (Thomas Gray). It also included truth *to* things, a sense of authenticity that beauty or vividness induces, or a new way to experience those "sensible images of things" that it is the poet's office "to exhibit continually."[25] If such truths come through taste, "the power of receiving pleasure from the beauties of nature and of art," then criticism, art's partner, must lead us "to reflect on the operations of the imagination and the movements of the heart; and increase our acquaintance with some of the most refined feelings that belong to our frame" (Blair 1:18, L2; 1:11, L1). From well-grasped art, readers accrued information, not only cultural capital. In turn artworks made for contemplation enjoy a guaranteed standing, constructed and hence appropriable aesthetic objects. The idea of influence within historical criticism aggrandizes the agency of artworks, too.

For "authentic," informational rather than mnemonic artworks, the aesthetic became a preferred context of reading. Its mode of utility didn't imply an artwork's being utilitarian, clever moral gadgetry. The liberal arts had once surpassed the mechanical arts ontologically, because they required more mental and less manual attention. By 1750 or 1800, mind and reason remained the chief bestowers of glory only for mathematics and philosophy, the publicly corrigible liberal arts. Between the remaining liberal arts and the mechanical arts, the line now divided mere craft objects in the world from aesthetic objects suffused with private, elevated meanings, far more clearly original (historical, novel), far more individuable. This aesthetic schema promotes those qualities that can most unquestionably be personal possessions. Feelings and imagination, which are private and not corrigible, outrank their old boss, reason. Eventually Romantic critics made art from craft, logically enough, by contriving a creative, imaginative corporate proprietor, "the Folk," inspired by its own "*Geist*."

4. REAL WORLD HISTORICAL MOVEMENT

As I envision it, British literary theory as it passes through the timespan 1650 to 1800 responds to a typical seventeenth-century effort to convert inherited truths into a working, codified research program. Could Civic principles give a descriptive understanding that accommodates tragicomedy, Shakespeare, and heroic plays? Within literature itself, changes in prestige were eroding the genre system's *raison d'être* certainly by 1600. This begot, one can guess, a social imperative that drove seekers for literary grandeur and dignity to clutch at codified "rules," the cultural equivalents of wavering sumptuary laws so as to keep the uncouth at bay. By the mid-seventeenth century, Civic efforts produced a byzantine literary etiquette, not the latitude that entered, for example, political theory, Anglicanism, and ethics after 1650. Failing to meet its clientele's demands for explanations and new ideas, a Civic program began to yield. As by fits and starts a slowly gelling Personal program supplemented and where possible supplanted the old truths, it offered new options to fill numbers of Civic functions. A Personal logic, unfolding and deployed within a range of situations, reinforced itself too by legitimating a broad range of ways to read. Through this process, Civic reading itself became semi-Personal, by turning into one consumer choice, not nature's law.

The Personal program had several advantages. It inherited from Civic critics a stock of starting points in "reason" and human nature. It accommodated issues of artistic detail, value, and grounding left aside by Civic theory. In tune with an unusual heterogeneity of ideas and a spurt in so-called "possessive individualism" after 1650, it harnessed tendencies increasingly present by 1600. It harmonized too with the (again, so-called) Scientific Revolutions of the seventeenth and late eighteenth centuries, and the Consumer Revolution of the mid-eighteenth. Consumerism defied the tiered, quasi-familial social assumptions of Civic theory, driven by new money, new standards of emulation, new social fluidity, and new ideas of using one's passions for one's interests.[26] Appealing in itself, then, Personal theory also explained and explored more facts.

The eighteenth-century boom in literary theory shows how well and fast an infusion of Personal logic renewed the credentials of criticism. In the cultural ecosystem, literary theorists found niches open for Personal theory in those that were familiar from the Civic program. New niches largely lay in fog unless controversies located them and bold new technology, conceptual or practical, showed how to exploit them. For instance, the fact of Ancients-Moderns conflicts pointed to a niche, enlarged by faith that Britain had "more and better Poets than ever *Greece* or *Rome* saw."[27] From Dryden's *Essay of Dramatic Poesy* (1668) through the work of Addison and the Jonathan Richardsons, father and son, on Milton, or Morgann and Twining on Shakespeare, for example, new bodies of ideas emerged for that niche. All were in keeping with the goals and vectors of Personal logic, for they lay within areas I have addressed above: historical criticism, genius and taste, and genre theory. Especially after 1700, they had lots of help from like-thinking critics' annotations, judicious appraisals, eulogies, and the like. Another niche was Lockean. By binding property to a labor theory of value and by portraying a psychological mode of personal labor in his *Essay,* a manual for work on minds' overlap and difference, Locke invited affective critical theory. Rational self-interest in property and esteem enhanced these niches. By midcentury, associationist psychology illuminated them.

Alongside new niches was a kind of change internal to the progress of critical theory. Literary theory *a fortiori* gained credibility after 1650 by both salvage of and lineage from the old. Much of it accepts some "neoclassical" disciplinary rosters, for it had no whole agenda, no great issue at hand, and no great founding figure except, obliquely, Locke. Yet one can consider the Personal program as a non-explicit analogue to the explicit programs of Descartes, Hobbes, and Newton. In resecuring things of the highest value—God, soul, sovereign, state, and cosmic law—these thinkers' new research programs began adapting all they could from older, colder, prior programs. So did a Personal research program. Like Descartes's or Hobbes's, it kept altering the elements it saved.

In the 1740s for example, Fielding authorizes *Joseph Andrews* with a preface referring to classical epics. Tragedy, the other genre with pride of place in an established hierarchy, features in Richardson's postscript authorizing *Clarissa.* But literary change—what counted as marketable writing—had changed what such references meant and did. By gluing high-generic labels to novels when the novel was the genre most open to invention, writers borrowed prestige for portraying the misadventures of distinctly private persons, what the genre hierarchy had been in part designed to exclude. The novelists' essays gained authority while evading its canonical basis. *Joseph Andrews* relies on the "epic" *Don Quixote,* a book that teases the epic mode with (speech-act) infelicity. Richardson jettisons the Aristotelian primacy of plot and public matters. He prefers a discomfiting, though maybe too comfortable, private voyeurism, arousing emotions, not purging them—this jibes with the changes in tragic theory I have mentioned. By redefining or rebalancing the old, now distended genres, the novelists also let one demote, though not discard, interest in genre assignments. To read classical epics and tragedies, one must know the works' weight in the genre system they presuppose. Fielding's and Richardson's readers can look at the novels otherwise. They have a double, heterodox genre tradition. One is that of the novel, where a reader can easily neglect genre and take emotional response or world-wisdom—and/or other "Personal" traits—as the works' core. The other is that of the old genres, which carry different weights according to how they're used in a given novel. They may, for example, be quite ancillary, no more than handy, apt, and classy vehicles for storytelling.

More modestly, mingling Civic and Personal programs, Blair redefines some Civic virtues toward the Personal. "Belles Lettres and criticism," he says, aid "us to support a proper rank in social life." They offer pleasures, chase ennui, and "bring to light various springs of action which, without their aid, might have passed unobserved." God's benignity grants us "Taste and Imagination," but Blair never mentions employing them wisely to winnow truth from rhetoric (1:51–52, L3). When Blair comes to virtue, no Civic moral fables materialize. Rather, we improve because taste raises the mind "above the attachments of sense, and prepare[s] it for the *enjoyments* of virtue" (emphasis mine). Therefore the wise always "tincture" youth with cultivated taste, a "liberal and elegant turn" favoring "many virtues." Non-aesthetes risk being "prone to low gratifications" and drudgery "in the more vulgar . . . pursuits of life" (1:11–14, L1).

In Blair's "virtue," Kuhnians might discover "revolutionary change," using the "touchstone" of "violation or distortion of a previously unproblematic scientific language."[28] They shouldn't. For cultural change, including literary theory, linguistic *lèse-majesté* is no touchstone, just a prime agent in opening options and cannibalizing old authority. These processes are most apt toward explaining how aggregate cultural movement grows, slows, and veers without breaks in substance. Breaks in style—yes, those occur in literary theory. Expository styles are stop-and-go, inflected by the cachet of the traditional or the trendy, the going jargon, and available metaphors. Here lie that pair of misprisions, "mirror" and "lamp." The small, bookish clientele for advanced literary criticism insures idiosyncrasy of style, common to highly tailored products or those with a steep curve of marginal utility. Although stylistic changes must affect substance in a Personal field, set by equipoise of its elements, quirks of verbal behavior aren't seismic. For a rational history of critical theory in and through the years 1650 to 1800, flowing unevenly but continuously, one might skip "revolutions" for easy co-options and fresh conceptual options, the result of trust-busting in the realm of thought.

If change depends on consumers' range of choices and pliable terms, a history requires Wittgensteinian lexicography, with the slogan "The meaning of a word is its use in the language." Eighteenth-century "use in the language" gains importance because the Personal program lacked a strong agenda and magisterial innovators. Shifting terms had to dislodge some Civic logic from its means of articulation. For some terms—imagination, sublime—we have accounts, but these can't readily register a semantic creep from the venues of the periodical press and popular talk. Addison's readership, far more democratic than Scaliger's, was far less steadied by shared tacit knowledge. The same spread of criticism let Johnson's Dick Minim declaim in a coffeehouse, not a college quadrangle, as he puffed out intellectual lint he'd vacuumed up. Unmoored terms, love of chic, and a swarm of Minims, one would imagine, elasticize words' uses "in an age when works of genius and literature are so frequently the subjects of a discourse, when every one erects himself into a judge, and when we can hardly mingle in polite society without bearing some share in such discussions" (Blair 1:10, L1).

Finally eighteenth-century theory moved to pluralize or diffuse ends and explore means. Many examples I have given entail this change, as to writers' ends as well as to readers', so I shall not discuss it at any length. Early seventeenth-century Aristotelian science specified that "the flux of generation and corruption received its rational ordering through final causes. To give a scientific explanation was to give an account of a thing's particular nature or form, and a thing's nature was only revealed by discovering the end toward which it strove." By the mid-to-late seventeenth century, however, "the [descriptive] rules governing nature's behavior take the place of the purposes for the sake of which that behavior occurs."[29] Just so, nearly all British social theorists from Hobbes through Spencer studied mechanisms. Starting from the propensities of individual human nature, they described not a telos but an interactive social field and an aggregate equilibrium within it.[30] Bearing out a conjoining of literary and social theory, the same empirical, corrigible, social process occurred in the art or science of literary theory. Affective criticism established an aesthetic field within which one could address heterogeneous modes, such as the novel and the serious play with a happy or mixed ending, and of multiple historical styles. As with opening new niches and democratizing criticism, such procedural change suited Personal priorities.

I again propose, in the simplest terms, that a gradual overall working out of Personal logic as detailed earlier, both rivaling and diluting Civic ideals, has drawn the twisting theoretical trendline, nonstop, from Dryden through Derrida. Readers may wish to test this proposal, using the vectors and ends I have suggested, to try to create a regression curve for literary theory over the last three hundred years depicting its conceptual initiatives and changing equilibria. Such a story of critical development needs no epistemic breaks or "paradigm shifts." It supposes that criticism and theory, like every other secular discipline in the seventeenth century, came to require codification in natural and rational, not authority-based, terms. This regrounding of Civic theory led to its gradual replacement. Since then, as with other secular disciplines, the empirical research program of criticism and theory has responsively changed with a market logic. To chart that program through a continuous narrative, from 1650 to 1800, the ideal types Civic and Personal theory serve well. They cleave to rational, not occult causes; they avoid the Cartesian vortices of isms; and, anti-Aristotelian, they require explanations for stasis, why things hold fast in a changing world. As yardsticks, these ideal types enslave no facts to hypotheses. Yet their logic indicates shifts and interconnections that in aggregate are reasonably likely to affect individual critical works. Most such works make retrospective sense, then, as to place. Interactive disciplinary logic and extradisciplinary history locate them, roughly, just as other logics and histories locate eighteenth-century road and canal systems, Twyford's flush toilets of the 1870s, Marcel Duchamp's ready-made "Bicycle Wheel" in the earlier twentieth century, or any other transporting artifact.

NOTES

1. References are to "On Writing the History of Criticism in England, 1650–1800" (1953), as reprinted in Crane, *The Idea of the Humanities and Other Essays Critical and Historical* (Chicago: University of Chicago Press, 1967), 2:157–75; and "English Neoclassical Criticism: An Outline Sketch" (1943), *Critics and Criticism Ancient and Modern,* ed. Crane (Chicago: University of Chicago Press, 1952), 372–88.

2. Crane, "English Neoclassical Criticism," 374.

3. Douglas Lane Patey makes the point nicely in "The Institution of Criticism in the Eighteenth Century," in *The Eighteenth Century,* ed. H. B. Nisbet and Claude Rawson, The Cambridge History of Literary Criticism (Cambridge: Cambridge University Press, 1997), 4:6–11. The thousand pages of this valuable if uneven volume offer up-to-date discussions of major issues in eighteenth-century criticism, with workable bibliographies. A good number of the issues, naturally, appear in my discussion, such as sublimity, imagination, the general and the particular, and the importance of increasingly widespread, popularized criticism. I won't duplicate the resources that the editors and authors here have generously made available to any interested reader; but rather, I'll turn my attention to what I don't think the volume provides, a narrative understanding of literary theory as a pragmatic, social discipline. For the "sister art" of painting, however, John Barrell presents an argument in many ways parallel to my own. Barrell, *The Political Theory of Painting from Reynolds to Hazlitt: "The Body of the Public"* (New Haven, Conn.: Yale University Press, 1986).

4. My model derives from Imre Lakatos' "research programmes," and Margaret S. Archer's model of homeostatic structure and contingent narrative, with feedback and feedforward. Lakatos, *The Methodology of Scientific Research Programs,* ed. John Worrall and Gregory Currie, Philosophical Papers Volume 1 (Cambridge: Cambridge University Press, 1978). Archer, *Culture and Agency: The Place of Culture in Social Theory* (Cambridge: Cambridge University Press, 1988).

5. René Bray, *Formation de la doctrine classique* (1926; reprint, Paris: Nizet, 1966), 126. God's will to save all humankind has, as secular sequel, a citizenry's "general will" to act in support of collective good. See Patrick Riley, *The General Will Before Rousseau: The Transformation of the Divine into the Civic* (Princeton, N.J.: Princeton University Press, 1986).

6. Before ca. 1650 the social ethics that my Civic logic entails was overwhelmingly obedience-based and theological, as demonstrated by J. B. Schneewind, *The Invention of Autonomy: A History of Modern Moral Philosophy* (Cambridge: Cambridge University Press, 1998).

7. Jean-François Lyotard and Jean-Loup Thébaud, *Just Gaming* (1979), tr. Wlad Godzich (Minneapolis: University of Minnesota Press, 1985), 9.

8. James Clifford, *The Predicament of Culture: Twentieth-Century Ethnography, Literature, and Art* (Cambridge, Mass.: Harvard University Press, 1988), 47, 58.

9. Rom Harré, *Personal Being: A Theory for Individual Psychology* (Cambridge, Mass.: Harvard University Press, 1984), 26.

10. The same holds true for social theory, expectably, because from it literary theory gets needed legitimation: "In Locke, Montesquieu, Rousseau, Price, most of the Scottish Enlightenment figures and the American founders . . . elements from" the old "republican" and new "juristic-liberal" modes—analogues to the Civic and Personal—"go hand in hand." Knud Haakonssen, "Republicanism," in *A Companion to Contemporary Political Philosophy,* ed. Robert E. Goodin and Philip Pettit (Oxford: Blackwell, 1993), 570–71.

11. John Guillory discusses this latter position, penetratingly and tendentiously, in his *Cultural Capital: The Problem of Literary Canon Formation* (Chicago: University of Chicago Press, 1993), 303–25.

12. James Engell, *Forming the Critical Mind: Dryden to Coleridge* (Cambridge, Mass.: Harvard University Press, 1989), 104.

13. Crane, "English Neoclassical Criticism," 382–86.

14. Hugh Blair, *Lectures on Rhetoric and Belles Lettres,* 8th ed. (London, 1801). In-text references give the volume and page number followed by the number of the lecture as "L1," "L2," and so forth.

15. Richard Fiddes, *A Prefatory Epistle Concerning Some Remarks to be Published on Homer's Iliad* (London, 1714), 68.

16. Leonard Welsted, "A Dissertation Concerning the Perfection of the English Language, the State of Poetry, &c." (1724), in *The Works, in Verse and Prose, of Leonard Welsted, Esq.,* ed. John Nichols (London, 1787), 129.

17. Lecturing on sublimity, Blair mentions the Bible, of course, but then Homer, Ossian, Milton, Virgil, and Shakespeare. *Lectures on Rhetoric,* 1:69–86, L4.

18. Julia Adeney Thomas, "Raw Photographs and Cooked History: Photography's Place in the National Museum of Modern Art, Tokyo," *East Asian History* 12 (December 1996): 129.

19. Sándor Radnóti, *The Fake: Forgery and Its Place in Art,* tr. Ervin Dunai (Lanham, Md.: Rowman and Littlefield, 1999), 51.

20. Engell, *Forming the Critical Mind,* 106.

21. [Thomas Parnell], *An Essay on the Different Stiles of Poetry* (London, 1713), 17, 19.

22. *London Journal* No. 421, 26 August 1727.

23. I have documented this process as to eighteenth-century artistic theory in "'Ideal Presence' and the 'Non Finito' in Eighteenth-Century Aesthetics," *Eighteenth-Century Studies* 9 (1976): 307–32. In other work of mine, discussion of conceptual substance versus explanatory rhetoric appears in "'Organicism,' Rupturalism, and Ism-ism," *Modern Philology* 85 (1988): 588–609. I discuss the relationship between diverse options and change further in "Diversity and Change in Literary Histories," in *Influence and Intertextuality in Literary History,* ed. Jay Clayton and Eric Rothstein (Madison: University of Wisconsin Press, 1991), 114–45. My "Broaching a Cultural Logic of Modernity," *Modern Language Quarterly* 61 (2000): 359–94 elaborates on the method I have advanced in discussing literary theory, 1650–1800, and on literature as information.

24. John Gilbert Cooper, *Letters Concerning Taste* (London, 1755), 12–13.

25. Henry Pemberton, *Observations on Poetry, Especially the Epic* (London, 1738), 75.

26. "Passions" and "interests" come from Albert O. Hirschman's classic *The Passions and the Interests: Political Arguments for Capitalism before Its Triumph* (Princeton, N.J.: Princeton University Press, 1977).

27. [Charles Gildon], *Miscellaneous Letters and Essays, On Several Subjects* (London, 1694), sig. A8[r].

28. Thomas Kuhn, "What Are Scientific Revolutions?" in *The Probabilistic Revolution,* vol. 1, *Ideas in History,* ed. Lorenz Krüger, Lorraine J. Daston, and Michael Heidelberger (Cambridge, Mass.: MIT Press, 1987), 21.

29. Peter Dear, *Discipline and Experience in the Mathematical Way in the Scientific Revolution* (Chicago: University of Chicago Press, 1995), 154–55.

30. Donald N. Levine, *Visions of the Sociological Tradition* (Chicago: University of Chicago Press, 1995), 133.

Contributors

Patricia C. Brückmann is Professor Emeritus of English at Trinity College, University of Toronto. She is the author of *A Manner of Correspondence: A Study of the Scriblerus Club,* as well as articles on Chaucer, Pope, Swift, Richardson, Fielding, Austen, Sterne, Nabokov, recusant literature, and history.

Michael J. Conlon teaches in the English Department of Binghamton University, the State University of New York, and directs the Binghamton University Scholars Program, a university-wide four-year undergraduate honors curriculum. He has published articles on the literature of Dryden, Swift, and Pope, and on the contexts of eighteenth-century satire.

Brian Corman is professor and chair of English at the University of Toronto and editor of the *University of Toronto Quarterly.* He has published articles on the plays of Behn, Centlivre, Cibber, Congreve, Dryden, Etherege, Shadwell, Tate, and Wycherley. He is the author of *Genre and Generic Change in English Comedy, 1660–1710,* and currently is writing a reception history of women novelists before Jane Austen.

Frank H. Ellis is Mary Augusta Jordan Professor Emeritus at Smith College. He has written *Sentimental Comedy: Theory and Practice* and numerous articles on Swift. He has edited two volumes of the Yale edition of *Poems on Affairs of State,* Swift's *Discourse of the Contests and Dissentions, Swift vs. Mainwaring: The Examiner and the Medley,* and *The Complete Works of Rochester.*

Stephen E. Karian has recently completed his dissertation on Swift and the practices of eighteenth-century authorship and has published several articles on Swift and eighteenth-century satire.

Maximillian E. Novak is professor of English at the University of California, Los Angeles. He has edited two volumes of the California edition of Dryden, as well as other eighteenth-century works and collections of essays regarding the eighteenth century. He has published extensively on Defoe, including *Defoe and the Nature of Man* and *Realism, Myth, and History in Defoe's Fiction.* His biography of Defoe will be published in 2001. His other projects include a forthcoming co-edited text of Defoe's *Consolidator* and a study of Congreve.

Claude Rawson is Maynard Mack Professor of English at Yale University. His books include *Henry Fielding and the Augustan Ideal under Stress, Gulliver and the Gentle Reader, Order from Confusion Sprung,* and *Satire and Sentiment 1660–1830. God, Gulliver, and Genocide: Barbarism and the European Imagination, 1492–1945* is forthcoming.

Hermann J. Real is professor of English and director of the Ehrenpreis Center for Swift Studies at the Westfälische Wilhelms-Universität Münster. He is editor of *The Battle of the Books* and co-editor of *Proceedings of the First Münster Symposium on Jonathan Swift, Swift and His Contexts, Reading Swift: Papers from the Second Münster Symposium,* and *Reading Swift: Papers from the Third Münster Symposium.* He has also co-authored a monograph on *Gulliver's Travels,* co-translated the *Travels* into German, and is editor of the annual *Swift Studies.*

Bruce Redford is University Professor at Boston University. His scholarship centers on the literary and visual culture of eighteenth-century Britain. He is the author of *The Converse of the Pen* and *Venice and the Grand Tour,* and has edited *The Letters of Samuel Johnson* and one volume of *The Life of Johnson* from Boswell's manuscript. His Lyell Lectures in Bibliography, *Designing the "Life of Johnson,"* are forthcoming from the Clarendon Press, Oxford.

Gerard Reedy, S. J., is Loyola Professor in the Humanities at Fordham University. He is the author of *The Bible and Reason: Anglicans and Scripture in Late Seventeenth-Century England* and *Robert South (1634–1716): An Introduction to His Life and Sermons,* as well as numerous articles and reviews in the area of seventeenth- and eighteenth-century theology and literature.

Eric Rothstein is Edgar W. Lacy Professor of English at the University of Wisconsin–Madison. He has edited *The Beaux' Stratagem* and co-edited *The Augustan Milieu* and *Influence and Intertextuality in Literary His-*

tory. His books include *George Farquhar, Restoration Tragedy, Restoration and Eighteenth-Century Poetry, 1660–1780, Systems of Order and Inquiry in Later Eighteenth-Century Fiction,* and the co-authored *Designs of Carolean Comedy.*

Peter J. Schakel is Peter C. and Emajean Cook Professor of English at Hope College, Holland, Michigan. He is the author of *The Poetry of Jonathan Swift,* of numerous articles on the verse satires of Dryden, Swift, and Pope, and has edited *Critical Approaches to Teaching Swift.* He has written two books on the fiction of C. S. Lewis and has edited two others. He also has co-authored a textbook, *Approaching Poetry: Perspectives and Responses.*

David L. Vander Meulen is professor of English at the University of Virginia and editor of *Studies in Bibliography.* He currently is preparing a descriptive bibliography and printing history of the writings of Alexander Pope, a study that began as a dissertation directed by Phillip Harth. The bibliography has given rise to his Engelhard Lecture at the Library of Congress, published as *Where Angels Fear to Tread: Descriptive Bibliography and Alexander Pope,* and *Pope's "Dunciad" of 1728: A History and Facsimile.* He has co-edited Johnson's previously unpublished translation of Sallust as well as Faulkner's novel *Mosquitoes,* and he has written a prize-winning history of the Bibliographical Society of the University of Virginia.

Howard D. Weinbrot is Ricardo Quintana Professor of English and William Freeman Vilas Research Professor in the College of Letters and Science at the University of Wisconsin–Madison. He has written numerous articles and reviews. His books include *The Formal Strain, Augustus Caesar in "Augustan" England, Alexander Pope and the Traditions of Formal Verse Satire,* and *Britannia's Issue: The Rise of British Literature from Dryden to Ossian.* He now is at work on a study of Menippean satire from antiquity to the eighteenth century.

James A. Winn is professor of English and chair of the Department of English at Boston University. His books include *A Window in the Bosom: The Letters of Alexander Pope, Unsuspected Eloquence: A History of the Relations between Poetry and Music, John Dryden and his World,* and *"When Beauty Fires the Blood": Love and the Arts in the Age of Dryden.* His most recent book is *The Pale of Words: Reflections on the Humanities and Performance,* an expanded version of the James Murray Brown Lectures at the University of Aberdeen.

James Woolley is Frank Lee and Edna M. Smith Professor of English at Lafayette College. He is editor of Swift and Sheridan's *The Intelligencer,* co-editor of *Swift and His Contexts,* and author of a number of articles on Swift and his contemporaries. He also is co-editor of the Swift Poems Project.

Index

The notes have been indexed selectively so as to supplement, not duplicate, references to the text pages. Except when they are directly quoted, authors of secondary works who are named in the notes alone have generally not been included.